To: هارل؟ جكسبا

know

the

truth

about

ISLAM

أساتيذ الشيخ حمد

Exposing the Truth about the Qur'an
THE REVELATION OF ERROR
VOL. 2 OF 2
The Stories of the Prophets
by Usama K. Dakdok

Exposing the Truth about the Qur'an, Volume 2

For copyright information:
Usama Dakdok Publishing, LLC
P.O. Box 244
Venice, FL 34284-0244

All scripture quotations, unless otherwise indicated, are taken from the New King James Version®. Copyright © 1982 by Thomas Nelson, Inc. Used by permission. All rights reserved.

ISBN: 978-0-9824137-7-7

Dewey decimal system number: 297, Islam

Published in the United States of America

Contents – Volume 2

Guide for Readers of This Book

1. Scripture taken from the New King James Version ®. Copyright © 1982 by Thomas Nelson, Inc. Used by permission. All rights reserved.

2. Qur'an verses are quoted from *The Generous Qur'an; An Accurate, Modern English Translation of the Qur'an, Islam's Holiest Book,* by Usama K. Dakdok, 2nd printing, (Venice, FL: Usama Dakdok Publishing, LLC, 2009).

3. Order of the text follows Ibn Kathir's book, *Stories of the Prophets* - this explains the somewhat erratic and occasionally repetitious nature of the content.

4. Frequent mention is made within the text of Mohammed or Muslim scholars copying from the Bible. In Mohammed's time the collected books of the Bible were not readily available in one document as we know it today and relatively few people had possession of actual manuscripts. While Muslim scholars writing in the following centuries no doubt had access to, and leaned heavily on, many of these manuscripts, it is more likely that Mohammed heard many of the scriptures recited verbally while on his various trading trips and that he got other information from his first wife's cousin, Waraka Ibn Nawfal, reportedly a heretical priest or monk familiar with much of the Old Testament manuscripts and some of the New Testament manuscripts, and who probably helped Mohammed create some of the Qur'an. Mohammed's frequent misspelling of names as well as the confusion of people and facts further suggests that he obtained much of his information verbally from others.

5. ✦ References are made to people being asked to **"revert"** to the original religion (Islam). Islam teaches that everyone is born Muslim, but some are taught by their parents to follow other false religions. Therefore if one leaves another religion to become a Muslim, they **revert** rather than **convert** to Islam.

[vi]

6. Definitions of:

Terms used as part of a name:

'Abd	"Servant (slave) of"
Abu	"Father of"
Al	"The"
Bin	Colloquial term for "Ibn" (son of)
Bint	"Daughter of"
Ibn	"Son of"
Oom	"Mother of"

Other terms frequently used in text:

Allah	Used in text for the god of the Qur'an, who has no son; is also the word used in the Arabic Bible for God, who is the Father of our Lord and our Savior, Jesus Christ.
Ayat	Plural of the word "ayah." It literally means signs or miracles and is often used to refer to the smallest units of the Qur'an; equivalent to "verses." Depending on context, it might also mean proofs, evidences, verses, lessons, revelations, etc.
Gabreel	An angel described in the Qur'an. Not spelled the same way in Arabic as the archangel Gabriel of the Bible.
'Iblis	Literally the Devil; Satan which is also known in Arabic as Shaytān.
'Isa	The name used in the Qur'an which Muslims falsely claim to be Jesus' name; actually in Arabic the correct translation of Jesus' name would be Yasua from Joshua in Hebrew, meaning "savior."
The People of the Book	A term used to designate Christians and Jews.
Surah	A portion of revelation; a division of the Qur'an corresponding essentially to "chapter."

DEDICATION

To my wife, whom I love, and partner in our calling and ministry for the last 22 years, thank you for your commitment of marriage to me and for your great support to our ministry. If it were not for you and your many sacrifices, the success of our ministry and the work of this book would not have been accomplished. I thank God for you each day of my life.

To my son, whom I praise God for you each day, I thank God for your love for Him and your maturity. I praise God that He has given you to me, and I thank you for your many sacrifices and willingness to travel for the past 12 years in our ministry from one state to another, having no steady friends like most other children and teenagers do. You have not complained, and you are an excellent student. I pray that the Lord will lead you into some ministry to carry the baton after me.

A special thank you to my brothers and sisters in Christ – without your hard work, dedication of time, and laborious efforts this book would not have been possible. I really appreciate all you have done for me, for The Straight Way of Grace Ministry, and most importantly for the Kingdom of our Lord and our Savior, Jesus Christ.

I also would like to acknowledge my professor and my friend, Dr. Jim Cogdill. He served the Lord through preaching and teaching his entire adult life. Thousands of students graduated under his direction, and I am proud to be one of them. Dr. Cogdill displayed Christian hospitality as he hosted me and my family in his home on many occasions. During these times spent in his home, as I dictated the words, he physically typed by his own hands Chapter 32, the story of Jesus. I can testify that he was the fastest two finger typist that I have ever known.

My prayer is that my dear Muslim believers, as they continue to read the rest of the stories in volume 2 of this book, will discover the truth - that the Qur'an is a counterfeit to the Holy Bible. My prayer for Christian believers is that, as they read and understand this book, they will be equipped to effectively reach out to Muslims with the truth of the Gospel.

With sincere thanks,
Usama K. Dakdok

INTRODUCTION

It is amazing that we see Westerners becoming Muslims while in the Middle East and around the world, Muslims, even Muslim scholars, are leaving Islam. When I share this fact with my Middle Eastern friends, they think one of the two things. First, I am lying; or second, I am joking. I understand why the Middle Eastern Christians feel this way, but I personally cannot understand why a free people, like Westerners, would imprison themselves in the cult of Islam. I have investigated this fact, for at least the past ten years, as I have met with Americans who have become Muslims. In investigating the techniques that Muslims use to lead Westerners to Islam, I found that Muslims are not using a gun or force to convert Westerners. Instead, they use deception. Muslims use a method which can be explained in a simple sentence. They cause Westerners to doubt Christian doctrine and faith by questioning the validity of the Bible. It is that simple. Muslims do not teach any truth about Islam or the teachings of Mohammed, but they instead try to make the Bible seem foolish. Then they use deception to make Islam appear wise, noble, and full of love and peace.

Some may think that Islam is only growing in the West among black Americans in prison or among uneducated people. However, that is not true for I personally have met with many Muslims who have been educated in worldly knowledge but not in biblical knowledge or spiritual truth. So, why do educated people become Muslims? Once again, it is through the deception of Satan, the god of this world, who can lead the weak, strong, wise, or foolish to Islam. As an example, I will share with you about a friend of mine who is a lawyer.

Almost four years ago, I met with Michael, a kind, godly brother in Christ, who was close to eighty years old. With tears and frustration, he shared with me his struggle over the loss of his son, Rob, to the cult of Islam. Rob was close to forty years old at the time.

Rob was raised in a Christian home and went to a Christian grade school. He was well educated, first with a degree in economics and then studied and obtained a law degree. Rob became successful but also became involved in several relationships with many different women. Then Rob met Donna at a restaurant. They began a long but troubled relationship. They argued frequently. However, Rob loved her, and they got married. Sadly, Donna would become verbally abusive after drinking wine, which she did frequently. These arguments led to separations and finally to divorce after about a year of marriage.

One of Rob's legal clients was a man named Nasar. He encouraged Rob to read the Bible, but what he was really doing was mocking the Bible by focusing Rob on all the apocryphal books of the Bible. The man talked continually, but Rob was fascinated by him.

Donna also met with Nasar, and he convinced her that the only way to get Rob back was to stop drinking and change her life by becoming a Muslim. About six years ago, she became a Muslim. Rob learned about this through Nasar. Rob still loved Donna and went to talk to her. However, Nasar said the only way Rob could talk to her was to remarry her according to Islam religion. Of course, it had to be a Muslim wedding, and Rob had to convert to become a Muslim. So they had a Muslim wedding, and since Donna had stopped drinking, they had a solid marriage.

Rob and Donna have been Muslims for about six years, but they refuse to discuss anything about their faith with Rob's dad, Michael. It is quite clear that they know very little about Islam and have been blinded by their mentor, Nasar, whom they all but worship. They are "Qur'an Only" Muslims and do not go to a mosque. Their marriage and life together got much better with Donna abstaining from drinking, and Rob has been a faithful husband. They even adopted a child from Africa, who is now three years old and a wonderful child.

The problem is clear when they make ridiculous statements such as "a lot of Islam can be found in our Constitution, such as equality." Rob even cut his father off from all e-mail contact since his dad kept trying to show him how Mohammed invented the Qur'an and how Islam violates human rights. These are the issues about Islam and the Qur'an we will be discussing in the final chapter of this book, the chapter of Mohammed.

Nasar, the teacher leading Rob and Donna, was married and had three children. Then his wife became a Christian and left him, taking two of the children. Nasar was left with one son who lives with him and is a Muslim.

It was two years ago that I first talked with Rob on his father's telephone while I drove with his father to have lunch. Michael was asking me to try and reach out to his son to lead him to Christ. He hoped that I could share the truth about Islam and the Qur'an with Rob. The conversation on the phone was not very long. Rob did most of the talking, and I could not get a word in edgeways to share anything with him.

[4]

Then a few weeks ago I was traveling to the city where both Michael and Rob live. As I got close to the city, the Lord led me to make a call to Michael. However, instead of Michael answering the phone, Rob answered. He desperately asked me to help him. At first, I did not know who he was. Then he told me that he, his wife, Donna, his three year old son, and his father, Michael, now over eighty years old, were stuck in a canoe on some river. They had been there for over five hours! Rob asked me to call 911 for help. I asked, "Why don't you call 911 yourself?" He said that his phone did not work. I said, "My friend, I am talking to you right now on your phone, so why do you say it does not work?" The truth is the connection I had to talk to Rob on his wet phone, which had no reception, was simply a miracle.

I only got the rough location of where they were stranded on the river because they themselves did not know exactly where they were. Because of this, I was not sure I could direct help to them in time. So before I hung up, I told Rob to try to call 911 himself, but I assured him that I would also call 911.

I did not learn until later that Rob's phone never worked again. However, 911 was able to respond and find them. The child and Michael were lifted by helicopter to the police waiting on the bridge. However, it was getting dark, and Rob and his wife could not be reached by helicopter. Still, a way was found in time to rescue Rob and his wife from the river. It was after 9:00 p.m. when I learned from the sheriff that they were all safe.

Rob called me the following day to invite me to his house to thank me for the little that I had done by making a phone call. He told me it was his son's birthday, and they had been celebrating by taking a trip in the canoe when they were stranded. So I took a simple gift to the child for his birthday.

As I held their son in my arms, feeling his curly hair, I saw the warmth in their hearts and their love for their child. They are a wonderful family who claim to follow Islam. It is sad that they do not know that this most noble thing which they had done to adopt this child stands contrary to the teaching of the Qur'an as we will see in the final chapter of this book.

We had cake and coffee as I tried to share with them about our ministry. It was like there was a huge wall between me and them that I could not go through. I learned from Donna, Rob's wife, that Islam is the religion of peace, equality, and human rights. She even shared the story of the woman who committed adultery when Jesus told the men there that if they had no sin they could stone her and how Jesus did not stone her either. She said that is what Islam is all about, love and forgiveness.

When I asked her where she learned Islam from, her answer was the Qur'an. Some watered down, sugar-coated translation of the Qur'an. However, when I asked either of them to share with me any verses from the Qur'an to support their beliefs about Islam, the answer was that it is their friend, Nasar, who knows about the Qur'an. All talk about Islam on that night for about two hours was really about the expertise and knowledge of Nasar.

I concluded that the only way to get through to them was through Nasar. They said that if I met with Nasar, he would destroy my arguments against Islam. Even though I was really planning to leave that night, I delayed my departure to the following day so I could meet with their teacher, Nasar. However, sadly the following noon, I received a phone call from Rob who informed me that Nasar would not meet with me, even though Rob explained to him that I am not just a talker but also a listener. Nasar declared that I would not listen to him, so he would not waste his time to meet with me.

Also, it is important to know that Nasar does not read Arabic. He has never read the Qur'an in Arabic. In other words, he is a blind man, knowing nothing about Islam, who led our dear friends to believe Islam to be what it is not.

Pray for Rob, his wife, and his son. Also, pray for the thousands of Westerners who have been deceived to believe in the cult of Islam, simply because they do not know Islam or the claims of the false prophet Mohammed.

I hope and pray that you have already read Volume 1. Now, here is the rest of the story, Volume 2. Here we can complete the work of exposing the truth about the Qur'an, and in the final chapter, we expose the truth about Mohammed, the claimed prophet of the Qur'an.

Ibn Kathir said that Joshua was the husband of Mary, the sister of Moses and Aaron.[1] This is an error. Mary, or Mariam to be correct, was not married to Joshua and apparently remained unmarried. Then Ibn Jarir stated that after Joshua, Ezekiel Ibn Youze was the one who was in charge of the matters of the Children of Israel. He called on Allah. Allah brought back to life those who left their homes, and there were thousands who feared death.

Although the name Ezekiel is not mentioned in the Qur'an, a single verse was used by Mohammed and his scholars to construct a story about the prophet. In Qur'an 2:243: *243Have you not seen those go forth from their homes, and they are thousands, for fear of death? So Allah said to them, "Die." Then he brought them to life. Surely Allah is bountiful to people, but most people do not give thanks.*

Ibn Kathir stated that Mohammed Ibn Isaac said that after Joshua died, he left Ezekiel in charge of the Children of Israel.[2] He was the one of whom Allah spoke in Qur'an 2:243. Ibn Kathir continued to explain how these people died.

An epidemic was in the land. Then Allah said to them, *"Die,"* and all of them died. After many centuries Ezekiel went by them and while he was standing, it was said to him, "Would you like to see them come back to life while you're watching?" He said, "Yes." He was commanded to call the bones that they could be covered with meat and the muscles would be attached to each other. He called them because Allah commanded him to. The entire people rose to life and shouted with one voice, "Allah Akbar."

Muslim scholars said the story behind Qur'an 2:243, in more detail, was that there was a village which was called Daor Dan. A disease or a plague was there, so most of the people of this village left. Of the ones who stayed, most of them died, but some stayed safe and sound. When they returned to the village, they returned safe and sound.

---

[1]Ibn Kathir, *Stories of the Prophets*, vol. 2, Abo Al Fida Ishamail Ibn Kathir Al Kurashi Al Damashce (Beirut: Dar Al-Arab Heritage, 1408 AH, 1988), 3.

[2]Ibid., 4.

Those who stayed behind said, "If we had left like the rest of you, we would all have lived; and if the plague comes again, we will leave with you." When it happened again, they all escaped. About thirty thousand came to a big valley. Two angels called to them from the top and the bottom parts of the valley, saying "Die." So they all died, but their bodies remained.

The Prophet Ezekiel went by them and saw them and began to contemplate. Allah revealed to him, "O Ezekiel, do you want to see me raise them to life?" He said, "Yes." He was still contemplating the wonder of the might of Allah over them. So it was said to him, "Call." So he called, "O you bones, surely Allah commands you to gather." So the bones began to fly until they became a skeleton.

Then Allah revealed to him to call, "O you bones, surely Allah commands you to be covered with meat." So they were covered with meat and blood and even with the same clothes they wore before they died. Then it was said to him, "Call." So he called, "O you bodies, surely Allah commands you to rise up." Then they rose up and said, "How great, O Allah, we praise you. There is no god but you." So they returned to their people who knew they were dead until their time came which was given to them, and they died again.

As for the number of those who were raised to life, Ibn Abbas said there were four thousand, but he also said there were eight thousand. Then he also said there were forty thousand. Ibn Abbas gave three different numbers, and Ibn Kathir quoted all three. However, Ibn Kathir also said that Abu Salah said there were nine thousand. *Where did all they come up with all these different numbers?*

Ibn Kathir stated that Mohammed applied this story to the Muslims to tell them that if there is a plague in a land, not to flee the land: "If you hear it is in another land, do not go there."[3]

What about the true account of Ezekiel in the Bible? First, I would like to encourage the reader to read the entire book of Ezekiel in the Bible because it is a great book of prophecy, especially if it is read with its commentary. The book contains forty-eight chapters; and, once again, I will repeat myself by stating that I am always amazed how Mohammed or Muslim scholars could have fabricated such a long interpretation to a simple verse (Qur'an 2:243) about

---

[3]Ibid., 6.

Ezekiel. It literally has nothing to do with Ezekiel. A book of forty-eight chapters is summarized by Mohammed into one ambiguous verse. As for the story of the bones, it is written in the book of Ezekiel 37. There was no village with a plague. Nobody left the village or stayed behind. Ezekiel was not contemplating, and the bones were very dry, which means they belonged to people who died long ago before Ezekiel's time. Therefore, when they came back to life, they did not go back to their people; and no one knew them.

In the paraphrase to follow, the question given by God to Ezekiel was not, "O Ezekiel, do you want to see me raise them to life?" But rather it was, "O Son of Adam, will these bones live?" His answer was, "O Lord God, you know." Then the Lord told Ezekiel to prophesy upon these bones and say to them, "O you dry bones, hear the word of the Lord." The Lord God said to the bones, "I will enter a spirit in you, so you shall live."

When Ezekiel prophesied, the bones were shaking and drew near one another, every bone to its bone. Ezekiel looked at the bones, and they were covered with muscles and flesh and skin. Notice Mohammed's scholars in their fabrication forgot the covering of their flesh with the skin. However, there was no spirit in them.

Then God said to Ezekiel, "Prophesy, O Son of Adam, and say to the spirits, 'Thus says the Lord God, O Spirit, come from the four winds, and come onto those who were slain so they may live.'" So the spirits came upon them. They lived, stood on their feet, and were an exceedingly great army.

Then the Lord said to Ezekiel, "These bones are the whole house of Israel." They said, "Our bones are dry, and our hope is lost. We are cut off." Then the Lord told Ezekiel to prophesy to them what the Lord said, "I will open your graves, and I will get you out of your graves and bring you to the land of Israel so you may know I am the Lord ..."

Notice the story of the rising of the dead bones is very clear. It requires neither interpretation nor fabrication as Muslim scholars tried to do.

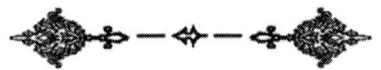

21 The Story of Elisha

Although there is no story for Elisha in the Qur'an, his name is mentioned twice and misspelled in the Arabic language. The first time he is mentioned is in Qur'an 6:86: *[86]And Ishmael and Alyas'a[1] and Yunus and Lūt,[2] and we preferred all those above the worlds.* Elisha's name is also written in error in Qur'an 38:48: *[48]And remember Ishmael and Alyas'a[3] and Za Al Kafel,[4] all from the chosen.* The real name in Arabic is Elisha not Alyas'a. Ibn Kathir stated that Mohammed Ibn Isaac said many other Muslim scholars said Elisha came immediately after Elijah, which is a direct contradiction to the previous section where Muslim scholars told us that Ezekiel came immediately after Elijah.[5]

They said that Elisha lived to call the people to Allah, following the same law of Elijah until Allah took his spirit, and sin grew exceedingly among the Children of Israel. They grew to be great Titans and killed the prophets. There was an overpowering king among them, and this king repented and entered the garden.

Who was Elisha? Ibn Kathir stated that Mohammed Ibn Isaac said he was Elisha Ibn Aktob.[6] Ibn Asakir said that Elisha was Ibn Aday, Ibn Shotlam, Ibn Ephraim, Ibn Joseph, Ibn Jacob, Ibn Abraham. If this genealogy is correct, that would make Elisha the great-greatgrandson of Joseph, which means he existed before Moses, which is nonsense.

Ibn Kathir continued by saying that it was said he was the cousin of Elijah and was hiding with him on Mount Kasuom. When Elijah was lifted up, Elisha became the new prophet to the Children of Israel, and Allah gave him the prophecy.

Ibn Kathir stated that Ibn Jarir said the sins of the Children of Israel increased greatly, and they began to kill the prophets of Allah.

---

[1]Elisha, non-Arabic word of Syriac/earlier Semitic origin
[2]Lot, non-Arabic word of Syriac origin
[3]wrong name, he meant Elisha
[4]wrong name, some Muslim scholars say he meant Isaiah, others say Ezekiel
[5]Ibn Kathir, *Stories of the Prophets*, vol. 2, Abo Al Fida Ishamail Ibn Kathir Al Kurashi Al Damashce (Beirut: Dar Al-Arab Heritage, 1408 AH, 1988), 6.
[6]Ibid., 7.

Therefore, Allah sent upon them powerful kings who treated them unjustly and shed their blood. Allah also sent upon them enemies, and whenever they fought any of the enemies, the Ark of the Covenant stayed with them. Thus they had victory over their enemies with the blessing of the Ark of the Covenant. When their enemies had victory over them in a war, these enemies took the Ark of the Covenant from their hand. When the king of the Children of Israel heard that the Ark of the Covenant was taken, he fell on his neck and died. The Children of Israel became like sheep without a shepherd until Allah sent from among them a prophet called Samuel. They asked Samuel to appoint a king over them so they could fight their enemies. So it happened.

Ibn Jarir continued by stating that from the time of the death of Joshua Ibn Noon until the days of Samuel was 460 years. He mentioned the names of the kings who were appointed over them, but Ibn Kathir stated that he refused to mention their names. I personally believe it is a great miracle for Muslim scholars to come up with the above story simply by reading a wrong name of a prophet in the Qur'an, for there is no hadith of Mohammed to even help them come up with this wonderful story of Elisha.

Was there any prophet killed before Samuel? Was there any powerful king before Samuel? When was the age of judges who ruled over the Children of Israel before Prophet Samuel appointed the first king, King Saul? What do Muslim scholars really know about Elisha? According to the lack of information in the Qur'an, Elisha is nothing but a wrong name. We encourage the reader to read about Elisha in 1 Kings 19 and 2 Kings in the Bible. *Did you know that Elisha had received a double portion of the ministry of the Prophet Elijah, and therefore he was supposed to perform double the miracles of Elijah?* Elijah performed seven miracles before he was taken into the chariot of fire.

Here is a list of the miracles performed by Elisha:

1. Parted the Jordan River, 2 Kings 2:14-15
2. Purified water, 2 Kings 2:19-22
3. Cursed mockers who were then savaged by bears, 2 Kings 2:23-25
4. Caused a flood to foil the Moabites, 2 Kings 3:14-25
5. Miraculous flow of oil for the poor widow, 2 Kings 4:2-7
6. Fertility for the woman of Shunem, 2 Kings 4:8-17
7. Raised a child from the dead, 2 Kings 4:32-37
8. Purified poisoned soup, 2 Kings 4:38-41

9. Multiplied of loaves to feed a large crowd, 2 Kings 4:42-44
10. Healed Naaman of leprosy, 2 Kings 5:1-19
11. Gehazi cursed with leprosy, 2 Kings 5:20-27
12. Made an iron axe head float, 2 Kings 6:1-7
13. Struck the Aramaeans with sun blindness and then cured them, 2 Kings 6:15-23

Therefore, Elisha would need to perform fourteen miracles, but he performed only thirteen miracles and died before he performed the fourteenth one. He was buried in the land of the Moabites. However, because the promise had been given to him, he was able to raise the dead while he was dead, as found in 2 Kings 13:21. This was the fourteenth miracle.

Because of the fulfillment of this fourteenth miracle, the prophecy of Prophet Elijah has been fulfilled. All these miracles performed are great evidence of a true prophet. Prophet Elisha himself gave the following prophecies which have been fulfilled:
1. Predicted the end of a famine, 2 Kings 7:1-2
2. Prophesied the death of Ben-Hadad and the rise of Hazael, 2 Kings 8:7-15
3. Predicted Israel would defeat Aram three times, 2 Kings 13:14-19

Mohammed ignored so many facts simply because he did not know them or they would make him look bad. Mohammed himself ✶ was not able to perform any miracles or prophecies.

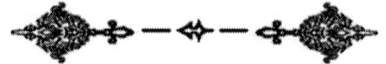

22 The Story of Samuel

Although the name Samuel is not mentioned in the Qur'an, Muslims claim to believe in him. They base their claims on one passage in Qur'an 2:246-251. This one passage has enough confusion of its own. It mixes the stories of Saul, the first king of the Jews, with Gideon as found in Judges 7:1-8. The request of Samuel for a king comes from 1 Samuel 8. The return of the Ark of the Covenant is found in 1 Samuel 6 and 7. This took place before the Jews asked for a king.

When we read such a passage as Qur'an 2:246, we cannot find any factual information about Samuel. Ibn Kathir himself showed his confusion when he interpreted verse 2:246.[1] Ibn Kathir stated that Qatadah said that this was the Prophet Joshua Ibn Noon. However, Ibn Kathir rejected this idea, with the excuse that the story here in verse 246 took place in a time far from Moses. This was during the time of David. He claimed the time between Moses and David was one thousand years. He ended the statement by writing *and Allah knows best.*

Then Ibn Kathir quoted Al Saddi by saying that this prophet was Simeon, which is another error. However, Mujahid said this prophet was Shamueel and gave lengthy names of genealogy for him. *Who was this Shamueel?* Of course, they meant Samuel, but misspelled his name in the Arabic text. Ibn Kathir wrote that he was Shamueel Ibn Bale, Ibn Al Cama, Ibn Yarhkom, Ibn Alehu, Ibn Tahu, Ibn Suff, Ibn Al Cama, Ibn Maahas, Ibn Amosa, Ibn Azrea.[2]

Wow, what a wonderful "scholar" Ibn Kathir was. *Once again, where did he come up with all these names? Now, if the name of Samuel isn't even in the Qur'an, where did he come up with such a list of names? Who was Samuel? Where did he come from? When did he live? What was his message and prophecy?* Once again, Ibn Kathir fabricated a story. He said Ibn Abbas and others said after the Amalekites from the land of Gaza invaded the land of Israel, they killed a large number of Israelites and took many of their children captive. Then the prophethood was stopped from the tribe of Levi.

---

[1]Ibn Kathir, *Stories of the Prophets*, vol. 2, Abo Al Fida Ishamail Ibn Kathir Al Kurashi Al Damashce (Beirut: Dar Al-Arab Heritage, 1408 AH, 1988), 7.

[2]Ibid., 7.

There was only one woman left from among them, and she was pregnant. She continued to call on Allah that he would give her a son. So she birthed a child and named him Ashameel which meant Ishmael in the Hebrew language and which means *Allah heard my call.* When he grew up, she sent him to the mosque (a place of worship) and gave him to a righteous man so that he could be with him, learning from his example and his worship. Ashameel lived with him until he became strong.

One night while Ashameel was asleep, he heard a voice come to him from the direction of the mosque. He became alert and frightened. He thought it was the righteous man calling him. So he asked him, "Did you call me?" So the righteous man said, "Yes, I called you, but go to sleep!" He commanded him, so Ashameel slept. He called him a second time and likewise a third time. So behold, Gabreel called him. So he came to him, saying, "Surely your lord has sent you to your people," and it was the command of Allah, as Allah said in his dear book.

As we have seen above, the great Muslim scholar Ibn Kathir wrote many errors in his interpretation. Now to the true account as it is written in the Bible. We advise the reader to read the entire account beginning in 1 Samuel.

Was Samuel a descendant of Levi? The answer is no because his father was Elkanah, son of Jeroham, son of Elihu, son of Tohu, son of Zuph, an Ephrathite. He was a descendant of Joseph, not Levi, as Ibn Kathir had stated. This man had two wives, one by the name of Hannah, who had no children, and the other by the name of Peninnah, who had children. Elkanah, the husband, used to go to Jerusalem every year to worship and offer sacrifices. He loved his wife Hannah, but the Lord had not opened her womb.

One year, Hannah was crying, for Peninnah made fun of her for not having any children. Her husband tried to comfort her, but she left and stood before the Lord at the temple. She prayed unto the Lord as she wept in her great sorrow. She made a vow before the Lord that if she would be blessed with a child, she would give him back to the Lord all the days of his life. Eli the priest thought she was drunk because she was praying by moving her lips but not speaking out loud. She answered him, "No, lord, I am not drunk. I am a sorrowful spirited woman." Eli, as he told her to go in peace, said, "The God of Israel will grant you the request of your heart." A year later, she had her first son. She called him Samuel because she said, "I have asked him of the Lord." Notice, here this story shows the fabrication of Ibn

[14]

Kathir's claim that she was already pregnant and that there was war, killing, and captivity; it is an error.

At this time Hannah refused to go with her son Samuel to Jerusalem, for she said to her husband, "I will not go to Jerusalem until the child is weaned." She intended to leave him in the temple, which is what she did when Samuel grew into a young child. At that time, she met with Eli and gave her son back to the Lord. She said, "As long as he lives, he shall be lent to the Lord." There is a beautiful prayer that is given by Hannah in 1 Samuel 2:1-10. (We encourage the reader to meditate on this prayer.) Then Elkanah and Hannah went back to their house, and the young boy served the Lord before Eli, the priest.

Eli had sons who did not know God. They had not served God as they should. Their sin was great before the Lord. The mother of Samuel made him a little coat and sent him another coat every year. The Lord blessed her with three more sons and two daughters (1 Samuel 2:21).

When Eli was getting very old, he heard about his sons' sins and rebuked them. As for the child Samuel, he continued to grow and have favor with the Lord (1 Samuel 2:27).

The word of the Lord in those days was precious, for there were no widespread prophetic visions. In the evening, Samuel was lying down to sleep near the Ark of the Covenant in the Tabernacle. The Lord called Samuel. Samuel said, "Here I am." He went to Eli because he thought Eli had called to him. Eli said, "No, I did not call you." (This is the opposite of what Ibn Kathir wrote in his book for he stated that Eli's answer was to tell him *yes* and to go back to sleep.) This happened three times. Then Eli knew the Lord was calling the child and said to Samuel, "If the voice calls to you again say, 'Speak, O Lord. I am your servant and I hear you.'" It was there the Lord spoke to Samuel of all the destruction to befall Eli's sons as a punishment for their sins because God had sworn that not even a sacrifice would remove the iniquity of Eli's house.

In the morning, Eli asked Samuel concerning the word of the Lord. Samuel told him all the things the Lord had spoken to him, as we read in 1 Samuel 3:18. Samuel grew, and the Israelites from Dan to Beersheba knew that Samuel was established to be their prophet. The Lord appeared again in Shiloh, revealed himself to Samuel, and spoke through Samuel.

Ibn Kathir interpreted Qur'an verse 2:246 by saying that the Children of Israel were so tired of many wars and that the enemies smote them, so they asked the prophet of Allah at that time to appoint a king over them.[3] They did this so they might fight the enemies under his leadership. The prophet said in Qur'an 2:246: [246]*Have you not seen the gathering of the children of Israel after Moses? When they said to a prophet for them, "Send to us a king, we will engage in war for the sake of Allah." He said, "Will it be that you would not go to war if engaging in war is decreed for you?" They said, "And why should we not engage in war for the sake of Allah, and indeed, we and our children are driven forth from our homes?" So when the engaging in war was decreed to them, they turned back except for a few of them. And Allah knows the unjust.*

Ibn Kathir said that they said, "We are fighting. It is justice for us to fight on the behalf of our lost, weakened, and captive children." Then Allah said when war was decreed to them, they turned back except for a few of them, and Allah knows the unjust. Ibn Kathir explained how this took place as few of them crossed the river with the king, but the rest of them turned away and rejected the fight.

There are so many errors and contradictions resulting from the ignorance of Ibn Kathir and other Muslim scholars. There was complete confusion on the part of Muslim scholars regarding the allegation of fear and cowardice of the Israelites concerning the crossing of the river with the king and a small number of forces because there was no king, but rather a judge by the name of Gideon. Also, it was not their choice, but God's commandment because God did not want them to think that they had won the battle by their numbers, but rather by the hand of Almighty God. The story of Gideon will be discussed a little later in another section.

As for Ibn Kathir's claim that the Children of Israel needed a king to fight for their children and their homes, this is a false statement. When we read the Scripture, we discover that the Children of Israel fought many battles with judges (not kings) years before Samuel was born because no monarchy had yet been established. Moreover, the entire story of Gideon, the crossing of the river, and the fight against the enemy did not take place during the time of Samuel, but rather more than a hundred years before Samuel became the prophet of Israel.

---

[3]Ibn Kathir, 9.

Here is the list of ten judges who judged over Israel before Samuel.[4]

Gideon	(Judges 6-8) Defeated Midianites with 300 men
Abimelech	(Judges 9) Only judge to win leadership through treachery
Tola	(Judges 10:1-5) Judged Israel for 23 years
Yair	(Judges 10:1-5) Judged Israel for 22 years
Jephthah	(Judges 10:17-12:7) Defeated Ammonites
Ibzan	(Judges 12:8-15) Judged people for 7 years
Elon	(Judges 12:8-15) Judge for 10 years
Abdon	(Judges 12:8-15) Ruled for 8 years
Samson	(Judges 13-16) Fought Philistines singlehandedly
Eli	(1 Samuel 1:9) Priest, ruled people from the sanctuary at Gilo
Samuel	(1 Samuel) Last judge before the kingdom came under the rule of Saul

Ibn Kathir provided an interpretation for Qur'an 2:247: *[247]And their prophet said to them, "Surely Allah has sent Tālūt[5] as a king to you." They said, "How can the kingdom be to him over us when we are more worthy of the kingdom than him, and he has no abundance of money?" He said, "Surely Allah has chosen him over you and has given him increase in knowledge and stature. And Allah gives his kingdom to whom he wills. And Allah is large, knowing."[6]* Ibn Kathir stated that Tālūt (wrong name, he meant Saul), according to Al Salabe, is Ibn Kesh, Ibn Afeel, Ibn Sorro, Ibn Afyeh, Ibn Annis, Ibn Benjamin, Ibn Jacob, Ibn Isaac, Ibn Abraham. He continued by stating that Akramah and Al Saddi said he

---

[4] The Shengold Jewish Encyclopedia, NY: Shengold, 1988, accessed January 14, 2013, http://www.jewishvirtuallibrary.org/jsource/History/judges.html.

[5] Saul, non-Arabic word created by Mohammed—apparently from a misunderstanding of the Hebrew word meaning *tall*

[6] Ibn Kathir, 9.

was a water pourer, but Wahab Ibn Monabah said he was a tanner. Ibn Kathir said that there were other opinions, *and Allah knows best.* Wow, what a "great" interpretation. Of course, *Allah knows best* simply because no one among the Muslim scholars knows and that is because none of this information is in the Qur'an or the hadith. Therefore, all we get is fabrication and confusion.

Ibn Kathir continued, explaining why the Children of Israel rejected Tālūt to be their king, by stating that the prophethood belonged to the tribe of Levi and the kingdom belonged to the tribe of Judah. However, because Tālūt was from the tribe of Benjamin, they did not like him; and they spoke against him saying, "We are more worthy of the kingdom than he is."

They also mentioned that he was poor, so how then could he become king? Ibn Kathir continued by saying, without telling us who said this statement, "Allah revealed to Shameel (Samuel) to measure all the Children of Israel with his staff, and whoever was the right height would be king." So there wasn't any among the entire house of Israel who was the right height except Tālūt. When Saul came to Samuel, he poured the oil on Saul and anointed him as king. It was said that Saul was the most beautiful physically and the most knowledgeable concerning warfare.

Ibn Kathir interpreted Qur'an 2:248: *[248]And their prophet said to them, "Surely the sign of his kingdom will be that the tābūt[7] will come to you. In it is tranquility from your lord and the relics left by the family of Moses and the family of Aaron. The angels will carry it. Surely in this is a sign to you if you were believers."[8]* Ibn Kathir said this man was a "blessing, for this good man, when he becomes a king, the Ark will be returned to them, for it was stolen by the enemy. Because of their possession of the Ark, they used to have victory over their enemies."

In response, this is false information, for according to the true account in the Bible, the Ark was returned before there was any king; and it did not bring good luck or blessings to their enemies, but the opposite: sickness and curse. That is why they returned it to the Children of Israel.

As for the saying *"In it is tranquility from your lord,"* Ibn Kathir said that some said that inside the Ark there was a basin made out of

---

[7]ark, non-Arabic word of Egyptian origin
[8]Ibn Kathir, 10.

[18]

gold. The chests of the prophets used to be washed in it. Others said tranquility is like the wind, and it was said it is like a cat; when it screamed in the time of war, the Children of Israel were assured of their victory.

When you search the Scripture, the Holy Bible, you will discover that this description of what was in the Ark is nothing but pure evidence of the ignorance of these scholars because the Bible clearly teaches, in the Old and New Testaments, that inside the Ark of the Covenant there was a gold jar of manna, Aaron's staff that had budded, and the stone tablets of the Covenant (Hebrews 9:4).

To further prove our assertion that the Muslim scholars were highly ignorant, Ibn Kathir said the Torah was also inside the Ark of the Covenant, and when they received it, they put it under the feet of the idol Dagon they had in their land. When they woke up in the morning, the Ark was on top of the head of the idol. So they put it under the feet on the second day, and when they woke up, they found the Ark again on top of the head. When this was repeated many times, they knew it was a command of Allah; therefore, they took it out of their city and sent it to one of their villages. However, a sickness took them in their necks and lasted for a long time.

Putting the Ark of the Lord under Dagon's feet and the discovery of the Ark on top of Dagon's head are further errors. The truth is that the Ark was put near Dagon, and in the morning they found Dagon fallen on his face. They raised Dagon up and put the statue back in its place. The following morning, he had fallen again with his head and his palms broken off on the threshold of the temple according to 1 Samuel 5:4. This was repeated with the god Ekron. As for the sickness that befell the Philistines, Ibn Kathir stated it was by the neck. However, as written in the Arabic Bible, it was not on the neck, but it was hemorrhoids; and you know where they are located. This is found in 1 Samuel 5:6, 9, and 12.

Ibn Kathir continued by stating that the enemy put the Ark on a wheel, tied it to two cows, and sent them away. So it was said that angels drove the cows until they came to the Children of Israel, who were watching it as their prophet informed them, *and Allah knows best* how this happened. It was clear that the angels were carrying the Ark by themselves, as it is clearly written in the verses of the Qur'an.

Notice also that this sign, which Mohammed put in the Qur'an as a sign of the king's kingdom, as written in verse 248, can be proven completely wrong by a simple reading of 1 Samuel 4-7. When we read these four chapters, we find the entire story of the war which took place between the Philistines and Israel and how Israel was smitten before the Philistines in which three thousand Israelites were killed, the Ark was taken by the Philistines, and the sons of Eli were killed that same day.

Eli died at the age of ninety-eight when he fell off a chair. As for the history of the Ark of the Lord, how it moved from one place to another and how God's hand was severe against the Philistines, this can be read in detail in 1 Samuel 4. The Philistines sent the Ark back as a gift to the border of Beth Shemesh. Notice that the Philistines returned the Ark; it was not stolen by the Israelites as Ibn Kathir stated. The Levites took down the Ark of the Lord and offered as a sacrifice the same two cows which had been pulling the cart that carried the Ark. They used the wood of the cart to burn the offering to the Lord. Then the Lord smote the men of Beth Shemesh, killing 50,070 men, because they had looked at the Ark of the Lord.

All this and more can be read in 1 Samuel 6. Notice that the Ark of the Lord was not carried by any angels but by two cows pulling a cart according to 1 Samuel 6:7. Neither Samuel nor King Saul had anything to do with the return of the Ark, for the Ark was returned because of the advice of the priests and diviners of the Philistines when they realized that the Ark of the Covenant brought sickness and torment to them. All these battles took place over a twenty-year time period, and the Prophet Samuel himself led the Children of Israel in many wars against the Philistines.

In 1 Samuel 7, as it is written, after twenty years the Prophet Samuel spoke to the people of the house of Israel saying, "Purify the house of Israel of all your false gods and worship the Lord God alone." As they all gathered, Samuel prayed for them. There was another battle between the Philistines and Israel, and the Children of Israel asked Samuel to cry out to the Lord for them that He would deliver them from the hand of the Philistines.

Then Samuel took a suckling lamb and offered it as a sacrifice before the Lord. He cried out to the Lord, and God answered his prayer. As the war began between the Philistines and Israel, the Lord sent a great thunder upon the Philistines. The Lord discomforted the Philistines, and they were smitten before Israel. The men of Israel followed the Philistines and attacked them until they came to Beth Car. There Samuel took a stone, set it up, and called it Ebenezer (which means *the stone of help*). Thus the Philistines were subdued and came no more onto the coast of Israel. The Lord's hand was against the Philistines all the days of Samuel.

[20]

Ibn Kathir stated that another proof that the king who Allah had chosen was a righteous king was that during his time the Ark of the Covenant would be carried by the angels.[9] This was a sign to the Jews "if they were believers."

This is an error, for the return of the Ark had nothing to do with the righteousness of the king or the Children of Israel, but as we mentioned above, this was the Philistines' own solution to get rid of their illness. Add to this, angels never carried the Ark of the Lord. Also, this story took place years before Saul was appointed as king. In his interpretation, Ibn Kathir did not clarify and apparently did not know who the ones were who had the Ark of the Lord. However, as we read in 1 Samuel 5, these were the Philistines, and obviously, none of the information given to us by Muslim scholars has a source in Islam. It is only hearsay.

Now let us look at the true account of how Saul became a king. In 1 Samuel 8, we read when Samuel had become old, his two sons, Joel and Abiah, were serving as judges in Beersheba. Unlike their father, they were unjust judges. The elders of Israel came to Prophet Samuel and asked him to appoint a king to rule over Israel. Prophet Samuel did not like the request for a king, but the Lord spoke to him saying, "Give them a king, for they have not refused you, but they refused Me to be king over them."

As for the matter of a king for the people of Israel, this is found in 1 Samuel 8:9-18. The people refused to hear the voice of Samuel and insisted upon having a king because they wanted to be like the other nations in having a king to judge and fight their battles for them. I believe Mohammed wrote his verses in Qur'an 2:246-251 from this portion of this story. Notice when we read this passage in the Qur'an, there are no names mentioned in these verses. I wonder how Muslim scholars come up with these names. *How did they then confuse and mix up the story of Samuel with other stories like the stories of Saul, Gideon, and David?*

To see how Saul was chosen as king, we encourage the reader to read 1 Samuel 9 and 10. Saul was the son of Kish, son of Abiel, son of Zerork, son of Bechorath, son of Aphiah, a Benjamite and a mighty man of power. He was impressive in appearance and a head taller than anyone else. Previously, Ibn Kathir stated that the prophethood belonged to the tribe of Levi and the kingdom belonged to the tribe of

---

[9]Ibn Kathir, 10.

Judah, but because Tālūt was from the tribe of Benjamin, they did not like him. There are so many lies in this statement.

First, the prophethood biblically does not belong to any tribe over other tribes, and as for the kingdom, the Bible clearly teaches that the king would be from among their brothers from any tribe. As the Bible states in Deuteronomy 17:15: *[15] You shall surely set a king over you whom the LORD your God chooses; one from among your brethren you shall set as king over you; you may not set a foreigner over you, who is not your brother.* I believe Americans should learn a great lesson from this verse. Having a foreign Muslim President over the land is leading to the fall of a great nation, and the coming years will prove my point. We are moving from a Christian nation, founded on Judeo-Christian principles, whose founders and for many years its elected officials were Christians, to now being a nation led by a Muslim President who wants to minimize or eliminate Christian influence in government. What a sorrowful state we are in.

I also believe the confusion among Muslim scholars comes from when the Bible talks about the priesthood belonging to the Levites, beginning with Aaron, the brother of Moses. However, this is the only office that belongs to a specific tribe and was not to be given to any other tribe.

When Kish lost his donkeys, he sent his son Saul to take one of the servants and go and search for them, but they could not find them. Notice that Saul was not a poor man, as the Qur'an and Muslim scholars describe him in verse 247: *"How can the kingdom be to him over us when we are more worthy of the kingdom than him, and he has no abundance of money?"* However, the Bible states that he came from a rich family who owned slaves and livestock and describes him as a son of a mighty man of power. They searched for the man of God that he might guide them to where the donkeys were.

Perhaps the confusion, leading to the conclusion that Saul was poor, resulted from verse 7 where Saul said to the servant that they had no gift for the man of God. This was not because they were poor but because Saul did not have a gift with him. They asked the young ladies who went out to draw water if there was a seer that they could meet. They met with Samuel, the prophet whom God had already told about the situation with Saul. Samuel asked Saul to "go up with him to eat and that the next day he would tell Saul all his heart desired."

Samuel told Saul that the donkeys which had been lost three days before had been found. Then Samuel told Saul that all the desire of Israel was upon him and all in his father's house. Saul responded that he was a Benjamite, the least and smallest tribe of Israel, and that his clan was the least of the clans in the tribe of Benjamin. Then Samuel took Saul and his servant and sat them at the place of honor among thirty men and told the cook to bring him the special portion of meat which had been laid aside and put it before Saul. So Saul ate with Samuel on that day. In the morning Samuel asked Saul to let the servant go ahead of them and for Saul to sit so that he could hear the word of God. Then Samuel poured the oil on Saul's head, kissed him, and explained to him that the Lord had anointed him to be leader over his inheritance, for he had been chosen to be king over Israel. Later, Saul was seen prophesying with the prophets, for the Spirit of God had come upon him.

In 1 Samuel 10:24, Samuel introduced King Saul to the people, but the children of Belial rejected Saul to be king for they despised him and did not give him gifts. Notice there was no stick to measure the height of every man in Israel as Ibn Kathir stated, but it is a completely different story.[10] Ibn Kathir also stated that Saul was chosen by Allah to be increased in knowledge and stature, meaning in fighting, but others said in his physical body. Perhaps Muslims really need to read the Bible, for that is the source from which Mohammed obtained information for his Qur'an and is also the same source where Muslim scholars used other stories to help interpret Mohammed's Qur'an.

Qur'an 2:249-251 states: [249]*So when Tālūt marched forth with his jund,[11] he said, "Surely Allah will test you by a river. So whoever drinks of it so is not of me, but he who does not taste it, so surely he is of me except who scoops a scoop by his hand so they drink from it, except a few of them." So when they had passed it, he and those who believed with him, they said, "We have no strength this day with Jālūt[12] and his troops." Those among them who thought that they would meet Allah said, "How many a small group have victory over a large group, by Allah's permission? And Allah is with the patient."*

[250]*And when they went forth against Goliath and his troops, they said, "Our lord, pour out patience on us and set our feet firm and give us victory against the infidel people." [251]So they defeated them by Allah's permission. And Dāwūd[13] killed*

---

[10]Ibn Kathir, 9.
[11]troops, non-Arabic word of Iranian/Aramaic origin
[12]Goliath, non-Arabic word, apparently of garbled Hebrew origin
[13]David, non-Arabic word of Aramaic origin

Goliath, and Allah gave him the kingdom and the wisdom. And he taught him from whatever he willed. And were it not that Allah gives conquest to some people over others, then the earth would have been vandalized. But Allah is the possessor of bounty to the worlds.

What a concoction of distortion and deceit! This passage alone shows us the ignorance of Angel Gabreel and Mohammed to the facts of the Scripture. Muslims cannot understand this confusion unless they read the history of King Saul in the Bible in 1 Samuel 9 through 31 and also the truth of what took place in Judge Gideon's life in the book of Judges 7:1-25. As for the killing of Goliath, one must read 1 Samuel 17.

For the sake of time and space, I will first point to Ibn Kathir's interpretation of the previous verses, Qur'an 7:249–250, and I will rebut them with a simple comment. First, Ibn Kathir said that Ibn Abbas, as well as many other interpreters, said that this river was the Jordan River, and Allah examined his soldiers and whoever drank from this river would not go with him for this invasion. Only those who drank by their hand could follow him.[14] Then Al Saddi said that the army was 80,000. Those who drank from the river were 76,000, and those who stayed with him were only 4,000. However, Al Bukhari said that Mohammed said 300 or a little more than that were believers.

Had Mohammed read the Bible, he would have discovered that King Saul never tested any soldier by any river. Imagine with me that perhaps this confusion took place because Mohammed or those who helped him to copy this story from 1 Samuel to the Qur'an, while in doing so, they took a break to drink a good cup of Arabian coffee. After the break, they continued to copy the Bible, but they did not realize that the wind, as it flew from the east to the west, had turned the pages of the Bible. Then Mohammed or those who helped him continued to copy the Bible now from the book of Judges 7:1-25. In this passage, Gideon was obeying God's command because God would not allow them to win the battle against the Midianites with a large number of fighters (32,000). God knew they would brag that they had won because of their numbers rather than giving credit to God (Judges 7:1-3).

The true account is much different from what Mohammed put in the Qur'an. The exam was only known by Gideon because God

---

[14]Ibn Kathir, 10-11.

wanted to eliminate all but a few of the most dedicated of the Israelites. We read in the Scripture that the Lord asked Gideon to announce to the men that whoever was afraid to let him go back. Thus 22,000 left, and 10,000 remained with Gideon.

Then the Lord told Gideon to take them down by the water. Notice that the Bible simply says *water* (Judges 7:4-5) but nothing about the Jordan River as Ibn Abbas said.[15] They were camping beside the well of Harod which is located southeast of Jezreel. There God told Gideon he still had too many men. God told him who to take and who to leave behind. The Lord said to separate those who lapped with their tongues, as a dog, from those who knelt on their knees to drink. Those who lapped by their tongue like a dog were exactly 300 men, not 310, and not 320, as Mohammed wrongly said. The others who knelt to drink were sent away. Then Gideon divided the 300 men into three sections and put trumpets in their hands along with empty pitchers and lamps within their pitchers.

Gideon and the 300 blew their trumpets, broke their pitchers, and shouted to the Lord and to Gideon. Then the entire Midianite army cried and fled. Then the Lord caused the Midianites to turn their swords against their own army. The Lord gave Gideon and the Israelites a great victory against the Midianites, including the two princes of Midian who were killed on that day. *What does this have to do with Saul?* Nothing at all. Of course, we can always blame the wind which may have turned the pages while they were copying the Bible in order to write the stories of the Qur'an.

As for the portion of the Qur'an, *"We have no strength this day with Jālūt[16] and his troops."* Ibn Kathir stated that because they were small in number and were weak, they were acknowledging that they had no strength to fight Goliath and his army.[17] However, those who were of strong faith and patient among them said, "Those among them who thought that they would meet Allah said, 'How may a small group have victory over a large group, by Allah's permission?'" Then when they met Goliath, Ibn Kathir interpreted it as to ask Allah to give them patience. Then Allah strengthened them and gave them victory over their enemy and Allah's enemy among the infidels. So the great, the mighty one, the hearer, the seer, the wise, the one who knows, gave them what they sought to have. All this was because,

---

[15] Ibid., 10.
[16] Goliath, non-Arabic word, apparently of garbled Hebrew origin
[17] Ibn Kathir, 11.

when they met Goliath, they said, "Our lord, pour out patience on us and set our feet firm and give us victory against the infidel people." In verse 251: *[251]So they defeated them by Allah's permission.* Amazingly, David showed up suddenly to kill Goliath.

Perhaps the wind this time moved from the west to the east, returning the pages of the Bible to the right spot where the story really belonged, missing only a couple of pages, to know how David came to this point. Verse 251 continues with: *And Dāwūd[18] killed Goliath, and Allah gave him the kingdom and the wisdom. And he taught him from whatever he willed. And were it not that Allah gives conquest to some people over others, then the earth would have been vandalized. But Allah is the possessor of bounty to the worlds.*

How did David come to this point in the story? Obviously, Muslim scholars would say, *and Allah knows best.* However, the Muslim scholar Ibn Kathir gave us more than enough details, which obviously have enough errors in themselves, such as when Ibn Kathir said that Al Saddi said, "David was the youngest of the children of his father, and they were thirteen males.[19] He heard King Saul saying, 'Whoever kills Goliath, I will give him my daughter as a wife and make him a partner of my kingdom.'"

What is wrong with this statement so far? There are plenty of errors. First, we must ask another question. *Where did Al Saddi come up with this information?* The answer is most likely the Bible, but here is the error. David did not have twelve brothers; he had only seven brothers. One can find this in the book of 1 Samuel 16:10-11. His second error was that Saul offered his daughter and his kingdom to be shared with whoever killed Goliath. The true account can be found in 1 Samuel 17:25, as the Scripture says that to the man who would fight and kill Goliath, the king would make him rich, give him his daughter as a wife, and grant his house to be free in Israel, meaning he would not pay taxes.

The entire true account can be found in 1 Samuel 17:1-54. We encourage the reader to read this story of David. In 1 Samuel 16, David was anointed king and took the kingship office, but he did not rule as a king until after the death of Saul. The rest of his life's story can be found in 2 Samuel. Ibn Kathir continued by saying that David used a sling shot, so a rock spoke to him: "If you take me, you will

---

[18]David, non-Arabic word of Aramaic origin
[19]Ibn Kathir, 11-12.

kill by me Goliath." So he took it. Then another rock said the same thing, so he took it, and then a third rock. *What is wrong with this picture?*

When we read the Bible, we find that David picked up five rocks, not three rocks, and none of the rocks spoke to David. Obviously, this could be a fairy tale to be told to children at bedtime. In 1 Samuel 17:40, we read that David chose five rocks and put them in his shepherd's bag. His sling was in his hand, but no rock talked to David at all.

Ibn Kathir continued by saying the two lines of opposing armies stood up when David went forward. Goliath said, "Return. I hate to kill you." David said, "But I love to kill you." Then he took the three rocks and put them in the sling. He swung it, they became one rock, and he threw it at Goliath. It opened his head, and Goliath's army ran as losers.

What is wrong with this picture? Lots of errors! First of all, the conversation between Goliath and David was more than "Go away, I hate to kill you" or "Come, but I love to kill you." The real account is recorded in 1 Samuel 17:41–51. The Philistine held a shield in one hand, while David only had a staff in his hand. When the Philistine saw David, he disdained him, for he was a youth, seemingly without fighting experience. Goliath asked David if he thought of him as a dog since David had come to fight Goliath with a stick. Then he cursed David by his gods, told David to come to him, and said he would feed David's flesh to the birds and the beasts of the fields. Then David stood and accused the Philistine of coming to him with the sword and the spear while David had come to the Philistine in the name of the Lord of hosts.

That day the Lord would deliver Goliath into David's hands, and David would cut off Goliath's head. David would then give the carcasses of the host of the Philistines to the birds of the heavens and the beasts of the fields. Then the whole earth would know that there is a God in Israel and that the battle is the Lord's.

Then David put his hand in his bag and took one stone, a stone, not three, not five stones, but one stone. He swung with his sling and the rock smote Goliath's forehead, and Goliath fell on his face to the earth. Notice the rock did not open his head but just hit him in his forehead. Since there was no sword in David's hand, he ran, stood on top of the Philistine, took Goliath's own sword, drew it out of the sheath, and slew him. Then he cut off Goliath's head. When the Philistines saw what happened to their champion, they fled. The men of Israel shouted, followed the Philistines, and killed many of them. Then they took the spoils out of the Philistines' tents.

Now let us go back to the lies of Ibn Kathir. After the killing of Goliath, King Saul gave his daughter to David and allowed David to rule the kingdom with him. He gave David a great position. The Children of Israel favored him over Saul, so Saul envied him and tried to kill him. However, he could not get to David because Saul's scholars forbade Saul from killing David. As a result, Saul killed many of the scholars until there were just a few of them left. Then he repented and cried.

Then Saul used to go out to the tombs and his tears were so much [wetting the tombs] from crying. The dead from the tombs called to him. The dead said that Saul had killed them, and now he harmed them by his tears, even when they were dead. That is why he cried more and more and was so afraid. He searched for a scholar to ask of him concerning this matter and if there was repentance. So it was said to him, "Have you kept any of the scholars alive?" He found a woman of those who were worshipers, so she took him to the tomb of Joshua. Ibn Kathir continued by saying they (we do not know who *they* are) said she called on Allah, and Joshua rose from his tomb and asked if the resurrection had happened. She said, "No, but this Saul wanted to ask you if there is any repentance." So Joshua said, "Yes. Saul will be removed from the kingdom, will fight for the sake of Allah, and will be killed." Then Joshua died again.

Saul left the kingdom to David. He went with thirteen of his sons, and they fought for the sake of Allah until they were killed, *and Allah knows best*. There are different opinions about the identity of the prophet whom Saul asked about the repentance. Mohammed Ibn Isaac said it was Prophet Elijah, but Al Salabe said that the woman brought him to the tomb of Samuel, which was more acceptable to Ibn Kathir. Perhaps he saw him in his sleep, for to see him alive in the tomb would be a miracle of a prophet, and this woman was not a prophet, *and Allah knows best*.

Ibn Kathir ended his story by saying that it was claimed by the people of the Torah that the kingdom of King Saul, until the killing of him and his son, lasted forty years, *and Allah knows best*. [20]

What are the errors in the rest of Ibn Kathir's story? There are plenty of errors. First of all, he never gave David a portion of the

---

[20] Ibn Kathir, 12.

kingdom. We must ask the same question again. *Where did Ibn Kathir and his fellow scholars come up with this information?* Nowhere, except in the Bible. In 1 Samuel 18 and 19, one can find where Saul tried to kill David three times, but David was able to escape. Then Saul found out from Doeg the Edomite, in 1 Samuel 22:9-23, that Ahimelech had helped David by giving him the sword of Goliath, along with some provisions.

Saul became angry and, as a result, killed eighty-five priests, and then he killed the entire city of Nob including the livestock with the edge of the sword. However, one young son of Ahimelech, by the name of Abiathar, escaped and fled to David. Obviously, that is what Ibn Kathir meant by the statement "scholars that King Saul killed." As for the story of the woman of the worshipers, who took Saul to the tomb to raise up for him Joshua, Elijah, or Samuel, this story is taken from 1 Samuel 28, beginning with verse 7. The reason Saul went to this medium, using the power of demons, was obviously because the spirit of God had departed from Saul, and he could no longer receive knowledge through the prophets.

This was not a dream, as Ibn Kathir mentioned, but was a true story, and the prophet the medium brought to life was Samuel, without any guessing of other prophets' names. There was a long conversation between Saul and Samuel, and in it he told Saul what would take place in the war with the Philistines. He explained to Saul that on the following day Saul and his sons would be killed. Saul fell to the ground at the words of Samuel because he had not eaten during the day or night. This woman gave Saul food. At first he refused to eat, but when she insisted, he ate. Saul and his servant ate, and then they left her house.

You can read the rest of the story of Saul in 1 Samuel 28-31. There you will discover the true account as written by the inspriation of the Holy Spirit from the true One and only true author, God himself, even though it is penned by human hands.

23 The Story of David

David is considered to be one of the most important prophets in Islam. *But who was David, according to Muslim scholars?* Ibn Kathir wrote about David in eleven pages in his book *Stories of the Prophets,* concerning David's life and death.[1] He began by stating that David was Ibn Isha (wrong name, the real name is Jesse), Ibn Oed (wrong spelling, he meant Obed), Ibn Abor (wrong name, the real name is Boaz), Ibn Salmon, Ibn Nashun, Ibn Aonynazb (wrong name, the real name is Amminadab), Ibn Arm (wrong spelling, he meant Aram), Ibn Nahshon, Ibn Perez, Ibn Judah, Ibn Jacob, Ibn Isaac, Ibn Abraham, the friend and the servant of Allah and his prophet.

We must ask a question: *Where did Ibn Kathir come up with all these names?* Neither Allah in the Qur'an nor Mohammed in the hadith mentions such names. One can find the real genealogy of King David in the Bible in many places in the Old Testament, but we choose to give the genealogy as it is written in one location, for the sake of simplicity, in the Gospel of Luke 3:31-38: *[31]The son of Melea, the son of Menan, the son of Mattathah, the son of Nathan, the son of David, [32]the son of Jesse, the son of Obed, the son of Boaz, the son of Salmon, the son of Nahshon, [33]the son of Amminadab, the son of Ram, the son of Hezron, the son of Perez, the son of Judah, [34]the son of Jacob, the son of Isaac, the son of Abraham, the son of Terah, the son of Nahor, [35]the son of Serug, the son of Reu, the son of Peleg, the son of Eber, the son of Shelah, [36]the son of Cainan, the son of Arphaxad, the son of Shem, the son of Noah, the son of Lamech, [37]the son of Methuselah, the son of Enoch, the son of Jared, the son of Mahalalel, the son of Cainan, [38]the son of Enosh, the son of Seth, the son of Adam, the son of God.* Notice, through the biblical account, we cannot only go from David to Abraham as Ibn Kathir did; but also, we can go all the way back to Adam, the first man who walked on the earth.

Muslims break the Book (the Bible) into the following three sections: the Torah of Moses, the Psalms of David (which is known in

---

[1]Ibn Kathir, *Stories of the Prophets*, vol. 2, Abo Al Fida Ishamail Ibn Kathir Al Kurashi Al Damashce (Beirut: Dar Al-Arab Heritage, 1408 AH, 1988), 13.

the Qur'an by the name Zabor), and the Gospel of Jesus ('Isā). (Muslims believe fragments of Jesus' message are contained in the existent gospels but that the majority of the original teaching has been corrupted or lost.) Mohammed and Muslims do not realize that the Bible is much larger than these seven books. The Torah, which consists of the first five books of the Old Testament (according to the Jewish faith), the Psalms, and the Gospels (Matthew, Mark, Luke, and John) of the New Testament account for only a portion of the Bible. They also do not know that Jesus did not write any books. He did not receive any gospel from God; rather He is the Gospel, the Good News, the Word of God.

How much can we learn about David from the writings of Mohammed? To begin with, the name David is mentioned sixteen times throughout the Qur'an, and four of those times it is simply mentioned, without any detail, or with one tiny detail or bit of information. See Qur'an 4:163; 6:84; 34:13; and 38:30.

The story of David is extensive; it can be found in the following books of the Bible: 1 and 2 Samuel, 1 and 2 Kings, 1 and 2 Chronicles, and Psalms. These books tell the entirety of the life of David, but he is also mentioned in other books of the Bible as well. The book of Psalms, on the other hand, was written mostly by David. If you were to study all of these books, which most Muslims do not even realize exist, you could discover everything that is known about David. There are some controversial times of his life which Muslims systematically discard, believing that they are errors added to his life as recorded in the Bible. Let me give you an example. When they read or hear about the sin of David with Bathsheba, Muslims immediately reject the story, not realizing that the same story is repeated in other parts of the Bible by other authors, consistently and without contradiction.

David and Goliath and David's Rise in Power

The story of David killing Goliath is found in Qur'an 2:251, but it contains no details about where, when, how, or why this occurred, as we have seen in the previous section above. One of the surprising things written by Ibn Kathir is the description of David. He wrote that Mohammed Ibn Isaac said David was a short, young man with blue eyes, little hair, and a pure and clean heart. *Where did Mohammed Ibn Isaac come up with this description?* The Bible states only that Samuel anointed David to be the king while he was still a shepherd boy. There is no information in the Bible concerning the height or the color of the eyes of David. All we know is that he was *"...ruddy, with beautiful eyes, and a handsome appearance"* (1 Samuel 16:12).

Now let us consider the details of the fight between David and Goliath from the original source. In 1 Samuel 17:1 we read that the place of the conflict was between Shochoh and Azekah, at Ephes Dammim, which means *boundary of blood*. Goliath, a huge man, six cubits and a span (9' 9"), challenged the Israelites by asking them to choose a man from among them to come out and fight him. Whoever won would be the master over the rest. There at Ephes Dammim, Saul and the Israelites fought in fear.

David was sent by his father to check on his brothers, taking some food with him (verse 18), and there he heard about the challenge from Goliath. In verse 26, he asked about the reward for the man who would kill Goliath. His brothers got angry at him for leaving the sheep and for his investigation into such a thing.

David stood before Saul, recounting killing a lion and a bear by himself (1 Samuel 17:34). When Saul brought him armor, he was not able to walk in it, so he removed this armor and picked up five smooth stones, a staff, and a sling (verse 40). He stood up before Goliath, the Philistine; and though Goliath made fun of David, threatening to give his flesh to the birds, David challenged him in return by saying in verse 45: *You come to me with a sword, with a spear, and with a javelin. But I come to you in the name of the LORD of hosts, the God of the armies of Israel, whom you have defied.* Then David slung the stone and hit Goliath in his forehead. When Goliath fell down onto the ground, David picked up Goliath's sword and cut off his head (1 Samuel 17:1-54).

Following Ibn Kathir's description of David, Ibn Asakir stated that when David killed Goliath, he killed him northeast of Damascus. Then the Israelites loved him and made him king over them. Allah gathered to him the kingdom and the prophethood. That is why Allah said in Qur'an 2:251: *[251]So they defeated them by Allah's permission. And Dāwūd[2] killed Goliath, and Allah gave him the kingdom and the wisdom. And he taught him from whatever he willed. And were it not that Allah gives conquest to some people over others, then the earth would have been vandalized. But Allah is the possessor of bounty to the worlds.*

When one reads a verse like this one and asks questions like where, when, how, why, and who concerning Goliath and David, the

---

[2]David, non-Arabic word of Aramaic origin

answer from Muslim scholars will be wrong, or they will say *Allah knows best*, simply because, as usual, the information does not exist in the Qur'an. Ibn Kathir stated that Ibn Jarir said Goliath challenged Talut (wrong name, he meant King Saul).[3] So Talut asked the people to fight him, and David killed Goliath. All the people removed Saul from power and made David the king over them. It was said that this was a command of Samuel, and some said Samuel appointed him as king before this incident. Ibn Kathir ended his interpretation by saying, *and Allah knows best*. Ibn Asakir said that Goliath was killed near the castle of the mother of Hakkum, *and Allah knows best*.[4]

Ibn Kathir mentioned the opinions of many Muslim scholars. Some of them stated that Wahab Ibn Monabah said the people leaned toward David to the point that Talut (Saul) became unimportant. The people removed him and appointed David as king over them. Some said it was an order from Samuel, to the point that they said they made him a king before the killing of Goliath.[5] My response is that this claim is not true, for David was never appointed as king while Saul was alive, as we read in the true account in the Bible. He was not a king until Saul and Jonathan died, as we will see in the coming pages.

Also, in Qur'an 21:78 the giving of the book of Zabor (Psalms) was mentioned when Allah said: *[78]And David and Solomon, when they judged concerning the crop when the sheep of the people pastured in it, and we were to their judgment a witness.* Here we see David was judging as king with his son, which makes no sense, for no two kings rule at the same time.

Prophet Samuel anointed David at God's direction. God had rejected Saul as king of Israel when he sinned against God by disobeying Him. He offered the sacrifice, which was not to be offered by the king, rather than waiting on Prophet Samuel to offer it. We see this in 1 Samuel 13:13: *And Samuel said to Saul, "You have done foolishly. You have not kept the commandment of the LORD your God, which He commanded you. For now the LORD would have established your kingdom over Israel forever."* Also, God asked him to destroy Amalek and all the animals, but Saul disobeyed God by sparing King Agag and the best of the sheep, cows, and lambs. Later,

---

[3]Ibn Kathir, 13.
[4]Ibid., 14.
[5]Ibid., 13.

he offered a sacrifice which he was not supposed to make because it was the God-given responsibility of Prophet Samuel as we read in 2 Samuel 15.

Saul became jealous, especially when the ladies sang to David in 1 Samuel 18:7: **"... Saul has slain his thousands and David his ten thousands."** We know from the Scripture that Saul tried many times to kill David (1 Samuel 19), but we also know that David was in a position to kill Saul on more than one occasion (1 Samuel 24 and 26). However, David never harmed Saul, for he believed that Saul was the anointed king of God.

David was never a king while Saul was still alive. Until Saul died (1 Samuel 31), he was the king of Israel. David wept over the death of Saul and his son Jonathan, whom he loved and with whom he had a great friendship (2 Samuel 1:17). David first became the king over Judah and then became king over all Israel (2 Samuel 2:5). Notice that none of these facts or information can be found in the Qur'an, hadith, or any Muslim sources.

The Bounty and Iron

In Qur'an 21:79-80, Allah said: *[79]So we caused Solomon to understand it, and to each of them we gave wisdom and knowledge. And we made subservient with David the mountains and the birds to praise, and we were the doers. [80]And we taught him the making of clothes for you to protect you from your violence. So are you thankful?*

Then in Qur'an 27:15: *[15]And indeed, we gave knowledge to David and Solomon, and they said, "Praise be to Allah who has favored us above many of his believing servants."* David was given knowledge by Allah, as all prophets were said to have received knowledge from Allah. In 27:16: *[16]And Solomon inherited David, and he said, "O you people, we have been taught the speech of the birds, and we have been given from everything. Surely this is the manifest bounty."* Solomon inherited the kingdom from David.

Also, in Qur'an 34:10-11, Allah subjugated the mountains to David and taught him to make war clothes. So he, the king, became a professional armor maker. Also, Allah was given bounty, and iron was made softened for David as written in these two verses: *[10]And indeed, we gave David a bounty from us: "O mountains, sing praises with him and the birds." And we softened the iron to him. ¹¹That, "Make suitable coats of sard⁶ and measure the length. And do a good deed. Surely I see what you do."* Also, see Qur'an 21:79-80 above.

Ibn Kathir stated that Allah helped David to make the armor of iron so he would be able to fight the enemy, and Allah taught him how to construct such armor. This is what has been shown in the previous verses. Al Hasan and Qatadah stated that Allah made the iron soft for him so he could work it by his hand and would not need any fire or sledge hammer to soften it.⁷ Qatadah said David was the first man who made armor from chain because before his time, it was made of solid breastplate armor. That is really amazing that a king worked as an armorer, and what mighty hands he had that he would not need fire or a hammer!

David's Wisdom and Speech of the Birds

In Qur'an 38:17-20: *¹⁷Be patient with what they say, and remember our servant David, a man with hands, surely he was repentant. ¹⁸Surely we made the mountains subservient with him; they will praise in the evening and in the sunrise. ¹⁹And the birds in obedience were all gathered to him ²⁰And we strengthened his kingdom, and we gave him the wisdom and the discerning speech.* Ibn Kathir's interpretation said the kingdom of David and his wisdom was very great. This has been proven by a made-up story by Ibn Abbas, who stated that two men disputed with each other concerning a cow.⁸ The men went to David and each one claimed that this cow was his. Then David asked them to leave until the evening. When the night came, Allah revealed to David to kill the one who was the liar. When the morning came, David said to him, "Allah revealed to me that I must kill you. So surely I am killing you, absolutely I must kill you." Then the man said, "O you prophet of Allah, surely you are telling the truth. I lied about the cow." So David commanded him to be killed. Then David was greatly and highly respected among the Children of Israel who were very obedient to him.

Scholars disagree concerning what the Qur'an says of Allah giving David wisdom. Some said the wisdom here is a prophecy, others said the right judging and understanding, and Wahab Ibn

---

⁶chain armor, non-Arabic word of Persian/Syriac origin
⁷Ibn Kathir, 14.
⁸Ibid., 16.

Monabah said evil and the false witness in Israel was great in David's time. That is why David was given a chain so he would be decisive in his judging, and this chain was spread from the heaven to the rock in the holy house. The chain was made of gold. So if there were two men in disagreement, the man with the truth would be able to reach the chain and the other would not be able reach it.[9] This was until a man gave another man a pearl, but then he refused to give it back to him. He got a staff and put the pearl inside the staff, so when they arrived at the rock, the one who was accused of stealing the pearl said to the other, "Take it by your hand," pointing to his staff. So he gave it to him, and he said, "O God, you know I gave the pearl to him." Then he reached out to the chain, and the chain became a problem to the Children of Israel (so it appears that the truth can be tricked); therefore, the chain was removed from among them. Wow! I can't believe that this man was able to trick Allah, the "all-knowing."

In their interpretation, Ibn Abbas and Mujahid stated that the hand of David was strong and was obedient to Allah by serving Allah and doing good deeds.[10] Then they compared Mohammed to David by saying that Mohammed loved praying to Allah as David loved fasting to Allah.

In verses 18 and 19, Allah commanded the mountain and the birds to worship with David at the beginning and the end of the day. This had been explained by stating that Allah gave David a strong voice that he had never given to anyone before him, and that when David sang by reading his book, the birds stopped in the air and sang the songs of David.[11] The mountains also answered him as they sang with him morning and night. Abd Allah Ibn Amir said that David was given the most beautiful voice, to the point that the birds and the animals stood next to him just to hear him, and they died thirsty and hungry because they did not want to leave him.

On the same line of thought, Wahab said when David used to read the Zabor (the Psalms), his voice was like no other voice to the point that the jinn, the humans, the birds, and the animals stood there until they died; some died of hunger. We must ask questions. *If they all got thirsty and hungry enough to die for the joy of listening to this*

---

[9]Ibid., 16.
[10]Ibid., 14.
[11]Ibid., 14-15.

beautiful voice of David, didn't David get hungry and thirsty? Why couldn't they eat and drink when David stopped singing and while he was eating?

In Qur'an 17:55: *And we gave David Psalms.* Ibn Kathir stated that the book of Psalms is a famous book.[12] Amazingly, Muslims believe in this book without knowing anything about it. As for Christians and Jews, they understand and know such a book since it still exists today in its fullness in the Bible. There are 150 chapters in the book of Psalms. Not all of them were written by David, but most of them were. Some of the psalms were written by Asaph, the family of Korah, Moses, Ethan, Heman, and others.

There is only one verse of the entire book of Psalms written in the Qur'an, which is found within 21:105: *[105]And indeed, we wrote in the Psalms after the reminder: "Surely my good servant will inherit the earth."* One of the amazing statements that has been said and repeated by Muslims is, "We believe in David and in the book of Psalms," but sadly, Muslims do not know David or the book of Psalms. If they knew David, they would know many of his prophecies concerning the coming of Jesus, the suffering Messiah, the One who would die on a cross and rise from the dead The message of Christianity is prophesied and written by David in the Psalms.

Advice for Muslim Readers

My simple advice to Muslims is to read the book of Psalms and see the Christian's face. I remember one time I was speaking at a college. A large number of Muslim students waited after my seminar to argue or debate with me. One of them was very sincere, and his question to me was, "If Jesus Christ is God, then why did He cry from the cross praying to God, seeking God's help by saying, 'My God, My God, why hast thou forsaken me?'" My answer to him was, "Do you believe in the book of Psalms, the book of Prophet David?" He said, "Yes, I do." But then he asked, "What does the book of Psalms have to do with Jesus crying on the cross?"

In his talk with me, I found a sincere heart and the usual level of ignorance among Muslims. He wanted to know the answer concerning why Jesus was crying to God. He believed in David, but at the same time he was ignorant of who David was and of David's prophecy. Then I asked him if he had ever read Psalm 22. The answer was that he had never read any of the Psalms. I explained to him that

---

[12]Ibid.

Psalm 22, at the time of Jesus, did not have the chapter number 22, but was instead known by the first verse which is, "My God, My God, why hast thou forsaken me?"

Like every other chapter in the book of Psalms, they were known by the first verse in the chapter. Another good example is Psalm 23 which was known by "The Lord is my shepherd," and so on and so on. Then I asked another Christian college student who stood next to us with a Bible in his hand to read to us the psalm's title: "My God, My God, why hast thou forsaken me?" It was eye opening to many of those who stood around us to hear the prophecy of David in Psalm 22.

As we move from Psalm 22 to Matthew, Mark, Luke, and John, we go between the prophecies of David which were written a thousand years before their fulfillment in the life of Jesus Christ. In Psalm 22:7-8: *[7]Those who see Me ridicule Me; They shoot out the lip, they shake the head, saying, [8]"He trusted in the LORD, let Him rescue Him; Let Him deliver Him, since He delights in Him!"*

This was the prophecy. I said they could see the fulfillment in Matthew 27:29: *[29]When they had twisted a crown of thorns, they put it on His head, and a reed in His right hand. And they bowed the knee before Him and mocked Him, saying, "Hail, King of the Jews!"* Also, in verse 39: *[39]And those who passed by blasphemed Him, wagging their heads.* Then in verse 43: *[43]He trusted in God; let Him deliver Him now if He will have Him; for He said, "I am the Son of God."*

Another prophecy in Psalm 22 is in verses 16-18: *[16]For dogs have surrounded Me; The congregation of the wicked has enclosed Me. They pierced My hands and My feet; [17]I can count all My bones. They look and stare at Me. [18]They divide My garments among them, And for My clothing they cast lots.* The fulfillment of this prophecy can be found in Matthew 27:35: *[35]Then they crucified Him, and divided His garments, casting lots, that it might be fulfilled which was spoken by the prophet: "They divided My garments among them, And for My clothing they cast lots."* Notice that crucifixion was prophesied by David a thousand years before the coming of Jesus. Moreover, crucifixion was an idea not yet developed at the time of David, as we have mentioned before.

Obviously, this young Muslim student was shocked to know that the crucifixion of Jesus was not the invention of Paul or some early Christians, but it was the fulfillment of prophecies which were written by many prophets hundreds of years before the time of Christ.

David and Bathsheba

    I watched a YouTube video about a Christian youth minister named Joshua Evans who converted to Islam.[13] The title of the video obviously captured my attention, but as I watched this video I could not help but discern that this "youth minister" was a fraud. Yes, he was an American who became a Muslim at the age of seventeen, and now he is traveling all over the country sharing his testimony on how he discovered all the errors of the Bible and how he became a Muslim.

    First, how can he prove that he was ever a youth minister? He did not finish high school according to his own testimony. *So when did he become a youth minister?* There were so many errors and contradictions in his testimony, to the point that any person with common sense could see it by watching his video. He said he studied all the theology books which belonged to his friend, who was a youth minister, so Joshua studied these books when he was only sixteen or seventeen years of age. The Bible teaches that a person much be qualified and trained and tested to minister. Today, this means that a person must first finish high school and then study at least four years of undergraduate studies, which would make a person twenty two years old. *So how did he study all of that while he was studying his own books for high school?*

    He claimed to know Greek and Hebrew while he was only seventeen, yet to know two such languages one must complete a master's program in a seminary. This would take at least another four years; that's simply a general study, not any doctrinal level studies. That will bring the person to a simple understanding of the biblical language of Hebrew and Greek, which would make the student at least twenty-six years old. But, remember, he became a Muslim when he was seventeen. *When did he study Hebrew and Greek? Was he ever in any seminary school?* Of course not! One of his claims was that he studied textual criticism. He went on and on about his knowledge of such a science. Considering these claims, this young man may need mental help; somebody should reach out to him and others like him. The important part of this testimony which fits into

---

[13]Joshua Evans, "How the Bible Led Me to Islam: The Story of a Former Christian Youth Minister," *Youtube,* September 9, 2009, accessed December 13, 2012, https://www.youtube.com/watch?v=IYMKQKSV0bY.

our topic here is why he left Christianity. According to him, it was when he began reading the Bible and discovered many of the errors in the Scripture.

Joshua stated that when he was a child, he learned about many stories of the Bible such as the story of David. He was so excited to learn about David and how he slaughtered Goliath, as taught to him in Sunday school class. Then when he began reading the Bible at age sixteen, he said that he began to discover many facts about David that no one had told him before, and it was shocking new information. He discovered that David committed adultery and committed a murder. Wow! *That's when he discovered that the Bible is a "corrupt" book?* So many Muslims, when they read the Bible, discover that there is sin in the life of the people, especially prophets or those whom Mohammed and Muslim scholars named prophets. *How can the Bible be the word of God when it shows incest and adultery?* This is what Joshua Evans said, and that is why he decided to leave Christianity and become a Muslim. I guess he had not read the Qur'an yet or studied the life of Mohammed, if he would lose his faith over such information in the Bible.

Did David commit adultery? Did David kill Uriah the Hittite? Who loved David more, Jewish people or Christians or Muslims? Who would know best the truth about David, David or someone else? If the Bible reveals sins committed by its people, kings, and prophets, does this prove that the Bible is a corrupt book or a true book? One may say, if any change ever took place in the Bible, it would have to be the removal of the sins and the evil acts of the kings and the prophets of the Bible. However, in doing so, this would create a contradiction in the teaching of the Bible because the Bible says all have sinned. "All" means *everybody.*

From Adam to the last person to be born, all have sinned. Not one is righteous, not even David. David wrote, as we read in Psalm 51:5: *⁵Behold, I was brought forth in iniquity, And in sin my mother conceived me.* The idea that the prophets did not sin, as taught by Muslims, not only contradicts the teaching of the Bible, but it also contradicts the teaching of the Qur'an. The Qur'an states that Adam sinned for he disobeyed Allah by eating from the tree which he was commanded not to eat. Moses sinned by killing the Egyptian, and David sinned by committing adultery with Bathsheba; but sadly, our friend Joshua Evans and many Muslims around the world do not know this.

What is amazing is Joshua Evans and all other Westerners who became Muslims do not know that the Qur'an, which they believe is a replacement for the Bible, teaches the same story about David sinning with Bathsheba. Not only this, but also it teaches that Mohammed, the prophet of Islam, was a sinful, yes, a very sinful man to the point that there was not one sin he did *not* commit. We will cover this in the section on Mohammed of this book, *Exposing the Truth about the Qur'an: The Revelation of Error*, but let us now study the story of King David sinning with Bathsheba as written in the Qur'an and as interpreted by Muslim scholars. Then we will share the true account of the Bible.

Qur'an 38:21-25 contains the story of David and Bathsheba, but it is missing much information, as well as being distorted from the original account in the Bible. The story of David and Bathsheba is written in 2 Samuel 11, and it is supported by Psalm 51. When we ask Muslims who the father of King Solomon was, they all know it was King David. However, they have no answer for the following question. *Who was the mother of King Solomon?* A simple search of the Bible will prove that he was the son of Bathsheba, the woman with whom David committed adultery and whose husband David had killed; she was also the woman who lost her first child, the child of adultery, through death. Now let us examine the verses of the Qur'an and the interpretation by Muslim scholars to see their story of David's sins against God with Bathsheba and her husband. Then we will study the truth as it is written by David in the Holy Bible.

We read Qur'an 38:21-25: *[21]And has the news of the two litigants come to you, when they entered the holy of holies? [22]When they entered into David, so he panicked because of them. They said, "Do not be afraid. Two litigants, some of us has wronged the others. So judge between us with the truth and do not act unjustly and guide us to a right way. [23]Surely this is my brother. He has ninety-nine sheep, and I had one sheep. So he said, 'Give it to me.' And he overcame me in the argument." [24]He said, "Indeed, he has done an injustice to you by asking for your sheep to his sheep, and surely many partners wrong one another, except those who believed and did good deeds, and few there are." And David thought that we only seduced him, so he asked forgiveness from his lord and fell down and bowed and turned. [25]So we forgave him this, and surely he had a nearness to us and a good return.*

It is amazing how Ibn Kathir interpreted such verses.[14] He simply said many interpreters from the past had mentioned interpretations of this passage, but he found this unacceptable and forbidden for these were lies because, he claimed, most of the interpretations were from the Jewish faith. He added, "We purposely refuse to put such interpretations in our book. We found that just telling the verses from the great Qur'an is enough, and Allah will guide whom he wills to a straight way."

Wow! What a scholar! *Why can't he give us an interpretation of the verses in his book, "The Stories of the Prophet," if he was a true scholar? Don't Muslims deserve to have an explanation of exactly what took place in David's life? The question we must ask here is why Ibn Kathir rejected or refused to interpret these verses? Is the interpretation of the verses not true, or are the verses of the Qur'an themselves not true? Why can't he interpret the verses that exist in his own Qur'an?* When I looked at Al Tabari's interpretation, I discovered that he got closer to the truth, but he still twisted it by saying that David had ninety-nine wives, that he used to have a warrior who had one wife, and that David took (had sex) this warrior's wife **after** her husband was killed.[15] In Al Tabari's interpretation of the words *"give it [her] to me"* (Qur'an 38:23), it was said that Ibn Zied said he meant divorce her so David could have her as a wife. Al Tabari's interpretation to the saying, *"...he overcame me in the argument"* (Qur'an 38:23), was that David was unjustly strong to take her away.

Al Tabari continued his interpretation of Qur'an 38:24 by saying that:

> David said this man had sinned when he asked the other man to give him his one wife to be added to his ninety-nine wives. In this interpretation, David fell down and bowed down to Allah to repent. He returned to Allah by repenting of his sin. Some scholars said that David remembered what Allah had given Abraham and Jacob, the respect among the people. He wished to have a similar position. Allah said to him that they were tempted and were patient. So David asked to be tempted and to receive the reward if he was patient.

---

[14]Ibn Kathir, 14-15.

[15]http://quran.al-islam.com/Page.aspx?pageid=221&BookID=13&Page=454, accessed January 24, 2013.

It was such a long time that David waited for Allah to tempt him that he almost forgot about it until one time, when David was in the Holy of Holies, a golden dove fell on him. He desired to take her. So the dove flew in the window of the Holy of Holies. He went to take her, but she flew away. Then David looked from the window and saw a woman bathing. So the prophet of Allah came down from the Holy of Holies, and he sent for this woman to come to him. David asked her about her husband and her matters. She told him that her husband was absent, and David sent to her husband's division and commanded that her husband be put in the war where all his friends were wounded except for him. David asked the commander again to send her husband to war. During this battle, all his companions were harmed. However, he was delivered again, and they won this battle.

There are different opinions by other scholars.[16] Others said David sent for the leader to command the man to fight against an enemy so that perhaps he may be killed, but he won the battle. Then David asked the commander to send him to a stronger enemy, perhaps he may be killed. However, he was not killed; he won again. So David asked the commander to send him a third time to an even stronger enemy, but this time he was killed.

Then David married this man's wife. After David married her, Allah sent to him two litigants (some other scholars said that these two litigants were angels in the shape of humans) while David was in the Holy of Holies. When David saw them, he became frightened. They said for him not to be afraid. They said they were arguing with each other. That is why they came to be judged by David, so they said for him to hear them. One of them said that this was his brother who has ninety-nine ewes, and he only has one. His brother wants to take his female sheep so that he can have a full one hundred sheep and leave him with nothing. He overcame him in the argument. Then David said that he has more need of his sheep than his brother and that his brother had dealt with him unjustly concerning his ewe. The two litigants (or angels) looked at each other and smiled.

Then David remembered his sin, so he sought forgiveness of his sin, fell down, and repented. Al Tabari continued by saying it was forty nights that he cried until the plants grew from the tears from his eyes. Then Allah strengthened to him his kingdom. A similar story is

---

[16]Ibid.

repeated by many other scholars, including Al Tabari, but all these interpretations have some fiction and fabrication.

Much interpretation has been given about these verses. Few of them make sense, although some are closer to the true account in the Bible, but much of what has been told is nonsense. I find it to be amazing that while Al Tabari and other Muslim scholars write pages of interpretation for these few verses, the great scholar Ibn Kathir ignored them completely. The important issue is acknowledgement of Muslim scholars of the sins of David. My heart's desire is that Muslims will read the interpretations of Al Tabari and others and that they stop using deception in trying to mislead Westerners by claiming the Bible is corrupted because their own interpretations mention that the prophets sinned, as seen here in the case of David.

A simple reading of Scripture gives us the true account, without second guessing, in 1 Samuel 16 through 2 Samuel 2. We will give a concise summary, but we encourage the reader to read the entire story in the Bible passage.

Now to the true account of the Bible in 2 Samuel 11. It was a time during which the kings would go out to war. David sent Joab with his servants to fight, but David stayed in Jerusalem. It was at evening time when David rose from his bed and walked on the roof of his house. This did not take place at the Holy of Holies, as Muslim scholars claim, for the Holy of Holies is not a place for David or any king to enter. Only the high priest could enter there and only once a year. Also, the Holy of Holies was not built in David's day but later by his son, King Solomon. Another gross error in the Muslim stories occurs when they describe David looking out of windows in the Holy of Holies when in fact the Holy of Holies did not have any windows.

When David saw a woman bathing, he asked about her and found out that she was Bathsheba, daughter of Eliam, the wife of Uriah the Hittite. Then David sent for her, took her, and lay with her. In verse 5, the Bible says that she conceived. When she told David that she was pregnant, he sent for her husband to come home so that he would lay with his wife in order to cover David's sin with Bathsheba.

However, her husband refused to lay with her, for he was an honorable man. Uriah said to David that he could not eat or lay with his wife when the army was on the battlefield. When David found out Uriah did not lay with his wife and did not even go to his house, David tried again. David fed him and gave him drink until Uriah became drunk, but still he did not go to his wife to lay with her. He stayed with the servant of his master David. Therefore, David sent him back to Joab with a message asking him to put Uriah in the front of the hottest battle so that he may be killed. Uriah carried the message in his own hand without knowing it, and there in the battlefield he was killed.

After the death of Uriah, David sent for Bathsheba and added her to his house. She became a wife to him and bore him a son. David's actions displeased the Lord. However, this was not the end of the story because in 2 Samuel 12, we read about a prophet by the name of Nathan who came and spoke to David. Nathan told David a story concerning two men. Notice it was not two men that met with David, as Mohammed and his Muslim scholars changed and fabricated the story in the Qur'an and its interpretation, but actually it was a prophet by the name of Nathan who told the story to David. The story was that one man, who had ninety-nine sheep, had a neighbor who was poor and had only one sheep. This rich man had a guest come to visit him, so he chose not one of his own sheep to prepare as a meal for his guest, but he took the one sheep of his neighbor to offer his guest.

At this point (verse 5), David became so angry that he said the man who did such a thing must be killed and four sheep must be returned for the one taken because he had done such a thing and had not shown compassion to his poor neighbor. Then boldly the prophet Nathan told David that *he* was that man. After all God had done for David, he did this evil work in the eyes of the Lord. Prophet Nathan told David that he killed Uriah the Hittite by the sword of the Ammonites. Therefore, the sword would not leave David's house forever because he took Uriah's wife. The Lord would take David's wives before his eyes and give them to his neighbor who would sleep with them in the middle of the day.

David then repented to Nathan. He said that he had sinned against the Lord. However, that was not the end of the punishment on David, for Nathan, the prophet, told David that his son who was born of this woman must die. The Lord struck the boy, and he became sick. David prayed and fasted, but on the seventh day, the young boy died. In verse 24, we read that David comforted Bathsheba and lay with her. She begot him a son whom all Muslims know, but they do not know that he was the son of David from Bathsheba. This son was King Solomon.

As for the tears of David, which were mentioned in some Muslim scholars' interpretations, we can read about this in Psalm 51. Amazingly, the title of this psalm is "A Psalm to David when the Prophet Nathan came to David after he lay with Bathsheba." It is a beautiful psalm, and we would encourage the reader to read and meditate on it. In it David confessed his sin and sought God's forgiveness, and God purified and cleansed him. David asked God to create a new heart in him and renew a right spirit in him. Yes, he had a broken spirit and a broken heart and that is an acceptable sacrifice to God as written in verse 17. Then God forgave him because he repented of his sin.

In one of his hadith concerning the fasting of David, Ibn Abbas said that David used to fast a lot.[17] He alternated fasting every other day. He said the apostle of Allah, Mohammed, said that the best fasting was the fasting of David. He used to read the book of Zabor (Psalms) with seventy voices and used to kneel during the night. He cried in his spirit and everything cried with his cry and with his voice he sent away the sorrow and the sickness.

The Length of David's Life
How many years did David live? Although there is no mention in the Qur'an of the length of David's life, the hadith, written by Ibn Abbas and Abu Horyrah, clearly teaches that after Allah created Adam, he touched his back with his hand and lights fell from his back representing his descendants.[18] Adam saw in them the prophets and among them a man represented as a small light. So Adam asked Allah, "Who is this?" Allah said, "That's your son David." So he said, "How old is he?" Allah said, "Sixty years." He said, "O Lord, add to his age." Allah said, "No. If I will add to his age, I have to take it away from your age."

Adam was supposed to live a thousand years. So Allah increased David forty more years. So when the time came for Adam to die, the angel of death came to him. Adam said, "Don't I have forty more years to live?" However, he had forgotten that he had given these forty years to his son David as a gift. So Allah fulfilled it to Adam a thousand years and to David one hundred years. Now one must ask some questions. *How many years did Adam live? How many years did David live according to the Bible?* First of all, this conversation between Adam and God did not occur. There is no such thing as God borrowing time from Adam's years to live and giving them to David.

Muslim scholars and Mohammed claim that Adam lived a thousand years. That is false, so they made up a story about Adam

---

[17]Ibn Kathir, 20.
[18]Ibid., 21.

giving forty years of his life to King David. This claim does not help them for if this claim were true, Adam must have lived 960 years. This number is still false. According to the Bible, Adam lived 930 years (Genesis 5:5). Muslim scholars and Mohammed claim that King David was supposed to live sixty years, but he borrowed forty years from Adam which means that King David lived a hundred years. That is also false, for he lived seventy years as we read in 2 Samuel 5:4-5.

How Did David Die?

Although the Qur'an does not mention anything about David's death, a humorous story was told by Abu Horyrah.[19] He said that Mohammed said David was a very jealous man, so if he left his house, he closed the doors so that no one could enter into the house to be with his wives until he returned. One day David left the house and closed the doors, and his wife looked inside the house. Behold, a man was sitting in the middle of the house, and she said to the people in the house, "Where did this man come from, and why are the doors closed? By Allah, we will embarrass David." So David came, and behold, the man was standing in the middle of the house.

So David said to him, "Who are you?" He said, "I am the one who did not fear the king, and I will not be forbidden by any door or wall" (meaning, closing the door of the house would not hinder him from being inside the house). Then David said, "By Allah, you are the death angel. Welcome. Was this the command of Allah?" But then he stayed until he took the spirit of David. When he prepared David's body, the sun rose up, and Solomon said to the birds, "Make shade on David." So the birds shaded him until the earth became dark. People complained to Solomon and that is why he said to the birds, "Gather one wing." Ibn Abbas and Ibn Jaber said that David died on Saturday, but Isaac Ibn Bashier and Qatadah said David died when he was one hundred years old on a Wednesday.

Although the story we read concerning how David died sounds like a funny fable, Muslim scholars still disagree on how it happened. Some said the angel of death came to him while he was in the Holy of Holies. Then David asked the angel of death to let him go down or come up (an attempt to stall the taking of his soul), so the angel of death said, "O prophet of Allah, the years and the months are gone." He said that David fell down worshiping and the angel of death took his spirit while he was worshiping. Isaac Ibn Bashier said, concerning

---

[19]Ibid.

the funeral, that the people who attended sat in the sun on a clear day. It was also said there were forty thousand monks who attended David's funeral.[20] (I wonder where they found all of those monks since they did not exist until the fourth century AD, after Christianity began – perhaps they came via time machine!)

So much can be written about David's life, but we only responded to what was written by Ibn Kathir in his book. We encourage the reader to go back to the Bible and study the truth about the life of King David as written in the Bible in 1 and 2 Samuel, 1 and 2 Kings, 1 and 2 Chronicles, and Psalms.

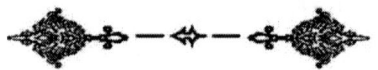

---

[20]Ibid, 22.

24 The Story of Solomon

Although Solomon and his life's story and history are written throughout the Bible in detail, the name Solomon is mentioned seventeen times, in sixteen verses, in seven portions of revelation (chapters) of the Qur'an without any verification or solid information. We will not present the entire biblical story of Solomon for it, in itself, is a long book. We will only use enough of it here to shed some light on some of the errors of the story of Solomon as it is written in the Qur'an, the hadith, and the interpretations of Muslim scholars.

Only the name Solomon is mentioned in the following verses, without any detail or further information. In Qur'an 4:163: *[163]Surely we have revealed to you as we revealed to Noah and the prophets after him. And we revealed to Abraham and Ishmael and Isaac and Jacob and the tribes and 'Isā and Ayyūb[1] and Yunus[2] and Aaron and Solomon, and to David we gave Zabor.[3]* Then in Qur'an 6:84: *[84]And we granted to him[4] Isaac and Jacob, both we guided, and Noah we guided before and among his descendants, David and Solomon and Job and Joseph and Moses and Aaron. And likewise, we reward the doers of good.*

Qur'an 21:78-82 and Qur'an 27:15-44 are the two longest portions pertaining to Solomon. We consider Qur'an 34:12-14 to be a small part of his story. Qur'an 38:30-40 contains another different short story of Solomon. Although the story is repeated in seven different locations in the Qur'an, it is severely lacking in details concerning who Solomon was, so his life is really unknown to the Muslims. One can see in this story a great example of how Mohammed added and took away much information.

Who was Solomon?

As we mentioned earlier, most Muslims know Solomon to be the son of David, but they do not know who his mother was. Certainly, if they knew who his mother was, Muslims would not mock the Old Testament and claim that it has been corrupted, especially when the

---

[1] Job, non-Arabic word of Greek/Syriac origin
[2] name mistakenly used when Jonah was meant
[3] in singular form = Psalms, non-Arabic word of Hebrew/Syriac origin
[4] Abraham

Holy Spirit exposed the sins of the people of the Old Testament as in the case of David committing adultery with Bathsheba. When we read in 2 Samuel 11, we discover the sin of King David with Bathsheba. In 2 Samuel 12:18, we read: *[18]Then David took Bathsheba to be his wife. Then she birthed him a son in adultery, and the child was severely ill and then died.* However, in verse 24, we read: *[24]David comforted Bathsheba his wife and then he knew her and she birthed him a son whom they called Solomon.*

Who do Muslims believe Solomon was? Ibn Kathir stated that he was Ibn David, Ibn Eshia, Ibn Owaid, Ibn Salmon, Ibn Nahshon, Ibn Omina, Ibn Dab, Ibn Aram, Ibn Hasron, Ibn Farris, Ibn Judah, Ibn Jacob, Ibn Isaac, Ibn Abraham.[5] Once again, we must ask a familiar question. *How did Ibn Kathir or Ibn Asakir come up with this genealogy of Solomon?*

The answer can be found in the Bible. We read in Matthew 1:1-6 that Solomon was the son of David, son of Jesse, son of Obed, son of Boaz, son of Salmon, son of Naasson, son of Aminadeb, son of Aram, son of Esrom, son of Phares, son of Judas, son of Jacob, son of Isaac, son of Abraham. This is the true genealogy. Notice the many similarities in the names within the two genealogies; one is simply written with different spellings in the Arabic language.

The first verse Ibn Kathir used in his book came out of Qur'an 27:16: *[16]And Solomon inherited David, and he said, "O you people, we have been taught the speech of the birds, and we have been given from everything. Surely this is the manifest bounty."* Ibn Kathir wrote that it was not an inheritance of money because David had many other sons, and he could not leave all his money to Solomon alone.[6] One must ask another question. *Though the kingdom can obviously be inherited, how can the prophethood be inherited?*

Solomon Communicates with the Animals

Ibn Kathir explained that Solomon knew the language of the birds and used to talk to them and translate what they said to the people. Abu Malik said that one time Solomon Ibn David walked by a male bird which was going in a circle around a female bird.[7] Solomon said to his followers, "Do you know what this bird says?" They said,

---

[5]Ibn Kathir, *Stories of the Prophets*, vol. 2, Abo Al Fida Ishamail Ibn Kathir Al Kurashi Al Damashce (Beirut: Dar Al-Arab Heritage, 1408 AH, 1988), 23.

[6]Ibid., 23.

[7]Ibid., 24.

"What did the bird say, O prophet of Allah?" Solomon said, "He engaged her to himself, and he said to her, 'Let me marry you. I will let you dwell in any room you choose in Damascus.'" Solomon said, "Every fiancée is a liar. Because the rooms in Damascus are built out of rock, no bird can live in it."

This is new information for me. What a "great" king and what "great" wisdom of Solomon! Ibn Kathir continued that this was the same with all other animals. (He meant Solomon was able to communicate with all other animals as we will see in the verses of the Qur'an.)

Ibn Kathir tried to prove his point using Qur'an 27:16: *[16]...we have been given from everything...* claiming that Allah gave King Solomon all he needed, including equipment, army, groups of jinn, humans, birds, beasts, satans (hosts of evil), knowledge, understanding, and interpretation concerning all creatures, those who talk and those who do not. This can be found in Qur'an 27:17: *[17]And to Solomon were gathered his troops of the jinn and the humans and the birds, so they were spread.*

Solomon and the Limping Ant

One day Solomon led his armies of the jinn and the people. The army of the birds was flying up above him to shield him from the sun. He put leaders over each of these troops until they came to a valley of ants. Ibn Kathir stated that Wahab said this ant's name was Jarsa. She was from the tribe named Children of Al Shesbyan, and she used to have a limp. Ibn Kathir continued by telling about a time when Solomon was riding on his horse with his military. The point of the story is that Solomon understood a conversation between this ant and her people. That is why he smiled about what she said because Allah had given him the good news to him alone, not to any of the others riding with him.[8]

Ibn Kathir gave an interpretation of Qur'an 27:18: *[18]until they reached the Valley of the Ants. An ant said, "O you ants, enter into your dwellings, lest Solomon and his troops crush you, and they do not feel."* Ibn Kathir said that some of the fools said, "All of the animals used to speak to the people before Solomon, until Solomon made a covenant with them and bridled them; therefore, they would never talk with people after that."

---

[8]Ibid.

I wonder if the writer of the *Bee Movie*[9] had learned this fact from these people whom Ibn Kathir called fools. Ibn Kathir said this was wrong, for if this had been true, then Solomon would not have had any privilege over the people. That is why Solomon said in Qur'an 27:19: *[19]So he smiled, laughing at her (the ant) sayings, and he said, "My lord, inspire me to thank your grace which you graced on me and on my parents, and that I do good deed that will be pleasing to you. And admit me, by your mercy, among your good servants."* Solomon asked Allah to make him give thanks for all that Allah had graced on him, what he gave him as a privilege over all others, and how Allah made the good work easy for him.[10] If Allah caused him to die, he would admit him with the righteous, and Allah has answered his prayer.

When Muslims read such verses as the ones above, do they use any logic at all? We see that Solomon was riding on a horse and his troops were marching. They were not walking quietly. *How in the world could Solomon hear the ant talking? Do you know that ants do not speak at all?* I have done the research, and you can too. Ants do not have lungs or a voice box. Ants communicate with each other by smell. The only time ants talk, and you can hear their voices very clearly, is when you watch cartoon movies made by Hollywood and others.

I wonder why Ibn Kathir did not include in his book the conversation which took place between the ants. The interpretation of Al Qurtobi added more detail to the unclear story in the Qur'an by stating that Al Shoabey said, "This ant used to have two wings, so it flew like a bird."[11] That is how Solomon knew her speech. Al Qurtobi was in agreement that she was limping, so she called the rest of the ants saying, *"O you ants, enter into your dwellings, lest Solomon and his troops crush you, and they do not feel."*

Al Zamakhary said, "Solomon heard her words from three miles away." He gave us a different name, though, for he named her Takyah. However, Al Zohaly said her name was Haramyah, and the fabrication goes on and on and on. I wonder why Muslim scholars disagree over the name of the ant. *Was this because they did not have a birth certificate for the ant?*

---

[9]*Bee Movie,* directed by Simon J. Smith and Steve Hickner, featuring Jerry Seinfeld and Renee Zellweger (Paramount Pictures, 2007).
[10]Ibn Kathir, 25.
[11]http://quran.al-islam.com/Page.aspx?pageid=221&BookID=14&Page=378, accessed January 24, 2013.

Do Muslims who read the previous interpretations realize that these Muslim scholars were not true scholars? I believe all of the misunderstanding is a result of what the Scripture teaches about Solomon being a wise man because he knew many parables and a lot about creatures. The Scripture teaches that there was no one wiser than Solomon. For example, in the book of Ecclesiastes 1:16, Solomon said that he was a man with more wisdom than all that had gone before him and that his heart had great experience with knowledge and great wisdom.

Then he also stated in Ecclesiastes 1:18 that *much wisdom is much grief. And the one who is increased in knowledge also has increase in sorrow.* Also, in the end of his writing in Ecclesiastes 12:9, Solomon stated that he was a wise man, taught the people knowledge, gave them good heed, and set in order many proverbs. Yes, Solomon was a wise man and knew a lot about many things.

In Proverbs 6:6-8, Solomon talked about the ants. Notice I said, he talked *about* the ants, not *to* the ants, for the lazy can learn many lessons from the ants. Solomon said that even though the ants do not have a leader, they prepare their food in the summer and gather the food during the harvest. No verse in the Bible tells us that Solomon ever talked to animals or birds. I believe the problem which Mohammed fell into was the result of another verse, 1 Kings 4:33. For the Bible stated that Solomon spoke of trees, the cedars of Lebanon, and the hyssop that grows from the wall, and he spoke of the beasts and the birds and of the creeping things and of the fish. Once again he spoke *about* all these creatures, not *to* these creatures.

As for the interpretation of Ibn Kathir concerning the saying in Qur'an 27:19, *"my parents,"* they were Solomon's parents (David and his wife), and his mother was a righteous servant.[12] Jaber said that Mohammed said, "The mother of Solomon said, 'O my son, do not sleep too much at night, for sleeping too much at night causes the servant to be poor on the day of the resurrection.'" What a strange statement! God made the night for the people to rest and sleep, especially in Solomon's day when there was no electricity or work at night. *What does sleeping at night have to do with the day of resurrection? How can a person be poor in the day of resurrection?*

Ibn Kathir wrote and repeated many stories concerning ants which went out to drink, lifting their arms to heaven, as if calling to

---

[12]Ibn Kathir, 25.

Allah.[13] He said that the prophet saw that Allah had answered the prayer of the ant, especially when the people who saw this did not interrupt the ant's prayer. The ant was praying. For example, Al Saddi said there was drought in Solomon's day, so people went out and there was an ant standing on her feet stretching her arms. She was saying, "O Allah, surely I am one of your creatures. And I have no riches, and we have no riches except for what you provide." Al Saddi said, "Therefore Allah sent the rain on them."

Solomon, the Hoopoe, and the Queen of Saba

Ibn Kathir interpreted the following verse in Qur'an 27:20a, *20And he inspected the birds, so he said,…* by saying that Solomon was commanding the hoopoe (a colorful bird that is found across Afro-Eurasia) like any of the armies of Solomon as they came to him to fulfill their duty by bringing to him and providing what he asked them to do.[14] Ibn Abbas said that the hoopoe's job was to search for water in the region when they were traveling. The hoopoe had been given the power by Allah to see if there was water under the earth, and if the bird found the water, he would inform them so they could begin digging the well.

After Solomon inspected the birds, he asked this question in Qur'an 27:20b-21: *20"…Why is it that I do not see the hoopoe? Or was he of the absent? 21Surely I will torment him with a severe torment. Or I will surely slaughter him, or he brings to me a manifest authority."* Ibn Kathir explained by saying, "Solomon asked why the bird was missing."[15] The scholars disagreed concerning the punishment with which Solomon threatened the bird, but Solomon gave the bird a way out to save him from such punishment if the bird would bring Solomon a manifested authority. The hoopoe was not gone for a long time, and he came to Solomon with true news from a faraway land, the land of Saba.

As it is written in Qur'an 27:22-23: *22So he did not tarry long, so he said, "I have gained the knowledge that you do not know, and I have come to you from Sabā[16] with sure news. 23Surely I have found a woman reigning over them, gifted with everything, and she has a great throne.* Ibn Kathir explained that the kingdom of Saba, which includes the country of Yemen today, was given to a

---

[13]Ibid.

[14]Ibid.

[15]Ibid., 26

[16]Sheba, non-Arabic word of probable Hebrew/Syriac origin

woman who was the daughter of the king who had not had any other children except for her.[17] Therefore, they made her a queen over them. Ibn Kathir interpreted the great throne here to mean a throne that is very ornate with lots of jewels and gold.

Ibn Kathir did not give interpretation to the following verses but simply quoted them. Qur'an 27:24-25: [24]*I found her and her people worshiping to the sun without Allah, and Satan adorns their works so that he prevented them from the way, so they are not guided.* [25]*Will they not worship to Allah who brings the secret things of the heavens and the earth, and who knows what you hide and what you reveal?*

I am astonished at how wise and how intelligent the hoopoe was in presenting the case of the queen and her people. His eloquent speech could be considered the best of the Qur'an writings. Notice that Mohammed, in the Qur'an, stated that if the humans and the jinn were gathered together, they could not come up with anything close to the writings of the Qur'an 2:23; 11:15; and 17:88. However, here the bird of Solomon was able to speak, literally much better than Solomon or Mohammed himself.

Ibn Kathir interpreted the following verse, Qur'an 27:26: [26]*Allah, there is no god but him, the lord of the great throne,"* by stating that the throne of Allah is the greatest throne which no creature has one that is greater. Ibn Kathir said that Al Salabe said her people crowned a man among them who allowed corruption to take over the land, so she sent for him, and he married her.[18] So she gave him wine, then she cut his throat, and she hung his head over her door. The people came to her and crowned her.

As for her father, Ibn Kathir stated he refused to marry any female from Yemen. Therefore, he married one of the females of the jinn. Her name was Rehanah. She birthed him a daughter, this woman, and her name was Talcamah; others said her name was Balkese. The latter was the name Mohammed chose for her. As for his saying that she was gifted of everything, Ibn Kathir said it meant she had all that the king would like to have.

In Qur'an 27:27, Solomon doubted the statement of the hoopoe by saying: [27]*He said, "We will see if you are truthful, or you were among the liars.* Then Ibn Kathir provided an interpretation of verse 28, [28]*Go with this my book. So throw it down to them, then turn*

---

[17]Ibid., 27.
[18]Ibid., 28.

away from them, so see what is their return," by stating that Solomon gave a letter to his miraculous bird, the hoopoe. The Qur'an used many words to describe the mission which Solomon gave to his messenger, the hoopoe, but then the Qur'an says, "Do not exalt yourself, and come to me as Muslims." Ibn Kathir stated that the meaning of these words was an invitation from King Solomon to the queen and her people that they may surrender to him or pay him without defying him.

Although the Qur'an does not give any details about the reaction of the people to the queen in Qur'an 27:29-30, *[29]She[19] said, "O you the leaders, a generous book has been thrown down to me. [30]Surely it is from Solomon, and surely it is, 'In the name of Allah, the merciful, the merciful...'"* Ibn Kathir gave more details as if he were there. For example, he said that the hoopoe carried the book into her castle, threw it to her when she was alone, and stood near her, waiting to learn what her response to the book would be. The reaction of the queen was in Qur'an 27:32: *[32]She said, "O you the leaders, consult with me in my affair. I was not to make any command unless you bear witness to me."*

Ibn Kathir continued by saying that she gathered all the princes and important people in her country and read to them the letter of Solomon. This was written as an interpretation of Qur'an 27: 30-31: *[30]"Surely it is from Solomon, and surely it is, 'In the name of Allah, the merciful, the merciful. [31]Do not exalt yourselves above me, and come to me as Muslims.'"* Then she took their advice on this matter, as she politely spoke to them while they were hearing her saying, as previously given in Qur'an 27:32: *[32]"O you the leaders, consult with me in my affair. I was not to make any command unless you bear witness to me."* This means she would not make a decision unless they were present.

Some said they were strong and could fight him, but they gave her the power to choose, as it is written in verse 33: *[33]They said, "We are imbued with strength and are imbued with mighty valor, and the command is to you, so see what you command."* Ibn Kathir then stated that she came with a better opinion than all of their opinions because she knew the author of the book she was reading, meaning Solomon. She could not have victory over him if she went to war against him, and she could not deceive him. Also, she knew what would happen if a king invaded a land, when she said in

---

[19]the queen of Sheba

verse 34: *³⁴She said, "Surely when kings enter a village they vandalized it and made the noblest of its family to be humiliated, and likewise, they do.* That is when she decided to send a gift to see what his response would be as she said in verse 35: *³⁵And surely I will send to them a gift, so I will see what the messenger will return."*

The Kingdom Throne

Ibn Kathir stated that this would not change anything or bring justice. That is why Solomon said in verses 36-37: *³⁶So when he (the bird) came to Solomon, he said, "Do you supply me with money? So what Allah has given to me is better than what he gave you, yet you rejoice in your gifts. ³⁷Return to them, for we will surely come to them with troops which they cannot withstand, and we will drive them from it humiliated while they are subdued."* Ibn Kathir stated, "Therefore, Solomon rejected her gift and returned it. He threatened that he would come in war against her and her people and would bring shame, dishonor, and destruction on them."

Ibn Kathir stated that when they heard his threat, all of them came to Solomon in that hour with their queen in obedience and submission.[20] When Solomon heard of their coming, he said to those who were under his power of the jinn what Allah said in Qur'an 27:38: *³⁸He said, "O you the leaders, which of you will bring me her throne before they come to me as Muslims?"* When Solomon asked the jinn to bring her kingdom to him, Ibn Kathir said that her throne was her bed, the one she sat on at the time of her judging.[21]

One of the ifrit (demon) of the jinn said, "I will bring it to you before you rise from your seat, and surely I am strong and faithful for it." We can read this in Qur'an 27:39: *³⁹An 'ifrīt[22] of the jinn said, "I will bring it to you before you rise from your seat, and surely I am strong and faithful for it."* Others said it would happen before the blink of an eye. This took place in the early morning, and this final jinni said, "I am faithful that I will not steal or lose any of the precious jewelry."

Who was this person who would bring her throne before the blinking of an eye to King Solomon? Ibn Kathir said it was Asf Ibn

---

[20]Ibid., 29.
[21]Ibid.
[22]demon, non-Arabic word of Persian, derived from Pahlavic origin

Barkya, the cousin of Solomon, but it was said he was one of the believers of the jinn. Then it was said that he was one of the Children of Israel, one their scholars. It was also said it was Solomon himself, which Ibn Kathir considered to be strange because this does not fit the style of the writing of the verse. The fourth opinion was that he was Angel Gabreel. Now we have four widely diverse opinions of who was making these statements. Here, I would love to insert the statement, *and Allah knows best.*

The interpretation went on and on and on. Somehow this last person was able to bring her throne all the way from Yemen to Jerusalem before the blink of Solomon's eye, as it is written in Qur'an 27:40: *[40]The one who had the knowledge of the book said, "I will bring it to you before the blinking of your eyes."* So when he saw it set before him, he said, "This is of the bounty of my lord, to test me, whether I will be thankful or become infidel, and who gives thanks, so surely he only gives thanks to himself and who became infidel. So surely my lord is rich, generous." Then Solomon commanded his people to change her throne, to determine her understanding as it is written in Qur'an 27:41: *[41]He said, "Disguise her throne for her. We will see if she will be guided or become one who is not guided."* Then in verse 42: *[42]So when she came, it was said to her, "Is your throne like this?" She said, "It looks similar to it." And we were given the knowledge before her, and we were Muslims.* Ibn Kathir interpreted this verse by saying that Solomon asked her, "Is this your throne or not?" Because she was very smart with deep understanding, she realized this could not be her throne for she had left it in the land of Yemen.[23] She did not know that anyone could do such wonderful, strange things.

Now, according to the saying in Qur'an 27:43: *[43]And what she was worshiping without Allah prevented her, surely she was among an infidel people.* Ibn Kathir interpreted the verse by stating that it was the sun that she and her people and their ancestors had worshiped. Ibn Kathir continued that Solomon had given command to build a building of glass, and he put in it all kinds of fish and animals which live in the water.[24] Then he commanded the queen to enter this building while Solomon was sitting on his bed.

---

[23]Ibn Kathir, 29.
[24]Ibid., 30.

Then in Qur'an 27:44: *⁴⁴It was said to her, "Enter the sarh."²⁵ So when she saw it, she thought it was a pool of water and uncovered her legs. He said, "Surely it is a palace paved with glass." She said, "My lord, surely I have been unjust to myself, and I surrender with Solomon to Allah, the lord of the worlds."* Ibn Kathir interpreted this verse by stating it was said that the jinn desired to make her look ugly before Solomon by showing her legs, so he would see her leg hair and then dislike her because they were afraid he might marry her for her mother was of the jinn. (If she married Solomon, she would have power over them.) Others said her toe nail was like the hoof of an animal, but Ibn Kathir stated this was a weak opinion, *and Allah knows best*. After all that, Solomon married her and made her the queen of the kingdom of Yemen.

Ibn Kathir said Solomon used to visit her every month. One time, he spent three days with her. He commanded the jinn to build three castles for him in Yemen, *and Allah knows best*. It was said by Ibn Isaac that he said some of the people of knowledge (scholars) said Solomon did not marry her but instead married her to the King of Hamdan. Solomon appointed her to the kingdom of Yemen. He made some of the jinn subservient to build her three castles, *and Allah knows best*.

What a wonderful story. I wonder how many Muslims believe this fairy tale. *Are any of these fabrications true?* When one knows the facts that there is no such thing as jinn and that ants do not talk and neither does the hoopoe, then maybe Muslims will realize Mohammed was not a prophet after all. Neither Jews nor Christians believe this fairy tale.

Yes, we know from the Bible in 2 Chronicles 9:1-12 that the Queen of Sheba heard of Solomon and his wisdom, and she came all the way to Jerusalem to meet with Solomon and gave him lots of gifts. She saw his life, the house he built, his servants, their clothes, and his sacrifices; and she was amazed by him. She did not believe what she had heard about him, but after she got there she found that she had not heard about even half of his wisdom and his fame. She noted how happy those men and servants were who stood before him to hear his wisdom. She also blessed his Lord who gave him the throne of his kingdom.

Another error is shown about Solomon's kingdom, when we read the interpretation above, where one comes to the conclusion that

---

²⁵tower, non-Arabic word of Ethiopian origin

Solomon was a warrior. However, during all his reign there was peace, and he never was involved in any war, not with the Queen of Sheba or any other ruler. This was the true account of the Queen of Sheba and Solomon, not the fairy tale of Muslim scholars or Mohammed's Qur'an.

To Pray or Not to Pray

Another part of the story of Solomon came from Qur'an 38:30-39. Let's begin with verse 30 when Allah said, *[30]And to David, we granted Solomon, blessed the servant, surely he was repentant.* Ibn Kathir said that Allah said he had given David his son Solomon who was repentant. Ibn Kathir explained that *repentant* meant he was an obedient returner to Allah. Ibn Kathir explained that this section of the Qur'an talks about the issues Solomon had with the fast horses. As for the section in this passage when Allah said that when they displayed the prancing horses before him in the evening, he said, *[32]"Surely I love the love of the good above the remembrance of my lord." Until it[26] was hidden behind the veil.* Muslim scholars explained that *"love of the good"* meant the love of the horses.

There were two different opinions of what was hidden behind the veil.[27] Some said the sun; others said the horses. As for those who came with the opinion that it was the sun, they believed the most accepted interpretation was that Solomon was busy in the afternoon examining his horses until the sun set. He did not miss the prayer of the afternoon on purpose or without excuse; he delayed the prayer because of the cause of jihad and the investigation and examination of the horses. Other Muslim scholars said one can delay the prayer if the fight is severe. Some said Mohammed had forgotten the prayer; therefore, it could be the same case with Solomon, *and Allah knows best.*

As for the second opinion, those who believed that the statement *behind the veil* meant to the horses, means that Solomon did not miss the prayer time. They said Solomon said, "Bring it back to me." When they displayed the prancing horses before him in the evening, he said, *[32]"Surely I love the love of the good above the remembrance of my lord." Until it[28] was hidden behind the veil.*

---

[26]the sun
[27]Ibn Kathir, 31.
[28]the sun

[33]*"Bring them back to me."* So he sat to stroke the legs and necks of the horses and then rubbed down the sweat from their necks.

Another opinion by Ibn Jarir and Ibn Abbas was that it was a large number of horses.[29] Some said it was ten thousand, others said twenty thousand horses, and others among them said there were twenty horses with wings. When Solomon asked his men to bring his horses to him, he killed all of the horses for they had hindered him from performing the prayer of the afternoon. Some scholars disagreed by saying there was no reason for killing these animals and the waste of money; but some Muslim scholars stated that in the past, when Muslims had excess animals from their spoils of war, it was acceptable to slaughter any amount of them, if it would distract the Muslim and cause the infidel to have victory over them.

Did you read what they said: "A horse with wings"? Even Mohammed himself did not know that such horses existed. As it is written in the hadith, Ibn Kathir stated that Aisha said, after the battle of Tabuk or Khaybar, that she was playing with her dolls (this indicates she was still a child during this battle).[30] Mohammed lifted up the cover of the basket where Aisha had her dolls. Then Mohammed asked her, "What is this inside this basket, Aisha?" She said, "These are my daughters."

Then Mohammed saw some horses with wings next to the dolls. So he asked her, "What is this in the midst of the dolls?" She said, "A horse." He said, "What is this on him?" She said, "Wings." There Mohammed was surprised and asked the question, "A horse with wings?" She said, "Haven't you heard that Solomon had horses with wings?" Then Mohammed laughed. He laughed so hard that she saw his molars. Some Muslim scholars stated that because Solomon left the horses, Allah substituted something better for him than the horses, which was the wind on which he used to travel, going and coming back, equal to a month, as Ibn Kathir stated. We will discuss this later in more detail.

Solomon Builds the Holy House

Now we turn to the saying of Allah in the following verses of Qur'an 38:34-35: [34]*And indeed, we seduced Solomon, and we placed on his throne a body, then he turned. [35]He said, "My lord, forgive me and grant me a kingdom which no one after me*

---

[29]Ibn Kathir, 31.
[30]Ibid., 32.

must have, surely you are the grantor." Ibn Kathir quoted Ibn Jarir and other interpreters saying that Solomon left his bed for forty days. When he returned to it, Allah commanded him to build the Holy House. So he built it perfectly.

I was surprised that Ibn Kathir skipped the interpretation of the section in his book *Stories of the Prophets*. Therefore, I would like to translate for you in the following paragraphs his interpretation as it is written on the Saudi website.[31]

Ibn Kathir said Allah seduced, meaning tested, Solomon by robbing him of the kingdom. He put on his throne another body. Ibn Abbas and others said it was a demon. Muslim scholars disagreed on the name of this demon. Some said his name was Rock. Some said his name was Asif. Some said his name was Hubaiq.

Here is the story of how Solomon was commanded to build the Holy House. It was said that he must build it without hearing the voice of iron. Obviously, this was taken from the Bible concerning the building of the altar as God commanded the Jewish people not to lift a chisel or hammer but to build it simply by piling up the rocks.

So Ibn Kathir continued by stating that Solomon asked his people to build the house under those conditions, but he was not able to do it this way. Then it was said to him, "There is a demon in the sea, his name is Rock." So he sought this demon. There was in the sea a spring to which the demon used to go once every seven days. Solomon removed the water from it and replenished it with wine. One day Solomon came, and it was wine. So he said, "You are a good drink, but you harm the kind person and you make the fool more foolish." Then he returned to it when he was very thirsty, repeating the same saying to the wine. Then he drank from it until his mind was dominated by the wine. He said he saw the ring (or he was sealed between his shoulders) so he was subdued, for his kingdom was in his ring.

Solomon came to him, and he said that we were commanded to build a house. It was said to us that we should not hear the sound of iron in it. So he said, "Bring an egg of the hoopoe and put a bottle above it." Then the hoopoe came, and he went around it because he desired to have his eggs. He went and brought a diamond, put it on the bottle, and cut it until he got to the eggs. So Solomon took the diamond, and they used it to cut the rock. *I wonder how the bird used a diamond to cut glass?*

In the Bible, God allowed Solomon to use a hammer and chisel in the construction of the temple. This is confused with Moses and others who constructed altars without using a hammer or chisel by God's order.

Solomon and the Kingdom Ring

Although there are many stories concerning the loss of Solomon's ring and kingdom written in Ibn Kathir's book, we will share just two of these with you.[32] When Solomon went to relieve himself in the woods or in the bathroom, he did not take the ring with him. One day he went to the bathroom and gave his ring to a demon. The demon threw the ring into the sea. A fish swallowed it, and the kingdom was taken away from Solomon. The kingdom was given to Satan who appeared to look like Solomon and came and sat on his throne and his bed. When Satan took over Solomon's kingdom, he put new women on the throne, and he began to judge between the people of Israel. The Children of Israel began to deny things about him (Satan who appeared like Solomon) until they said the prophet of Allah had been subdued.

There was a man among them who looked like Omar Ibn Khattab in his strength. He said, "I swear by Allah I will test him." So he said, "O prophet of Allah, one of us became impure in a cold night, but he purposely did not wash until the sun rose. Is there any wrongdoing in that?" Then he said *no*. It was like that for forty nights until Solomon, the prophet of Allah, found the ring in the belly of a fish, he took the ring, and he came back to his kingdom.

In another story, it was said that Solomon had 100 women, and he trusted one of these women named Jarada. It was said when Solomon went to the bathroom, he would take the ring off his finger and give it to her. He never gave it to anyone else because he trusted her. One time he went to the woods to go to the bathroom, and Satan appeared in the form of Solomon and said to her, "Give me the ring," so she gave it to him. Then he went and he sat on Solomon's throne. Later, Solomon came back from the woods and asked Jarada to give him the ring. She said to him, "Didn't I give it to you before?" He said, "No." Then he went out as if he were lost.

---

[32]Ibn Kathir, 32.

Satan sat and judged between the people for forty days, but the Children of Israel rejected his judgment. The scholars of the Children of Israel gathered until they met with Solomon's wives and said to the women, "We deny this. If he were Solomon, so indeed he lost his mind, and we reject his judgment." So the women cried, came to him (Satan, whom they thought was Solomon), surrounded him, and began to read the Torah. He flew from among them until he fell out the window and the ring was with him. Then he flew until he arrived at the sea where the ring fell from his hand into the sea. One of the fish swallowed it.

Solomon came in the same condition as he was, until he met with one of the fishermen of the sea, and he was very hungry. So Solomon asked him about their catch, and he said, "Surely I am Solomon." One of them hit him with a stick, and he was cut. Solomon washed his blood at the shore of the sea. The companion of the man who hit Solomon rebuked him for hitting Solomon and said to him, "What you have done for beating him was not good."

He said that this man claimed to be Solomon. Then they told him to give Solomon two fish from what they had caught. Solomon was not worried about the beating, and he went to the shore near the water and cut open the fish to wash it. He found the ring in the belly of one of the fish. Then he wore the ring, and Allah restored his honor and his kingdom. Then the birds came hovering above him, and the people knew that he was Solomon.

When I read such stories, they remind me of cartoons or Disney stories. *Can a bird use diamonds to cut rocks? Was the building built without using chisels or hammers? Is the kingdom in a bed? Do kings rule from their beds? Is there really a kingdom in a ring? If a king removes a ring from his finger, will he lose his kingdom? Will a king remove his rings from his fingers and give them to his wife every time he goes to the bathroom?* These are nothing but fairy tales. Mohammed and his so-called scholars filled their books of interpretation with them.

Ibn Kathir gave the hadith that a man came to Mohammed and asked him, "Which mosque was built first?" Mohammed answered, "The Forbidden Mosque."[33] The man said, "Then which was next?" He said, "The Holy House Mosque." Then the man asked, "What was the length of time from one being built until the other was built?" Mohammed answered, "Forty years." Ibn Kathir concluded this

---

[33]Ibid.

[64]

hadith by stating that it is known that Abraham built the Forbidden Mosque more than a thousand years before Solomon built the Holy House in Jerusalem. I wonder how Ibn Kathir reconciled Mohammed's answer of forty years with the length of time between Abraham and Solomon being more than a thousand years. Here is another example of how ignorant Mohammed was of historical timelines.

Mohammed also said in the hadith that when Solomon was building the Holy House, his lord asked him to ask three requests.[34] Allah gave him two of them, but Mohammed wished to receive the third request. Solomon asked for wisdom and a kingdom like no one had received before him. Then Allah gave both to him. As for the third request, if a man left his house, not desiring any but the prayer in this place of worship, his sin would be removed from him, as in the day his mother gave birth to him. Mohammed concluded this hadith by saying that he hoped Allah would give him this third request. Once again, Mohammed copied the request of Solomon for wisdom found in the Bible in 1 Kings 3:5-14, but then he added the requests about a strong kingdom and the prayer.

The Wisdom of Solomon

The story of Solomon's request for wisdom can be found in 1 Kings 3:5-15. We encourage the reader to read the entire account from the Bible. First of all, it was a dream. Second, it was not during the building of the temple but took place before the temple was built. Third, Solomon acknowledged that he was a little child, not knowing how to lead this large number of people, so large they could not even be counted; therefore, he asked God for an understanding heart to judge the people and that he may discern between good and evil. That is the only thing he asked God for.

God said because Solomon did not ask for long years or riches or the lives of his enemies but sought only wisdom, God would give Solomon his request. There would be no one like him, not before him or after him. God would also give him riches and honor. As for living a long life, God told Solomon that if he walked in God's ways and kept His statutes and His commandments, as his father David had done, then God would give him a long life. Notice there were not three requests as Mohammed mentioned above.

---

[34]Ibid., 33.

As for the wisdom which Allah gave to Solomon, Ibn Kathir quoted Qur'an 21:78-79: *[78]And David and Solomon, when they judged concerning the crop when the sheep of the people pastured in it, and we were to their judgment a witness. [79]So we caused Solomon to understand it, and to each of them we gave wisdom and knowledge. And we made subservient with David the mountains and the birds to praise, and we were the doers.*[35] Ibn Kathir interpreted these verses by quoting the judge and other scholars by saying that one day there was a group of people who owned a vineyard. Some other people's sheep went into the vineyard by night and ate all the vines, so they went to David to judge between them. David judged that the owner of the sheep would replant the vineyard. When they went out from the presence of David, they met with Solomon, and so they asked him what the prophet of Allah's judgment was. So they told him what happened between them and David.

Then Solomon said, "If I had judged between both of you, I would have given the sheep to the owner of the vineyard that he may use its milk and its wool until the owner of the vineyard begins to harvest again and the vineyard is in the same condition as it was before the sheep ate the vines." When David heard of this judgment, he judged with the same judgment.

My response to this story is with the true account as recorded in the Bible. Solomon never ruled or judged during the reign of his father David. The person who stole the kingdom from David was another of his sons, Absalom. There is no record of King David ever judging concerning sheep and vineyards. After becoming a king, the only time that David was discussed along with sheep was when the Prophet Nathan brought judgment against David concerning King David, Bathsheba, and Uriah the Hittite. This is the story of the ninety-nine sheep.

There is another story written by Ibn Kathir, concerning the wisdom of Solomon, in which he stated that Mohammed said in the hadith that two women had two sons and a wolf took one of the two children.[36] The women disputed with each other concerning the other son. The older woman said, "The wolf took your son." However, the younger said, "No, he took your son." They went to David so he could judge between them. David gave the child to the older. Then

---

[35]Ibid.
[36]Ibid., 32.

they went out and met with Solomon who said, "Give me a knife, and I will cut the child into halves and give one half to each of you." Then the youngest said, "Do not do that. May Allah have mercy on you. He is her son." So Solomon gave the child to the older woman.

Obviously, this story is taken from the Bible with many errors and important things left out as Mohammed always did. Typically, Mohammed completely missed the point of the story. The true mother of the child loved it so much that she would rather give it to the other woman than see it killed, but Mohammed's story is without a message as the child is given to the wrong woman. Sadly, if Muslims do not read the Bible, they cannot recognize that this story, along with most other stories Mohammed shared in the Qur'an or the hadith, is simply a counterfeit of the stories of the Bible. The story about the two women comes from 1 Kings 3:16-28. It did not take place when David was still alive but after his death. We encourage the reader to go and read the entire story.

Here is the true account. There were two harlots who lived in the same house. They had two babies born within three days of each other. One of the women rolled onto her baby during the night and killed him. Obviously, there was no wolf that took the baby. She took the other baby and put her dead child with the other woman. In the morning, the other woman discovered the child at her breast was dead, but it was not her child. The first woman said, "Your son is dead, and the living child is mine."

They told their story to Solomon who requested a sword to cut the living child into two halves so that each woman could take one half. Then the mother of the living child was overwhelmed with her love for her child, and she pleaded to Solomon, "No, lord, give her my son; do not kill him." As for the other woman, she said, "This child will be neither yours nor mine." Then Solomon gave the order to give the child to his real mother. When Israel heard of the wisdom given by King Solomon, they were in awe for they saw the wisdom of God in him.

Now, let us go back to Ibn Kathir's interpretation. As we mentioned previously, because Solomon left the horses to seek the face of Allah, Allah rewarded him with a better method of traveling which is known as *the wind*. Here are the passages of the Qur'an to show such theories.

Qur'an 21:81-82: [81]*And to Solomon, the strongly blowing wind will run according to his command to the earth which we blessed in it, and we were knowing of all things. [82]And some of*

the satans, who would dive for him and they would do works
without that, and we were keepers for them. Qur'an 38:36-40:
*36So we made the wind subservient to him, it ran softly by his
command wherever he directed it. 37And of the satans every
bannā́[37] and diver 38and others were bound in chains. 39"This is
our gift, so we give or withhold without accounting." 40And
surely he was near to us and had a good return.*

Qur'an 34:12-13: *12And to Solomon the wind. Its going a
month and its coming a month. And we made a fountain of
molten brass to flow for him. And some of the jinn who work
between his hands, by the will of his lord, and whoever of them
deviated from our command, we will cause him to taste the
torment of the blaze. 13They made for him whatever he willed,
of synagogues and statues, deep dishes like jāwib,[38] and
immovable boiling pots: "Work, O family of David, thankfully;
and few of my servants are the thankful."* We chose the following
title to describe the previous verses as interpreted by Ibn Kathir.

The Super-Colossal Flying Platform

Ibn Kathir interpreted such verses by stating that Allah replaced
the horses with the wind which is a faster way to travel and stronger
and greater.[39] Allah commanded it to run with Solomon's command
wherever he wished, from one country to another country. He made a
platform from wood, large enough to fit in it all that he needed for
buildings, castles, tents, luggage, horses, camels, heavy loads, men of
human and jinn, and other things such as animals and birds.

This comes from a Jewish mythological story in which God gave
Solomon a large carpet, sixty miles long and sixty miles wide, made
of green silk interwoven with pure gold and ornamented with figured
decorations.[40] Surrounded by his four princes—Asaph ben Berechiah,
prince of the men; Ramirat, prince of the demons; a lion, prince of the
beasts; and an eagle, prince of the birds—Solomon sat upon the
carpet until he was caught up by the wind and sailed through the air
so quickly that he ate breakfast in Damascus and had supper in
Medina.

---

[37]builder, non-Arabic word of Akkadian origin
[38]cisterns, non-Arabic word of Syriac origin
[39]Ibn Kathir, 34
[40]Jewish Encyclopedia, s.v. "Solomon," accessed January 24, 2013, http://www.
jewishencyclopedia.com/articles/13842-solomon.

If Solomon decided to travel for fun or for killing his enemies from any other country, by Allah's will, he would carry all of the things mentioned above on this platform of wood. Then he would command the wind to go underneath the wood and lift it up so it would stay between the heaven and the earth, and the wind would move the platform for him. If he desired to go faster, he would command the storm to carry him at a faster speed. Since traveling in one afternoon is equal to traveling one month, he could stay there for one afternoon. Then the wind would take him back to his house.

When I read such verses from the Qur'an and their interpretation by so-called Muslim scholars, it saddens my heart and breaks my spirit, for there are over a billion Muslims who believe in Islam without knowing the truth about the fairy tales of Islam, for if Muslims knew Mohammed, the Qur'an, and the Muslim scholars' interpretation of the Qur'an, they would not remain Muslims. We are not talking about a 747 airplane, we are talking about a huge ship like the one built by Noah. However, Noah's ship was not moving very fast, but rather it moved slowly in the water. Mohammed lied to Muslims with whatever verses he claimed in the Qur'an to be a perfect revelation, and sadly, the educated ones among the Muslims follow the same steps of Mohammed and continue to deceive the simple, innocent Muslims.

As for the work of the jinn, Ibn Kathir and other scholars write on and on about how the jinn possessed the skills of working, making statues, and making jawib (cisterns) and boiling pots. Some of the jinn were divers, bringing pearls and gems up from under the water. Once again, it is amazing how Muslim scholars not only believe such lies, they also teach it to others.

Ibn Kathir said that Abu Horyrah said that Mohammed said, "Yesterday, Ifreet (a demon) tried to cut my prayer, but Allah gave me strength over him, so I seized him and I desired to tie him to one of the pillars of the mosque so that all of you may see him.[41] But then I remembered the call of my brother Solomon, 'Lord, forgive me, and give me a kingdom you have not given to anyone after me,' so I released him as a loser."

As for the number of women Solomon had, Muslim scholars disagree on how many there were. Ibn Kathir said that Solomon had a thousand women of which seven hundred were wives and three

---

[41]Ibn Kathir, 35.

hundred were concubines.[42] However, in the next sentence in Ibn Kathir's book, he said there were actually three hundred free women and seven hundred slaves.

Abu Horyrah said that Mohammed said, "Solomon said to one hundred women: 'I will have sex with all of you tonight, and each of you will give me a son who will strike with the sword for the cause of Allah.'" Mohammed said that Solomon did not say "if Allah wills." Mohammed continued by stating that Solomon did have sex with all of them. None of them gave birth to a son except for one woman who bore him half a human. Isaac Ibn Bashier said that Abu Horyrah said that Solomon Ibn David had four hundred wives and six hundred concubines. He also said, "Tonight I will have sex with a thousand women so each one will give me a fighter who will perform the jihad for the sake of Allah," but he did not say "if Allah wills." Mohammed said if he had said "if Allah wills," he would for sure have had a thousand jihadists who would fight for the sake of Allah. I cannot imagine how someone could even begin to imagine thinking that Solomon could physically have sex with a hundred or a thousand women in one night.

The Death of Solomon

Ibn Kathir inserted the following verse, Qur'an 34:14: *[14]So when we decreed the death on him, nothing showed them that he was dead but a small creature of the earth that ate away his staff which supported his corpse. So when he fell, the jinn perceived that, if they had known the unseen, they had not continued in this shameful torment.*[43] Then he stated that Ibn Jarir said Ibn Abbas stated that Mohammed said when Prophet Solomon used to pray, he saw a tree growing between his hands. So he said to it, "What is your name?" It told him, but we do not know what it said. Then he said, "Why were you made?" It answered saying that if it is planted, it will grow as a plant for medicine.

One time while Solomon was praying, he saw a tree growing between his hands. So he asked her, "What is your name?" She said, "Carob." So he asked her, "Why were you made?" She answered, "For the destruction on this house." Therefore Solomon said, "O Allah, hide the news about my death from the jinn, for the humans know that the jinn do not know the unseen." So he carved the tree into a staff. He leaned on it for a year after his death. The jinn continued to work until the earth rotted the staff, and then the humans knew that the jinn do not know the unseen because if they knew the unseen, they would not have worked shamefully for an entire year after Solomon died.

The Qur'an teaches in the previous verses that an animal or worm of the earth ate the staff. One must ask some questions here. *What kind of king was Solomon? What kind of kingdom did Solomon rule?* For a king to be dead, leaning on a staff for an entire year, is unacceptable even to the most foolish person of the earth. *Did Solomon have children or grandchildren?* I believe Solomon was a very wise man, but I do not believe wisdom continues after death. When we read the story of Solomon in the Bible, we read completely different information than that of the Qur'an.

The same hadith is repeated using different words in which Ibn Kathir assured the Muslim reader Solomon was dead for an entire year, but no one knew he was dead. Lots of fairy tales are written about Solomon and his conversation with the angel of death.

As for how long Solomon lived, as usual, Muslim scholars disagree. Isaac Ibn Bashier said Solomon lived fifty-two years and was a king for forty years.[44] However, Ibn Abbas said that Solomon was a king for twenty years, *and Allah knows best.* Ibn Jarir said Solomon lived a little over fifty years. Ibn Kathir ended the story of Solomon by stating that Solomon began the building of the Holy House in the fourth year of his kingdom. Then his son, Rehoboam, became a king after him for seventeen years. After he died, the kingdom of Israel split. Once again, I wonder what verse in the Qur'an or what hadith Ibn Kathir used to bring us such information.

The true account of Solomon's decline and death can be found in 1 Kings 11 where we can read that Solomon loved many foreign women from the nations from which God had commanded the Israelites not to have relations. God knew that the Children of Israel would follow those nations' gods and would sin against Him, and that was exactly what happened to Solomon. He had seven hundred wives and three hundred concubines. They made his heart turn toward their gods in his old age. He did evil in the sight of the Lord; he built the high places to worship the gods of the foreign women.

The Lord was angry with Solomon for his heart had turned from the Lord God. That is why God said to Solomon, "I will surely tear

---

[44]Ibid., 39.

the kingdom from you, and I will give it to your servant." It was because of God's love for King David that He did not take the kingdom away during Solomon's lifetime, and even then He kept one tribe for Solomon's son. The length of Solomon's reign over his kingdom was forty years (971-931 BC.).

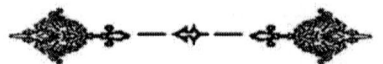

The Story of Isaiah

The next six chapters in Ibn Kathir's book are a total fabrication from him and those who claim to be Muslim scholars. There is simply no mention whatsoever of these stories in the Qur'an or in the hadith. Ibn Kathir inserted these chapters under the title "The Mention of a Group of Prophets from the Children of Israel after David and Solomon and before Zacharias and Yahya." (Yahya was the wrong name because he meant John the Baptist).

Ibn Kathir began these chapters with Isaiah. Again, Ibn Kathir was doing everything he could to help his prophet, Mohammed, write about another prophet, one who is very well known to the Jews and very important to the People of the Book. This man wrote his own book, the book of Isaiah, which is one of the larger books of the prophets. The book includes sixty-six chapters full of many prophecies. This is a book which, if it were read and understood by Muslims and Jews, they would come to realize that the Christian faith is the fulfillment of prophecies written there seven hundred years before Christ and thirteen hundred years before Mohammed claimed to be a prophet.

Ibn Kathir stated that Mohammed Ibn Isaac said Isaiah lived before Zacharias and John the Baptist and that he was one of those who prophesied about the coming of 'Isā (wrong name, he meant Jesus) and Mohammed.[1] Now we ask the question. *How did Mohammed Ibn Isaac know this information?* As we stated earlier, there is no mention whatsoever in the Qur'an or the hadith about Isaiah. On the other hand, when we read the prophecies in the book of Isaiah, we see many prophecies about Jesus but none about Mohammed because the name of Mohammed is not mentioned in the book of Isaiah or anywhere else in the Bible.

Ibn Kathir stated that Mohammed Ibn Isaac said that in the days of Prophet Isaiah, a man named Hezekiah ruled over the Children of Israel in Jerusalem. The king was obedient to Prophet Isaiah. King Hezekiah became sick, and during his sickness, the king of Babylon,

---

[1]Ibn Kathir, *Stories of the Prophets*, vol. 2, Abo Al Fida Ishamail Ibn Kathir Al Kurashi Al Damashce (Beirut: Dar Al-Arab Heritage, 1408 AH, 1988), 40-41.

Sennacherib, desired to conquer and take over Jerusalem. The people were very frightened because of the large numbers of invading Babylonians.

Hezekiah asked Isaiah to seek Allah to see what would happen concerning the king of Babylon and his soldiers. Prophet Isaiah said that Allah had not revealed anything to him yet, but then Allah revealed to him to let King Hezekiah know that he must find a successor because the time had come for Hezekiah to die. When Prophet Isaiah informed the king of this, the king prayed and cried to Allah with a sincere heart. Then Ibn Isaac made up a prayer, and Allah answered the king's prayer, gave him an extra fifteen years to live, and delivered him from his enemies, the king of Babylon, Sennacherib, and his soldiers. The king was relieved from his pain and his sorrow. Once again Ibn Isaac made up another prayer. Then Allah revealed to Prophet Isaiah to take water (sap) from a fig tree and put it on the king's sore so that he would be healed. Allah sent death on the army of Sennacherib so that they were all destroyed except Sennacherib and five of his companions. One of them was Nebuchadnezzar.

Then the king of Israel brought them into the countries and humiliated them for seventy days, and he fed each of them two loaves of barley bread every day. Then he put them into the prison. Then Allah revealed to Isaiah to command the king to send these Babylonians to their own countries to warn their people and to warn their sorcerers and their priests. The sorcerers and priests reminded their king, Sennacherib, "Did we not inform you about these people and their Lord and their prophet, and you did not listen to us? They are a nation no one can have victory over because of their Lord." So Allah used this affair to scare the Babylonians. Then King Sennacherib died seven years later. Ibn Isaac also stated that after King Hezekiah died, the Children of Israel sinned against Allah, and their evil was great. So Allah told Prophet Isaiah to preach to them and remind them about Allah, and Isaiah warned them of Allah's might and his punishment if they disobeyed him or considered him a liar.

When Prophet Isaiah ended the war against their enemies, his people searched for him to kill him. So he escaped from them, and he walked by a tree. The tree was opened, so he entered the tree. However, Satan caught up to him and held onto the edge of his clothes so that it showed outside of the tree. The Children of Israel saw it. They brought a saw and cut the tree and Isaiah. So he died.

[74]

Once again I would like to ask a question. *How did Mohammed Ibn Isaac know all of this information?* The answer is very simple. He, like Ibn Kathir and like Mohammed, the prophet of Islam, copied many stories of the Bible and added many of their own fabrications, as well as taking out many other facts from the accounts of the Bible. Sadly, the average Muslim will read this writing and will never ask questions concerning the source of the information of the Qur'an nor the source of the Muslim scholars' writings. There are many errors in these fabrications, or what I call a foolish counterfeit, of the story of the Prophet Isaiah.

The true account of King Hezekiah can be found in 2 Kings in chapters 18-20, in 2 Chronicles in chapters 29-33, in the book of Isaiah in chapters 36-39, and also in the book of Jeremiah in chapters 15 and 26. We encourage the reader to read the entire account in the Bible.

Notice that the problem was not between the Babylonian Kingdom and Israel but between Israel and the Assyrian Kingdom. The Assyrian king, Shalmaneser, invaded Samaria and conquered it at the end of three years because the people of Samaria had not obeyed God and had transgressed His covenant and all that Moses, His servant, had commanded. This took place in the sixth year of King Hezekiah's reign.

In the fourteenth year of Hezekiah's reign, the Assyrian king, Sennacheriab, came up and took the cities of Judah. Because of the harsh conditions, King Hezekiah surrendered to the king of Assyria. Hezekiah rented his clothes, and he sent Eliakim and Shebna and the elders of the priests to Prophet Isaiah to ask him to pray for the remnant of people that was left. The Lord spoke through Prophet Isaiah immediately, not as written in the fabrication of Muslim scholars' writing. The Lord said that this Assyrian king would return to his own land and there would be killed by the sword. The details of this account can be read in 2 Kings 19.

The prayer King Hezekiah lifted up to the Lord in 19:15 was not because of his sickness, as Muslim scholars fabricated, because he was not sick at this time. Also, the words of the prayer of the king are completely different than the prayer made up by Mohammed Ibn Issac as stated in verses 15-19. The Lord spoke through Prophet Isaiah and assured King Hezekiah that his prayer was answered and that God had also assured the king that they would plant vineyards and eat its fruit in the third year. The remnant of the house of Judah would return, and the Lord would do this because He is a jealous

[75]

God. In simple words, the threat of King Sennacherib to destroy the city of Jerusalem and carry off its people would not be fulfilled.

Then we read in verse 35 that the angel of the Lord killed 185,000 soldiers of the camp of the Assyrians that night. So King Sennacherib left for Nineveh. One day he was worshiping his god, Nisroch, when two of his sons, Adrammelech and Sharezer, killed him with the sword. Then his son, Esarhaddon, became the new king. This, obviously, proves that the story written in Ibn Kathir's book was nothing but a fabrication because King Sennacherib never returned to Babylon because he was not a Babylonian. He was an Assyrian and was killed in Nineveh. God never revealed to Prophet Isaiah to command King Sennacherib to return to his people, and the conversation between King Sennacherib and his priests and sorcerers never took place.

As for the sickness of King Hezekiah, this did not take place until after the death of King Sennacherib. The details of this story can be found in 2 Kings 20 where we can read how Prophet Isaiah prophesied to King Hezekiah that he would die. Hezekiah's prayer can be found in verses 2-4. God answered his prayer by adding fifteen years to Hezekiah's life. His sickness was not a sore but a boil. Isaiah's command was that they take a lump of figs and put it on the boil, not the water of the fig, as Ibn Kathir stated.

As for the sin of Hezekiah and the punishment of God on his children, this can be read about in 2 Kings 20:12-20. The king died as we read in verse 21, and his son Manasseh reigned in his place.

We encourage the reader to read about Isaiah in the Bible. His account is found, not only in the sixty-six chapters of Isaiah, but also in 2 Kings and 2 Chronicles.

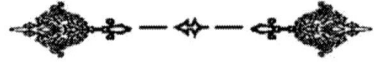

26 The Story of Jeremiah

As in the case of Prophet Isaiah, so it is the same with the story of Prophet Jeremiah. There is no mention of the story or name of Jeremiah in the Qur'an or the hadith. Ibn Kathir wrote only one paragraph, giving scarcely any information, as he quoted Ibn Asakir saying that it was said that Jeremiah stood up on top of the blood of John the Baptist, Ibn Zachariah, as his blood was flowing in Damascus, and Jeremiah called on the blood to stop until it disappeared.[1] *What is the connection between Jeremiah, John the Baptist, and Damascus?* There is no record that either man was ever in Damascus; also, they lived over five hundred years apart.

John the Baptist was born in Judah, and his ministry was along the Jordan River. He was born 2-6 BC and died AD 32-36. Jeremiah was from Anathoth, born 649 BC, preached in Jerusalem from about 628 BC to 586 BC, and then lived in Egypt where he apparently died, although the date is unknown.

We advise the reader to read about Prophet Jeremiah in Jeremiah 1 through 52 and also in 2 Kings 1, 2 Chronicles, Ezra, Nehemiah, and Daniel. To read his writings, we also encourage the reader to read the five chapters in his other book in the Bible, Lamentations.

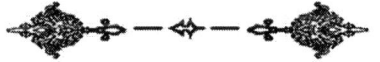

---

[1]Ibn Kathir, *Stories of the Prophets*, vol. 2, Abo Al Fida Ishamail Ibn Kathir Al Kurashi Al Damashce (Beirut: Dar Al-Arab Heritage, 1408 AH, 1988), 41.

Ibn Kathir quoted Qur'an 17:2-8.[1] I do not find any connection between these verses and the title pertaining to the destruction of Jerusalem. Here are the verses: [2]*And we gave Moses the book, and we made it a guidance to the children of Israel that: "You would take no other guardian than me."* [3]*The offspring whom we carried on with Noah, surely he was a thankful servant.* [4]*And we decreed to the children of Israel in the book: "Twice you will vandalize on the earth, and you will be lifted to a big height."* [5]*So when the first promise came to them, we sent against you our servants with substantial, great strength, so they invaded the innermost parts of the homes, and the promise was accomplished.* [6]*Then we gave you back what was turned against them and aided you with money and children, and we made you large in number.* [7]*If you do good, you do good to yourselves; and if you do evil, so for it. So if the promise of the hereafter came to grieve your faces, and they enter the mosque as they entered the first time and bring about tatbīr.*[2] [8]*Perhaps your lord will have mercy on you. And if you return, we return. And we made hell a prison for the infidels.*

Although there is no connection, as I stated previously, between these verses and the destruction of Jerusalem, Ibn Kathir inserted the following passages of Wahab Ibn Monabah, who said that Allah revealed to Prophet Jeremiah that because of the sin of the Children of Israel, they have hearts but do not understand, eyes but do not see, and ears but do not hear. Allah had compassion on the children because of the good of their parents. Then Allah asked them whether it was a hardship for them when they obeyed him and whether any of them found good when they disobeyed him.

Wahab Ibn Monabah went on and on concerning the army which would come to destroy them and which would not show them mercy, an army that did not speak the same language as them. Isaac Ibn Bashier took the baton from Wahab Ibn Monabah to tell more about

---

[1]Ibn Kathir, *Stories of the Prophets*, vol. 2, Abo Al Fida Ishamail Ibn Kathir Al Kurashi Al Damashce (Beirut: Dar Al-Arab Heritage, 1408 AH, 1988), 42.

[2]utter destruction, non-Arabic word of Aramaic origin

Prophet Jeremiah concerning the destruction of Jerusalem and how Allah talked to Jeremiah about the prophecies of what would take place.

Some may look at verse 5 as stated in the previous passage: *⁵So when the first promise came to them, we sent against you our servants with substantial, great strength, so they invaded the innermost parts of the homes, and the promise was accomplished,* to say that this verse is talking about the destruction of Jerusalem in Jeremiah's day. However, when we look at the interpretation of this verse by Ibn Kathir online, he stated that those people of strength whom Allah chose to destroy the homes of the Jews were Goliath's people, but then Allah gave David the victory over Goliath when King David killed him.[3]

Now we must ask a question. *What is the relationship between Goliath, King David, Prophet Jeremiah, and the destruction of Jerusalem?* The answer is *nothing*. There is no relationship whatsoever. This shows the level of ignorance among Muslim scholars concerning the account of the Bible, for David died hundreds of years before the destruction of Jerusalem.

So much has been written concerning Jeremiah which is nothing more or less than fabrications about Jeremiah, his conversation with their enemy, Sennacherib and his army, and how Allah sent Jeremiah to the Children of Israel.[4] Jeremiah said that he was weak and could not go to Israel and that he needed the help and strength of Allah. Then Allah encouraged Jeremiah by saying that he was in charge of the seas and waves. Allah told Jeremiah that he would be with him and would reward him. None of this information even exists in the Qur'an. Similar to previous incidents, Muslim scholars were fabricating this information by twisting the words of God in the Bible as they went on and on in their writings in seven pages of Ibn Kathir's book. We encourage the reader to go back to the book of Jeremiah, which includes fifty-two chapters, and also in his second writing, Lamentations, which includes five chapters, to learn the truth about Jeremiah. From these true words of God, readers will discover the ignorance of Allah, Angel Gabreel, Mohammed, and Muslim scholars, who do not know who Jeremiah was.

---

[3] http://quran.al-islam.com/Page.aspx?pageid=221&BookID=11&Page=282, accessed January 24, 2013.
[4] Ibn Kathir, 43-44.

Another foolish error was the mention of the monks.[5] Allah, Mohammed, and their ignorant scholars did not know that the Jews did not have monks. Allah also described how wicked the kings and the princes were. The Jews did not have princes, which is another error. Muslim scholars keep telling us what Allah told the prophets as if they were there, hearing the conversation. Maybe they forgot and thought that they were also prophets, like Mohammed their prophet. Kaab and Isaac continued to write more about what took place between Allah and Jeremiah.[6]

Even though Ibn Kathir found what was written there to be strange, he did not deny it. Hasham Ibn Al Kelby continued the story of Jeremiah when he mentioned the killing of the fighters and the taking of captives and how Jeremiah was found in prison.[7] Then he explained how the Children of Israel were scattered throughout the land. At the end of all this fabrication, he ended with the famous words, *and Allah knows best.*

I can simply say "no" because Allah knows nothing. It is the Jews and Christians who know best, but Muslims and everyone else can know by simply reading the true account of the destruction of Jerusalem, the Babylonian captivity, and all the wars which took place in the history of the Jews as is written in the Old Testament. This will remove any doubt that the Bible is the true word of God.

I find it to be a waste of time and space to translate such lies and fabrications of Muslim scholars. If someone desires to know what Jeremiah said, I believe that the best and only way is to read what Jeremiah himself wrote, not what someone else stated about what he wrote.

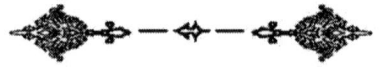

---

[5]Ibid., 44.
[6]Ibid., 46-47.
[7]Ibid., 48.

Ibn Kathir said that Ibn Abu Al Donya said Nebuchadnezzar put two lions in a den.[1] Then he threw Daniel into the den. So he stayed there, but "we do not know for how long." Then he became hungry and thirsty. Then Allah revealed to Jeremiah, who was in Sham (region in the Near East bordering the Eastern Mediterranean Sea or the Levant), that he was to prepare food and drink for Daniel. He said, "O lord, I am in the Holy Land, and Daniel is in Babylon in the land of Iraq." So Allah said, "Do what I command you so surely I will send to you who will carry you and what you prepared."

Jeremiah did what Allah said, and he was carried to the mouth of the den. Then Daniel said, "Who is that?" He replied, "I am Jeremiah." So Daniel asked, "Why are you here?" He said, "Your lord sent me here." Then Daniel said, "Did my lord remember me?" So Jeremiah said, "Yes." So Daniel gave thanks and prayed a long prayer.

Ibn Kathir said that Yunus Ibn Bakyar said that Abu Al Alayah said when Muslims invaded Taster, "we found a bed in one of the houses.[2] On this bed was a dead man, and by his head there was a book. So we took this book to Omar Ibn Khattab, and he transcribed it in Arabic:

> I was the first man who read it. Its reading was exactly what was written in the Qur'an. So I said to Abu Al Alayah, 'What was in it?' He said, 'Your issues and the melodies of your words and what is happening.' The book is still there. So I said, 'What did you do with the dead man?' He said, 'We dug thirteen graves in the daytime, but we buried him at night and we covered the graves, so people will not know where he is buried and they will not take him out.' So I said, 'What do they hope to get from him?' He said, 'When there is no rain, they would put his bed out so they would receive rain.' So I said, 'Who do you think this man was?' He said, 'This man was Daniel.' Then I said, 'How long has this man been

---

[1]Ibn Kathir, *Stories of the Prophets*, vol. 2, Abo Al Fida Ishamail Ibn Kathir Al Kurashi Al Damashce (Beirut: Dar Al-Arab Heritage, 1408 AH, 1988), 49.
[2]Ibid.

dead?' He said, 'Three hundred years.' I said, 'Has anything changed about him?' He said, 'No, except a few hairs from the back of his neck for the flesh of the prophet will not be corrupted by earth, and it will not be eaten by wild animals.'

Ibn Kathir said this was a true hadith, except he had a problem about Daniel's age at death. Perhaps he was another man, not Daniel himself, for the time between 'Isā (Jesus) and Mohammed is not what is written according to Bakhari. The time between them was 400 years, it was also said 620 years, and then it was said 800 years, which is near to the time of Daniel. Ibn Kathir asserted that if it was not the time of Daniel, that means he was another prophet or another righteous man, but most surely he was Daniel.

Ibn Kathir stated that Abu Al Alayah said this prophet's nose was one span.[3] Anas Ibn Malik said his nose was one cubit which means that he must be one of the old prophets long before this time, *and Allah knows best*. Another proof that he was Daniel was that Mohammed said Daniel called unto his lord, asking to be buried by the people of Mohammed. Abu Moses said when he found him and he was told that this dead man in the bed was Daniel, he hugged and kissed him. Then he washed him with water, put a shroud on him, and buried him in a tomb; but no one knows its location.

As for the ten thousand dirham that was found with him, it was returned to the house of money. Then Abu Moses ordered four captives to build a dam on a river (to stop the flow of water), and they dug another grave in the bottom of the river and buried him in it. As for the four captives who buried Daniel, Abu Moses *struck their necks* (decapitated them). Therefore, no one knows where Daniel was buried except Abu Moses.

Ibn Abu Al Donya said that Abd Al Rhaman Ibn Abu Al Zenad said that his father saw on the hand of Abu Moses a ring and on its insignia was the drawing of two lions licking a man. Abu Bardah said this was the ring of the dead man which the people of the city claimed to be Daniel. Abu Moses took this ring when he buried him. The reason Daniel was thrown into the lions' den was that the astrologers and the people of knowledge said to the king that there would be a child born, and this child would speak against the king's kingdom and destroy it. So the king said, "I swear by Allah, I will kill every one of the young men." Then they took Daniel and threw him into the lions' den, so the lion and the lioness spent this night licking him. Then his

---

[3]Ibid., 50.

mother came to him and found the lions licking him. That is why the scholars of this village drew the lions licking him on his ring so that he would not forget the grace of Allah on him.

That was the fairy tale of Ibn Kathir, his scholars, and his prophet concerning the story of Prophet Daniel. Obviously, if Mohammed or Ibn Kathir had read the book of Daniel carefully, which is only twelve chapters in the Old Testament, they would not have exhausted themselves writing such fabrications. Once again, we encourage the reader to go to the Bible and read the true account of Daniel.

Here is a short summary of the true account of Daniel as it is written in the Bible. Notice the exact details of the story. In the third year of the reign of King Jehoiakim, the king of the Jews, King Nebuchadnezzar, the king of Babylon, besieged Jerusalem. He gave the order to Ashpenaz to bring from the Children of Israel the noble young men who were without blemish, skillful, and wise, so that they may serve the king of Babylon. That is why they were taught the writing and the tongue of the Chaldeans.

The best food and drink were offered to them, but there were four young men from the Children of Israel by the name of Daniel, who received the new name of Belteshazzar; Hananiah, who was called Shadrach; Mishael, called Meshach; and Azariah, called Abed-Nego. They refused to eat and drink the ungodly food of the king. Instead, they ate high protein beans and seeds and had water to drink instead of wine. After ten days of doing this, they looked much better than the rest of the young men.

These four young men were the wisest men. That is why they stood before the king. The king had a terrible dream, and he brought the wise men and the astrologers to tell him the dream and its interpretation, but he refused to tell them his dream. If they were not able to tell him his dream, they would be cut into pieces. They said, "There is not one man on earth who can tell what this dream was and its interpretation. Your request is too difficult." Now the king became angry and gave the order to slay all the wise men. Daniel asked the king's captain, Arioch, to give him some time to come up with an answer to the request of the king. Then Daniel met with his three friends and prayed with them, and the Lord gave Daniel the dream and its interpretation (Daniel 2:31-49).

In Daniel 3, we read that the king made a statue and commanded that all people worship the statue when the music was played. Anyone who refused to worship the statue would be put in a burning, fiery furnace. Because the three young men, Shadrach, Meshach, and

Abed-Nego refused to worship the statue, they were thrown into the fiery furnace. Since they had said that they would not obey the king but would only obey the Lord their God, the king became angry and ordered the fire heated seven times hotter. Later, when the king went to see them, they were not consumed by the fire. There were four in the furnace, and the result was that King Nebuchadnezzar believed that the fourth was the angel of the Lord who saved them. He believed in the God of Israel, and he said, "Blessed be the God of Shadrach, Meshach, and Abed-Nego." He made a decree that no one would speak anything against the God of Israel, or they would be cut into pieces. The reader can read in Daniel 4 about the rest of Nebuchadnezzar's life, how he lost his mind, and how he regained it.

After King Nebuchadnezzar died, his son Belshazzar became king. He gave a command to make Daniel the third highest ruler in the kingdom, but then on the same night, Belshazzar was killed. His kingdom was divided into Medes and Persians.

Darius the Mede took over the kingdom at the age of sixty-two (Daniel 5). He appointed 120 princes over his kingdom. Three of these princes were administrators, and Daniel was preferred above all of them. Because of their jealousy, the princes and the administrators tried to implicate Daniel in wrongdoing. They met with King Darius, giving him the advice that, in the subsequent thirty days, anyone in his kingdom who would ask a petition from any god except King Darius would be thrown in the lions' den. King Darius signed the decree, but Daniel continued to kneel and pray to the God of Israel. Therefore, the administrators came to the king and told him, "Daniel did not give any honor to your decree, O King Darius."

King Darius was very angry at himself and desperately looked for any way possible to save Daniel, but he knew that the statute could not be changed. That is why the king gave the order for Daniel to be thrown into the lions' den. A large stone was put at the mouth of the den. The king did not eat or sleep that night. In the early morning, he went to the lions' den. With a sorrowful voice, he cried, "O Daniel, servant of the living God, was your God able to deliver you from the lions?" Daniel answered, "Live forever, O king. My God sent His angel, and He shut the lions' mouths." Then the king was glad and gave the order to bring Daniel out of the den. As for Daniel's accusers, they were thrown into the lions' den with their entire families and were crushed and eaten by the lions. The king became a believer and proclaimed that the God of Israel, who performed a great miracle to save Daniel from the mouth of the vicious lions, is the true God.

As for the rest of the story of Daniel, we encourage the reader to read the book of Daniel in the Bible. There you will read the true account of his life as it is written with the guidance of the Holy Spirit by the hand of Daniel through the power of the only true author, God Himself.

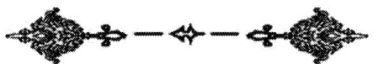

29   The Story of
The Rebuilding of Jerusalem
and the Return of the Jews

Although nothing is written in the Qur'an by this title, Ibn Kathir quoted Qur'an 2:259 and tried to make of this verse as if Allah was telling the story.[1] Here is the verse: [259]*Or like this one who passed by a village, and it was empty on its roof.*[2] *He said, "Will Allah give life to this after its death?" So Allah caused him to die for a hundred years and then raised him to life. And Allah said, "How long were you waiting?" He said, "I have waited a day or part of a day." He said, "Yet you have waited a hundred years. So look at your food and your drink, they are not corrupted, and look to your donkey. We would make you a sign to people. And look on the bones, how we raise them, then clothe them with flesh." So when this was shown to him, he said, "I know that Allah has might over all things."*

This verse is nothing but a bunch of nonsensical words. This does not even satisfy the definition of a parable. A parable is a short story that uses familiar events to illustrate a religious or ethical point. *What is the actual story? Does the story illustrate a point, or is there just a statement made after some rambling words? Furthermore, what does it have to do with Jerusalem?* Moreover, it cannot be a true story. There is nothing in its contents that would lead us to conclude that it is talking about Jerusalem or the entire two kingdoms of Israel. Ibn Kathir may have been unaware that there were two kingdoms at the time of Jeremiah—the northern and the southern kingdoms. It was not just Jerusalem which had been destroyed. All that this verse refers to is a village.

The death of this man for a hundred years and the description of the food, drink, and the donkey is nothing but a made-up story or, as I said earlier, an attempt at a parable. All that I can see is that we can perhaps connect Ezekiel, but certainly not Jeremiah, to this verse and what is written at the end of the verse concerning the bones and the

---

[1]Ibn Kathir, *Stories of the Prophets*, vol. 2, Abo Al Fida Ishamail Ibn Kathir Al Kurashi Al Damashce (Beirut: Dar Al-Arab Heritage, 1408 AH, 1988), 51.

[2]crumbled

clothing of the bones with flesh (Ezekiel 37). God is not a god of confusion, for if the Qur'an is the word of God and God wants to tell people facts about the past of the Children of Israel, He would do so in a clear and concise manner, as in the case of the Bible, not as it is written here in this verse. The interpretation of the Word of God is clear and elaborates on the information in the verses; it is not fabricating stories.

Now let us look at the writings of Ibn Kathir, and his Muslim scholars, for he stated that Hasham Ibn Al Kelby said that Allah revealed to Jeremiah that he would rebuild Jerusalem.[3]

> So Allah asked Jeremiah to go to Jerusalem because it was destroyed. He said to himself, "Allah commanded me to come to this country, and he said that he would rebuild it. So when will he rebuild it?" So he slept, and his donkey was with him. He also had a basket, and in it there was food. He slept seventy years until Nebuchadnezzar died, and the king who came after him, Lahrasb, and his kingdom was 120 years. His son rose up after him, and his name was Bashtasb.

King Nebuchadnezzar died in his country, so Jeremiah told Bashtasb about the countries of the Levant and how they were destroyed. That is how the wild animals filled Palestine[4] and no humans lived there. He called to the Children of Israel in Babylon, "Whoever desires to return to the Levant, let him return." Then he appointed a king, a man from the family of David, and he commanded him to return to Jerusalem and rebuild its temple. They returned and rebuilt it.

When Allah opened the eyes of Jeremiah, he looked at the city, saw how it was built, and saw how it was repopulated. Then he went back to sleep until a hundred years were completed. Then Allah brought him back to life, but he did not think that he had slept more than an hour. He had seen the destruction of the city, but when he looked at it, it was rebuilt by the people. He said, "I know that Allah is able to do everything." So the Children of Israel lived in it and stayed there until the Byzantine kings had victory over them.

---

[3] Ibn Kathir, 51-52.

[4] The editor of the 1988 revision of Ibn Kathir's writings, which we are using, apparently changed the word *Israel* to *Palestine* to support Muslim claims on the land, but it is well known that Palestine did not exist at the time of the writing of the original document in the eighth century.

However, they did not have unity or authority after the Christians took them over.

Ibn Kathir said that Ibn Jarir mentioned that King Lahrasb was a just king.[5] People, countries, kings, and leaders drew near to him. He was a man with good opinions on the following: regional architecture, rivers, and fortresses. When he became too weak to manage his kingdom a hundred years later, he left the throne to his son Bashtasb. During Bashtasb's days, the religion of the Magi began. It began with a man named Zardsht. He was a friend of Jeremiah but had made Jeremiah angry, so when Jeremiah cursed him, he became leprous. He went to the land of Azerbaijan, became friends with Bashtasb, and taught him the religion of the Magi, which he had invented. King Bashtasb accepted the religion and forced the people to accept the religion. If anyone refused, he was killed. After King Bashtasb died, his son Bahman became the king. He was one of the heroic and famous Persian kings. Ibn Kathir ended this story with, "May King Nebuchadnezzar live longer than these three kings. May Allah make his face ugly."[6]

Ibn Kathir concluded the story by writing that Ibn Jarir knew that the man who walked by the village and who slept a hundred years was Jeremiah, but other scholars like Ibn Abbas and Qatadah said that he was Uzair. This is a famous opinion among them, *and Allah knows best*. That in itself is the proof of the point that I mentioned earlier. No one really knows anything about such a story because there is no story. The Allah of the Qur'an is a god of confusion, for the words of the Qur'an are great evidence, in and of themselves, that the Qur'an is not God's words. These words are made up by Muslim scholars and are not a true interpretation, especially when they cannot even agree on the person about whom the verse is written and when their words have nothing to do with the verse of the Qur'an.

Did Jeremiah sleep a hundred uninterrupted years; or did he sleep seventy years, wake up, and then sleep another thirty years? Was it really Jeremiah or was it Ezra? Qur'an 2:259 has nothing to do with Jeremiah or Ezra. It is just a jumble of words with no true story.

---

[5]Ibid., 52.
[6]Ibid.

Dear reader, do you want to know the true story of the rebuilding of Jerusalem and the return of the captives from Babylon? You must read the account in the Bible. I encourage you to read the story of Nehemiah which is thirteen chapters long. Nehemiah told us the story which anyone can read and easily understand. It does not require fabrication or interpretation like *the hundred years of sleep!*

Nehemiah was in captivity during the month of Chislev in the twentieth year of the reign of King Artaxerxes. When he was in the fortress Shushan, he met with Hanani, one of his brethren. They were from the tribe of Judah. He asked Hanani what was left of those who escaped captivity and what was left of Jerusalem. There he received the sad news that the country was in great evil and shame, the walls of Jerusalem were broken, and the gates were burned with fire. Nehemiah wept and fasted before the God of heaven. He prayed a lengthy prayer which can be read in Nehemiah 1. He stood before King Artaxerxes, and the king saw that Nehemiah was sick. His face was sorrowful, and he told the king about the situation. He asked the king to send him to his city so he could rebuild it. The king and queen thought it was a good project, so not only did they allow him to go back, they also sent letters to the kings beyond the river to help him rebuild the city.

When Sanballat the Horonite, Tobiah the Ammonite official, and Geshem the Arab heard of it, they were upset and gave Nehemiah a hard time in rebuilding. They made fun of him and scorned him, but the answer of Nehemiah was, "The God of heaven will prosper us; therefore, we his servants will rise up and build. You will have no part of it."

Each Jewish group stood up before the walls. With one hand they worked, and with the other hand they held their swords. Sanballat and Tobiah came to wage war against Nehemiah. They tried to stop the work, but Nehemiah made the people work with bows and spears in their hands. Nehemiah encouraged the people, and when the enemy knew that Nehemiah was ready for battle against them, they left. Then Nehemiah was able to go back to the wall, and everyone returned to work. He divided the people into two groups, half to work and half to hold the spears, from the rising of the sun to the appearance of the stars at night.

Disputes took place among the Jewish people. People were mortgaging their land, borrowing money, and even selling their children into slavery to their Jewish brothers in order to buy grain. When Nehemiah was informed about this, he became angry and then wept. He brought the people together and accused these nobles and officials of exacting usury against their brothers. The people fell silent. He then asked the people to promise to restore the vineyards and olive yards and homes back to their brothers. He called unto the priests and leaders to take an oath to do according to their promises.

Jerusalem was rebuilt and the city was restored because of the hard work and the faithfulness of Nehemiah and those who stood with him. Notice that it was Nehemiah, not Jeremiah or Ezra, who rebuilt the city of Jerusalem. We encourage the reader to read the entire book of Nehemiah in the Bible.

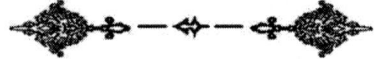

Once again, Ibn Kathir introduced a story for which there is no preceding mention in the Qur'an or the hadith.[1] It is the story of Prophet Al Uzair (Ezra). He began his writing by stating that Al Hafaz said that Al Uzair was Ibn Gerowah, but it was also said he was Ibn Soreeq, Ibn Adya, Ibn Job, Ibn Darzana, Ibn Arey, Ibn Taqee, Ibn Asboa, Ibn Finhas, Ibn Al Uzair, Ibn Aaron, Ibn Amran. According to archeology, Uzair's tomb is on the plains of the Tigris River at Al-'Uzair in Iraq. Most Muslim scholars did not know whether or not he was a prophet.

Ibn Kathir said that Ibn Abbas said Uzair was one of those taken into captivity by Nebuchadnezzar when he was a young man.[2] When he turned forty years old, Allah gave him wisdom, and no one memorized the Torah better than he. His name used to be with the prophets until Allah removed his name because he asked Allah about destiny (things to come). Ibn Kathir said this part of the story is weak and evil, *and Allah knows best.*

Ibn Kathir said that Isaac Ibn Bashier said Uzair was the servant which Allah caused to die for a hundred years and then brought back to life. Somehow this made-up story about someone who was dead for a hundred years and then brought back to life by Allah is written in Qur'an 2:259. *[259]Or like this one who passed by a village, and it was empty on its roof.[3] He said, "Will Allah give life to this after its death?" So Allah caused him to die for a hundred years and then raised him to life. And Allah said, "How long were you waiting?" He said, "I have waited a day or part of a day." He said, "Yet you have waited a hundred years. So look at your food and your drink, they are not corrupted, and look to your donkey. We would make you a sign to people. And look on the bones, how we raise them, then clothe them with flesh." So when this was shown to him, he said, "I know that Allah has might over all things."* Muslim scholars said he was Ezekiel,

---

[1]Ibn Kathir, *Stories of the Prophets*, vol. 2, Abo Al Fida Ishamail Ibn Kathir Al Kurashi Al Damashce (Beirut: Dar Al-Arab Heritage, 1408 AH, 1988), 52.

[2]Ibid., 53.

[3]crumbled

Jeremiah, or Al Uzair. Isaac Ibn Bashier also quoted many other scholars who said that Al Uzair was a wise, good servant.

One day Al Uzair went to a place in the afternoon. He became so hot that he had a heat stroke, so he went inside of some ruins there on his donkey. He got off the donkey with a basketful of figs and another basketful of grapes. As he sat in the shade of the ruins, he got a bowl and began to squeeze the grapes into it. He took out a dry piece of bread and put it in the bowl to soften it in order to eat it. Then he lay down on his back, put his legs up on the wall, and looked up at the ceilings of the houses. Then he saw the destruction of the houses, for their occupants were destroyed. He also saw the dry bones. He said, "Will Allah give life to this after its death?" He did not doubt that Allah could give the bones life, but he said it in wonder.

Therefore, Allah sent the angel of death who caused him to die for a hundred years. Many things happened to the Children of Israel during this time. Then Allah sent an angel to Uzair to create a new heart in him, so that he could understand and new eyes so he could see with them; therefore, he would understand how Allah gives life to the dead. Then he put his creation together while Uzair was watching. Then he covered his bones with meat and hair and skin. Then he blew the spirit into him. All this was done while Uzair was watching and understanding.

So the angel said to him, "How long did you stay?" And he said, "A day or part of a day." That is because he died in the afternoon and was raised at the end of the afternoon and the sun did not set. The angel said, "No, you stayed one hundred years."

The angel said to him, "Look at your food and your drink," meaning the hard bread and the juice which was in the bowl. Behold, they were in the same condition. Likewise, the figs and the grapes had not changed. So the angel said to him, "Look at your donkey." Behold, the donkey was dry bones. Then the angel called to the bones of the donkey. So the bones answered him and gathered together from every place as the angel put the bones together, and Uzair was watching the angel. Then the angel dressed the donkey with the veins and nerves, then with meat, skin, and hair. Then he blew into the donkey so the donkey rose up and lifted up his head and his ears to the heavens, and he brayed for he thought that the day of resurrection had come. That is why Allah said, "And look to your donkey. We would make you a sign to people. And look on the bones, how we raise them, then clothe them with flesh." So when he saw this, he said, "I know that Allah has power over all things, and I know he is able to raise the dead."

Isaac Ibn Bashier continued by stating that Uzair rode his donkey and came to his place, but the people did not know him. He did not know the people until he came to his house. There he saw an old woman who was blind. She was 120 years old and was as a mother to the people. Uzair left when she was twenty. So he said to her, "O you, is this the house of Uzair?" She said, "Yes, this is the house of Uzair." Then she cried and said, "I have not seen anyone for many years." All the people had forgotten Uzair.

He said, "I am Uzair for Allah put me to death for one hundred years and then brought me back to life." So she said, "Great is Allah for surely we missed Uzair for one hundred years, and we never heard anything about him." So he said, "Surely I am Uzair." She said, "Surely Uzair is a man whose prayer Allah answered. He called for the sick and the people who have trouble with healing. So call on Allah for me that Allah will bring my sight to me that I may see you. So if you are Uzair, I will know you." So he called on his lord and wiped his hand over her eyes so they were healed; and he reached out, took her by her hand, and said, "Arise with the will of Allah."

So Allah healed her legs, and she stood up in a healthy condition. She looked and said, "I bear witness, surely you are Uzair." So she went to the place, where the Children of Israel were located in their clubs and councils, where Ibn Uzair was an old man at the age of 118 years and his grandchildren were old in the council. So she said, "This is Uzair. He came to you." They called her a liar. She said, "I am So-and-so, your leader. Uzair called on his lord for me so I got my sight back and my feet were healed and he claimed that Allah caused him to die for one hundred years and then he raised him back to life."

Then the people stood and came near him and looked at him. His son said, "My father has a black mole between his shoulders." So he looked between his shoulders, and behold, he was Uzair. So the Children of Israel said, "Surely no one is among us who memorized the Torah except Uzair and Nebuchadnezzar, and nothing is left of it except what the men memorized. So write it for us. His father was Srokha."

Srokha had buried the Torah in the day of Nebuchadnezzar, and no one knew except Uzair. He took them to the place, they dug into the ground, and he took the Torah out. The pages were moldy. He studied the book, they sat in the shade of a tree, and the Children of Israel sat around them.

Thus Uzair renewed to them the Torah. Two flames came from heaven and went into his stomach, he remembered the Torah, and he renewed it to the Children of Israel. Then the Jews said, "Uzair is the son of Allah." Because of the event of the two flames and the renewal of the Torah and because he took care of the matter of the Children of Israel, he renewed that Torah to them in the land of the vast monastery of Ezekiel, and the village in which he died was called Sairabaz.

Ibn Kathir said that Ibn Abbas said, as Allah said, "We would make you a sign to people."[4] The meaning here is that Uzair was a sign to the Children of Israel for he used to sit with his sons, and they were old men; but he was a young man, for he died when he was forty years old. When Allah raised him from the dead, he was in the same condition as when he died. Ibn Kathir continued by saying that Uzair was a prophet from among the prophets of Israel and lived between the days of David and Solomon and Zachariah and John the Baptist.

Because not one of the children memorized the Torah, Allah revealed to him to memorize it. Wahab Ibn Monobah said Allah commanded an angel who came down with knowledge of light so that he threw it into Uzair, so he wrote the Torah letter by letter until he finished it. Ibn Abbas said, concerning Allah, "The Jews said Uzair is the son of Allah," which is in Qur'an 9:30: *[30]And the Jews said, "Uzair is the son of Allah." And the Nasara (Christians) said, "The Christ is the son of Allah." This is their saying with their mouths; they repeat the sayings of those who became infidels before. Allah engages in war with them. How perverted they are!* The reason they called him the son of Allah was because Moses was not able to give the Jews the Torah except in a book, but Uzair gave them the Torah without a book. Ibn Kathir shed some light on a very important disagreement among Muslim scholars concerning when Uzair left. Some said he left during the life of Nebuchadnezzar; others said at the time of Moses.[5]

I am assuming, only from the similarity in the name, that the prophet of Islam which Mohammed and his Muslim scholars were talking about was Ezra. I am astonished at how Muslim scholars can interpret Qur'an 2:259 to be the story of Nehemiah, Jeremiah, Ezra, and who knows who else. Once again, the verse does not give any

---

[4]Ibn Kathir, 55.
[5]Ibid., 55-56.

details or information about any prophet, but Muslims use it to come up with several fabrications. No Jew ever called Ezra the son of God.

I will now summarize the major points of the book of Ezra in an attempt to help the reader to know the true account of Ezra. Prophet Ezra lived during the reign of King Cyrus, the king of Persia, at which time the Lord had asked the king to rebuild Solomon's temple in Jerusalem. He gave permission for the people to go back to Jerusalem to rebuild the temple. He asked people to give all that they could of silver and gold, animals, and goods as a free will offering to the Lord so they could rebuild His house in Jerusalem.

Hundreds and thousands of people came back from all over Cyrus's kingdom to Jerusalem to rebuild the house of the Lord. People gave even above their ability to give to the treasury in order to build the House of the Lord. The people were gathered as one man to build the altar for the Lord. In the second year of their return to Jerusalem, they began to rebuild the foundation of the temple of the Lord. The fathers and the elders who saw the first temple cried when they began to lift up the foundation of the temple. People could not discern between the voice of weeping and the voice of joy, for the cry was very loud.

Some complained and tried to stop the rebuilding of the temple. They sent a letter to the new king, Artaxerxes, and stated that if the city would be completely rebuilt with its walls, the people in the land would not pay the tribute. These people were acting as if they were friends of the king and as if they were concerned about his wellbeing. Therefore, the king sent an answer to their letter commanding that all building be stopped until the king gave a new command.

The godly men of Jerusalem responded with a letter to the new king, King Darius. In their letter they explained all the things that had taken place concerning King Nebuchadnezzar and when they were taken into captivity. They told how King Nebuchadnezzar took the gold and silver vessels of the temple, how the Lord had spoken to King Cyrus to rebuild the temple, how King Cyrus gave an order to rebuild the temple, and how he also gave the vessels of gold and silver back to the temple. They requested that the king search to see if this information was true or not. Then they asked the king to send his response to them.

King Darius investigated the matter and found the godly men's account to be true. Therefore, he commanded the work to be continued. He supported the construction with more financial gifts. He gave an order that any man who would hinder the work must be hung on a timber from his own house. Then his house would be a dunghill. The elders of the Jews prospered and were determined to rebuild the temple as it was ordered by the God of Israel and commanded by Cyrus, Darius, and Artaxerxes. The temple was completed in the sixth year of the reign of King Darius. The Children of Israel kept the Passover in the fourteen days of the first month.

As for the identity of Ezra, according to the list of the names in Ezra 7:1-5, he was one of the descendants of Aaron the chief priest. He was living in Babylon and was an excellent writer of the laws of Moses. Ezra, some of the priests and Levites, along with some other Children of Israel came to Jerusalem in the seventh year and fifth month of the reign of Artaxerxes the king. The king gave an order that whatever Ezra the priest and the scribe of the law of the God of heaven needed, it must be given to him. Anyone who would not obey the law of the God of Ezra and the law of the king would be punished quickly by death, banishment, confiscation of his goods, or imprisonment. Hundreds of people left Babylon with Ezra and returned to Jerusalem. However, there were no Levites there. Ezra sent for Levites to come, and hundreds came to Jerusalem. Ezra and his people prayed, fasted, and humbled themselves before God. God protected them, and they arrived in Jerusalem.

Because Ezra saw that the people of Israel had intermarried with the Gentiles, he tore his clothes, pulled out his hair, and tore out his beard. He waited till the evening and prayed to the God of heaven, confessing his sin to God and the sin of his people. When he prayed, all the people of Israel wept bitterly. Then the men of Israel made a covenant with God to put away all their Gentile wives. They called for the people in Judah and Jerusalem to gather in three days. All the people gathered, and Ezra asked all the people to repent and to separate themselves from these strange wives. It was organized, for the people were large in numbers. This work of removing these wives required more time than just a day, and it was the time of rain. So, all the foreign wives were removed from among them.

Notice that Ezra did not die for a hundred years and come back to life, nor did he have a donkey. As for the claim that the Torah was lost or burned by Nebuchadnezzar, that is just fabrication. Ezra was a priest and was a skilled writer of the law. He did not write the law because of the law being lost, as Muslims claim, but because he was a priest and a scribe, well-versed in the law, as written in Ezra 7:6, 11-12: *⁶This Ezra came up from Babylon; and he was a skilled scribe in the Law of Moses, which the Lord God of Israel had given. The king granted him all his request, according to the hand of the Lord his God upon him.* [11]*This is a copy of the letter that King Artaxerxes gave Ezra the priest, the scribe, expert in the words of the commandments of the LORD, and of His statutes to Israel:* [12]*Artaxerxes, king of kings, To Ezra the priest, a scribe of the Law of the God of heaven: Perfect peace, and so forth.* A scribe copied the manuscripts of the law to preserve them.

Finally, Ezra did not have any sons who were older than he, as stated in the fabrication of Muslim scholars. To learn more details about Ezra, we encourage the reader to read the book of Ezra which includes ten chapters.

The Story of Zacharias and John the Baptist

Who was Zakariyya, and who was Yahya? As was the habit of Mohammed, he often rewrote the history and the stories of the Bible. He also changed the names of the stories' characters. For example, he changed the name of John the Baptist to Yahya. If we ask any Hebrew scholar the name of the son of Zacharias, the answer will be, in the Arabic language, Uhana (*John* in English), not Yahya.

Who did Ibn Kathir say Zakariyya was? Ibn Kathir stated that he was Zakariyya Ibn Barkhya.[1] Ibn Kathir also said others said he was Zakariyya Ibn Dan. Ibn Kathir further stated that it was said (by others) he was Zakariyya Ibn Laden, Ibn Muslim, Ibn Sadook, Ibn Hashban, Ibn David, Ibn Solomon, Ibn Muslim, Ibn Sadekah, Ibn Barkhya, Ibn Balatah, Ibn Nehor, Ibn Shalom, Ibn Bahshafat, Ibn Rhabaam, Ibn Solomon, Ibn David, the father of Yahya the prophet. *Where did this list come from? I believe Ibn Kathir made up these names.*

Ibn Kathir continued by stating that Zakariyya was seeking his son in Damascus, for he was in Damascus when his son was killed. Ibn Kathir ended his account with the usual words, *and Allah knows best.*

Although Ibn Kathir used a lot of his book to give us a genealogy of every prophet, without having any source for his information, here we find that he made a long list of wrong names. When we read the Scriptures, all we can find concerning the genealogy of Zacharias, the father of John the Baptist, was that he and his wife Elizabeth (Mohammed did not mention her name in the Qur'an) were the descendants of Levi which gave Zacharias the right to be a priest. They were from the division of Abijah (Luke 1:5). It is very important to note that there is not one man by the name of *Muslim* in the entire existence of the Jewish nation.

The other important error we see in Ibn Kathir's writing was the location of their home. He stated that they lived in Damascus. The truth is that Zacharias and his family lived on the mountain of Judah

---

[1]Ibn Kathir, *Stories of the Prophets*, vol. 2, Abo Al Fida Ishamail Ibn Kathir Al Kurashi Al Damashce (Beirut: Dar Al-Arab Heritage, 1408 AH, 1988), 57.

(Luke 1:39). John the Baptist had his ministry in the villages surrounding the Jordan River (Luke 3:3).

The story of Zakariyya and his son Yahya is mentioned in the Qur'an in four different places. In Qur'an 6:85 only their names are mentioned: *⁸⁵And Zacharias and Yahya² and 'Isā and Iliyas,³ all were from the good.*

The second mention of Zakariyya can be found in Qur'an 21:89-90 which is a short version of the story: *⁸⁹And Zacharias, when he called on his lord: "My lord, do not leave me alone,⁴ and you are the best of the inheritors." ⁹⁰So we answered him and granted him Yahya,⁵ and we fixed his wife for him. Surely they were hastened in the good deeds, and they called on us with affection and fear. And they were humble to us.* Ibn Kathir interpreted these verses by stating that Allah *fixed* Zakariyya's wife, meaning that she was not having menstrual cycles and he caused her to have them. Ibn Kathir said that others said there was uncleanliness in her tongue.⁶

The third mention is in Qur'an 19:1-15. Ibn Kathir stated the purpose of Allah instructing Mohammed to tell the story of Zakariyya and how he and his wife had a son in their old age was to show Allah's mercy, that no one should lose hope in the bounty of Allah.

It is written in Qur'an 19:2-3: *²A reminder of your lord's mercy to his servant Zacharias. ³When he called on his lord with a whispered calling.* Ibn Kathir said that Qatadah said Allah knows the pure heart, and he can hear the soft whisper. He continued by saying that Zakariyya stood up in the middle of the night calling his lord; he said, "O lord, O lord, O lord." Allah answered him, "Here I am; here I am; here I am." One must ask a question. *How did Qatadah know the words of the prayer of Zakariyya and the answer of Allah?*

Zakariyya continued talking to Allah in Qur'an 19:4 by saying: *⁴"My lord, surely my bones are brittle, and my head is aflame with gray hair....* Ibn Kathir interpreted these words by saying that Zakariyya was weak and old in age and no longer had black hair. As for the saying of Zakariyya in the rest of verse 4,...*And I was not miserable with my calling on you*, Ibn Kathir said that Zakariyya

---

²John the Baptist
³name mistakenly used, Elijah was meant
⁴without offspring
⁵the Baptist
⁶Ibn Kathir, 59.

knew that Allah was able to give him a child even though he was old. When he was watching over Miriam, the daughter of Amran, "Mary the mother of Jesus," Zakariyya always noticed that Allah provided her with fruit which was not in season. In other words, if Allah could provide Mary with off-season fruit which was a miracle, Allah would also be able to provide Zakariyya with a son even though both he and his wife were old.

Continuing the story in Qur'an 19:5-6, the Qur'an states: *⁵And surely I have fears for my relatives after me, and my woman [wife] was barren. So grant me from yourself an heir, ⁶to inherit me and inherit the family of Jacob, and make him pleasing, my lord."* Ibn Kathir interpreted the statement, *"And surely I have fears for my relatives after me ...,"* by saying that Zakariyya was afraid of the action of his people after him, that they would live in a way that was not acceptable to the law of Allah, and they would be disobedient to Allah.[7] That was why Zakariyya was seeking a son from his own flesh who would live right to please Allah, inherit the prophecy and wisdom for the Children of Israel, and continue the traditions of the family of the descendants of Jacob. It was not to inherit the money but the prophethood and the wisdom.

When you read this interpretation, you could draw the conclusion that Zacharias was a prophet who was in charge of the nation of Israel, or he would not have been concerned that there would not be a righteous prophet or leader in Israel after his death. The fact was that he was a priest, one of many priests. He served in the temple only twice a year, and if the lottery fell on him, he would serve one time in his life in the Holy of Holies.

In Ibn Kathir's explanation, prophets did not bequeath any inheritance to their children because they were poor. He said that Zakariyya was a carpenter and that he ate from the profit of the work of his hands, as it was in King David's case. Prophets did not work hard to make excessive profit but just enough to be able to live; therefore, they would not have any inheritance for their children. Ibn Kathir proved from the hadith that Zakariyya was a carpenter.[8] Imam Ahmed said that the apostle of Allah said, "Zakariyya was a carpenter." This was also said by Muslim and Ibn Magah and others.

All the above information is an error. Zacharias was not a carpenter. Mohammed showed his ignorance of the simple facts about

---

[7]Ibid., 58.
[8]Ibid., 59.

Judaism, for Zacharias was a priest, a Levi, who did not work, not as a carpenter nor as a fisherman.

Let us continue the story in Qur'an 19:7: [7]*"O Zacharias, surely we give you good news of a son; his name is Yahya.*[9] *That name we have given to none before him."* When we read this verse, we discover that Allah here was speaking to Zakariyya, and Allah gave Zakariyya the good news of a son. Allah was telling him that his name would be Yahya. Allah was explaining to him that no one had ever had the same name before him. However, look closely in Qur'an 3:38-39: [38]*Thereupon Zacharias called his lord and said, "My lord, grant me from yours a good descendant. Surely you are the hearer of the calling."* [39]*So the angels called to him while he stood usalle*[10] *in the holy of holies: "That Allah gives you good news of Yahya,*[11] *confirming by a word from Allah, and a master, celibate, and a prophet from among the good."*

Notice that the prayer of Zakariyya in Qur'an 3:38 is written in a different wording than the prayer which he offered in Qur'an 19:4-6. Also, the answer of his prayer in Qur'an 19:7 was by Allah, not as it was written in Qur'an 3:39 where it was answered by the angels, and also the words in the answer of the prayer were different. We must ask these questions. *Which of the previous prayers is correct, Qur'an 19:3-6 or Qur'an 3:38? Who answered the prayer? Was it Allah as it was stated in Qur'an 19:7, or was it the angels as written in Qur'an 3:39?*

Memorizing the Qur'an is an easy thing to do, even for people who cannot read or write, but understanding the Qur'an after studying it is difficult for a person with common sense. He or she would have to accept all these inconsistencies and contradictions without coming to the conclusion that the Qur'an is not from God.

Let us continue to look at the rest of the story in both locations. In Qur'an 19:8-9: [8]*He said, "My lord, how can I have a son, and my woman [wife] was barren and, indeed, when I have now reached old age?"* [9]*He said, "Likewise, your lord says, it is easy for me; and indeed, I created you before, and you were not anything."* Compare this with Qur'an 3:40: [40]*He said, "My lord,*

---

[9]wrong name, he meant John the Baptist
[10]praying, non-Arabic word of Syriac origin
[11]wrong name, he meant John the Baptist

how can I have a son and, indeed, the old age has come to me and my wife is barren?" He said, "Likewise, Allah does what he wills."

Here is the question. *Why was Zakariyya praying?* The answer is so that Allah would give him a son. Allah answered his prayer by telling him that he would have a son; but then, surprisingly, Mohammed said that Zakariyya asked, "How can I have a son?" Although the saying of Zakariyya is different between Qur'an 19 and Qur'an 3, as stated above, I am more astonished at his response when Allah answered his prayer. Instead of saying *thank you* for giving him an answer to his prayer, he asked, "How can I have a son when I am an old man and my wife is barren?" *Was Zakariyya drunk when he asked Allah in his prayer to give him a son, or was this just a bunch of words by Mohammed to make the poetry in the Qur'an?*

Was the answer of Allah in Qur'an 19:9: *[9]It is easy for me; and indeed, I created you before, and you were not anything*? Or was the answer of Allah in Qur'an 3:40: *[40]...Allah does what he wills"*? My dear friends, this is the problem with the Qur'an. Whenever the story is repeated, it is always written with different words or, as in the following case, along with gestures by Zakariyya as in verse 3:41.

In Qur'an 19:10-11: *[10]He said, "My lord, give me a sign." He said, "Your sign will be that you will not speak to the people three nights together." [11]So he came out of the holy of holies to his people, so he revealed to them to praise morning and evening.* Also, in Qur'an 3:41: *[41]He said, "My lord, give me a sign." He said, "Your sign that you will not speak to the people for three days except gestures. And remember your lord much, and praise in the evening and in the morning."* Here we find Zakariyya asking his lord for a sign. Although the question was the same, the answer of Allah was a little different in Qur'an 19:10; he would not speak to the people for three straight nights. In Qur'an 3:40, Allah said that Zakariyya would speak to them with gestures.

You might say that both answers were the same, but which words did Allah say? Also, is there any truth in such a story when compared to the true account in the Bible? In his interpretation of the statement, *he revealed to them to praise morning and evening,* Ibn Kathir said that it was an easy command. Perhaps Zakariyya showed them by writing or with gestures. Some Muslim scholars such as Mujahid and Qatadah and others said the tongue of Zakariyya was imprisoned without any sickness. Others like Ibn Saeed said that he was able to read and praise Allah, but he could not talk to people.

Let us have a quick look at the true account as it is written in the Bible as we recommend to the reader to read the entire story in the book of Luke 1:5-25, 39-80; 3:1-20; and 7:18-35. We can read about the death of John in the book of Matthew 14:1-12 and in Luke 9:7-9.

Throughout the reading of the previous Scriptures, we found that Zacharias and his wife Elizabeth were righteous people, not that they did not have sin but that they had lived according to the law by offering the sacrifices for their sins. That was why they were acceptable before God. They were of old age and without any children.

After Zacharias was chosen by lot to serve in the temple, he was in the temple offering prayer and incense when the angel of the Lord appeared to him from the right side of the altar of incense. Zacharias was afraid when he saw the angel, but the angel said to him to not be afraid. He gave Zacharias the good news that his prayer was answered by God because he and his wife Elizabeth would have a son. The angel told Zacharias that he should call his son John for he would bring joy, not only to Zacharias but to many; he would be great before the Lord. He would not drink wine, and he would be filled with the Holy Spirit from his mother's womb. He would lead many of the Children of Israel to their God. Zacharias, however, showed his doubt by asking how he would know this, for he was an old man and his wife was an old woman.

Obviously, he had stopped praying for a child a long time before, but God hears our prayers and is able to answer them in His time. What could seem late to us is just the perfect timing of God. The response of Angel Gabriel to Zacharias's doubt was a little harsh. He said to him, "You will be mute until the day this baby is born for you did not believe my words." Notice that Zacharias did not ask for a sign, as it is written in the Qur'an, but rather this was a punishment from Angel Gabriel. Also, he was mute for at least nine months, not three days as Mohammed claimed in the Qur'an.

While all this took place, the people were outside wondering why Zacharias was late coming out of the temple. When he came out, he spoke to them with gestures. After he finished his two weeks of service in the temple, he traveled to his house. His wife Elizabeth became pregnant, and she hid herself for five months.

At the birth of John the Baptist, the joy and greatness of God's mercy were upon Elizabeth and her neighbors. After eight days, they took the child to the temple for circumcision, and they named him Zacharias like his father; but his mother said, "No, you shall name him John." They said to her that no one in her family had such a name, so they went to his father and asked Zacharias what the baby's name should be. He asked for a board and wrote down *John*. They wondered what this young man would be like. Then Zacharias praised the Lord as he was full of the Holy Spirit. His praise can be found in Luke 1:67-79, but verse 80 ends with John growing in the Spirit. John lived in the wilderness until he appeared to the people of Israel.

In Qur'an 19:12: *12O Yahya, take the book with strength, and we gave him the wisdom [as] a child,* Ibn Kathir stated that Allah declared that the child existed and that the good news from Allah to his father Zakariyya was that Allah taught him the book and the wisdom when Yahya was a child.[12] As for the statement, *and compassion from us,* found in verse 13, Ibn Abbas said he did not know what it meant, but Ibn Kathir also said that Ibn Abbas and others said it meant the mercy from us (Allah) which we (Allah) used to show to Zakariyya. That is why Allah gave him his son, but Akramah said it meant love on him because Yahya was compassionate towards people, especially his father and his mother.

As for the zakat (alms giving), it was for the purity of his character and his obedience to Allah and also for his parents as it is written in verse 14: *14and righteous to his parents, and he was not powerful, disobedient.* The final verse of this passage is 15: *15And peace be on him the day he was born and the day he dies and the day he is raised alive.* Ibn Kathir interpreted these verses by saying that these are the three hardest times in a man's life, for in them a man will be moved from one world to another. A man will lose the first world after he gets used to it and knows it and then moves to the other world. That is why he cries when he leaves his mother's womb and comes to this world where he can meet its sorrow. The second hard time is when he leaves this world to live in the world of death, as he lived with the people of the tombs until the time when they waited for the angels to blow the trumpet. Finally, the third time is when men will move to the resurrection, and there people will meet their destiny when some will be pleased, some will be sorrowed, some will be living in the gardens and others in hell.

Ibn Kathir stated that "Yahya (John the Baptist) met with 'Isa (wrong name, he meant Yasua or Jesus), and 'Isa told Yahya, 'Ask

[12]Ibn Kathir, *Stories of the Prophets*, 60.

forgiveness for me. You are better than me.' Yahya said, 'No, you ask forgiveness for me. You are better than me.' Then 'Isā said, 'You are better than me. You greeted me, and Allah greeted you.' So he knows, and Allah preferred both of them."[13]

The response to the previous fairy tale, this conversation between Jesus and John the Baptist written above, is a lie invented by Ibn Kathir because Jesus is the only human who never sinned. He is the only one who is able to say, "Who can convict me of sin?" *Therefore, how can Jesus ask John to seek forgiveness for His sin?* Jesus Himself is the only one who can forgive sin.

In Matthew 3:13-17, Jesus came from Galilee to the Jordan River to be baptized by John, not to seek forgiveness from John. That is why John protested, "I need to be baptized by you, and you are asking me to baptize you." But Jesus asked John to baptize Him so that all righteousness would be fulfilled. Then the heavens were opened when Jesus was baptized, the Spirit of God came upon Him as a dove, and the voice of God from heaven said, "This is my beloved Son in whom I am well pleased." Notice John's opinion of Jesus in Matthew 3:11 when he said to the Jewish people who came out to see him by the Jordan River: *[11]I indeed baptize you with water unto repentance, but He who is coming after me is mightier than I, whose sandals I am not worthy to carry. He will baptize you with the Holy Spirit and fire.*

As for the statement, "*a master, celibate, and a prophet from among the good,*" Ibn Kathir said that Yahya was a celibate, meaning he did not have any relationships with women. This was supported by Imam Ahmed who quoted the hadith of Mohammed who said, "All the sons of Adam sin or desire to sin except Yahya Ibn Zakariyya…" This was also repeated by the hadith, which was told by Mohammed Ibn Isaac, in which Mohammed said, "All sons of Adam will come on the day of the resurrection and have sin, except Yahya Ibn Zakariyya."

Ibn Kathir continued to write many of the sayings of Mohammed, known as the hadith, concerning Yahya. For the sake of time and space, I choose to bypass them, since the reader is by now aware that there are plenty of fabrications that add nothing to these stories except for numerous contradictions.

---

[13]Ibid., 61.

As for the death of Zakariyya, Ibn Kathir stated that Muslims disagree about how he died.[14] *Was he killed, or did he die naturally?* Some say that Zakariyya escaped from his people and hid inside a tree. Then they came and sawed the tree until they cut him into pieces. However, others said he died of natural causes. Although the Bible does not mention anything concerning the death of Zacharias, we know there is no basis for believing that he hid inside a tree or that he was sawed inside the tree. The absence of comments to the contrary suggests he died naturally from old age.

As for the killing of Yahya, Ibn Kathir stated there are many reasons given for his death. The most famous one is that one of the kings of Damascus chose to marry one of the forbidden women which was unlawful. Yahya forbade him to marry her. She hated Yahya's opinion of her marriage to the king, and she asked the king to shed Yahya's blood. So the king sent for Yahya, and then brought Yahya's head to her in a tub. It was also said that the king's wife loved Yahya. She sent for him so that he might come and be with her, but he refused. When she gave up on having him, she went to the king with mockery, asking the king to bring Yahya to her. Then the king killed Yahya and brought his head and his blood to her in a tub.

There are other variations of stories about his death, such as when the king sent for Yahya in order to kill him for his wife. A warner went ahead of them and told Yahya, so he ran for his life, but Satan was leading them to capture Yahya. The tree called to Yahya, "To me, to me, come inside me." So when the tree closed on him, his robe was still outside of the tree. That is how the Children of Israel found out he was inside the tree. The Children of Israel said, "Let's burn the tree." However, Satan said, "No, cut the tree with the saw." Mohammed said that was how Yahya was cut with the tree. In the interpretation of Qur'an 17:1, when Mohammed ascended to heaven, he asked Yahya, "Did the saw hurt when they cut you in the tree?" He said, "No, but I found the tree in which Allah put my spirit."

Scholars also disagree about where the killing of Yahya Ibn Zakariyya took place.[15] Ibn Kathir stated that Alsuri said Yahya was killed at the Dome of the Rock. He also said there were seventy prophets killed on the rock by the holy house. One of them was Yahya Ibn Zakariyya, but others like Abu Obdiah said he was killed in Damascus, *and Allah knows best.*

---

[14]Ibid., 63.
[15]Ibid., 66.

Ibn Kathir gave us yet another story of how Yahya was killed. He said that Al Hafaz said King Hadad Ibn Hadad of Damascus married his son to the daughter of his brother; her name was Areal, the queen of Sayda. His son divorced her three times and then desired to bring her back as a wife, so he questioned Yahya Ibn Zakariyya. Yahya said to him, "It will not be lawful for you to have her as a wife until she has had sex with another husband." This is the teaching of Islamic law concerning divorce. See Qur'an 2:229-230, which contradicts the teaching of the law in the Bible in Deuteronomy 24:1-4. We will cover this in more detail in the session on Mohammed.

That was why the queen hated Yahya, and she asked the king to bring his head on a serving tray. After Yahya was beheaded, his head spoke and said, "It is not lawful for him until she has sex with another husband." The woman carried the dish that contained Yahya's head on her head and brought it to the hands of her mother. He again said the same thing. The mother wept, and the servants wept and slapped their faces. The story continues to go on and on from this point, but I will not waste more space on it.

What is the real story of how John the Baptist died according to the Bible? We can read the true account of the death of John the Baptist in Matthew 14:3-12. I will share the story with you in simple words. King Herod had captured John and imprisoned him because of Herodias, the ex-wife of his brother Philip, of whom John said to Herod, "It is not lawful to you to take her as wife." Herod desired to kill him, but he feared the people because John was a prophet to them. There was a birthday party for Herod, and the daughter of Herodias danced. Herod was pleased with her dance, so he gave an oath that he would give her "whatever she asks." Her mother told her to ask for the head of John the Baptist. The king became sorrowful in his heart, but because he had given an oath before all of his guests, he sent to the prison and the head of John the Baptist was brought to the young lady on a platter. As for his body, his disciples took it and buried it.

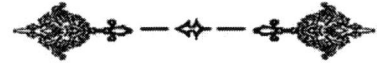

The Story of Jesus

*[Note to reader: When Muslims say 'Isā as written in the Qur'an, they mean **Jesus**.]*

Ibn Kathir opened his writing concerning the story of Jesus, whom Mohammed called 'Isā, by stating that Allah revealed this portion of Qur'an 3 to respond to "the Nasara (Christians), the curses of Allah be upon them, who claimed that Allah had a son. Allah is exalted above what they said, very highly, that 'Isā was just a slave whom Allah created."[1]

A group of them from Najran came to the apostle of Allah (Mohammed) mentioning this vanity of teaching of the trinity to him. They were claiming that Allah is the third of three, the holy person (God the Father), 'Isā (Jesus the Son), and Miriam (Mary the mother of Jesus) according to their different denominations.

Therefore, Allah, his glory is exalted, gives this portion of this revelation in which he clarified that 'Isā is a servant from the servants of Allah. He created him and fashioned him in the womb as he fashioned all other creatures, and he created him without a father as he created Adam without a father or a mother. And he said to him, 'Be,' so he was. Glory be to Allah, and may he come. And he clarified the source of the birth of his mother Miriam and what was in her situation and how she became pregnant with her son 'Isā. Likewise, he simplified this in Qur'an 19, as we will speak in all of this with the help of Allah and the best of his success and his guidance.

What a wonderful way to start the writing of Ibn Kathir concerning Jesus. I wish Muslims in the West would study the Qur'an and its interpretation by Muslim scholars like Ibn Kathir before they travel all over the West telling the Westerners that they believe in Jesus and the Gospel. Such an introduction could end the lies spread by Muslims all over the West, for the Qur'an and Mohammed in the hadith clearly deny the deity of Jesus Christ beginning with calling him 'Isā, a non-Arabic name without any meaning in the Arabic

---

[1]Ibn Kathir, *Stories of the Prophets*, vol. 2, Abo Al Fida Ishamail Ibn Kathir Al Kurashi Al Damashce (Beirut: Dar Al-Arab Heritage, 1408 AH, 1988), 67.

language. We can only wonder if Mohammed had known that the real name for Jesus in Arabic is Yasua not 'Isā, which in the Hebrew language is the name Yeshua (Joshua), meaning *Savior*, would Mohammed still have denied Jesus' deity or His work, which is His death and resurrection for the sin of the world. *Or did Mohammed deliberately use the wrong name to conceal his identity as the Savior?*

The Birth of the Mother of Jesus

Qur'an 3:33-37 contains one of the most confusing passages of the Qur'an. It says: *³³Surely Allah chose Adam and Noah and the family of Abraham and the family of 'Imrān,² above the worlds, ³⁴their offspring, some from the other. And Allah is hearing, knowing. ³⁵When the wife of Amran said, "My lord, surely I vow to you what is in my belly is to be devoted [to you]. So accept it from me. Surely you are the hearing, the knowing." ³⁶So when she had given birth to her, she said, "My lord, surely I have delivered her a female, and Allah knows of what I have birthed. And the male is not like the female. And I have named her Mary, and I seek refuge for her and for her offspring from the rajim³ Satan." ³⁷So her lord accepted her with a good acceptance and planted her a good planting. And Zakariyyā⁴ took responsibility for her, and every time Zacharias entered into her in the mihrab,⁵ he found that she had provision. He said, "O Mary, where did this come from?" She said, "It is from Allah. Surely Allah provides for whom he wills, without accounting."*

In his interpretation, Ibn Kathir stated that Allah had chosen Adam.⁶ Then from his offspring he specially chose the family of Abraham as he preferred from this good and purified house, and they were the family of Amran. Amran here was the father of Mary, peace be on her. *Is that true?* Obviously, Ibn Kathir, Mohammed, Angel Gabreel, and Allah did not know the true story. Mohammed thought that Mary, the mother of Jesus, was the same Mary (Miriam) who was the sister of Moses and Aaron. See also Qur'an 19:28 and 66:12. According to the Bible, the only woman who vowed her child in her

---

²Amran, non-Arabic word of Syriac origin
³stoned, non-Arabic word of Ethiopian origin, originally meaning cursed
⁴Zacharias, non-Arabic word of Syriac origin
⁵holy of holies in Solomon's temple
⁶Ibn Kathir, 68.

belly to the Lord was Hannah, the mother of Samuel. See 1 Samuel 1:1. Miriam, the daughter of Amran, never married nor had children.

The real name of Miriam, Moses, and Aaron's father was not Amran but Amram (see 1 Chronicles 6:3). Not only did Mohammed confuse Mary, the mother of Jesus, and Miriam, the sister of Moses, he did not get the father's name right either. Also, Mohammed did not know the time period between these two Marys was fifteen hundred years. *What about the real name of the father of Mary, the mother of Jesus?* When we read Luke 3:23, we discover that his name was Heli. *What is the big difference between Mohammed's knowledge and true biblical knowledge?* Perhaps Mohammed would not have been confused if he had read the account of Jesus from the Bible.

Mohammed was apparently influenced by a novel contained in the apocryphal books which stated that the parents of Virgin Mary were very old and that her mother was barren, which was considered shameful in the Jewish society at that time.[7] However, the Lord performed a miracle in which Mary's mother became pregnant with Mary. So she made a vow that she would give Mary to God. So when Mary was born, her mother offered her to serve in the Temple of Solomon.

Actually, no females lived in the temple. In fact, they were only allowed as far as the outer courtyard. Because it was God's house, the worshipers could not enter the holy place which was reserved for priests and other worship leaders, much less in the holiest place (Holy of Holies) which was to be entered by the high priest only once a year. (See Leviticus 16 and Hebrews 9:6.)

When we read the genealogy of Amran by Muslim scholars as presented by Ibn Kathir, we see how much more confused these scholars were.[8] For example, Mohammed Ibn Isaac said that Amran was Amran Ibn Bashm, Ibn Imon, Ibn Missiah, Ibn Hazkua, Ibn Ahreck, Ibn Mosam, Ibn Azazyah, Ibn Amsya, Ibn Yahwish, Ibn Ahriho, Ibn Yazem, Ibn Yahoshfat, Ibn Esha, Ibn Iyan, Ibn Rahbaom, Ibn Solomon, Ibn David.

On the other hand, Abu Al Qusim gave a long updated genealogy by telling us that Miriam was the daughter of Amran Ibn Masan, Ibn El Other, Ibn El Ude, Ibn Akner, Ibn Saduke, Ibn Azazuse, Ibn El Yakem, Ibn Ebode, Ibn Zaryabeel, Ibn Shaltal, Ibn Uhina, Ibn

---

[7] http://www.fatherbakhoum.com/archive/index.php/t-6717.html, accessed February 24, 2013.

[8] Ibn Kathir, 68.

Bursha, Ibn Immoon, Ibn Mishia, Ibn Hazka, Ibn Ahaze, Ibn Mosam, Ibn Azrya, Ibn Uram, Ibn Ushafat, Ibn Esha, Ibn Eyba, Ibn Rahbaom, Ibn Solomon, Ibn David.

Notice the list of names given by Mohammed Ibn Isaac is a completely different list of names from the list of Abu Al Qusim. Moreover, the first list of names contains eighteen generations from Amran to David, but the second list has twenty-six generations. Even though there were eight generations difference between these two completely different sets of genealogy, Ibn Kathir did not have any problem with the discrepancy. He said there was "no difference; surely these names are descendants of David, peace be on him."

Ibn Kathir continued by saying that Amran, the father of Mary, was a man of prayer, and he said that Mary's mother was Hannah the daughter of Facude, Ibn Capeal, one of the servants, and Zacharias was the prophet at that time and was the husband of the sister of Mary. Ibn Kathir said others said that he was the husband of her aunt. Then he concluded his interpretation of confusion by saying, *and Allah knows best.*

He obviously erred in saying that Mary's mother was Hannah, for Hannah was the mother of Prophet Samuel, not Mary's mother, as we stated previously (1 Samuel 1:1-20). The proof that Ibn Kathir, Mohammed Ibn Isaac, and others were confused between Hannah, the mother of Samuel, and Mary's mother is seen in the following statement. They said that Mary's mother could not conceive any children, but one day she saw a bird with its babies, so she coveted having a son. She made a vow to Allah that if she became pregnant she would give her son to serve Allah in the holy house. They said that she immediately started to menstruate. When she became pure, her husband had sex with her, and she became pregnant with Mary, peace be on her.

As stated earlier in the discussion of Qur'an 3:33-37, when Mary's mother had her baby and found out it was a girl, she said that the male is not like the female and then named her Mary.[9] Then she prayed her prayer, which Allah answered, when she said, *and I seek refuge for her and for her offspring from the rajim*[10] *Satan.* This is also supported by the saying of Mohammed in the hadith from Abu Horyrah when he said that Mohammed said, "There is no birth that takes place but Satan touched the baby before it is born, so the baby

---

[9]Ibid., 68.
[10]stoned, non-Arabic word of Ethiopian origin, originally meaning *cursed*

cries from the touch of Satan, except in the case of Mary and her son."[11] This is also supported by another hadith that states that Mohammed said, "All children of Adam are poked on their sides before they were born, except 'Isā son of Mary; when Satan went to poke him, he poked (Mary's) hymen."

Ibn Kathir stated that many interpreters said that after Mary's mother birthed her, she wrapped the baby in cloth.[12] Then she took her to the mosque (temple) and gave her to the servants that were living there. Because she was the daughter of their leader, the one who prays for them, they fought over who would take care of the baby. Although the statement above did not mention anything about breastfeeding baby Mary, Ibn Kathir inserted a statement about the obvious appearance of Mary's mother who had taken the baby to the temple after she breastfed her.

When the baby arrived at the temple, those who lived there had a dispute because they all wanted to raise this baby. Prophet Zacharias wanted to take her and have full charge of her since his wife was Mary's sister or aunt, so they decided to cast lots. Ibn Kathir stated that they cast the lot three times by using pins. First, they asked a little boy to choose one of the pins, and he picked Zacharias's pin. The second time they threw the pins in the river, and the sign was that the pin that would move to the opposite side of the river would be the winner. Again, it was Zacharias's pin. The third time, they did the opposite by asking that the pin that would go with the flow of the water would be the winner. Again, it was Zacharias's pin, and the other pins went in the opposite direction of the water. By law, then, it was the right of Zacharias to take charge of baby Mary. As for the rest of verse 37: *and every time Zacharias entered into her in the mihrab,[13] he found that she had provision. He said, "O Mary, where did this come from?" She said, "It is from Allah. Surely Allah provides for whom he wills, without accounting."*

Ibn Kathir said that the interpreter said Zacharias chose a noble place in the temple. No one entered there except for her, and she worshiped in it. When her time came to serve, she served in the house. She served night and day to the point that the Jews used Mary as an example of how service should be.

---

[11]Ibid., 68-69.
[12]Ibid., 69.
[13]holy of holies in Solomon's temple

Mary had a noble way of life and description, and every time Prophet Zacharias went into her place of worship to check on her, he found that she had strange provision, such as fruit not in season. He found the fruit of winter in the summertime and the fruit of summer in the wintertime. That was when Zacharias hoped that Allah would give him a son although he was old in age. As Ibn Kathir stated, some of the scholars said that Zacharias said, "O you who give Mary the fruit out of season, give me a son even though I am old."

What a story of confusion! I wonder where Muslim scholars came up with this information. I understand that when Mohammed made up stories, he claimed to be a prophet and that Angel Gabreel gave him such stories. *But when the scholars made up stories, are they also claiming to be prophets as well?*

When we read the account in the Bible, we discover that Mary and Elizabeth were cousins; Elizabeth was not Mary's aunt or sister. *Where did Mohammed or his scholars get the idea that Mary's mother did not have any other children?* As we stated earlier, the woman who could not have children was Hannah, the mother of Samuel, not Mary's mother.

Where did Mohammed and his scholars get the idea that Mary lived in the temple in some honorable place when the teaching of the Old Testament and the tradition of life in the temple allowed no woman to live or even enter there? The truth is that Mary lived a normal life with her family, not in any temple. No female children lived in the temple. Zacharias was just a priest and not a prophet, as Mohammed's scholars claimed.

We encourage Muslims to read the Bible. The time of ignorance is gone, and it is time for Muslims to open other books to investigate what is in the Qur'an and compare it to the real source of the stories Mohammed copied and inserted in his book, *The Generous Qur'an.*

The Birth of Jesus

The story of the birth of Jesus is written in two different locations in the Qur'an. In Qur'an 3:42-51, which was written in Medina, the tone of these verses is completely different from that which was written in Qur'an 19:16-37, which was written in Mecca during the time of Mohammed's first thirteen years of claiming to be a prophet. During this time in Mecca, Mohammed was trying to reach out to the Christians, but later in Medina he emphasized that Mary and her son were not gods at all.

When Muslims read these verses, they do not see any inconsistencies in these two passages for several reasons. First, they do not believe the Qur'an contains any inconsistencies because they believe that the Qur'an is from Allah and because Allah said in Qur'an 4:82: *[82]Do they not consider the Qur'an? If it was from other than Allah, they would have found in it many inconsistencies.* To a Muslim, that proves there are not any inconsistencies in the Qur'an.

Second, as we have mentioned before, Muslims do not study the Qur'an with any critical thinking or any questioning. It is not appropriate in the Islamic religion to question Allah's word, the Qur'an. In fact, a Muslim sins by questioning the Qur'an.

Third, most educated Muslims memorize the Qur'an so they can have perfect pronunciation when reading its verses. Therefore, they will concentrate on the recitation of the verses and not consider the material or the subject matter of the verses. This can sometimes be seen in how Muslim believers sit on their knees and cover their ears with their hands and display with their body language their focus on diction and technique—from shaking their heads from left to right to rocking back and forth—while they are reciting the Qur'an aloud.

As we present the account of the birth of Jesus in these two locations in the Qur'an, we will include the interpretation of scholar Ibn Kathir and shed light on the inconsistencies. First, let us look at the passage in Qur'an 3:42-51.

[42]And when the angels said, "O Mary, surely Allah has chosen you and purified you and chosen you above the women of the worlds. [43]O Mary, be devout towards your lord and worship and kneel with the kneelers." [44]This is from the unseen news that we reveal to you. And you were not with them when they cast their aqlam[14] for which of them should take responsibility of Mary, and you were not with them when they disputed. [45]When the angels said, "O Mary, surely Allah gives you the good news with a word from him. His name is the Christ, 'Isā, son of Mary, exalted in this world and in the hereafter, and of the nearer. [46]And he will speak to the people from the cradle and in his old age. And of the good."

[47]She said, "My lord, how can I have a son when no man has touched me?" He said, "Likewise, Allah creates what he wills. When he makes a command, so he surely only says to it,

---

[14]pens, non-Arabic word of Greek/Ethiopian origin

'Be,' so it will be. ⁴⁸And he will teach him the book and the wisdom and the Torah and the Gospel. ⁴⁹And a messenger to the children of Israel." "Indeed, I came to you with a sign from your lord. I create for you the figure of a bird from the tīn.¹⁵ So I breathe into it, so it will become a bird by Allah's permission. And I heal the blind and the leper, and I raise the dead by Allah's permission. And I inform you about what you eat and what you store in your houses. Surely in this is a sign for you, if you were believers. ⁵⁰And confirming what is between my hands from the Torah, and make lawful for you some of the things that were forbidden to you. And I came to you with a sign from your lord. So fear Allah and obey me. ⁵¹Surely Allah is my lord and your lord, so serve him. This is a straight way."

Ibn Kathir began his interpretation by stating the angels had given the good news to Mary that Allah had chosen her from all the women of her time, he would bring a boy from her without a father, and she was given the news that this boy would be a noble prophet.¹⁶ *Was this a fair interpretation in that Mary was the best woman during her life on earth or was she the best young lady of all human life? If not, can Ibn Kathir or any other scholar tell us who the best woman to ever walk on earth was? Could it be Eve who ate from the tree and caused sin to enter into the world? Could it be Mohammed's mother, the one who is burning in hell forever, according to Mohammed's own words?* Perhaps the reason that Mary was the best in her time is because Muslims believe that the wives of Mohammed are the best women on earth.

What does the Bible state? In Luke 1:28, the Bible clearly states that the angel of the Lord said to Mary that she was highly favored, that the Lord was with her, and that she was blessed among all women. Notice it was Angel Gabriel who came to her and spoke to her in the sixth month in the city of Nazareth. We know where and when this took place and with whom Mary met. At the time, she was engaged to a man from the house of David whose name was Joseph, whom obviously Gabreel, Mohammed, and Muslim scholars knew nothing about or chose to ignore. We encourage the reader to read the entire story in Luke 1 and 2.

When we look at the verses of the Qur'an as written above, we see that Mohammed said it was many angels who talked to Mary

---

¹⁵mud, non-Arabic word of N. Semitic origin
¹⁶Ibn Kathir, 71.

[115]

although there are no details of the conversation, but Allah had chosen her, purified her, and chosen her once again. I wonder why Mohammed used the word *chosen* twice. Ibn Kathir stated that it was suggested that she was chosen from the females of her time. However, I believe that these verses, which were written about the angels speaking to Mary, were given by Mohammed and were stated for one purpose and one purpose only. As Ibn Kathir wrote, she was commanded to serve, to worship, to kneel, to be equivalent to such honor, and to give thanks to such grace that it was said that she used to pray until her knees hurt.

Ibn Kathir went on to express the wish that Allah might be pleased with her and that Allah's mercy might be upon her and her mother and father. The whole point of the writing about Mary in the Qur'an and the interpretation of it was, I believe, to emphasize that Mary was not a god; she was just a human. This can be found throughout the Qur'an; and, thank God, we Christians do not believe that Mary was a god. The whole problem is that Mohammed met with some members of a cult who used to worship Mary; and, without verification, Mohammed assumed that all Christians believed the same. Even to this day Muslims that read the Qur'an believe that Christians worship Mary as a god.

Ibn Kathir contradicted himself by saying that perhaps Allah had chosen her above the women of the world and that she was the favorite over all the other women since she was a prophetess as was Sarah, the mother of Isaac, and as was the mother of Moses.[17] There was no objection to her being better than Sarah and the mother of Moses, *and Allah knows best*.

Ibn Kathir contradicted himself once again by saying that the prophethood, as some Muslim scholars stated, was to belong to males only, that females had no portion of the prophethood.[18] However, the Qur'an says in 5:75: *[75]The Christ, son of Mary, is nothing except a messenger; indeed, other messengers have gone before him, and his mother is a siddīqah.*[19] Ibn Kathir's interpretation of this verse does not suggest that she was the best of the famous righteous women of those who lived before her and those who lived after her. Ibn Kathir concluded his paragraph by saying, *and Allah knows best*.

---

[17]Ibid.

[18]Ibid., 72.

[19]person of integrity, non-Arabic word of Aramaic origin

Finally, Ibn Kathir contradicted other scholars by comparing Mary to other women of Mohammed's day, such as his first wife Khadijah, stating that she was the best woman of her lifetime. However, other scholars say that Fatimah, Mohammed's daughter, was one of the four best women, along with Mary, Pharaoh's wife, and Khadijah. There are many other lists of women, and here also is one of the amazing, shocking, astounding sayings of Mohammed.[20] He told his first wife Khadijah on her deathbed that Allah had given him Mary, daughter of Amran and the mother of Jesus, as a wife, and also Asyah, daughter of Mazaham, and the wife of Pharaoh, and Kalsom, the sister of Moses. *Was Mohammed thinking that Allah would give him all these women in heaven?*

The Birth of the Slave, the Messenger, 'Isā, Son of Virgin Mary

In the summer of 2010, I was invited by friends to a church in Orlando, Florida, to attend a meeting held by Muslims inside a liberal church. At the beginning of the meeting, a young Muslim lady stood up and read the story of the birth of Jesus. She read it first in Arabic; then she read it in English. I looked around as people listened to the story, and people were wonderfully surprised that the story of Jesus' birth was written in the Qur'an. Muslims always emphasize that they believe in Jesus, the virgin birth, the great miracles of Jesus, and how Jesus was a good teacher, a good man, and a good prophet.

The people of this church did not listen carefully to the story of Jesus as it was presented to them. The other important issue is that the people of this liberal church must not know the true story of Jesus as it is written in the pages of the Holy Bible. I know they did not, for if they did, they would never have fallen for the counterfeit Jesus in the Qur'an.

Let us look to the story of Jesus as it is presented once again in the Qur'an in 19:16-36. Notice that this story presents Jesus' virgin birth, for he was a messenger created by Allah, but he was not portrayed as Allah's son. Note that this story is repeated in Qur'an 5:110-120, but we will look at this passage later.

First, let us look at the passage in Qur'an 19:16-36: *[16]And remember in the book Miriam, when she went apart from her family to an eastern place. [17]So she took a veil apart from them. So we sent our spirit to her, so he appeared to her a normal human. [18]She said, "Surely I seek refuge with the*

---

[20]Ibn Kathir, 72-75.

merciful from you if you were a fearer." [19]He said, "Surely I am only a messenger of your lord that I may grant to you a righteous son." [20]She said, "How can I have a son when no man has touched me, and I was not unchaste?" [21]He said, "Likewise, your lord says, 'It is easy for me, and we will make him a sign to the people and a mercy from us.'" And it was a decreed matter.

[22]So she conceived him, so she withdrew with him to a remote place. [23]So the pain of childbirth came on her by the trunk of a palm tree. She said, "Oh, I wish that I had died before this, and I was forgotten, forgetting." [24]So he called her from below her, "Do not grieve. Indeed, your lord has made a creek under you. [25]And shake the trunk of the palm tree toward you; it will drop fresh, ripe dates on you. [26]So eat and drink and please eye. So if you see any human, so say, 'Surely I have vowed a fast to the merciful, so I will not talk to any human today.'"

[27]So she came to her people with him, carrying him. They said, "O Mary, indeed, you have brought a strange thing. [28]O sister of Aaron, your father was not an evil man, and your mother was not unchaste!" [29]So she pointed to him. They said, "How can we talk with him who was in the cradle, an infant?" [30]He said, "Surely I am the servant of Allah; he gave me the book and made me a prophet. [31]And he made me blessed wherever I was and commanded me with the prayer and the legal alms as long as I live [32]and [to be] righteous to my mother. And he has not made me powerful, miserable."

Did you notice the subtitle of this section as it was given by Ibn Kathir? He did not call Jesus Messiah, good teacher, good man, good prophet, or Mr. Jesus; he simply called him a slave. First, Ibn Kathir asked for the curse of Allah to be on all Christians, and then he called their Jesus a slave.[21] He continued in his interpretation by saying that, after the angels gave the good news to Mary that Allah chose her, he would give her a pure son, a noble son, who would be supported by performing miracles.[22]

Ibn Kathir said Mary was surprised that she could have a son when she did not have a husband. The angels told her that Allah is able to do all things. If he commanded a matter, he only says "Be,"

---

[21]Ibid., 77.
[22]Ibid., 78.

and it would be, so she surrendered to Allah's command. She knew it would be a great hardship because people would speak against her, for they did not know the truth about this situation.

Ibn Kathir stated that she never left the mosque (temple) except during the time of her menstruation or for an important need like getting food or water. He said that Zacharias had chosen for her a special honorable place that no one could enter except her. Ibn Kathir continued by saying that one day Mary went out to take care of some matters alone. She went to the east of the Al-Aqsa mosque. Allah sent to her the faithful spirit Gabreel.

Gabreel appeared to her as a normal human so that when she saw him, she said, "I seek refuge with the merciful from you if you were a fearer." The rest of the dialogue between this angel and Mary is written in verses 19-21 above. Ibn Kathir emphasized that Allah would create a young man from her without a father. He continued to explain that there are different creations. Allah created Adam without any male or female. He created Eve from a male without a female. Then he created 'Isā from a female without a male.

Ibn Kathir tried to separate the telling of the story of Jesus in Qur'an 19 from the story of Jesus in Qur'an 3 as we covered earlier, but they are not two separate incidents.[23] They are repeated as one story in the Qur'an. When you read two stories found in two separate places, you may not see any problem, but when we read both stories side by side at the same time, we see many inconsistencies.

For example, we see in Qur'an 3:42: [42] *...the angels said, "O Mary..."* (Notice it was not one angel, as it is written in Qur'an 19:17, who spoke to her as a normal human). As for the rest of the dialogue between Mary and the angels, Qur'an 3:42-51 and Qur'an 19:17-21 are similar, but they use different words. Qur'an 3:47 states: [47]*She said, "My lord, how can I have a son when no man has touched me?"* The same question is repeated in Qur'an 19:20: [20]*She said, "How can I have a son when no man has touched me, and I was not unchaste?"*

Which question did she really ask? Did she ask this question to one human who was really an angel or to a group of angels? How about the answer to Mary's question? Was it as it is written in Qur'an 3:47-49? Notice it is no longer a group of angels talking to Mary (as it had been presented in the beginning of the dialogue in verse 42 and in the middle of the dialogue in verse 45). The noun has been changed

---

[23]Ibid.

in verse 47 from plural (angels) to singular (he): ...*[47]He said, "Likewise, Allah creates what he wills. When he makes a command, so he surely only says to it, 'Be,' so it will be. [48]And he will teach him the book and the wisdom and the Torah and the Gospel. [49]And a messenger to the children of Israel."*

Is this what <u>he</u> really said to Mary? When I read the answer to Mary's question in Qur'an 19:21, I read completely different words: *[21]He said, "Likewise, your lord says, 'It is easy for me, and we will make him a sign to the people and a mercy from us.'"* You see, my dear readers, if we skim the Qur'an without deep study, we will not catch such deep contradictions. And remember, for Muslims, every word of the Qur'an must be taken as the literal word of Allah without error.

Ibn Kathir continued to state that 'Isā "will be a mercy from Allah."[24] This meant that Allah would use him to give mercy to the servants for he will call them to Allah from his early age as a child to his old age as a decrepit old man by teaching them to serve Allah alone and not add a girlfriend, child, partner, or equal in opposition to Allah.

As for his saying, *and it was a decreed matter,* Ibn Kathir interpreted this phrase by saying perhaps the words of Gabreel were fulfilled and that is what was written in Qur'an 66:12: *[12]And Mary, the daughter of Amran, who guarded her sexual parts, so we breathed into it[25] from our spirit, and she believed in the words of her lord and his books, and she was among the obedient.* There are many different interpretations, or what I call *fabrications*.

As for the statement, *we breathed into it,* it refers to Mary's vagina. The question is how Allah put his spirit in Mary's vagina. A very simple reading of the verse does not require such fabrication by Muslim scholars. *We* refers to Allah. *Breathed into it* refers to Mary's vagina. *Our spirit* is the spirit of god. There is no existence of Gabreel in this verse.

Similar verses, as we mentioned earlier in the book, such as when Allah breathed into Adam from his spirit, can be found in Qur'an 15:29 and 38:72. No interpreter said that Allah breathed his spirit into Adam by Angel Gabreel. *So why in Qur'an 66:12 did Ibn Kathir and others insert Gabreel to do the work of the breathing on behalf of Allah?* That is not what the verse says.

---

[24]Ibid., 77.
[25]her sexual parts

The question remains: How could Allah breathe his spirit into Mary's vagina? Not only did Ibn Kathir insert Gabreel instead of Allah to do this job, but he also fabricated another way in which the spirit of Allah could be put into her vagina. He said that Gabreel breathed under her arm and that the breath entered into her vagina immediately.

Ibn Kathir also said that "he breathed into her in her mouth and the one who was speaking to her was the spirit and he entered into her from her mouth."[26] He also made the point that his last interpretation is not in agreement with the understanding of the passage in the Qur'an. Ibn Kathir insisted that the angel who had been sent to her was Gabreel and he breathed into her and the angel did not face the vagina; but he breathed into her pocket, and the breath went through it (the vagina), not her mouth and not in her chest as many other interpreters claim.

Here is another question. *Why do we not find any Muslim scholars with interpretations, such as the ones made from the verses of the Qur'an when Allah breathed into Adam from his spirit?*

There are many ways in which the Spirit of God fills the human body. We can read about it in many places in the Bible. We see where people were filled with the Holy Spirit sometimes with the laying on of hands on their heads after being baptized, as found in Acts 8:17, when Peter and John laid hands on the believers of Samaria. Sometimes people were filled with the Holy Spirit before being baptized while listening to the preaching of the Word, as in the case of Cornelius and his family (Acts 10:44). Sometimes it was with the blow of a breath into their faces as related in John 20:22 when Jesus blew His Spirit into the disciples.

Sometimes God gave the breath of life by simply breathing it into the nostrils, as in the case of Adam in Genesis 2:7. Sometimes the Spirit of the Lord fell on people after the anointing of oil, as in the case of David when Prophet Samuel anointed him to be a king over Israel in 1 Samuel 16:13. Sometimes it happened without any wind or breath, as in the case of King Saul who had just met with the prophets and immediately was filled with His Spirit, as in 1 Samuel 10:6. So, after all, there are many ways the Spirit of God can fill a human, but as for the teaching of the Qur'an where Allah breathed his spirit into Mary's vagina, I do not know what to say.

---

[26]Ibn Kathir, 77.

Ibn Kathir continued by saying that Allah said, "So she conceived him, and she withdrew with him to a remote place."[27] The reason Mary went away, Ibn Kathir said, was because she was distressed, and she knew many of the people would speak against her honor. Ibn Kathir said Wahab Ibn Monabah said that the first man who noticed Mary was pregnant was Joseph, Ibn Jacob, the carpenter.[28] He was her cousin. He was very surprised for he knew about her religion, her integrity, and her worship; and he knew that she did not have a husband.

One day he told her, "O Mary, can it be a plant without seed?" She said, "Yes. So who created the first plant?" Then he said to her, "Can there be trees without water or rain?" She said, "Yes. So who created the first trees?" Then he said to her, "Can there be a son without a male?" She said, "Yes, surely Allah created Adam without male or female." Then he said to her, "So tell me your news."

Then she said, "Surely Allah had given me the good news with a word from him. His name is the Christ, 'Isā, son of Mary, exalted in this world and in the hereafter and of the nearer. And he will speak to the people from the cradle and in the old age and of the good." Ibn Kathir mentioned similar dialogue between Zacharias and Mary and ended with the statement, *and Allah knows best.*[29]

When I read such a story, I have to laugh. *What does the Bible say about Mary's pregnancy?* In Luke 1:26-35 and Matthew 1:18-25, we can find the true account of Jesus' birth. We encourage the reader to go back to the Bible and read the entire account.

Let us begin with the account as told in Luke. It was the sixth month, and Angel Gabriel was sent by God to the city of Nazareth (not to the temple because the temple was in Jerusalem and Mary never lived in the temple) to a virgin by the name of Mary who was engaged to a man by the name of Joseph from the house of David. Notice that Joseph was her fiancé, not her cousin, as fabricated by Ibn Kathir. The angel said to her in Luke 1:28b: *Rejoice, highly favored one, the Lord is with you; blessed are you among women!* When Mary saw him, she was disturbed and wondered what kind of greeting this was.

So the angel told Mary not to be afraid, for she had received grace in the eyes of God. She would become pregnant, have a son, and

[27]Ibid.
[28]Ibid., 78.
[29]Ibid., 79.

name him Jesus. He would be great and would be called the Son of the Most High. The Lord God would give him the throne of David, His father. He would be king over all the house of Jacob forever. His kingdom would have no end.

Are you reading this carefully? Do you see the description in such an announcement? Many times, when I talk to Muslims, they question where the Bible gives the information that Jesus is the Son of God: "Show me where this is in the Bible. Where in the Bible did Mary say that Jesus, my son, is God?" The angel said to Mary, in verse 32, that He would be great and He would be called the "Son of the Most High." The Lord God would give Him the throne of David, His father. He would be king over all the house of Jacob forever. Notice the words between Angel Gabriel and Mary are completely different from those written in the Qur'an.

Muslims will say that this is because the story of the Qur'an is the true story and the account in the Bible has been corrupted. Once again I will remind my Muslim friends that not only does the story in the Qur'an contradict the account in the Bible, but the story of the Qur'an contradicts the Qur'an, as we saw in Qur'an 3:42-51 when compared to Qur'an 19:16-21.

Now, let us go back to the true account in the Bible, in Luke 1:34, where Mary asked the angel how she could have a son if she had not known a man. The angel told her that the Holy Spirit would come upon her and the power of the Most High would shadow her. Therefore, the Holy One who would be birthed of Mary would be called the Son of God. *Did you hear what the angel said to Mary, that the Holy One who would be birthed of her would be called the Son of God?*

How about Joseph the fiancé? Although the Qur'an does not mention Joseph at all, we read about him in Matthew 1:18. The Bible says that the birth of Jesus Christ was during the time when Mary, His mother, was engaged to Joseph but before they came together as a husband and wife because she was pregnant from the Holy Spirit. Since Joseph her husband was a righteous man and did not desire to expose her, he desired to leave her in secret. He would leave her in secret because no one knew that she was pregnant, contrary to what some Muslims claim. However, in verse 20, the Bible said that while he was thinking on this problem (the pregnancy of Mary) that the angel of the Lord appeared to Joseph in a dream and told him not to be afraid to take Mary as his wife because she was pregnant from the Holy Spirit. She would conceive a son, and Joseph was instructed by the angel to name the baby Jesus (Joshua in Hebrew, which means Savior). *Why that name specifically?* Because the angel said He would save His people from their sin.

This was the fulfillment of the prophecy by Isaiah, the prophet, that a virgin would have a baby, and they would call Him Emmanuel. Jesus' name is Emmanuel which means *God with us*. Notice what the Bible says in Matthew 1:24-25 concerning when Joseph woke up from his sleep. He did what the angel of the Lord asked him. He took Mary as his wife but did not know her until she had her firstborn son, and he called Him Jesus. When we read such verses as Matthew 1:21-25, we cannot help but come to the conclusion that Mary was married to Joseph, but he was not intimate with her until after the birth of her first baby, Jesus. Also, she had other children by Joseph because the Scripture said that Jesus was her ***firstborn son***. If there were no other children, the Scripture would not say He was her *firstborn son* but would say her *only son* or just *her son*.

How can we support this from the Scripture? James, the brother of the Lord, was His brother from His mother, as written in Galatians 1:19. Also, we see that His mother and His brothers were in the early church, as written in Acts 1:14. Another example was when His mother and His brothers could not get to Him while He was preaching because there was a large crowd around Him, as written in Luke 8:19.

Also, another proof from the Scripture is found in John 6:42, in that the Jews knew Jesus and His earthly father, and they grumbled against Jesus because He said that He was the Bread of Life that came down from heaven. Their rejection of His claim was nothing about being a bastard but rather that they knew Him, and they knew His father and mother, as evidenced by the fact they asked if he were not indeed *Jesus, son of Joseph*. Since they knew His father and His mother, how could Jesus then say that He came down from heaven?

Even in His own town of Nazareth where He grew up, although He performed great miracles there and with all of the wisdom He showed to them, they refused to believe in Him. They knew Him only as the son of the carpenter and His mother Mary and that His brothers were James, Joseph, Simon, and Judas. They did not believe in Him, and Jesus said to them that no prophet has honor in his country or in his house (Matthew 13:55).

I know that there are many Christians who love Virgin Mary. They give her high respect because she was a most honorable woman whom God chose even before the creation of the world to bring His Son into this world through her. Because of their sincere love for her, they reject the idea that she would have been married to Joseph and had other children. I extend my love and high respect to them for their respect for Virgin Mary, but their love and respect is without knowledge, fact, or biblical support. The Bible clearly teaches that Mary was a sinner and needed Jesus as a Savior just like anybody else, for the Bible says that all have sinned and fallen short of the glory of God (Romans 3:23). That is why Mary said that she rejoiced in God her Savior (Luke 1:47) because God had saved her through His Son Jesus, the Son of Mary in the flesh.

I would like to tell a little about how and where the birth of Jesus took place. The answer comes from Luke 2. Caesar Augustus told all the people to go to their home city for a census; therefore, Joseph traveled to Bethlehem to be recorded with Mary his espoused wife, to whom he was engaged at the time, and who was pregnant by the Holy Spirit. While she was there, the time of childbirth came. Because there was no room in the inn, she put her firstborn son in a manger after she wrapped him in cloth. Notice that Joseph was there with Mary and everyone thought he was the father of Jesus. Mary did not have baby Jesus under some palm tree, as Mohammed falsely stated in Qur'an 19:23. As for the angels and the shepherds, you can read the entire account about them in the Bible. We encourage the reader to read Luke 2.

Ibn Kathir said that Al Saddi said, "One day Mary visited her sister, and her sister asked her, 'Do I feel like I'm pregnant?' Mary said, 'I feel that I am pregnant, also.' So she hugged her, and the mother of Yahya (John the Baptist) said to her, 'I feel that what is in my belly bows down to what is in your belly.'"[30] Ibn Kathir said that this is Allah's word in the Qur'an "confirming by a word from Allah." He also said that the *worshiping* here is the obedience and the honor as when people worship (bow down) when greeting others, as was in the case when Allah commanded the angels to worship Adam.

What Ibn Kathir did not know was that the word *osjodo* as it was written in the Qur'an is a non-Arabic word of Aramaic origin which literally means *worship*. We can read the true account in the Bible. When Mary went to visit Elizabeth, not her sister or her aunt but her cousin, she left Nazareth and went to the hill country of Judah. She entered the house of Zacharias and greeted Elizabeth. When Elizabeth heard the greeting of Mary, the child within her leaped in her belly.

---

[30]Ibn Kathir, 78.

We encourage the reader to go back to Luke 1:39-45 to read the account, but the following is a short summary.

Elizabeth was filled with the Holy Spirit, and she shouted with a great voice. She exclaimed that Mary was blessed among women and the child she was carrying was blessed. Elizabeth was honored that the mother of her Lord had visited her. When Mary came and greeted her, Elizabeth's baby jumped for joy at the sound of Mary's voice. Mary was blessed because she believed in what the Lord had told her. *Did you notice that what Elizabeth said was by the power of the Holy Spirit and that it was not Elizabeth's words?* It was the Holy Spirit through her when she called Mary the mother of her Lord, for Jesus is Lord.

Ibn Kathir stated it appeared that Mary was pregnant with Jesus for the full nine months as is natural for women and that "if it was not that, the Qur'an would have mentioned it."[31] Really! There are so many things that the Qur'an does not mention, and Ibn Kathir stated different interpretations and different opinions in so many verses of the Qur'an simply because the verses themselves were incomplete thoughts. To prove my point, which obviously is very clear here, he stated that the time of pregnancy of Virgin Mary was nine months; but, in the following sentence, he contradicted his own words when he said that Ibn Abbas and Akramah said, "Mary was pregnant with Jesus for eight months." Ibn Kathir continued with further contradictions by saying that Ibn Abbas said Mary was pregnant with Jesus and birthed him immediately. Yet again, Ibn Kathir said that others said Mary was pregnant with Jesus for nine hours.

When Mohammed recited the Qur'an and when Ibn Kathir wrote his book, *Stories of the Prophets*, they did not have the technology which is available today to discover the truth about embryology through observation. To prove the level of ignorance in the teaching of the Qur'an concerning the stages of pregnancy, I will do the following: state the verses, give the interpretation of Ibn Kathir, and then point out the errors in his interpretation.

Ibn Kathir interpreted Qur'an 23:14: *[14]Then we created the nutfah into a clot. So we created the clot into a piece of flesh, so we created the piece of flesh into bones, so we clothed the bones with flesh. Then we made it another creature. So blessed be Allah, the best of the creators.*[32] He said these are four

---

[31]Ibid., 79.
[32]Ibid.

[126]

stages of embryonic development. Also, he said the duration of each one of these stages is forty days. What a great interpretation which makes the time of pregnancy only approximately five months and ten days, not nine months.

Now I would like to ask a question. *What is nutfah?* According to the Qur'an, it is the combination of two fluids, one produced by the male and one by the female. The male's fluid comes from his backbone while the female's fluid comes from the breasts. This can be found in the Qur'an 86:5-7: *⁵So let the human look to what he was created from. ⁶He was created from gushing water; ⁷it comes out from the backbones³³ and the breasts.³⁴* This is another error that proves the Qur'an is not the word of God.

Now I would like to share the four errors concerning human reproduction as described in Qur'an 23:14. The first is: *¹⁴Then we created the nutfah into a clot. Nutfah,* as Muslims understand it, is in error; females do not produce any fluid from their breasts for conception. Conception involves an egg which has nothing to do with the breasts. Man's sperm does not come from the backbone. Sperm do not mutate into blood cells. The cells in the embryo which form blood, much less blood-clotting agents, do not begin formation until the fourth week of pregnancy. During this first month, many other cell types have to form prior to blood and clotting.

The second error is: *so we created the clot into a piece of flesh.* This is an error since the Qur'an presents the idea that human life is grown from a clot into a later collection of other cells (piece of flesh). As mentioned above, that is not the case.

The third error is: *so we created the piece of flesh into bones, so we clothed the bones with flesh.* The order presented in the Qur'an is fertilization, blood (or cell) formation, bones, and then flesh. This is absolutely false. Cells for organs and flesh actually begin formation before bone development. Later, as the fetus grows, bone structures begin to develop along with organs and flesh.

Finally, the fourth error is: *then we made it another creature.* As mentioned above, cellular division which forms bone tissue takes place after flesh and organs begin developing. The picture painted in the Qur'an is very different.

Every modern observation of fetal formation demonstrates conclusively that the Qur'an's order of events is completely

---

³³of the male
³⁴of the female

erroneous. *In conclusion, can the Qur'an be the word of God and yet be wrong about reproduction which God created?*

Ibn Kathir continued by quoting Mohammed Ibn Isaac who said the rumor spread and became well known among the Children of Israel that Mary became pregnant and that some of the ungodly people accused her of being impregnated by Joseph.[35] He used to worship with her in the temple. Mary hid from them and left to a faraway place. As we have seen above, this is far from the truth, for everyone in the entire neighborhood of Nazareth where Mary and Joseph lived believed that Jesus was their son, as it is written in the Bible, and no one ever believed that Mary became pregnant outside of marriage. Only Joseph and Mary knew the truth. Also, Elizabeth spoke through the power of the Holy Spirit by calling Mary the mother of her Lord; therefore, she could not have been a sinful woman who would have committed such an act.

Ibn Kathir continued to interpret the verses of the Qur'an in 19:23: *[23]So the pain of childbirth came on her by the trunk of a palm tree. She said, "Oh, I wish that I had died before this, and I was forgotten, forgetting."*[36] He stated that she was forced and pushed to go to the palm tree when the delivery time came. Her wishing to die is proof that it was acceptable for one to wish death at a time of hardship or when rumors were spread by some honorable person. She knew that people would accuse her and would not believe her. They would call her a liar when she brought them the baby, and she was among the servants in the temple who stayed in the temple all the time. Because of all of that, she was so worried that she wished she would die or had never been created.

Ibn Kathir continued by interpreting the following verses in Qur'an 19:24-26: *[24]So he called her from below her, "Do not grieve. Indeed, your lord has made a creek under you. [25]And shake the trunk of the palm tree toward you; it will drop fresh, ripe dates on you. [26]So eat and drink and please eye. So if you see any human, so say, 'Surely I have vowed a fast to the merciful, so I will not talk to any human today.'"*[37] He stated two different interpretations concerning who the person was who called her and talked to her from below her. He said that Ibn Abbas said it was Angel Gabreel, and I wonder why Angel Gabreel had to talk to

---

[35]Ibn Kathir, 80.
[36]Ibid.
[37]Ibid.

[128]

her from below her. *Was this a normal way for Angel Gabreel to talk to people, from below them?*

The second interpretation was that it was baby 'Isā who talked to her as stated by Mujahid, Ibn Jarir, and others.[38] As for the palm tree and the strength of the new mother, this would have been a powerful miracle. What makes this miracle even greater is that Ibn Kathir said that the tree was a dead tree without fruit, while others said that it was a fruitful tree. He closed his statement by saying, *and Allah knows best*. Ibn Kathir stated that perhaps it was a palm tree, but it did not have fruit at that time because 'Isā was born in the time of winter; that was not the time of season for the palm tree to have dates, and there is nothing more beautiful to the soul of man than fresh, ripe dates.

Ibn Kathir quoted a hadith by Ali Ibn Abu Talib who said that Mohammed said, "To honor your aunt, the palm tree, so surely it was created from the same clay which Adam was created from…" Mohammed also said to feed your new mothers from the ripe dates "…for there is nothing better or more generous than the palm tree under which Mary, daughter of Amran, sat." Here I would like to correct Ibn Kathir, concerning the birth of Jesus, for the Bible clearly teaches that Jesus was not born in the winter. Ibn Kathir was repeating a fourth century error in determining the time of Jesus' birth, but the time of Jesus' birth was in the spring or early summer because the Scripture teaches that the angels went to the shepherds who were watching over their sheep. It is known that shepherds do not go out into the fields with their sheep during the winter (Luke 2:8-20).

Perhaps if Mohammed or Ibn Kathir had read the account in the Bible correctly, they would have saved themselves from falling into so many errors, and they would know Jesus for who He is and what He came to do. The shepherds would not go out into the fields in winter but in March through November. That is when baby Jesus was born. Jesus was not born under a palm tree, nor did He talk to His mother as a new baby. He was born in Bethlehem when His mother Mary and her fiancé Joseph went there to be counted in the census. Because there were no rooms, they stayed in the stable with the animals. While they were there, her baby was born. Then she wrapped the baby with cloth and put Him in the manger.

We encourage the reader to read the entire account, beginning in Luke 2:9, when the angel of the Lord with his bright light and glory

---

[38]Ibid.

stood before the shepherds and announced the good news to them. Yes, the shepherds were very afraid, but they did not run away for the angel told them that the Savior, Christ the Lord, was born that day in the city of David. *Did you just read what I wrote?* He is the Savior, Christ the Lord. Then the angel was joined by a multitude of angels. They were singing to God and declared, ***Glory to God in the highest, peace on earth, good will to men!***

According to Scripture, the shepherds hurried to Bethlehem and saw the baby Jesus wrapped and lying in the manger as the angels had told them, not under a palm tree as Mohammed said in his Qur'an. When they saw the baby, they told what took place between them and the angel of the Lord. All who heard wondered, but Mary kept all of this in her heart. Then the shepherds returned rejoicing and glorifying God.

Notice that baby Jesus did not talk, but rather He grew as a normal child. It would be miraculous for an infant to actually talk; and if it were true, the Bible would have recorded it. The opposite was true. The Scriptures said that the first miracle Jesus performed was when He was thirty years of age when He changed the water into wine at the wedding in Galilee. Readers can read the entire story in John 2:1-11.

Although Ibn Kathir did not know who talked to Mary from below her, he said that after he said to her, [26]*So eat and drink and please eye...* that the mystery person (Jesus or Gabreel) said, ...[26]*So if you see any human, so say, 'Surely I have vowed a fast to the merciful, so I will not talk to any human today.* [69] Ibn Kathir was skillful and deceitful. He tried to fix a problem in the wording of the Qur'an for the following question. *How can a person say that he or she is fasting after eating and drinking?* Therefore, Ibn Kathir came up with this great idea that in the Jewish religion they do fast of eating and fast of talking. Therefore, Ibn Kathir said that she was fasting of talking and was pantomiming to those who came to see her.

The question one must ask is this: *Why did she fast from talking?* The Qur'an clearly said that she said, *'Surely I have vowed a fast to the merciful.'* Notice that in the case of Zacharias, he was not able to talk but spoke to the people at the temple by gestures for the Qur'an was clear that he used pantomime. However, in the case of Mary, she was actually talking. Moreover, there is no such thing in

---

[39]Ibn Kathir, 81.

the Jewish religion as fasting from talking. The problem is very simple. Mohammed made Jesus teach his mom to lie, for eating and drinking breaks the fast. Mohammed was only worried about the rhythm of the verses of the Qur'an, not considering the topic or the subject. For, even if there was such a thing as fasting from talking, when Mary spoke to the people, she broke her fasting of talking.

Qur'an 19:27-28: *²⁷So she came to her people with him, carrying him. They said, "O Mary, indeed, you have brought a strange thing. ²⁸O sister of Aaron, your father was not an evil man, and your mother was not unchaste!"* Ibn Kathir interpreted these verses, but he first claimed that the People of the Book said that when they missed Mary, they searched for her.[40] They came by the place where she was staying, and the lights were around her. When they confronted her and her son who was with her, they said to her, *"O Mary, indeed, you have brought a strange thing,"* meaning what a great evil she had done for they claimed that she had committed adultery. Ibn Kathir said this is what the People of the Book said, but this is a contradiction because, as it appears in the Qur'an from its dialogue, Mary is the one who carries the baby to her family. Ibn Abbas said she did this after she waited forty days. I don't know where Ibn Kathir came up this so-called saying of the People of the Book, for there is not one Christian scholar or any writing in the Bible that teaches such lies. Once again, we encourage the reader to read the account of the birth of Jesus, as it is written in Matthew 1 and Luke 1 and 2.

Ibn Kathir continued his interpretation by saying that when they called her in verse 28, *²⁸O sister of Aaron,* it was because "Aaron was a godly man. She used to be as good as he in worshiping Allah."[41] The other opinion of who this Aaron was is the exact opposite, as Ibn Kathir said that they compared Mary to a very wicked man in their lifetime by the name of Aaron. This is a great contradiction. *Was Aaron a good man or a wicked man?* Then Ibn Kathir stated that Saeed Ibn Jaber said he meant by this Aaron the brother of Moses; they compared her to him in the worship. Ibn Kathir continued that Mohammed Ibn Kaab claimed that she was the sister of Moses and Aaron. That is a great error for the period of time between Moses and Mary was approximately fifteen hundred years.

---

[40] Ibid.
[41] Ibid.

He was confused because the Torah said Moses and Aaron had a sister by the name of Miriam (Mary), who was the one who played the tambourine when Pharaoh drowned. I personally believe that Mohammed Ibn Kaab was the only one who interpreted the statement *O Sister of Aaron* correctly for many reasons. First, there is no agreement among Muslim scholars about who Aaron was. Second, as we read earlier, Mohammed called Mary the daughter of Amran, who obviously was the father of Moses, Aaron, and Miriam. Notice that the name Mary and Miriam are one name in the Arabic language. Notice also that in the Bible his name is Amram not Amran as is written in Qur'an 3:35. The problem is not the Muslim scholars' interpretation but the confusion of Mohammed and Angel Gabreel. As we mentioned earlier, the real name of Mary's father is Heli not Amran. Also, Mohammed gave the name Amran, not **Amram,** erroneously for both Moses' father and Mary's (the mother of Jesus) father.

Ibn Kathir continued to defend the error of the Qur'an concerning the statement *O Sister of Aaron* by stating that "the correct hadith stated that Mary used to have a brother by the name of Aaron, and there was nothing in the story of her birth from her mother which disproves that she had a brother, *and Allah knows best*."[42] Imam Ahmed said that Alkamah said the prophet of Islam, Mohammed, sent him to Nijran (to the Christian community there). The people there asked him concerning the statement *O Sister of Aaron*. They asked him how this could be when Moses was before 'Isā by many years (the real length of time between Moses and Jesus was approximately fifteen hundred years). So Alkamah returned to the prophet of Islam, Mohammed, and asked Mohammed. Then Mohammed said, "Did you inform the Christians of Nijran that Jews used to be called by the name of the prophets and the righteous before them?" Obviously, it is a very weak answer with no proof, and we cannot find anywhere in the Bible any proof for this claim.

Ibn Kathir continued by saying that Qatadah said they used to name many people Aaron to the point that, one day at a funeral, there were forty thousand men there named Aaron who came to pay their respects.[43] This is quite an amazing statement! As we have seen in the section on Moses, Aaron was not a very righteous man. He was the one who led the Jews to sin when he made the golden calf for them to

---

[42]Ibid., 82.
[43]Ibid.

worship. *If this idea were true, why do we not hear of thousands of people named Moses, or Elijah, or Jeremiah, for that matter?* After all, Moses was the prophet, not Aaron, and Moses was a righteous man.

Ibn Kathir said that Ibn Jarir said they accused Zacharias of being the father of 'Isā.[44] They tried to kill him, but he ran away from them. So the tree opened for him, he entered the tree, and the tree closed on him. However, Satan held the edge of his clothes on the outside of the tree and that is how they cut him inside the tree with a saw and killed him.

Some of the hypocrites accused Mary of adultery with her cousin Joseph, Ibn Jacob, the carpenter. However, when things got very difficult, there was no hope except to depend on Allah, the one who has all the glory and honor. Mary pointed to 'Isā, as if to say, "You talk to him. He will answer you." This is told in Qur'an 19:29-33: [29]*So she pointed to him. They said, "How can we talk with him who was in the cradle, an infant?"* They responded as if she were making fun of them, for how could they talk to a little baby who still breastfeeds, and why would she not answer their accusations? Then the baby spoke. [30]*He said, "Surely I am the servant of Allah; he gave me the book and made me a prophet.* [31]*And he made me blessed wherever I was and commanded me with the prayer and the legal alms as long as I live* [32]*and [to be] righteous to my mother. And he has not made me powerful, miserable.* [33]*And the peace be on me the day I was born and the day I die and the day I am raised alive."*

Ibn Kathir stated that these words were the first words that came from the lips of 'Isā, son of Mary.[45] When he said that he was the servant of Allah, 'Isā was confessing here that Allah was his lord and he was the servant of Allah. This brought honor to Allah concerning the saying of the unjust or the wicked who claim that he was the son of Allah. 'Isā was his servant and messenger and he was the son of Allah's servant Mary and he proved the innocence of his mother from what the ignorant prescribed to her of committing adultery. 'Isā stated that Allah gave him the book and made him a prophet, for surely Allah would not give the prophethood to one who was as they claimed, meaning if 'Isā was the son of adultery.

---

[44]Ibid.
[45]Ibid.

Ibn Kathir called on them by saying, "May Allah's curse be on them."[46] He also said that they were infidels as in Qur'an 4:156: *[156]And because of their infidelity and their saying against Mary, a great slander.* But Allah made 'Isā a blessing, for he called to worship Allah alone without any partner, and he honored him as he explained that Allah did not have a girlfriend or a son. Allah encouraged 'Isā to pray and give the legal alms as long as 'Isā lived, for this was the job of the servants.

Ibn Kathir stated:

> Almsgiving contained within it the purification of the soul and the body, the purification of the money as the person gives to the needy with their varieties, and the hospitality of the visitors and the wives and others. 'Isā was righteous to his mother and that was by proving her rights towards him since there was no other parent for him but her. He proved her innocence and he gave every soul its guidance and 'Isā was not arrogant or miserable. He was not harsh, and he did not say or do anything in the opposite of the commands of Allah.[47]

Ibn Kathir closed by saying that the interpretation for the saying of 'Isā, *[33]"And the peace be on me the day I was born and the day I die and the day I am raised alive,"* was covered in the section on Yahya. He concluded by quoting the verses of Qur'an 19:34-35: *[34]This is 'Isā, son of Mary, the saying of truth about which they doubt. [35]It was not to Allah to take some son. Praise be to him. When he decrees a matter, so surely he only says to it, "Be," so it will be.*

Ibn Kathir continued by quoting from Qur'an 3:58-63: *"[58]This we recite to you from the verses and the wise reminder.[48]" [59]Surely the example of 'Isā with Allah is like the example of Adam. He created him from dust. Then he said to him, "Be," so he will be. [60]The truth from your lord, so do not be of the doubters. [61]So who disputes with you about him? After that the knowledge has come to you, so say, "Come. Let us call our sons and your sons, our women and your women, and ourselves and yourselves. Then will we invoke, so we make Allah's curse on the liars." [62]Surely this is the true story, and*

---

[46]Ibid., 83.
[47]Ibid.
[48]Qur'an

there is no god except Allah. And surely Allah is the dear, the wise. [63]*So if they turn away, so surely Allah knows the vandals.*

After he quoted these verses, Ibn Kathir told the story of some sixty Christian men who came from Nijran but who were represented by fourteen of them.[49] Three of them were the most noble among them and were named Al Aakab, Al Sayed, and Abu Harthah, and they debated concerning the Christ. Ibn Kathir said that was why Allah descended Qur'an 3 where he showed the story of the Christ, the beginning of his creation, and the creation of his mother before him. At the end of this debate, they surrendered.

Ibn Kathir said that Al Aakab confessed Mohammed to be a prophet.[50] They asked Mohammed to force a tribute on them, and Mohammed sent with them Abu Ubaydah Ibn Al Jaraḥ as a faithful man. When we read such a story, we are surprised how easily the Christians in Mohammed's day gave in to Islam or surrendered to Mohammed. *Are any of these stories true?* Obviously not, for as we have seen, all that Mohammed claimed to receive from Allah concerning the story of Jesus not only contradicts the account in the Bible, but it contradicts the Qur'an elsewhere as Mohammed repeats the story. Also, such stories made by Ibn Kathir contradict the fact that Mohammed ordered the slaughter of many Christians and Jews as the command came from above from Allah himself.

Once again, I want to shed some light on the previous passage of Qur'an 3:59: [59]*Surely the example of 'Isā with Allah is like the example of Adam. He created him from dust. Then he said to him, "Be," so he will be. Is there any truth in such a statement? Is the example of 'Isā like Adam?* First, we know that the Qur'an stated that Allah created Adam from dirt. *Did Allah create Jesus from dirt?* Absolutely not, Jesus is not a created being. *Did Allah in the Qur'an create Adam by telling him to "Be"?* Absolutely not. As it is written in the Qur'an, when Allah made Adam, he did not say to him "Be," but Allah made Adam and breathed into him (Adam). So it was the same in their story of the case of Jesus when Allah breathed his spirit into Mary's vagina (Qur'an 66:12). There were no such words or commands; Allah fashioned Adam by his hand and breathed into him his spirit.

---

[49]Ibn Kathir, 84.
[50]Ibid.

Ibn Kathir continued by quoting the following three verses from Qur'an 19:34-36.[51] *[34]This is 'Isā, son of Mary, the saying of truth about which they doubt. [35]It was not to Allah to take some son. Praise be to him. When he decrees a matter, so surely he only says to it, "Be," so it will be.* He interpreted these two verses by stating that there is nothing that hinders Allah. He is able to do all things he wishes. As for 'Isā saying, as recorded in the next verse, *[36]And surely Allah is my lord and your lord, so serve him. This is a straight way,* it is exactly what the baby 'Isā said, informing them that Allah was his lord and their lord and that Allah was his god and their god.

As for the doubt mentioned in verse 34, Ibn Kathir interpreted it by saying that Jews disagreed about who 'Isā was. Some of them said that he was the son of an adulteress. They continued in their infidelity and disobedience; but others, who became infidels, said that 'Isā was God. Others said, "He is the Son of God." But the believers said he was the servant of Allah and the son of his servant Mary, and he was the word of Allah given to Mary and a spirit from Allah; these were the saved ones, the victors.

Anyone who disagrees with the third group, the believers of Allah, in anything, they are the infidels, the lost, and the foolish. That is why Allah the great, the wise, the knower threatened them by saying, "Woe to those who became infidels from this terrible great day." By this, Allah meant the punishment of the great Judgment Day. Ibn Kathir quoted Al Bukhari's hadith of Mohammed in which the prophet of Allah said, "Whoever witness there is no god but Allah, no partner with him, and that Mohammed is his servant and that 'Isā is the servant of Allah and his messenger and his word given to Mary and a spirit from him and the garden is truth and the fire is truth, Allah will cause him to enter the garden according to what he has done."[52]

According to this interpretation and this hadith, all Christians who do not believe in Mohammed, those that believe that Jesus is God or the Son of God, are nothing but infidels; and on the Day of Judgment, they will surely burn in hell forever and ever.

In 2012, I was speaking in a church in the state of Ohio where young Muslim men came to the church. They had not attended my seminar, but they asked about what I was teaching. The topic of my

---

[51]Ibid.
[52]Ibid.

seminar was "Revealing the Truth about Islam: Is Islam a Loving Peaceful Religion?" They came with the appearance of doves to tell a group of believers that were standing around me that there are many common beliefs between Islam and Christianity. They said they, like Christians, believe in Jesus, the son of Virgin Mary. At that point I asked the question in a bold tone, "Do you believe that Jesus Christ is the Son of God, God Almighty who came in flesh, died on the cross, and rose from the dead?"

One young Muslim stood quietly, hesitant to answer my question. After repeating the question, his other friend answered, "No we do not, and we will not give any apology for such beliefs." In that moment, the truth was told. There is no such common ground between Christianity and Islam, for if the Jesus of the Bible is true, Islam is nothing but the work of Satan.

It Is Disrespectful to Say that Allah Has a Son

In this session Ibn Kathir tried to prove his point as it is written in the verses of the Qur'an that Jesus is not the Son of God and Allah has no partner.[53] He begins by quoting Qur'an 19:88-95: *[88]And they said, "The merciful has taken a son." [89]Indeed, you have brought a wicked thing. [90]The heavens might almost be torn apart from it. And the earth splits, and the mountains fall to pieces [91]because they ascribe a son to the merciful. [92]It must not be to the merciful that he takes a son. [93]That all what is in the heavens and the earth but comes to the merciful as a slave. [94]Indeed, he counted them and numbered them numbering. [95]And all of them will come to him on the resurrection day alone.* Ibn Kathir added his interpretation: "Allah revealed that he must not have a son because he created everything, and he is the owner of everything. And everything is in need of him, obedient and subdued to him, all the inhabitants of the heavens and the earth are his servants, and he is their lord. There is no god but him, and there is no lord but him."

Then Ibn Kathir quoted Qur'an 6:100-103: *[100]And they made to Allah partners the jinn and their creation. And they made up for him sons and daughters without knowledge. Praise be to him, and he is exalted above what they describe. [101]The inventor of the heavens and the earth, how can he have a son when he has no female companion? And he created everything, and he*

---

[53]Ibid., 85.

is the knower of all things. *[102]That is Allah your lord. There is no god except him, the creator of all things. So serve him, and he is the guardian of all things. [103]No vision can reach him, and he reaches the visions. And he is the kind, the aware.*[54]

Ibn Kathir added that Allah showed that he is the creator of all things, so "how can he have a son? And the son cannot be except to be between two equal things and there is none equal to him and there is none like him. He does not have a female companion (a girlfriend); therefore, he does not have a son" as Allah said in Qur'an 112:1-4: *[1]Say, "He is Allah the one of. [2]Allah is absolute. [3]He does not birth, neither was he birthed, [4]and there is no one equal to him."*

Ibn Kathir continued by stating that Allah is the one:

> …who has no one like him, not in his deity nor his likeness nor his work. He is the absolute. He is the master. His knowledge and his wisdom are complete. So are his mercy and his likeness. He never begat a son, and he was never born of anything before him.[55]

What I like about his interpretation to these verses is the assurance of Ibn Kathir that there is no one like their god Allah, not in his likeness or his work, but it is funny that when we read the Qur'an, we discover that 'Isā and Allah have many similarities in likeness and work.

Even in the Bible, some of these attributes are not given to Jesus, as the Son of Man as in the case of Qur'an 43:61 when Allah said, *[61]And surely he ('Isā) is the knowledge of the hour, so do not doubt it,…* for the Bible stated that Jesus does not know the hour, meaning the time of the Second Coming and the beginning of the new heaven and new earth. Some other attributes can be seen in Qur'an 3:49: *"[49]And a messenger to the children of Israel." "Indeed, I came to you with a sign from your lord. I create for you the figure of a bird from the tīn.[56] So I breathe into it, so it will become a bird by Allah's permission. And I heal the blind and the leper, and I raise the dead by Allah's permission. And I inform you about what you eat and what you store in your houses. Surely in this is a sign for you, if you were believers."*

---

[54]Ibid.
[55]Ibid.
[56]mud, non-Arabic word of N. Semitic origin

Why did Ibn Kathir ignore this verse? I believe it was simply because we see four things Jesus performed which, according to the Qur'an, are attributes for Allah alone. Jesus said he will create, heal, raise the dead, and inform (tell the future or what is hidden). Allah alone "creates, heals, raises the dead, and tells the future." *So how can Jesus share such attributes with Allah?* Ibn Kathir included that there is none like Allah by stating that there is not any equal to Allah.[57] Therefore, Allah cannot have a son because a son cannot exist except for two equal things, and Allah is greater and higher than all things.

Ibn Kathir moved on to another passage from the Qur'an to prove his point concerning who 'Isā really is.[58] Qur'an 4:171-173: *[171]O People of the Book, do not exaggerate in your religion and do not speak against Allah, except the truth. Surely the Christ 'Isā, son of Mary, is only a messenger of Allah and his word, which he cast to Mary, and a spirit from him. So believe in Allah and his messengers, and do not say, "Three."[69] Cease; it is better for you. Surely Allah is only one god. Praise be to him that there would be to him a son. To him what is in the heavens and what is on the earth, and Allah is a sufficient guardian. [172]The Christ does not disdain to be a servant of Allah, nor do the angels who are close. And whoever disdains his service and is proud, so he will gather them all to himself. [173]So as for those who believed and did good deeds, so he will pay them their wages in full, and he will increase them from his bounty. And as for those who are disdainful and proud, so he will torment them with a painful torment. And they will not find a friend or helper other than Allah.*

Ibn Kathir interpreted these verses by saying that Allah forbade the People of the Book from exaggerating the Christ, so Allah cursed them.[60] Qur'an verse 4:171 contains an astonishing error. In this verse Allah is stating that the People of the Book (Christians and Jews) exaggerated their belief of Jesus. This is an error because Jews do not believe Jesus to be either the Son of God or God. It would be more accurate if Allah would begin verse 171 by stating "O Nasara" which means "O Christians," for they are the only ones who believe Jesus to be the Son of God, God Almighty, who came in the flesh.

---

[57]Ibn Kathir, 85.
[58]Ibid., 86.
[59]Trinity
[60]Ibn Kathir, 86.

Ibn Kathir continued by stating that "all those who believed that Jesus is the Son of God or God, may the curse of Allah be on them, for they exaggerated and made claims about Christ which exceeded all limits. It was right for them to believe that he is a servant of Allah and his messenger and that he is the son of his mother, Virgin Mary, who kept her chastity when Allah sent Angel Gabreel to her, he who breathed into her and with one breath she became pregnant by it with her son 'Isā."

Ibn Kathir interpreted "the angel came to Mary with the spirit of Allah" by explaining that the word *spirit* added to Allah is an honorable addition, for the spirit is one of the created things of Allah, as it is said in the following cases: the house of Allah and the donkey of Allah. It is the same in the case of 'Isā. He was named the word of Allah, for this is to honor 'Isā. Ibn Kathir continued his interpretation by stating that 'Isā was named by it because he existed by it without a father, and it is the word from which he was created and because of which he exists, as it is written in Qur'an 3:59: *[59]Surely the example of 'Isā with Allah is like the example of Adam. He created him from dust. Then he said to him, "Be," so he will be.* Also in Qur'an 2:116-117: *[116]And they said, "Allah has taken a son. Praise be to him." Yet to him all of what is in the heavens and the earth, all are obedient to him. [117]The originator of the heavens and the earth. And if he decrees an affair, so surely he only says to it, "Be," so it will be.*

First, let us look at what is written in Qur'an 4:171-173. *Did Mohammed know the true Christian doctrine of God?* Obviously, he did not. From reading the Qur'an, one can come to the conclusion that Mohammed's concept was that the trinity consisted of god the father, god the son, and god the mother (female companion or a girlfriend), which can be supported by Qur'an 5:116: *[116]And when Allah said, "O 'Isā, son of Mary, did you say to the people, 'Take me and my mother as two gods, other than Allah'?" He said, "Praise be unto you. It is not for me that I say what is not true for me; if I had said it, so indeed, you know it. You know what is in my soul, and I do not know what is in your soul. Surely, you are the knower of the unseen."*

This is a very astonishing question from Allah, supposedly the knower of all things, as Jesus even stated in his answer. *Has any true born-again Christian or any verses in the Bible taught that Mary is a god?* Absolutely not! As we read in Qur'an 4:171, the true trinity is this: God the Father (if Allah was actually God, as Muslims claim), God the Son (Jesus, His Word), and God the Holy Spirit (His Spirit).

Neither Mohammed nor the Qur'an said that Jesus was a word *from* God but rather the Word *of* God, based on the premise that Allah is God. Jesus, according to the Bible, is the Word of God who became flesh as it is written in John 1:1: *¹In the beginning was the Word, and the Word was with God, and the Word was God.* Notice John 1:3: *All things were made through Him, and without Him nothing was made that was made.* The Bible is very clear that "*All things*" is *everything ever created* including heaven, earth, everything in the universe, angels, humans, animals, birds, sun, moon, and stars. Everything was created by the Word of God. In the Word of God was life. In John 1:14 we read: *And the Word became flesh and dwelt among us, and we beheld His glory, the glory as of the only begotten of the Father, full of grace and truth.* Here the Bible clearly states that the Word of God became flesh, and we have seen His glory, the glory of the One from the Father, full of grace and truth. This is our Jesus, the Word of God. Jesus is not a man that Christians made a God, but He is God who became a man. This was the humility of God.

God humbled Himself and became a man as Paul wrote in Philippians 2:6-11. We encourage the reader to read the passage in Philippians, but here is a summary of these verses. Jesus was equal to God, but He did not demand or cling to His rights as God, rather He made Himself as nothing by taking the form of a human. He did so in order to be the sacrifice for all humans as He died for all our sins. Therefore, God raised Him up and gave Him a name above all names. Every knee will bow down to Him, and every tongue will confess Him as Lord for the glory of God the Father.

Notice that when people honor the Son and confess Him as Lord, God the Father receives the glory for there is no jealousy between God the Father and God the Son since they are together with the Holy Spirit as one God. Some may say that this is just a false teaching of the New Testament. No, my friend, this is the fulfillment of the prophecies of the Old Testament as it is written in Isaiah 9:6 which was written seven hundred years before the coming of our Lord and Savior to this world in the flesh. *What does the Bible say?* A child will be born to us. A son will be given. The government will be on his shoulder. Notice the titles that would be given to this child and son: Wonderful, Counselor, *Mighty God*, Everlasting Father, and Prince of Peace.

When was the beginning of Jesus? Some may claim that Jesus' existence began two thousand years ago, and if that were true, then that would prove that Jesus is not God. *But what did Prophet Micah say, four hundred years before Jesus came to this world, as he foretold in Micah 5:2 that this Messiah would be born in Bethlehem?* Micah 5:2: ***But you, Bethlehem Ephrathah, though you are little among the thousands of Judah, yet out of you shall come forth to Me the One to be Ruler in Israel, <u>whose goings forth are from of old, from everlasting.</u>*** That means He has no beginning and no end. That is why Jesus said that He is the Alpha and Omega (Revelation 22:13). The beginning and the end is the same statement which is said by God the Father (Revelation 1:8). Much more can be told about this, and that is why we encourage the reader to read both the Old and New Testaments.

Is the Word of God created or eternal? The only true answer is that it is eternal. God is unchangeable. He is the same yesterday, today, and forever. There was no time that God existed without His Word. God in Genesis 1:1 is the same God in John 1:1, Jesus, who is the Word of God.

What about the Spirit of God? According to the Bible, He is known as the Holy Spirit. He is God. In the Qur'an, we see *the spirit of Allah* (as Muslims claims that Allah is God), but neither Mohammed nor his scholars know who he is. There are nineteen interpretations as to whom the Holy Spirit is and no one knows. Some Muslim scholars said that it is the word of the Torah or the Gospel or the word of the Qur'an. Some said that it is some angel or high supreme creature. Many Muslim scholars agree that it is Angel Gabreel.

Let me show you that even what they agreed on is not true. As we stated in the section on Creation, when we talked about the creation and Adam in Qur'an 15:29: *"[29]So when I have fashioned him and breathed into him from my spirit, so fall down, worshiping him." [30]So all the angels worshiped him* … Notice that the god of the Qur'an put his spirit into Adam and that Angel Gabreel bowed down to Adam because he is one of the angels. Therefore, the spirit of Allah in the Qur'an cannot be Angel Gabreel or any of the other interpretations presented by Muslim scholars. The one god as one person does not exist in the Qur'an for we see the Word of God is eternal, the Spirit of God is eternal, and God Himself is eternal. Therefore, I repeat the same teaching by using the capital G, not the small g. The Scripture teaches that we Christians cannot say or claim who God is, but God Himself declared to us what to believe about His nature.

If He had declared in His word that He was ten persons, we would believe in the *tenity*, but since He declared Himself a triune God, we Christians believe in what we call the Trinity. Although the word *Trinity* does not exist in the Bible, the three Persons of God exist in both the Old and New Testaments of the Bible as God, the Spirit of God, and the Word of God. The plural and the singular of God also exist throughout the Bible many times in the same sentence. It could only be explained in two ways. Either throughout the Scripture, in the Old Testament written in Hebrew and in the New Testament written in Greek, all these writers had very bad grammar or there is a doctrine of Trinity.

Biblical Foundation for the Trinity

The study of the doctrine of the Trinity is by nature a very expansive subject. Throughout history, many books have been written about it. To provide a complete analysis of the doctrine would require an entire book. However, I have chosen to lead the reader to some of the verses in the Bible that will hopefully enlighten you on this important doctrine. I encourage you to investigate this topic in depth by reading and studying other resources as well. First of all, we must understand that the Bible in its entirety teaches that there is one God. Both the Old and New Testaments declare the oneness of God. In the Old Testament, we read in Deuteronomy 6:4-5: *⁴Hear, O Israel: The Lord our God, the Lord is one! ⁵You shall love the Lord your God with all your heart, with all your soul, and with all your strength.* Then in 1 Kings 8:60: *⁶⁰That all the peoples of the earth may know that the Lord is God; there is no other.* Also, in Isaiah 45:6: *⁶That they may know from the rising of the sun to its setting that there is none besides Me. I AM the Lord, and there is no other.*

The same teaching can be found in the New Testament pages where, in Mark 12:29, Jesus answered, *²⁹The first of all the commandments is: "Hear, O Israel, the Lord our God, the Lord is one."* This is also taught by Paul in Romans 3:30: *³⁰Since there is one God who will justify the circumcised by faith and the uncircumcised through faith.* Again it is taught by James in James 2:19: *¹⁹You believe that there is one God. You do well. Even the demons believe-- and tremble!* Finally, I quote what Paul taught Timothy

[143]

in 1 Timothy 2:5: *5For there is one God and one Mediator between God and men, the Man Christ Jesus.*

On the other hand, as we read the Holy Bible, we find many passages that refer to the plurality of the Godhead. I would like to share some of these passages with you. My hope and my prayer is that you will open the Bible and read it for yourself. May this be a good study, leading you to know the God of the Bible as He teaches about Himself in His Word. In Genesis 1:26, God said, *26Let Us make man in Our image.* In Genesis 3:22, God said, *22Behold the man has become like one of Us.* In Genesis 11:7, God said, *7Come let Us go down.* In Isaiah 6:8, the Lord said, *8Whom shall I send, and who will go for Us?* In Isaiah 48:16, Isaiah said the Lord said, *16God and His Spirit have sent Me.* The Lord who is speaking here is the Alpha and Omega—Jesus Christ. We can see in this verse the three parts of the Trinity; God, the Father; His Spirit, the Holy Spirit; and *Me*—Jesus.

In Psalm 45:6-7, which is quoted in Hebrews 1:8, God the Father is speaking about Jesus: *6Your throne, O God, is forever and ever; a scepter of righteousness is the scepter of Your kingdom. 7You love righteousness and hate wickedness; Therefore God, Your God, has anointed You With the oil of gladness more than Your companions.* In Psalm 110:1 (and repeated in Matthew 22:41-46): *1The Lord said to my Lord, "Sit at My right hand, till I make Your enemies Your footstool."* In Malachi 3:1-2, God said, *1Behold, I send My messenger, and he will prepare the way before Me. And the Lord, whom you seek, will suddenly come to His temple, even the Messenger of the covenant, in whom you delight. Behold, He is coming, says the Lord of hosts. 2But who can endure the day of His coming? And who can stand when He appears? For He is like a refiner's fire and like launderers' soap.*

These are verses from the Old Testament. Now I would like to share some verses from the New Testament which present the plurality of the Godhead. In Matthew 3:16-17, Matthew wrote: *16When He had been baptized, Jesus came up immediately from the water; and behold, the heavens were opened to Him, and He saw the Spirit of God descending like a dove and alighting upon Him. 17And suddenly a voice came from heaven, saying, "This is My beloved Son, in whom I am well pleased."* Jesus said in Matthew 28:19-20: *19Go therefore and make disciples of all the nations, baptizing them in the name of the Father and of the Son and of the Holy Spirit, 20teaching them to observe all things that I have commanded you; and lo, I am with you always, even to the end of the age. Amen.*

In the following two passages from the Gospel of John and from Ephesians, the Bible clearly teaches that all three Persons of the Godhead indwell in the believers. We read in John 14:19-24: *[19]A little while longer and the world will see Me no more, but you will see Me. Because I live, you will live also. [20]At that day you will know that I am in My Father, and you in Me, and I in you. [21]He who has My commandments and keeps them, it is he who loves Me. And he who loves Me will be loved by My Father, and I will love him and manifest Myself to him. [22]Judas (not Iscariot) said to Him, "Lord, how is it that You will manifest Yourself to us, and not to the world?" [23]Jesus answered and said to him, "If anyone loves Me, he will keep My word; and My Father will love him, and We will come to him and make Our home with him. [24]He who does not love Me does not keep My words; and the word which you hear is not Mine but the Father's who sent Me."*

In Romans 8:9, Paul writes: *[9]But you are not in the flesh but in the Spirit, if indeed the Spirit of God dwells in you. Now if anyone does not have the Spirit of Christ, he is not His.* 1 Corinthians 12:4-6 states: *[4]There are diversities of gifts, but the same Spirit. [5]There are differences of ministries, but the same Lord. [6]And there are diversities of activities, but it is the same God who works all in all.* According to 2 Corinthians 13:14: *[14]The grace of the Lord Jesus Christ, and the love of God, and the communion of the Holy Spirit be with you all. Amen.* Ephesians 4:4-6 states: *[4]There is one body and one Spirit, just as you were called in one hope of your calling; [5]one Lord, one faith, one baptism; [6]one God and Father of all, who is above all, and through all, and in you all.*

Peter wrote in his first letter, 1 Peter 1:2: *[2]elect according to the foreknowledge of God the Father, in sanctification of the Spirit, for obedience and sprinkling of the blood of Jesus Christ: Grace to you and peace be multiplied.* Finally, Jude wrote in his letter, Jude 1:20-21: *[20]But you, beloved, building yourselves up on your most holy faith, praying in the Holy Spirit, [21]keep yourselves in the love of God, looking for the mercy of our Lord Jesus Christ unto eternal life.*

In 2011, as we traveled in our ministry, we were in the state of Texas. There I met with a group of Christians who called themselves the *Oneness*. I did not know up to this point anything about this cult. As we sat and talked, myself and the preacher of this group, I came to understand their belief in the oneness of God. They believe that there is one God. The Father is the Son is the Holy Spirit. They do not believe in anything called Trinity as they claimed that the doctrine of the Trinity was invented by the Catholic Church. As I shared the following verses with them, they could not respond back to me.

Read carefully the following verses which clearly teach the opposite of what this cult teaches. These passages in the Bible prove the distinction of the three Persons, for the Father is neither the Son nor the Holy Spirit. The Father, the Son, and the Holy Spirit are three separate Persons. First, we can see the distinction between the Father and the Son in Matthew 28:19: *[19]Go therefore and make disciples of all the nations, baptizing them in the name of the Father and of the Son and of the Holy Spirit.* We also see the distinction between the Father and the Son in John 1:1-2: *[1]In the beginning was the Word, and the Word was with God, and the Word was God. [2]He was in the beginning with God.* 1 John 2:1: *[1]My little children, these things I write to you, so that you may not sin. And if anyone sins, we have an Advocate with the Father, Jesus Christ the righteous.* Finally, in Hebrews 7:25: *[25]Therefore He is also able to save to the uttermost those who come to God through Him, since He always lives to make intercession for them.*

The distinction between the Father and the Holy Spirit is seen in Matthew 28:19: *[19]Go therefore and make disciples of all the nations, baptizing them in the name of the Father and of the Son and of the Holy Spirit.* Also, see John 14:26: *[26]But the Helper, the Holy Spirit, whom the Father will send in My name, He will teach you all things, and bring to your remembrance all things that I said to you.* Finally, in Romans 8:27 we read: *[27]Now He who searches the hearts knows what the mind of the Spirit is, because He makes intercession for the saints according to the will of God.*

Now I would like to look at the final distinction, which is between the Son and the Holy Spirit. We see this once again in Matthew 28:19: *[19]Go therefore and make disciples of all the nations, baptizing them in the name of the Father and of the Son and of the Holy Spirit.* Also, in John 16:7: *[7]Nevertheless I tell you the truth. It is to your advantage that I go away; for if I do not go away, the Helper will not come to you; but if I depart, I will send Him to you.*

Muslims always ask, "Where can you show me in the Bible that Jesus is God?" They challenge me as if there is no proof in the Bible that Jesus is God. But when I show them many verses in the Old and New Testaments, their response is "the Bible is corrupt." *Were they really seeking an answer or just throwing a challenge to me?* We have already proven in this book that the Bible is the infallible Word of God and cannot be changed. Now, I would like to share with you the deity of God the Father, God the Son, and finally, God the Holy Spirit.

Passages that Prove that God the Father Is God

In the Old Testament in Isaiah 63:16: *[16]Doubtless You are our Father, though Abraham was ignorant of us, And Israel does not acknowledge us. You, O Lord, are our Father; our Redeemer from Everlasting is Your name.* Also, as seen in Malachi 2:10: *[10]Have we not all one Father? Has not one God created us? Why do we deal treacherously with one another by profaning the covenant of the fathers?*

Now I would like to share the following verses from the New Testament: Matthew 6:9: *[9]In this manner, therefore, pray: Our Father in heaven, Hallowed be Your name.* According to Matthew 23:9: *[9]Do not call anyone on earth your father; for One is your Father, He who is in heaven.* John 6:27 states: *[27]Do not labor for the food which perishes, but for the food which endures to everlasting life, which the Son of Man will give you, because God the Father has set His seal on Him.* John 8:41 states: *[41]You do the deeds of your father. Then they said to Him, "We were not born of fornication; we have one Father—God."* Ephesians 4:6: *[6]one God and Father of all, who is above all, and through all, and in you all.*

Passages in the Bible that Prove that Jesus Is God.

Isaiah 9:6 proclaims: *[6]For unto us a Child is born, unto us a Son is given; and the government will be upon His shoulder. And His name will be called Wonderful, Counselor, Mighty God, Everlasting Father, Prince of Peace.* Isaiah 40:3 states: *[3]The voice of one crying in the wilderness: "Prepare the way of the Lord; make straight in the desert a highway for our God."*

As for the passages in the New Testament, John the Baptist said in Matthew 3:3: *[3]For this is he who was spoken of by the prophet Isaiah, saying: "The voice of one crying in the wilderness: 'Prepare the way of the Lord; make His paths straight.'"*

John 1:1-4: *[1]In the beginning was the Word, and the Word was with God, and the Word was God. [2]He was in the beginning with God. [3]All things were made through Him, and without Him nothing was made that was made. [4]In Him was life, and the life was the light*

[147]

of men. John 1:14: *[14]And the Word became flesh and dwelt among us, and we beheld His glory, the glory as of the only begotten of the Father, full of grace and truth.*

Turning to John 5:16-17, we learn that because Jesus was working on the Sabbath, the Jews were persecuting Him: *[17]But Jesus answered them, "My Father has been working until now, and I have been working."* The Jews then desired even more to kill Jesus, not only because He worked on the Sabbath, but because He made Himself equal to God. Jesus' response was that the Son cannot do anything by Himself. He only does what he sees the Father do because everything the Father does the Son can do also. The Father loves the Son, and He will show Him all the work and do even greater things. People will wonder at these things for exactly as the Father raised the dead and gave them strength, the Son can do the same things, as he wishes.

The judgment is given only to the Son so that everyone will honor the Son exactly as they honor the Father. For when the Son is honored, the Father Who sent Him will also be honored. Whoever hears the words of the Son and believes in the Father who sent Him will have eternal life. He will not be condemned for he has passed from death into life. When the dead hear the voice of the Son of God, they will come to life for the Father and the Son have life in themselves. When the dead hear His voice, they will come out. The one who did good will have eternal life, and the one who did evil will be judged. This means that the one who accepts the Son and follows the will of God will have eternal life, and the one who denies the Son and defies the will of God, because Jesus hears and judges justly, will not have eternal life.

Jesus only seeks the will of the Father who sent Him. The Father testifies for Jesus, as it is written in the Scripture. If people just search in the Scripture, they can find eternal life. Jesus said that He came in the name of the Father, but people rejected Him; but if someone else came in his own name, people would accept him. Then Jesus asked them how they could believe if they only glorify each other and do not seek the glory of God. Jesus also said that He will not accuse anyone to the Father, but Moses will because the people put their hope in him. See John 5:45. If people believe in the writings of Moses, they will also believe in the words of Jesus.

In the following verses, the Jews were going to stone Jesus for His blasphemy in calling Himself God. John 8:58-59: *[58]Jesus said to them, "Most assuredly, I say to you, before Abraham was, I AM."*

[59]Then they took up stones to throw at Him; but Jesus hid Himself and went out of the temple, going through the midst of them, and so passed by. Also, we encourage the reader to read the passage in John 10:22-30 which I have paraphrased here. Jesus was in Jerusalem during the Feast of the Dedication. While he was walking in the temple, the Jews asked him if He was the Christ. He replied that if He were to tell them, they would not believe. The works of Jesus testified for Him. The reason they did not believe in Him is because they were not of His sheep. Jesus' sheep hear His voice, and He knows them. He gives them eternal life, and no one can take them away from Him because His Father is the One who gives them to Jesus. No one can steal them from His Father's hand, for Jesus and His Father are One.

Now let us turn to a few of the other Bible verses which prove that Jesus is God. In John 14:7-11, Jesus is speaking: *[7]If you had known Me, you would have known My Father also; and from now on you know Him and have seen Him. [8]Philip said to Him, "Lord, show us the Father, and it is sufficient for us." [9]Jesus said to him, "Have I been with you so long, and yet you have not known Me, Philip? He who has seen Me has seen the Father; so how can you say, 'Show us the Father'?" [10]Do you not believe that I am in the Father, and the Father in Me? The words that I speak to you I do not speak on My own authority; but the Father who dwells in Me does the works. [11]Believe Me that I am in the Father and the Father in Me, or else believe Me for the sake of the works themselves.*

John 20:28 states: *[28]And Thomas answered and said to Him, "My Lord and my God."* Romans 9:5 states: *[5]of whom are the fathers and from whom, according to the flesh, Christ came, who is over all, the eternally blessed God. Amen.*

I believe the problem with our dear Muslim friends can be summarized in simple words. They believe Jesus to be a good prophet, good teacher, and good man whom Christians made into a god. However, the truth in the Scripture is that Jesus is God who chose to become a man. We can see this clearly in the following passage. Philippians 2:5-11: *[5]Let this mind be in you which was also in Christ Jesus, [6]who, being in the form of God, did not consider it robbery to be equal with God, [7]but made Himself of no reputation, taking the form of a bondservant, and coming in the likeness of men. [8]And being found in appearance as a man, He humbled Himself and became obedient to the point of death, even the death of the cross. [9]Therefore God also has highly exalted Him and given Him the name which is above every name, [10]that at the name of*

Jesus every knee should bow, of those in heaven, and of those on earth, and of those under the earth, [11]and that every tongue should confess that Jesus Christ is Lord, to the glory of God the Father.

Colossians 2:9 declares: *[9]For in Him dwells all the fullness of the Godhead bodily.* Also, in Titus 2:13: *[13]Looking for the blessed hope and glorious appearing of our great God and Savior Jesus Christ.* In the book of Hebrews 1:3: *[3]Who being the brightness of His glory and the express image of His person, and upholding all things by the word of His power, when He had by Himself purged our sins, sat down at the right hand of the Majesty on high.* Continuing with Hebrews 1:8: *[8]But to the Son He says: "Your throne, O God, is forever and ever; A scepter of righteousness is the scepter of Your kingdom."* Finally, 2 Peter 1:1: *[1]Simon Peter, a bondservant and apostle of Jesus Christ, to those who have obtained like precious faith with us by the righteousness of our God and Savior Jesus Christ.*

In the following verses we see Jesus as a creator. In Colossians 1:16: *[16]For by Him all things were created that are in heaven and that are on earth, visible and invisible, whether thrones or dominions or principalities or powers. All things were created through Him and for Him.* Hebrews 1:10 states: *[10]And You, Lord, in the beginning laid the foundation of the earth, and the heavens are the work of Your hands.*

Jesus accepted the worship of His disciples. We see this throughout the Bible, which is great internal evidence that He is God. Matthew 2:11 shows that Jesus was worshiped as a child. Matthew 14:33 shows that Jesus was worshiped as a man prior to the resurrection, and Matthew 28:9 shows that Jesus was worshiped after the resurrection. However, in the Qur'an, Allah states that anyone who accepts worship will burn in hell forever. Since Jesus accepted worship, according to the Qur'an, He will burn in hell forever. Also, anyone who worships a human rather than Allah will burn in hell forever. All Christians worship Jesus; therefore, according to the Qur'an, all Christians will burn in hell forever. We can see this clearly in Qur'an 21:98-99: *[98]Surely you and whatever you serve, without Allah, will be the fuel of the fire for hell, and into it you will arrive. [99]If those were gods, they would not enter it, and everyone in it will abide there forever.*

<u>Passages in the Bible that Prove that the Holy Spirit Is God</u>

Unlike Muslim scholars who claim that the Holy Spirit is Angel Gabreel, the Bible teaches that the Holy Spirit is God, for He existed before creation along with God. In the Old Testament, Genesis 1:2, we see the Holy Spirit in the creation: *²The earth was without form, and void; and darkness was on the face of the deep. And the Spirit of God was hovering over the face of the waters.* Here we see the Holy Spirit is omnipresent, but Angel Gabreel cannot be omnipresent. Psalm 139:7-8: *⁷Where can I go from Your Spirit? Or where can I flee from Your presence? ⁸If I ascend into heaven, You are there; if I make my bed in hell, behold, You are there.*

Additional proof that the Holy Spirit is God can be found in the following verses. In Matthew 28:19: *¹⁹Go therefore and make disciples of all the nations, baptizing them in the name of the Father and of the Son and of the Holy Spirit.* John 3:5-7: *⁵Jesus answered, "Most assuredly, I say to you, unless one is <u>born of water and the Spirit</u>, he cannot enter the kingdom of God. ⁶That which is born of the flesh is flesh, and that which is born of the Spirit is spirit. ⁷Do not marvel that I said to you, 'You must be born again.'"* When we compare this passage with 1 John 3:9, we see that the Holy Spirit is God: *⁹Whoever has been <u>born of God</u> does not sin, for His seed remains in him; and he cannot sin, because he has been born of God.*

In Acts 5:3-4: *³But Peter said, "Ananias, why has Satan filled your heart to <u>lie to the Holy Spirit</u> and keep back part of the price of the land for yourself? ⁴ While it remained, was it not your own? And after it was sold, was it not in your own control? Why have you conceived this thing in your heart? You have <u>not lied to men but to God</u>."*

Consider Acts 5:9: *⁹Then Peter said to her, "How is it that you have agreed together to test <u>the Spirit of the Lord</u>? Look, the feet of those who have buried your husband are at the door, and they will carry you out."*

According to 1 Corinthians 12:4-6: *⁴ There are diversities of gifts, but the same Spirit. ⁵There are differences of ministries, but the same Lord. ⁶And there are diversities of activities, but it is the same God who works all in all.* Also, in 2 Corinthians 13:14: *¹⁴The grace of the Lord Jesus Christ, and the love of God, and the communion of the Holy Spirit be with you all. Amen.* Other verses that show that the Holy Spirit is God are listed below.

Ephesians 4:4-6: *⁴There is one body and one Spirit, just as you were called in one hope of your calling; ⁵one Lord, one faith, one baptism; ⁶one God and Father of all, who is above all, and through all, and in you all.*

1 Peter 1:2: *²Elect according to the foreknowledge of God the Father, in sanctification of the Spirit, for obedience and sprinkling of the blood of Jesus Christ: Grace to you and peace be multiplied.*

Again, we look to Jude who wrote in his letter according to the following passage 1:20-21: *²⁰But you, beloved, building yourselves up on your most holy faith, praying in the Holy Spirit, ²¹keep yourselves in the love of God, looking anxiously for the mercy of our Lord Jesus Christ unto eternal life.*

*What about the interpretation of Ibn Kathir that the Word of God or the Spirit of God is simply to honor the word **Word** or the word **Spirit** by adding the word **God** to them, as in the case of the house of God, the donkey of God, and the servant of God?*[61] Notice the word *Word* in the Arabic language is a feminine word which always is followed by the pronouns *she* or *her*, but when the Qur'an talks about Jesus as the Word of God in Qur'an 3:45: *⁴⁵When the angels said, "O Mary, surely Allah gives you the good news with a word from him. His name is the Christ, 'Isā, son of Mary, exalted in this world and in the hereafter, and of the nearer,"* the Qur'an does not say *her* name is the Christ, but *his* name which is a masculine pronoun.

The statement *a word from him* in Qur'an 3:45 is not a *talk* from God but the *Word* of God Himself which is eternal as we understand it in John 1:1: *¹ In the beginning was the Word...* In the English language the word *Word* has no gender, but in the Arabic language, the original language of the Qur'an, it makes a big difference. The word *Word* is feminine which must follow in the Arabic grammar with the word *her name,* but in the Qur'an it is followed by *his name* which is proof that the statement does not mean a simple talk but the *Word* of God Himself. The word used for Jesus as the Word of God which is given to Mary is not just a simple talking of God as any spoken words, but it is a very unique one Word, the existence of God Himself. Therefore, Allah used the pronoun *his,* breaking the grammar rule of the Arabic language by not using the pronoun *her* in the statement, *His name is the Christ.*

---

[61]Ibn Kathir, *Stories of the Prophets*, 86.

As for Ibn Kathir's statement, *the house of God*, there is no such thing as God having a house in which to dwell; this is only a figurative speech as it is written in the Bible when it states in Isaiah 66:1: *¹Thus says the Lord: "Heaven is My throne, and earth is My footstool. Where is the house that you will build Me? And where is the place of My rest?"* We sometimes say many things and mean something else. When we say that we are going to the church, we mean that we are going to the church building, but that is wrong. *Why*? The Bible says that the church is a body of believers for the church is the Body of Christ. Christ is the head of the church. Therefore, we cannot really go to the church for we are the church, and the Spirit of God dwells in the church (the believers), not in the walls and structure of the physical building which we call the church building.

As for Ibn Kathir's statement, *the donkey of Allah,* I could not find any reference in the Qur'an or the Bible that God ever needed a donkey to ride upon. Even when God came in flesh in the person of our Lord and Savior Jesus Christ and entered Jerusalem, the Bible, in Luke 19:28-38, did not call the donkey that Jesus rode upon *the donkey of Allah or the donkey of 'Isā.*

As for Ibn Kathir's interpretation of *the servant of God,* assuming that God is Allah, although we do not believe so, no one will claim that, as a servant of God, we exist immortally. We are mortal, but God is immortal. *Does God need us to be His servants to help Him? Or are they just playing with words to convince the reader that the Word of God and the Spirit of God are just words?* We added the word *God* to it to honor it, like the house of God or the donkey of God or the servant of God. This is an unsuccessful argument, as we have seen in the Scripture. Jesus is the Word of God who is eternal, the Spirit of God is eternal as God the Father Himself is eternal, and They are Three in One.

<u>Key Verses</u>

Deuteronomy 6:4; 2 Chronicles 30:12; and Malachi 2:10. *One* is the first of the ordinal numbers in Hebrew. As a cardinal number, the word occurs in the account of the tower of Babel when the peoples of the earth had *one* language (Genesis 11:1). As an ordinal number, the term *first* often marks significant events in biblical history (the completion of the Tabernacle, Exodus 40:2, 17; certain feast days, Numbers 29:1). As an adjective, the word may mean lone, single, unique, or certain (Judges 4:16; 13:2; 1 Samuel 1:1). The kinship of

the Hebrew tribes as descendants of Abraham and the covenant ceremony at Mount Sinai established the oneness of Israel as the people of God (Exodus 19:6; 24:3). This meant that there was only "one" law (Exodus 12:49) and that God would grant the people "one" heart to obey His commands (2 Chronicles 30:12; Jeremiah 32:39).

The first line of the Shema of Judaism identifies God as *one* Lord (Deuteronomy 6:4). The word *one* is not so much a title as an adjective of quality. God is *one* in the sense of being complete and unique. Theologically, *oneness* is a distinctive quality of the Hebrew God in contrast to the polytheism of most other ancient religions. The Old Testament does not explicitly teach a doctrine of the Trinity. The plurality of the Godhead is implicit, however, in the language of the Old Testament and in the descriptions of worship offered to the differing manifestations of God (Genesis 1:26; Exodus 3:5–6; Judges 13:18–22; Isaiah 63:10).

Carpenter and Comfort gave this information:

> The Prophet Malachi argued poignantly for fidelity in the marriage covenant on the basis of the oneness of God. Since God is the sole Creator of the material world, all human beings have equal standing before him. Malachi echoes the Genesis ideal in acknowledging the 'one' Father of all humanity as the God who created man and woman to be 'one flesh' (Malachi 2:10; see also Genesis 2:24). The New Testament affirms that 'God is one' (Galatians 3:20) and articulates a Trinitarian understanding of the Godhead in the distinctive names and work of the three divine persons: Father, Son, and Holy Spirit (Matthew 28:19; 2 Corinthians 13:14). All Christians are one in Christ Jesus, and hence the church is called to a bond of unity and peace (Galatians 3:28). There is "one Lord, one faith, one baptism, one God and Father of all…" (Ephesians 4:5-6).[62]

Do Jews Really Believe Ezra Is the Son of God?

Not only did Mohammed misunderstand the Christian doctrine of the Trinity by claiming it to be father, mother, and son; but he also fabricated a doctrine for the Jews, teaching that the Jews believed Ezra to be the son of God. Therefore he considered them to be polytheists, giving him the right to engage in war with them. Ibn

---

[62]E. E. Carpenter and P.W. Comfort, *Holman Treasury of Key Bible Words* (Nashville: Broadman & Holman Publishers, 2000), 133.

Kathir moved on with his teaching, quoting Qur'an 9:30: *³⁰And the Jews said, "Uzair⁶³ is the son of Allah." And the Nasara (Christians) said, "The Christ is the son of Allah." This is their saying with their mouths; they repeat the sayings of those who became infidels before. Allah engages in war with them. How perverted they are!⁶⁴* Here Ibn Kathir interpreted by stating that Allah reported that the Jews and the Nasara (Christians), on them the curse of Allah, claimed a lie against Allah. They claimed that he had a son, and Allah showed that none of them had the evidence of what they thought or what they claimed. It was just a saying. They are exactly like those before them, who were in such error saying that their hearts are alike (believe the same).

I wonder where Mohammed came up with this information. As I searched throughout the beliefs of the Jews, I could not find any Jews, even those who left the Jewish faith, whom we call heretics, who believed that Uzair, or Ezra for that matter, is the son of God. Moreover, no one before them ever believed in anyone to be the son of God. I understand there are many families whom people have claimed to be gods, but they are a father and a mother and a child, three completely separate entities, as in the case of the Egyptian gods Osiris, Isis, and Horus. The father is a god, the mother is a god, and they have a physical son who is a god. They are not one god, but three entities whom their believers claimed to be gods. None of the Egyptians believed that they collectively were one god, but rather that they were three distinct gods. However, Christians believe that the Father and the Son and the Holy Spirit are three Persons and one God.

Ibn Kathir continued by calling the Arabs foolish because they believed that the angels are the daughters of Allah who had married the jinn, and the result was that many angels were born.⁶⁵ Then he quoted Qur'an 43:19: *¹⁹And they have made the angels, who are servants of the merciful, females. Have they witnessed their creation? Their testimony will be written, and they will be asked.* I wonder who is actually foolish. Mohammed himself followed the saying of the people of his day by believing in the jinn who, as we covered earlier, Ibn Kathir himself claimed were created two thousand years before Adam and also shed blood, although in reality there are no such things as jinn.

---

⁶³Ezra, non-Arabic word of Hebrew origin
⁶⁴Ibn Kathir, 86.
⁶⁵Ibid.

Ibn Kathir quoted another passage from the Qur'an, in 37:149-160: *[149]So consult with them, "Do daughters belong to your lord and to them the sons? [150]Or have we created the angels females, and they were witnesses?" [151]Is it not surely from their own lie they say, [152]"Allah has birthed." And surely they are liars. [153]Has he then chosen the daughters over the sons? [154]What is [the matter] with you? How do you judge? [155]Do you not remember? [156]Or do you have a manifest authority? [157]So bring with your books, if you were truthful. [158]And they made a kinship between him and the jinn, and indeed, the jinn know that they will surely be brought. [159]Praise be to Allah about what they describe, [160]except for the faithful servants of Allah.*[66]

Then Ibn Kathir quoted the following verses from Qur'an 21:26-29: *[26]And they said, "The merciful has taken a son, praise be to him." Yet they are honorable servants. [27]They do not go before him with the speech, and they work with his command. [28]He knows what is between their hands and what is behind them, and they do not intercede except to whom he pleases. And they tremble from his fear. [29]And whoever says from among them, "Surely I am a god, without him." So such a one we will reward him hell; likewise, we reward the unjust.*

In Qur'an 18:1-5: *[1]The praise be to Allah who has sent down the book on his servant and has not made in it crookedness, [2]valuable to warn of a grievous woe from him and to give the believers good news, those who do good deeds, that they will have an excellent wage; [3]wherein they will dwell forever. [4]And he warns those who said, "Allah has taken a son." [5]They have no knowledge of this, neither their fathers, a dreadful word to come out of their mouths that they say except a lie.* Also Qur'an 10:68-70: *[68]They said, "Allah took a son, praise be to him." He is the rich, to him what is in the heavens and what is on the earth. Do you have authority for this? Do you say against Allah what you do not know? [69]Say, "Surely those who forge the lie against Allah do not prosper." [70]Enjoyment in the world, then to us is their return. Then we will make them taste the severe torment because they were infidels.*

Ibn Kathir stated that all of these Meccan verses include the answers to the infidels, philosophers, and the idolaters among the Arabs, Jews, and the Nasara (the Christians), those who claim

---

[66]Ibid., 86-87

"without knowledge that Allah had a son, and Allah is above what they say. They are the unjust, the sinful ones. Because of the Nasara (Christians), the curse of Allah be on them, the famous one among them believed in such lies. The Qur'an mentions much more to answer them because of their contradictions and the little knowledge they had and they are foolish. Their sayings were varied in their infidelity. That is because their vanity was much entwined and has differences and contradictions, but the truth comes without disagreement or worries."[67]

As Allah said in Qur'an 4:82: *[82]Do they not consider the Qur'an? If it was from other than Allah, they would have found in it many inconsistencies.* It is amazing how many Muslims I have met who will quote this verse, thinking in their hearts or their minds that just because the Qur'an says that there is no inconsistency in it, that the Qur'an is true without error. That is a very foolish statement because, as we have shown many times in this book, there are hundreds of inconsistencies in the Qur'an. To prove my point that Ibn Kathir is foolish, notice this verse in Qur'an 4:82 where he interpreted it by saying that this verse "proved that the truth united and agreed, but the lies disagreed and confronted each other."

Speaking of Christians, Ibn Kathir said that "a denomination among them went in their error and in foolishness claiming that the Christ is God and another denomination said that He is the son of God and a third denomination said that He is the third of three." Not only did Mohammed not know the true nature of God and the biblical understanding of God, but his scholars were even more foolish. Ibn Kathir did not understand that all Christian denominations, the Catholics, the Orthodox, and the Protestant, accept as true the three different beliefs mentioned above. All Christians believe that Jesus Christ is God and the Son of God and He is the Second Person of the Trinity because God is God the Father, God the Son, and God the Holy Spirit, and they are one God. The problem is that this belief requires man to be broken before God after the repentance of sin and turning away from his wicked ways and believe in Jesus, and then the Holy Spirit will fill him. Then he will believe who God is, for no one can even believe Christ is God except by the Holy Spirit.

I remember on one occasion traveling and speaking in Seattle, Washington, when a group of Muslims showed up. Although the topic this night was "Women in Islam," in the question-and-answer

---

[67]Ibid., 87.

session a Muslim man stood to ask a question. I later found out that he was the president of CAIR in Seattle which is nothing but a Muslim jihadist group (Brotherhood who dress in suits and ties), a wolf dressed in sheep skin, and what the liberal media call *moderate Muslims.* Instead of him asking a question, he stood up to make fun of me by claiming that I teach hate, and he read one of the early Meccan verses of the Qur'an. In it he claimed the following:

> Christians, Jews, and Muslims are good, and that we worship one God. There is so much more in common among us to unite us than there is to divide us. He said that Muslims believe in Prophet Jesus, in the miraculous birth of Jesus, and in the Gospel; and Muslims also believe in Prophet Moses and the Torah.

There I stopped him. I simply asked him two questions. *First, did he believe that Christians who gather in this church are infidels?* His answer was, "Absolutely not." Then he accused me of teaching hate between Christians and Muslims. Then I asked him the second question. *"Do you believe that all the people in this church should be beheaded?"* Again, he answered, "Absolutely not." Then I asked him to sit down because I wanted to talk to the people of the church. I asked the people of the church two questions and asked them to answer these questions by simply raising their hands.

First, I asked if anyone in the church believed that God is the Christ, Son of Virgin Mary. Without hesitation all the people in the church raised their hands, except the ten persons who were Muslims. I asked the Muslim man to look around and see the answer of the body of Christ. Then I asked the church if they believed that God is a Triune God, which is to believe in the Father, Son, and Holy Spirit, one Triune God. Once again, the entire church raised up their hands. I looked at the man who stood just a few minutes ago to call me a hate speaker. He was sitting with hands covering his face, for he knew where I was going with such questions.

Then I quoted the following Qur'an verses as Ibn Kathir had quoted in his book, *Stories of the Prophets.* First, Qur'an 5:17 states: *[17]Infidels, indeed, are those who said, "Surely Allah is the Christ, the son of Mary." Say, "So who could have anything against Allah if he desired to destroy the Christ, son of Mary, and his mother and all who are on the earth?" And to Allah the kingdom of the heavens and the earth and what is between them. He creates what he wills. And Allah has might over all things.*[68]

Also, the following verses in Qur'an 5:72-75: [72]*Infidels, indeed, are those who said, "Surely Allah is the Christ, son of Mary." And the Christ said, "O children of Israel, serve Allah, my lord and your lord." Surely whoever partners with Allah, so indeed, Allah forbids him the garden. And his abode is the fire, and the unjust will have no helpers.* [73]*Infidels, indeed, are those who said, "Surely Allah is the third of three." And there is no god except one god, and if they do not refrain from what they are saying, a painful torment will touch those who became infidels among them.* [74]*Do they not repent to Allah and ask his forgiveness? And Allah is forgiving, merciful.*[75]*The Christ, son of Mary, is nothing except a messenger; indeed, other messengers have gone before him, and his mother is a siddīqah.*[69] *They were eating the food. Look at how we show the verses to them, then look at how they turn away!*

After I finished quoting these verses, I quoted another verse to prove to my Muslim friend that it is not I who teaches hate but their book, the Qur'an. As we saw above, the Qur'an calls the Christians *infidels*. Not only did the Qur'an call Christians infidels but *infidels indeed* which means *for sure*. I could not help but to quote Qur'an 47:4: [4]*So when you meet those who became infidels, so strike the necks (decapitating) until you have made a great slaughter among them. ...* What a "loving" book, and what a "loving" religion.

Then there was a wonderful Muslim lady who sat next to this gentleman. She stood up and said that she was a Muslim and had lived in this country for over thirty years, and she had never killed any Christian; she had never even killed a chicken in her life. My response to her was, "I'm sorry. You have not been a good Muslim."

Ibn Kathir closed the previous verses in Qur'an 5:17 and 5:72-75 by stating that "Allah has judged the Christians who believe that Jesus is God or in the Trinity as infidels. This false teaching came from them although the messenger that came to them was 'Isā, Son of Mary. He showed them that He was a created servant, formed in the womb, who called to the servant of Allah alone without any partner.

---

[68]Ibid., 87.
[69]person of integrity, non-Arabic word of Aramaic origin

He threatened them that if they did the opposite of that, they will have the fire and they would not win the garden, but shame and disgrace."[70] In Qur'an verse 5:73: *[73]Infidels, indeed, are those who said, "Surely Allah is the third of three."* Ibn Kathir said that Ibn Jarir and others said he meant that "they are the three persons, the Person of the Father, the Person of the Son, and the Person of the Word which came from the Father to the Son according to their different denominations, and may the curse of Allah be on them."

Here once again, Muslim scholars prove to the world that they are nothing but foolish. Mohammed thought falsely that the Trinity is father (god), mother (Mary), and son (Jesus). Here his scholars in later days came up with a new trinity in which no Christian believes. This trinity is father, son, and the word which is great proof that those who are Muslim scholars had no idea what Christians believe. They did not understand that the Son is the Word of God, and they failed to mention the Holy Spirit as the third Person of the Trinity.

We do not believe in father, son, and the word, but Father, Son (the Word), and Holy Spirit. Ibn Kathir stated that they will talk about the differences among Christians in a later place in his book, and I will respond to him at that time.[71] Ibn Kathir pointed to the threat, which Allah gave to those who believe in such infidelity, as the Qur'an stated "they must repent and ask forgiveness from Allah, the forgiver, the merciful." He continued by stating that Christ was a servant and his mother was a friend, meaning that she was not wicked as the Jews claimed; and therefore, may the curse of Allah be on the Jews. He stated that some of the scholars claimed that she was not a prophetess. As for the saying of Allah in Qur'an 5:75, *they were eating the food,* he meant Jesus and Mary. This is a proof that the food came out of them as food comes out of anyone else. He meant that they relieved themselves. Ibn Kathir asked how a god could be in such a condition.

Ibn Kathir stated that Al Saddi said in his interpretation for this statement of Qur'an 5:73: *[73]Infidels, indeed, are those who said, "Surely Allah is the third of three..."* that is their (Christians') claim that 'Isā and his mother are two gods with Allah.[72] Allah *proved* that they are infidels when he said in the following verses of Qur'an 5:116-118: *[116]And when Allah said, "O 'Isā, son of Mary, did you*

---

[70]Ibn Kathir, 87-88.
[71]Ibid., 88.
[72]Ibid.

say to the people, 'Take me and my mother as two gods, other than Allah'?" He said, "Praise be unto you. It is not for me that I say what is not true for me; if I had said it, so indeed, you know it. You know what is in my soul, and I do not know what is in your soul. Surely, you are the knower of the unseen. [117]I did not tell them except what you had commanded me, 'That serve Allah, my lord and your lord,' and I was a witness among them as long as I was with them. So when you caused me to die, you were the watcher over them, and you are the witness of all things. [118]If you torment them, so surely they are your servants; and if you forgive them, so surely you are the dear, the wise."

In Ibn Kathir's interpretation, there was some excellent fabrication evident to anyone who knows Arabic.[73] You will see in the Arabic grammar that this conversation between Allah and 'Isā took place in the past tense, saying *when Allah said,* not *when Allah will say,* as some falsely translated into English in the future tense. So Ibn Kathir stated that Allah will ask 'Isā on the day of resurrection in a way to honor Jesus and to rebuke those who worshiped him as many have lied against him and claimed that he is the son of god or that he is god or that he is a partner of Allah. So Allah will ask 'Isā, *and Allah knows best* that this did not derive from him but is intended to rebuke those who lied against him as in, *[116]"...did you say to the people, 'Take me and my mother as two gods, other than Allah'?"*

Jesus answered the question. Ibn Kathir said that the conversation was very polite, and in the answer found in the rest of verse 116: *He* ('Isā) *said, "Praise be unto you. It is not for me that I say what is not true for me; if I had said it, so indeed, you know it. You know what is in my soul, and I do not know what is in your soul. Surely, you are the knower of the unseen.* By this, 'Isā meant that he only told them what Allah had commanded him when Allah sent him to them, that is to worship Allah alone, and Allah was a witness over them; *[117]... So when you caused me to die, you were the watcher over them, and you are the witness of all things.*

Ibn Kathir interpreted the words *caused me to die* by saying "when you lift me up to you, when they desired to kill me and crucify me surely you have shown mercy to me and have saved me and you have put my image on one of them."[74] So they killed him (meaning

---

[73]Ibid.
[74]Ibid., 89.

they killed someone other than 'Isā), and then he ('Isā) proposed to Allah to do whatever he (Allah) wished with those infidel Christians. He could punish by tormenting them or forgiving them. Ibn Kathir slanted his interpretation toward Allah tormenting them and not forgiving them. His proof was that 'Isā ended his saying to Allah with, *[118]....you are the dear, the wise,"* not "the forgiving, the merciful." Ibn Kathir's proof of this was the hadith in which Mohammed said, "He asked Allah's intercession for his people. So Allah gave it to him, and it is to whom does not associate anything with Allah."

Obviously, we Christians, according to the Muslim belief, associate Jesus, God's Word, and Mary with God. Therefore, according to Islam, there is no intercession for us, and we will burn in hell forever.

In the following four passages of the Qur'an, we see that Mohammed's rejection of the sonship of Christ is built on the misunderstanding of who God is. Ibn Kathir listed these passages: Qur'an 39:4-5: *[4]Had Allah desired to take a son, he could surely have chosen whomever he wills from whom he had created. Praise be to him. He is Allah, the one, the dominator. [5]He created the heavens and the earth with the truth. He makes the night roll over the day and makes the day roll over the night and has made the sun and the moon subservient. All run to their assigned times. Is not he the dear, the forgiving?* Qur'an 43:81-82: *[81]Say, "If to the merciful was a son, so I would be the first to serve him." [82]Praise be to the lord of the heavens and the earth, the lord of the throne, from what they describe.*

Qur'an 17:111: *[111]And say, "Praise be to Allah who has not taken a son, and it was not for him to have a partner in the kingdom. And it was not for him to have a friend from the humiliated." And magnify him[75] magnificently.* Also Qur'an 112:1-4: *[1]Say, "He is Allah the one of. [2]Allah is absolute. [3]He does not birth, neither was he birthed, [4]and there is no one equal to him."*

On the same page of Ibn Kathir's book, there are many hadith written following the previous verses where Mohammed assured his followers that Allah had no son, as when Mohammed said that Allah said, "Son of Adam, it was not for him to disown me so he claimed that I have a son, but I am the only one, the absolute. I have no

---

[75]that is to call "Allah Akbar," i.e. Allah is bigger

begotten son, I was not born, and there is none like me."[76]
Mohammed also said, "No one is more patient when harmed than
Allah, for when they made him to have a son, he still provided for
them and healed them."

As I said earlier, Mohammed did not understand the nature of
God. As he stated in the first passage of Qur'an 39:4: *[4]Had Allah
desired to take a son...,* Allah did not desire to take a son; rather
God is Father, Son, and Holy Spirit. That is the nature of God, as God
described it Himself in the Holy Bible and as we have proven above.
In the following verse, Qur'an 43:81: *[81]Say, "If to the merciful was
a son, so I would be the first to serve him,"* the word *if* for the
hearer does not prove that Allah does not have a son. The Son of God
is *the first* and *the last* (Revelation 1:17). He was worshiped in the
Old Testament before the incarnation, and He was worshiped after He
came in the flesh, as recorded in the New Testament. He will be
worshiped forever and ever.

The problem is not if God has a Son, but the problem is
Mohammed did not believe that Jesus is the Son of God. Qur'an
17:111 states: *[111]And say, "Praise be to Allah who has not taken
a son...."* If Mohammed was worshiping Allah the lord of this world,
as it is written in Qur'an 1:1, and here he was repeating the praise to
this god, then we discover that he was praising Satan for the god of
this world is nothing but Satan himself; and Satan did not take a son.
See 2 Corinthians 4:4 and many passages throughout the Bible which
show that the god and the lord of this world is Satan.

As for the last statement in Qur'an 112:1 quoted earlier,
Mohammed did not say *Allah wahad* which means *God is one*, but he
said *Allah ahad*. Allah is *one of*, for the word *ahad* in the Arabic
language can only be translated *one of*, as in the statement, *John is
one of the students.*

But as we have seen before, Allah, the god of Mohammed
throughout the Qur'an, is not the absolute one. We have seen in the
Qur'an the spirit of Allah and the word of Allah; this would make
Allah three. In simple words, Mohammed did not understand the
nature of God as we see it in the Bible. This problem not only began
with Mohammed, but it exists today in his followers, the Muslims.

Ibn Kathir closed this section with several verses of the Qur'an,
as we see, with a threat of a painful punishment to all Christians,

---

[76]Ibn Kathir, 89.

whom the Qur'an calls unjust, because they lie about Allah and are infidels.[77] Here are the verses Ibn Kathir listed:

Qur'an 11:102: *[102]And likewise, your lord seized, if he seizes the villages while they are unjust. Surely his seizing is painful, severe.*

Qur'an 22:48: *[48]And how many a village have I delayed to it,[78] and it was unjust; then I seized it, and the final return is to me.*

Qur'an 31:24: *[24]We give them enjoyment for a little while. Then we will force them into a thick[79] torment.*

Qur'an 10:69-70: *[69]Say, "Surely those who forge the lie against Allah do not prosper." [70]Enjoyment in the world, then to us is their return. Then we will make them taste the severe torment because they were infidels.*

Qur'an 86:17: *[17]So give the infidels a delay. Delay them leisurely.*

'Isā, from Childhood until Receiving the Revelation

Ibn Kathir stated, "As we have said before that 'Isā was born in Bethlehem near the holy house, but then he said a man by the name of Wahab claimed he was born in the land of Egypt and that Mary had traveled with Joseph, Ibn Jacob, the carpenter as she was riding on a donkey."[80] However, Ibn Kathir stated that the Wahab story is not true for 'Isā was born in Bethlehem not Egypt. Although Ibn Kathir did not believe in Wahab's story, he continued to tell his story by saying Wahab said that when 'Isā was born all the idols from the east and the west of the earth bowed down, and demons wondered why this happened until the great Satan discovered for them the matter of 'Isā. They found him in the lap of his mother and the angels were staring at him and there appeared a great star in the heavens. The King of Persia feared his ('Isā's) appearing, so he asked the priests about that (he meant what happened). They told him that this was a great birth on earth.

Then the King of Persia sent his messengers with gold and myrrh and incense as a gift to 'Isā. The king of the land asked them why they had come, and they told him. He asked them about the time of the birth of 'Isā, son of Mary, in the holy house. 'Isā became very

---

[77]Ibid.
[78]its punishment
[79]great
[80]Ibn Kathir, 90.

famous because of him being able to speak as a baby. So the king sent the messengers to 'Isā along with some others so that they could kill him after the messengers left. When they arrived, they gave Mary the gifts and then left. Then it was said to Mary that the messengers of the king of the land came only to kill her son. So she carried 'Isā, and they went to Egypt until he became twelve years old. *I wonder where Ibn Kathir and Muslim scholars came up with this information for none of this information comes from the Qur'an or the hadith?* Perhaps someone told Ibn Kathir the true account in the Bible, and as usual, Muslim scholars added and took away from the truth.

Continuing, Ibn Kathir said that 'Isā was blessed by miracles even when he was a little boy.[81] Al Dahqan, the man 'Isā and Mary stayed with in Egypt, said that he lost money from his house and only poor and weak people and the needy lived in his house. Because of the loss of his money, Mary and everybody were upset. When 'Isā saw this, he went to a blind man and another one who was crippled. 'Isā said to the blind man, "Carry this crippled man, and stand up with him." The blind man said, "I cannot do that." 'Isā said, "Yes, you can just as you did when you both took the money from this window of the house." When he said that, they believed him and brought the money back. So 'Isā became great in the eyes of the people when he was very little.

Then Ibn Kathir stated that Al Dahqan made a party and hosted the people because of the circumcision of his children.[82] When the people gathered, he fed them and desired to give them a drink, meaning wine, as they used to do in that day. However, he could not find any wine in his stone pots so he became upset. When 'Isā saw this, he stood up and walked by these stone pots, passing his hand over the openings. Every time his hand passed over the openings of the stone pots, they were filled with the best wine. Then the people were very amazed and offered him and his mother lots of money, but they refused to take any money. They left and went to the holy house, *and Allah knows best.*

When I read such confusion, I realize why Muslims are Muslim. This was written by Ibn Kathir, the great scholar for the Muslim world. I wonder if Ibn Kathir truly read the life of Jesus in the Bible. I cannot imagine living in Saudi Arabia or any other Muslim country and knowing nothing about the true account of Jesus. The gentleman

[81]Ibid., 91.
[82]Ibid.

who gave me the hard copy of Ibn Kathir's book, the one I used to write this book, thought if I would read this book, I would become a Muslim. The people of Yemen believe that. *Why are Muslims Muslim?* It is simply because they have no knowledge of Jesus. All that they know is what I have just shared with you from the book of their scholar Ibn Kathir.

If they just knew the truth of the Bible, they would find that their scholar was not a scholar at all. A simple reading of the Bible does not require the statement, *and Allah knows best,* for I believe the real meaning of the statement, *and Allah knows best*, is **we don't know**. Yes, God knows and through forty men, whom He inspired with the Holy Spirit, wrote to us the entire account of the Bible. *I wonder what source Ibn Kathir used for all of the information above?*

Here is a summary of the true account as it is written in the Bible. After Jesus was born in Bethlehem, the magi came from the East to Jerusalem asking where the newborn king was because they had seen His star in the East. When Herod the king heard that, he was upset. He gathered the leaders of the priests and asked them where the Christ was to be born. Obviously, they knew the prophecy of the Bible, saying that the king would be born in Bethlehem. In secret, Herod met with the magi, asking them to search for the baby. With deception he told them to bring back word to him when they found the baby, so that he could worship Him too. When the magi found the baby, they worshiped him and gave him their gifts of gold, frankincense, and myrrh; but it was revealed to them in a dream not to go back to Herod. So they went another way back to their countries.

Notice how the story we have written here is completely different from what was written by Ibn Kathir above. The biblical account names the specific king, people, and cities.

Then the angel of the Lord appeared to Joseph, commanding him to take Jesus and His mother and to escape to Egypt because King Herod desired to kill the child. That is exactly what happened. Herod gave an order to kill all male children of Bethlehem two years old and younger, which fulfilled a prophecy from the Old Testament. Later, the angel of the Lord appeared to Joseph after the death of King Herod and told them to go back to the land of Israel. However, because of Joseph's fear of the son of King Herod and having been warned by God in a dream, he turned aside into the region of Galilee. Joseph lived there with Jesus and his mother in Nazareth. We encourage the reader to read the entire account in the Bible in Matthew 2.

Ibn Kathir described in detail the prayer of baby 'Isā, as he tried to emphasize the miracle that 'Isā was able to talk shortly after birth.[83] The prayer is very long and ends by 'Isā saying the verses of Qur'an 112: *¹Say, "He is Allah the one of. ²Allah is absolute. ³He does not birth, neither was he birthed, ⁴and there is no one equal to him."* Ibn Kathir stated that Isaac Ibn Bashier said Ibn Abbas said, "'Isā stopped talking until he became a toddler (the normal age of learning to speak). Then Allah caused Him to speak with wisdom and understanding, and the Jews spoke against him and his mother, and they used to call Him 'the son of a whore'" as in Qur'an 4:156: *¹⁵⁶And because of their infidelity and their saying against Mary, a great slander.*

The claim that Mary was called a whore is not true, as we have proven before. Throughout the reading of the Gospel, one can clearly see that Mary was married to Joseph and had other children after the birth of Jesus. No Jew ever believed that Jesus' birth was the result of sin, but rather they always knew him as the son of Joseph. No Jew ever called Him *Jesus the son of Mary*, as if he were fathered by some unknown man, as Mohammed stated in the Qur'an. Jesus was also known as the brother of James, Joseph, Simon, and Judas, as we have covered this point in detail (Matthew 13:55). I wonder how Muslims would react if we called Mohammed the son of Amnah (which would be more accurate since Mohammed's claimed father had died four years before his birth). Calling a man by his mother's name in the Arabic culture is very insulting because it means that his mother is a prostitute or a whore. Only the Qur'an and Mohammed called Jesus the son of Mary. Jews know Him as the son of Joseph, and Christians know Him as the Son of God.

Ibn Kathir continued by saying when 'Isā became seven years old, his mother put him in school.[84] 'Isā asked the teacher a question, but the teacher did not know the answer. Then 'Isā said, "How can you teach me if you do not know the answer?" Then 'Isā taught the teacher the answer to the question.

Perhaps the source for this story was taken from Luke 2:41-52 that describes when Jesus was twelve years old, not seven years old, He was left behind in the temple after the family visited Jerusalem, not attending some school as Muslim scholars claim. He was sitting in the temple in the midst of the teachers asking them questions and

---

[83]Ibid., 91-92.
[84]Ibid., 92.

teaching them, and they were astonished at His knowledge. We encourage the reader to read the entire account in the book of Luke.

Another story as told by Ibn Kathir was that 'Isā was able to tell the young boys he played with about what their mothers had hid from them.[85] The parents of these boys became upset and refused to let their children play with 'Isā. One day 'Isā went to seek some of these children to play with them, but the parents closed their doors. The children were not allowed to play with 'Isā. When 'Isā knocked at the door and heard the noises inside the house, the parents lied and told him that the children were not home and that the noise was the voices of pigs and monkeys. Then 'Isā said, "O Allah, may they be," and the children were transformed into pigs and monkeys.

Muslim scholars have attributed many miracles to Jesus. Some are taken from the Bible, and others are just myths. However, according to the Bible, Jesus did not perform any miracles at an early age. As we see in the Scriptures, Jesus did not perform any miracles before the age of thirty. We read in John 2 that at the wedding in Cana in Galilee, not at the time of the circumcision of some children, Jesus changed the water into wine, and not as we read earlier in the fabrication of Ibn Kathir's writings. The miracle and the wedding were not in Egypt when Jesus was a boy but in Galilee when Jesus was thirty years old.

Ibn Kathir quoted Ibn Abbas who said that 'Isā was empowered to see (perform) miracles since his childhood from Allah.[86] This became known to the Jews, so the Children of Israel desired to kill him. His mother feared for his life, and then Allah revealed to her to take him to the land of Egypt. In Qur'an 23:50: *[50]And we made the son of Mary and his mother a sign, and we sheltered them in a high place with security and with a spring.*

There is a question we must ask here. *How did Ibn Kathir use this verse to prove that Jesus' mother took him to Egypt because she feared for his life when the verse does not even mention the country of Egypt?* As we mentioned previously, the one and only time Jesus went to Egypt was when He was an infant and King Herod desired to kill him. Ibn Kathir closed this section by stating that scholars disagreed on what the *high place* with all the springs of water was.[87] I can see total confusion because, not only did the scholars disagree on

---

[85]Ibid.
[86]Ibid.
[87]Ibid., 92-93.

what place, they also disagreed about which time. *Was Jesus a boy or only a newborn baby?* Following this rendition, Ibn Kathir quoted Qur'an 19:24: *²⁴So he called her from below her, "Do not grieve. Indeed, your lord has made a creek under you."*[88]

As for the place where 'Isā was born, under the palm tree, some scholars said there were small rivers, and Ibn Kathir stated that Ibn Abbas said it was the rivers of Damascus.[89] It was also said it was in Egypt as the People of the Book (Christians) claim, and he closed his statement with, *and Allah knows best.*

Ibn Kathir ended this session by saying that Isaac Ibn Bashier said that when 'Isā became thirteen years old, Allah commanded him to return from the land of Egypt to the house of Elijah. *If this was Elijah the 9ᵗʰ century BC prophet, how could his house exist 900 years later?* Obviously, Ibn Kathir, like Mohammed, did not know the timeline between the prophets.

Ibn Kathir continued by stating that Joseph, the cousin of his mother, came with 'Isā and Mary, riding on her donkey, to Elijah's house. They stayed there until Allah gave 'Isā the gospel, taught him the Torah, and gave him the miracle of resurrection of the dead, the healing of the sick, and the knowing of the unseen. People were shocked by the miracles that he performed. He called them to Allah, and the news became known to all of them.

The Descending of the Four Gospels and the Timeline

Ibn Kathir said that Abu Zarah Al Damascus said somebody said the following:

> The Torah descended on Moses in six nights, not in the month of Ramadan. The Zabor (Psalms) descended on David in twelve nights, not in the month of Ramadan and 482 years after the Torah. The Ingeel (Gospel) descended on 'Isā, son of Mary, in eighteen nights, not in the month of Ramadan and 1,050 years after the Psalms. The Discriminator (the Qur'an) descended on Mohammed in twenty-four days in the month of Ramadan.[90]

We discover, from this statement, they believe only three books are in the Bible which are the Torah and the Zabor (Psalms) and the Ingeel (Gospel). This statement is repeated throughout the Qur'an and

---

[88]Ibid., 93.
[89]Ibid.
[90]Ibid.

the hadith, and it is a critical error. The time between Moses and David is roughly five hundred years. *What about all the other Scriptures which were between Moses' writing the first five books of the Old Testament (the Torah) and the Zabor (Psalms)?* There are ten more books during this period: Joshua, Judges, Ruth, 1 and 2 Samuel, 1 and 2 Kings, 1 and 2 Chronicles, Ezra, Nehemiah, Esther, and Job. *What about all these books?*

The Qur'an very clearly teaches that all the men who came before Mohammed were inspired. As it is written in Qur'an 16:43: *[43]And we did not send before you any except men that we inspired, so ask the people of the reminder,[91] if you were not knowing.*

As for the book of Psalms written by David, which Muslims believe in, there is another error. Muslims claim that the entire book of Psalms was written by David, but that is not true for there were many writers of the book of Psalms. For example, Psalms 42, 44, 45, 46, 47, 48, 49, 84, 85, 87, and 88 were written by the descendants of Korah. Psalms 50, 73, 74, 75, 76, 77, 78, 79, 80, 81, 82, and 83 were attributed to Asaph. Psalms 72 and 127 were written by Solomon. Psalm 89 was written by Ethan the Ezrahite. Psalm 90 was written by Moses. We see then that David was not the only writer of Psalms, but rather there were many others.

Another error is concerning what was written after Psalms. The assumption that the Ingeel (Gospel) was written after the Psalms and there was no Scripture between them is a critical error, for obviously neither Mohammed nor Muslim scholars were aware of the number of books that were written in the six hundred years after David. When we study the manuscripts, we discover the following books are in the Holy Scripture: Proverbs, Ecclesiastes, Song of Solomon, Isaiah, Jeremiah, Lamentations, Ezekiel, Daniel, Hosea, Joel, Amos, Obadiah, Jonah, Micah, Nahum, Habakkuk, Zephaniah, Haggai, Zechariah, and Malachi.

Notice that after the book of Malachi there were four hundred years of silence in which God did not send any prophets or messages. Many Muslims believe in many of the prophets that we named simply because the Qur'an mentions their names as prophets. However, Muslims do not know about the lives or the writings of these men. For example, they believe in Job and in the book of Job, but they do not have access to this information. It is the same with David. They believe in David and the book of Psalms, but they have no access to

---

[91]Jews and Christians

who David was or anything about his life and writings. All that they know is the few words written in the Qur'an that are mixed with error and confusion, as we have previously seen in the section on David.

Now for the gospel, Ibn Kathir said that Ibn Jarir wrote that 'Isā was thirty years old when he received the gospel and that he ascended when he was thirty-three years old.[92] Muslims believe the gospel was a book descended on 'Isā simply because they do not know what the word *Gospel* means or who 'Isā is. If Muslims knew that the term *The Gospel* means the *Good News* and Jesus is the Word of God who became flesh, and if they knew that the name Jesus in the Hebrew language is not 'Isā but *Yeshua* which means *Savior*, then they would know that the Good News is Jesus who will save His people from their sin.

Saving those who believe in Him from eternal death to have eternal life is the Good News, the Gospel. If Muslims would only realize that Jesus is the suffering Messiah, the Anointed One, and if Muslims could see that Jesus is the one who came to fulfill all the prophecies which were written throughout the thirty-nine books of the Old Testament, then they would believe in Him and understand that the Discriminator (the Qur'an) is not from God descending in Ramadan or any other month. There is no value or honor in a book which is given and written by Satan, containing repeated and corrupted stories, and full of error and inconsistencies. Muslims would realize this if they would just read, study, and understand the Qur'an, not just memorize it.

The Tree of Toby

Ibn Kathir described a tree which he called *The Tree of Toby* without any information about where he came up with this story.[93] He began by telling about a dialogue between Allah and 'Isā concerning this tree and saying that Allah planted it by his hand. 'Isā asked Allah if he could drink from it because Allah had said that anyone who drank from it would never again be thirsty. Allah, however, told 'Isā that he could not drink from it nor could any prophet until the Gentile prophet of Islam (Mohammed) drank from it. It was even forbidden to all the nations until Mohammed's nation drank from it.

Then Allah told 'Isā, "I will raise you up to me." 'Isā said, "Why do you raise me?" Allah said, "I will raise you up, and then I will

---

[92]Ibn Kathir, 93.
[93]Ibid., 94.

send you down in the end of time to see the wonder of the nation of this prophet and that you may help them to kill the cursed false prophets…"[94] Then there is a long dialogue between Allah and 'Isā concerning the Muslim nation, and Allah describes the Muslim nation as being "the best, the most humble, and the most worshiping." Obviously, there is no such tale found in the Scriptures or the history of the church, for Jesus never talked to God concerning Mohammed or his followers. It is a Muslim folk tale.

Ibn Kathir stated that Abu Dawood said Satan came to 'Isā, son of Mary, and said, "Do you not claim that you are the truthful? Here is the height so throw." 'Isā answered, "Woe to you. Did he not say, 'O sons of Adam, do not ask me the destruction of your soul? I will surely do whatever I wish.'"[95]

In the next paragraph of Ibn Kathir's book, Abu Tobah said that Kaled Ibn Yazed said Satan worshiped with 'Isā ten years or two years. One day they were on the top of a mountain, and Satan said, "See if I throw myself from the top, will anything harm me except what is prescribed for me?" 'Isā said, "Surely I will not test my lord, but if Allah wills, he will test me," and 'Isā knew him that he was Satan, so Satan left him. There are many hadith like the one above with long detailed conversations between 'Isā and Satan. Some of the hadith said Angel Gabreel alone or Gabreel and Angel Mika'il together helped 'Isā have victory over Satan by slapping him with their wings. Sometimes the wings took him to the sun and sometimes to the hot muddy spring (where Mohammed claimed the sun set in the evening causing darkness) and sometimes to the seven seas. Satan ended by leaving 'Isā. In another hadith, Satan said to 'Isā, "No one has seen what I have seen from you, O son of Mary." (Every time Satan talked to a prophet, he was punished; but when he talked to 'Isā, he was punished the most.)

It is pathetic to read so many contradictions of sayings concerning the temptation of Jesus by Satan. If those who call themselves scholars had truly read the Bible, they would have found the true account as it is written in Matthew 4:1-13.

We know from the Scripture that Jesus left the Jordan River and spent forty days in the wilderness and was tested by Satan. He fasted these forty days and forty nights, and finally He became very hungry. Satan tempted Jesus three times. First, Satan said to Jesus that if He is

---

[94]Ibid., 94-95.
[95]Ibid., 95.

the Son of God, then command this rock to be bread; but Jesus answered him by what is written in the Bible, Mathew 4:4: *[4]...**"It is written, 'Man shall not live by bread alone, but by every word that proceeds from the mouth of God.'"***

In the second temptation, Satan took Jesus to the pinnacle of the temple. This time Satan used the Scripture to tempt Jesus by telling Jesus that if He is the Son of God, to throw Himself down from the temple for the angels would protect Him, and He would not be harmed. Jesus answered him, *[7]...**It is written again, "You shall not tempt the Lord your God."***

In the third temptation, Satan took Jesus to a high mountain and showed Him the kingdom in a moment. Then he said to Jesus that he would give Jesus this entire kingdom if He bowed down and worshiped Satan. Jesus answered him, *[10]...**"Away with you, Satan! For it is written, 'You shall worship the Lord your God, and Him only you shall serve.'"*** The Scripture states that Satan left Jesus for a while.

You see, my friends, here is the true account. Jesus was not shouting or crying for help. None of the angels, Gabreel, Mika'il, or Israfeel, came to fight for Him by slapping Satan with their wings or to take Him to the sun or to the depths of the valleys as Ibn Kathir stated in his book.

Ibn Kathir gave us another story which had been told by Abu Hozeyafah who said Satan met with his demons, and they told him, "Our master, you are tired."[96] He said that this (Jesus) is infallible. "I do not have a way against him, but I will use him to lead many astray. I will put in them different desires, and I will make them many groups. They will make him and his mother gods, other than Allah. Allah sent what he supported 'Isā with and kept him from Satan," as is written in the Qur'an to show his grace on 'Isā, when it says in Qur'an 5:110: *[110]When Allah said, "O 'Isā, son of Mary, remember my grace on you and on your mother when I supported you with the holy spirit ..."*

Notice here, it was Satan's plan according to this teaching that all Christians would be led astray simply by believing that Jesus and his mother are gods. No Christian believes in such a thing. Only Mohammed and his Muslim followers made this assumption, as we have shown many times in the past, for no true Christian believes in the trinity of the father, mother, and son. If only Muslims knew the

---

[96]Ibid., 97.

true Christian doctrine concerning the nature of God as Father, Son, and Holy Spirit, they would not accept Mohammed and his false teaching.

In Ibn Kathir's book, he stated that 'Isā did not have a known place to live in since he was traveling in the land.[97] As for how 'Isā performed the first miracle of raising the dead, he described it in the following paragraphs.

One day while he was walking, he went by a woman who sat near the tomb crying. So 'Isā asked this woman, "What is wrong with you, woman?" She said, "My only daughter died, and I made a covenant to my lord; I will not leave this place until I die or until Allah brings her back to me alive. So look at her." 'Isā answered her, "If I look at her, will you then return?" She said, "Yes." They said that 'Isā prayed kneeling twice (the style of Muslims' prayer which is evidence that he was a Muslim). Then he came and sat by the tomb and called, "O so (he called her by her name), arise by the permission of the merciful, so come out." Ibn Kathir stated that the tomb moved, and 'Isā called a second time. So the tomb moved with the permission of Allah, and he called the third time, so she came. She said, "When you shouted the first shout, Allah sent an angel, and he put me together. And when you shouted the second shout, my spirit came back to me. So when I received the third shout, I was afraid for I thought that it was the shout of the resurrection, so my hair and eyebrows became gray for I was afraid of the resurrection."

Obviously, I believe that this story is just a simple fairy tale, for how did she know what happened in the first shout if she was still dead? Now let's go back to the story.

Then she went to her mother, and she said, "O my mother, why did you want me to taste the distress of death twice? O my mother, be patient; I have no need of the life of this world. O spirit of Allah and his word (speaking to 'Isā/Jesus), ask my lord to return me to the hereafter and make the distress of the death easy on me." So 'Isā called his lord and Allah took her to him and the earth became flat over her. The Jews knew that, and they became very angry against 'Isā.

The Children of Israel asked 'Isā to raise Shem, Ibn Noah. 'Isā called to Allah and prayed to Allah, so Allah raised Shem to life, and he told about the ark and the entire matter. Then 'Isā called again, and Shem returned to dust. Ibn Kathir continued by stating that Al Saddi

---

[97]Ibid., 98.

said that Ibn Abbas said there was one of the kings of Israel who died, and he was carried on his bed. So 'Isā, peace be on him, came and called to Allah. So Allah raised him from the dead. Then the people saw this wonderful thing and this beautiful appearance.

What a wonderful telling of the miracles of Jesus, raising a lady and returning her back to death, raising Shem and returning him to dust, and finally, raising one of the kings who was carried on his bed. I wonder what sources Ibn Kathir or these men used to tell these stories, for there is no mention of such miracles in the Qur'an or in the hadith.

Jesus performed many miracles, and we encourage the reader to go to the Bible and read about the following miracles. Here are the miracles and their references in the Bible: changing the water into wine in John 2:1-11; the healing of the son of a nobleman in John 4:43-54; the healing of the man from demon possession in Mark 1:21-28 or Luke 4:34-43; the healing of Peter's mother-in-law and others in Matthew 8:14-17, Mark 1:29-34, or Luke 4:38-41; the healing of the leapers in Matthew 8:1-4, Mark 1:40-45, or Luke 5:12-16; the healing of the cripple in Matthew 9:1-8, Mark 2:1-12, or Luke 5:17-26; the healing of a man at the pool of Bethesda in John 5:1-47; the healing of the withered hand in Matthew 12:9-13, Mark 3:1-6, or Luke 6:6-11; the feeding of the multitude at the Sea of Galilee in Matthew 14:14-21 or Mark 6:35-44 & 8:7-12; the healing of the Centurion's servant in Matthew 8:5-13 or Luke 7:1-10; the raising of the son of the widow of Nain in Luke 7:11-17; the healing of the woman, who was bent over for eighteen years, on the Sabbath in Luke 13:10-17; the healing of the man with dropsy in Luke 14:1-14; the raising of Lazarus four days after his death in John 11:1-44; the healing of the ten lepers in Luke 17:11-19; the healing of the blind men in Matthew 20:29-34, Mark 10:46-52, or Luke 18:35-43; the healing of the soldier's ear on the Mount of Olives in Luke 22:51; and many other miracles that, according to the Scriptures, if they were all written down, the world itself could not contain all the books that would be written (John 21:25).

Do you know why? The simple answer is that Jesus has no beginning and no end. He is the Alpha and Omega; therefore, the eternal life of God the Son cannot be limited within books because from Jesus' day to today millions of miracles are performed by the power and name of Jesus.

Although Jesus performed these wonderful miracles, they are not the reason He came into this world. The main purpose for Him to

[175]

come into this world in the flesh was to perform the greatest miracle which is the fulfillment of the meaning of His name, Jesus, Savior. That miracle is not the destruction of His physical body caused by death, but raising Himself from death as Jesus prophesied in John 2:19 when He told the Jews: ***Destroy this temple, and in three days I will raise it up.***

The Jews did not understand that Jesus was speaking of His own flesh. They were thinking that He was talking about the Temple of Solomon which took forty-six years to build. However, when Jesus rose from the dead (John 2:22), the disciples remembered His words concerning His resurrection for they believed in the book (the Old Testament prophecies) and believed in the words which Jesus spoke. I know there are many Muslims who believe in Jesus, but not my Jesus. To believe in Jesus is to believe in who He is and what He has done. He is God who came in flesh, died, and rose again.

Ibn Kathir returned to the Qur'an citing 5:110-111: *[110]When Allah said, "O 'Isā, son of Mary, remember my grace on you and on your mother when I supported you with the holy spirit; you spoke to people in the cradle and [as] an old man. And when I taught you the book and the wisdom and the Torah and the Gospel, and when you created from the mud the likeness of the bird by my permission, so you breathed into it, so it will become a bird by my permission. And you healed the blind and the leper by my permission. And when you brought forth the dead by my permission, and when I withheld the children of Israel from you, when you came to them with the proofs, so those who became infidels among them said, 'That this is but an obvious sorcery.'" [111]And when I revealed to the Hawārīyūn:[98] "That believe in me and in my messenger." They said, "We believed and bear witness that surely we are Muslims."[99]*

He interpreted these two verses by stating that Allah reminded 'Isā of his grace and his goodness and how he created him without a father from a mother without a male, and he made him a sign to the people. Also, Allah reminded him of how he chose 'Isā and his mother for this great grace and of how he proved that they were innocent of all that the foolish had brought against them. That is why

---

[98]white or pure—Mohammed used it to mean disciples of Jesus, non-Arabic word of probable Abyssinian origin
[99]Ibn Kathir, 99.

he said: *I supported you with my holy spirit.* Ibn Kathir emphasized that the holy spirit is the Angel Gabreel who gave 'Isā's spirit to his mother and made 'Isā speak as a baby and that 'Isā called the people to Allah since he was an infant until he was very old. Also, he told how Allah taught 'Isā the book and the wisdom, meaning the writing and the understanding of the Torah and the Ingeel (Gospel).

As for the saying, *You create from the mud the likeness of the bird,* Ibn Kathier interpreted this by stating that he shaped the bird and formed it from mud, as it was supposed to look, by the order of Allah. As for his saying, *You breathed into it so it will become a bird by my permission,* Ibn Kathir interpreted this as meaning *by my command.* Allah assured that the permission was given to 'Isā, so no one assumes that it was 'Isā who did it on his own. As for his saying, *You healed the blind,* Ibn Kathir interpreted this as meaning those who were born blind and there were no doctors that could heal their eyes with medicine.

As for the lepers, those who the sickness became so severe, in the saying, *When you brought forth the dead,* Ibn Kathir interpreted this as meaning to bring them alive from the tomb by my permission. *And when I withheld the children of Israel from you,* he interpreted this as that's when they desired to crucify 'Isā, but Allah delivered him from their hand by raising him up to himself so he saved him from any harm. Finally, *when you (Allah) revealed to his disciples,* Ibn Kathir's interpretation was this meant that he guided them to the *right mind.* It was also said it was *revelation through the messengers* as he guided them in their hearts to accept the truth. This was the completion of Allah's grace on his servant 'Isā, son of Mary, when he made for him helpers to guide him and gave victory and called others with him to serve Allah alone without partners.

In my humble opinion, Ibn Kathir was doing everything he could to remove the evidence that Jesus shares many of God's characteristics, but he was not very successful. The evidence that Ibn Kathir tried to remove proves that Jesus is God, for no one can share these characteristics with God, like creation and raising the dead. There are also more errors, for Jesus never spoke as a baby and did not grow to a very old age (the Arabic word used here for *old* means someone who is at least past 90-100 years). We know that Jesus left earth when He was thirty-three years old.

Ibn Kathir continued by quoting a similar passage to the previous one in Qur'an 5:110-111 which is Qur'an 3:48-54: [48]*"And he will*

[177]

teach him the book and the wisdom and the Torah and the Gospel. [49]And a messenger to the children of Israel." "Indeed, I came to you with a sign from your lord. I create for you the figure of a bird from the ṭīn.[100] So I breathe into it, so it will become a bird by Allah's permission. And I heal the blind and the leper, and I raise the dead by Allah's permission. And I inform you about what you eat and what you store in your houses. Surely in this is a sign for you, if you were believers. [50]And confirming what is between my hands from the Torah, and make lawful for you some of the things that were forbidden to you. And I came to you with a sign from your lord. So fear Allah and obey me. [51]Surely Allah is my lord and your lord, so serve him. This is a straight way."

[52]So when 'Isā sensed infidelity on their part, he said, "Who are my allies in Allah's cause?" The Hawārīyūn[101] said, "We are Allah's allies. We believed in Allah and bear witness that we are Muslims. [53]Our lord, we believed in what you sent down, and we followed the messenger. So write us among the witnesses." [54]And they deceived, and Allah deceived. And Allah is the best deceiver.[102]

Ibn Kathir interpreted these verses by stating that every prophet's miracles during his time were matched with the people of his time. Moses' miracles matched his time when there were smart sorcerers, so he was sent with miracles which shocked the eyes and caused their necks to be humbled because the sorcerers were very skilled with the art of sorcery. Allah empowered Moses to do more miracles by his hand, so they believed in him and surrendered to him.

So it was in the case of 'Isā, son of Mary, Ibn Kathir wrote. There were many wise men, so he was sent with miracles that they could not perform. He showed that he was wise in the case of healing the sick, like the blind and the leper and those with all diseases, and how someone could move from the act of creating to the raising of the dead from the tomb. Every one of these miracles was proof that whoever performed them was truthful and was proof of the mighty power of Allah who sent them.

The same was the case with Mohammed when he was sent. It was within the time of the poets, so Allah sent on him the great Qur'an:

---

[100]mud, non-Arabic word of N. Semitic origin

[101]white or pure—Mohammed used it to mean disciples of Jesus, non-Arabic word of probable Abyssinian origin

[102]Ibn Kathir, 100.

which does not have any vanity, not between his hands or from behind him. It is the descending, the wise, the praised. Its words are miracles. It challenged the people and the jinn to bring a sura (a portion of revelation) like it or ten suras like it; and he challenged them, but they were not able to do it, meaning he challenged them to write some portion like the Qur'an in Mohammed's time or the future. Because they could not do it, that is the proof that the Qur'an is the words of the creator. There is none like it in the description or its work.

There is much to respond to in the previous claims of Ibn Kathir concerning the statement "that every prophet came to match his time." As for Moses' example, we may say that the Egyptians were sorcerers that performed their sorcery and were able to make snakes out of the rods. Notice here that it was not Moses, as Mohammed erred in the Qur'an, but it was Aaron who performed this miracle (Exodus 7:8-13). There are ten other miracles or, as the Bible calls them, plagues on the Egyptians that neither Mohammed nor his scholars knew about. We encourage the reader to read in Exodus 7-12 about the plagues of changing the water into blood, the frogs, the gnats, the flies, the destruction of the livestock, the boils, the hail, the locusts, the darkness, and the most important one, the death of the firstborn. Obviously, the Egyptian sorcerers could not compete with Moses, especially after these ten plagues. When Moses crossed the Red Sea, the Egyptian pharaoh and his army drowned.

We move on to Jesus' time. *Was there anyone who performed miracles in Jesus' time? What was the condition of the Jews in Jesus time? Were they high-tech or medically advanced?* The obvious answer is *no.* They were under Roman occupation. Jesus was a carpenter, not a doctor. His people were simple farmers and fishermen who lived a simple life, riding donkeys and walking on foot. *So what was the challenge for Jesus?* He did not perform miracles to compete with other people who performed miracles but to show compassion to those who lived in His day.

In Matthew 20:34, we read: ***So Jesus had compassion and touched their eyes. And immediately their eyes received sight, and they followed Him.*** Here we see that Jesus opened the eyes of the two blind men, even though people rebuked them and told them to be quiet. However, the men kept shouting for Jesus to have mercy on them. There was no doctor to heal their eyes or some magician to compete with Jesus, but Jesus healed their eyes simply because He was filled with compassion towards them.

There were people who came before Jesus who performed similar miracles and even some greater, as when Elisha performed his fourteenth miracle because he was promised by Elijah that he would perform double the number of miracles. Since Elijah performed seven miracles before he died and Elisha only performed thirteen miracles before he died; therefore, he had to perform one more miracle after his death. In 2 Kings 13:21, the dead body of a soldier touched the bones of Elisha and came back to life and stood on his feet.

The point is there was no challenge in the time of either Prophet Elijah or Prophet Elisha to perform any miracles; it was only a sign from God that the people would know that these were men of God. Jesus also promised his disciples that they would do greater miracles than He (John 14:12): ***Most assuredly, I say to you, he who believes in Me, the works that I do he will do also; and greater works than these he will do, because I go to My Father.***

As for Mohammed's time and the miracle of the poetry of his Qur'an, first of all, there is no such miracle of any poetry when it is so full of errors, no matter how wonderful it sounds in its original language. The Qur'an is full of geographical, botanical, historical, moral, theological, legal, social, scientific, and linguistic errors. *How can someone delude themselves about such errors to believe in such a lie that the poetry of the Qur'an is a miracle?*

As for the challenge which Mohammed put in the Qur'an, that the human and the jinn cannot write even a portion of the Qur'an, this challenge has already been equaled in quality many times, for there are books, not just portions of revelation, that have been written with the same style of poetry. The only difference is that they present the Christian message without any of the above errors of the Qur'an.

This leads us to another important question. *Is writing poetry a proof of prophecy?* I wonder if Muslims have ever read the poetry of the British poet Shakespeare or the French poet Voltaire. Neither one claimed to be a prophet, nor did the British or French ever think that these two men were prophets. I encourage Muslims, especially those who memorize the Qur'an, to study its content to see for themselves if the claims that the Qur'an is a miracle, or an evidence of Mohammed's prophecy, are valid.

Ibn Kathir stated that the meaning or the purpose of 'Isā performing the miracles was to give the evidence and proof to the Jews, but that most of them continued in their infidelity, errors, and disobedience.[103] Some of them though were good, and they helped him. They followed him and gave him advice. Then some of the Children of Israel bribed the kings at that time because "they determined to kill and crucify him." Allah delivered 'Isā from the Jews, raised 'Isā up to himself, and made one of his companions to look like 'Isā. They took him, killed him, and crucified him thinking that they had killed 'Isā, but they were wrong; and they were proud against the truth (meaning they bragged about killing Jesus, but they did not kill Jesus; instead they killed the other man that looked like Jesus). Many of the Nassara (Christians) surrendered to them and to what they claimed, and both were wrong as Allah said in Qur'an 3:54: *[54]And they deceived, and Allah deceived. And Allah is the best deceiver.*

I will not believe in a god, no matter how truthful he is, if he is a deceiver. For such a god does not deserve or have the right to earn worship, even from a sinful man like me. It is amazing that Muslims believe in such a lie which has no evidence, not historical or biblical or qur'anical; yet, Jewish and Greek historians wrote that Jesus died, rose again, and all of his followers, not *some* as Muslims claim, believed in His death, His burial, and His resurrection. As a matter of fact, all of His disciples, those who Mohammed called Hawārīyūn, except Apostle John who was imprisoned on the Isle of Patmos, were killed for this very same reason, for believing in Jesus' death, burial, and resurrection.

It is amazing how many references throughout the Qur'an and how many hadith (Mohammed's sayings) concerning Mohammed's personal issues bring nothing but shame to him and his followers. Moreover, Allah and Gabreel neglected to give Mohammed details about who the person was who took Jesus' place on the cross and how this happened. If I were Allah and had dictated the Qur'an, I would have made sure that the true story of Jesus would be put throughout the Qur'an beginning with the very first verse; therefore, the details of the story would be told to the people so that there would not be any confusion or mystery.

The stories of the Qur'an were taken out of the Bible, twisted, and repeated over and over again, without any point, as we have seen throughout this book. However, when Mohammed talked about Jesus' crucifixion, he put in only one ambiguous verse. I enjoyed reading the interpretation of this lonely verse as scholars disagreed about how it

---

[103]Ibn Kathir, 101.

happened, by whom, when it happened, or why. We will talk about this in detail later. *What kind of a god is Allah to deceive millions of Christians for over six hundred years, and when he sent his true prophet (Mohammed), he did not tell him exactly what took place?*

Ibn Kathir proceeded by quoting the following verses in Qur'an 61:6-8: *⁶And when 'Isā, son of Mary, said, "O children of Israel, surely I am a messenger of Allah to you, confirming what is between my hands from the Torah and to give you the good news of a messenger to come after me. His name is Ahmad.*"[104] *So when he came to them with the proofs, they said, "This is obvious sorcery." ⁷And who is more unjust than he who forged the lie against Allah when he is being invited to Islam, and Allah will not guide the unjust people. ⁸They desire to extinguish the light of Allah with their mouths, and Allah will fulfill his light, even if the infidels hate it.*[105]

Islam will be victorious over all religions until it is the only religion. In Qur'an 61:14: *¹⁴O you who have believed, be the helpers of Allah as 'Isā, son of Mary, said to the Hawārīyūn, "Who is my helper with Allah?" The Hawārīyūn said, "We are the helpers of Allah." So a group from the children of Israel believed and another group became infidels. So we supported those who believed against their enemy, so they became triumphant.*

Ibn Kathir interpreted these verses by saying that 'Isā was the seal (last) of the prophets to the Children of Israel.[106] He preached to them and gave them the good news of the seal of the prophets to come after him (he meant that Jesus was prophesying about Mohammed). He told them his name that he described to them so they may know him and follow him when they saw him. That is showing goodness from Allah to them as Allah said in Qur'an 7:157: *¹⁵⁷"Those who follow the messenger, the Gentile prophet whom they will find described for them in the Torah and the Gospel. He will command them with fairness and forbid them from the evil and make good things lawful for them and prohibit the impure for them and will ease them of their burdens and of the yokes which were on them so that those who believed in him and*

---

[104]Muslims claim that Ahmad is the same name as Mohammed, which is not true, and that 'Isā, whom they claim to be Jesus, prophesied his coming

[105]Ibn Kathir, 101.

[106]Ibid.

strengthened him and helped him and followed the light which has been sent down with him, those are the prosperous."

Ibn Kathir said that Mohammed Ibn Isaac said Kaled Ibn Madan said the companion of the apostle of Allah said, "O messenger of Allah, tell us about yourself."[107] He said, "The call of Abraham my father, the announcement of 'Isā, and when my mother conceived me, it was like light that came out of her that lit up the castles of Bosra and the land Sham (old Syrian border)." And that is when Abraham built the Kaaba. He prayed as it is written in Qur'an 2:129: *[129]Our lord, and raise to them a messenger from among them....* Ibn Kathir continued by stating that when the prophethood ended among the Children of Israel, 'Isā stood up preaching to them announcing to them that the "prophethood has stopped among them (the Jews); but it would continue after him in his Gentile Arab Ahmed, the absolute final prophet of all, and he is Mohammed Ibn Abd Allah from the descendants of Ishmael Ibn Abraham."

As for the statement that Mohammed is the "descendant of Ishmael, the father of all the Arabs," we have discussed this in detail in the section about Abraham, so there is no reason to repeat it here. There is no connection between Ishmael and the Arabs or Mohammed. *As for Mohammed saying, "When he was conceived by his mother a light came out of her," then why did Mohammed's mother never proclaim him to be godly or a prophet; and why did his mother not believe in him?* He himself said that she would burn in hell forever. There was no witness to prove Mohammed's account. As usual, there was no witness to all the miracles and the wonders which the Muslims say he performed. We will cover this in detail in the section concerning Mohammed.

In Qur'an 61:6: *[6]...So when he came to them with the proofs, they said, "This is obvious sorcery."* Ibn Kathir interpreted this by stating that there are two different interpretations of who *he* is. Some say it is 'Isā, peace be on him, or maybe Mohammed, Allah's prayer and peace be on him. When Muslims say 'Isā, they only say "peace be on him." However, every time they mention the name of Mohammed, they literally say, "Allah's prayer and peace be on him," which means there must be a greater god who Allah can pray to for Mohammed. It is amazing how Muslims translate this sentence in English; they lie, and purposely ignore the word *prayer,* so they only

---

[107]Ibid., 102.

say, "May Allah's peace be on him." *Obviously, the true translation makes no sense to the English reader, for how could Allah pray upon Mohammed?*

When American Muslims or any Muslims, speak to Westerners, they claim *Sala Allah Alyhe Wa Salam* means *peace be on him*. They know that is not true, for they purposely leave the word *prayer* out, but they are following their Mohammed who is following their Allah, the best deceiver.

Ibn Kathir interpreted that Mohammed provoked the believers to give victory to Islam and its people (the Muslims) and to give victory to its prophet (Mohammed), that is, to stand with him and help him to raise their religion and spread it through invitation.[108] As it is written in Qur'an 61:14: *[14]O you who have believed, be the helpers of Allah as 'Isā, son of Mary, said to the Hawārīyūn, "Who is my helper with Allah?" The Hawārīyūn said, "We are the helpers of Allah...."* Ibn Kathir stated that this took place in a village called Nazareth. That is why they were called *Nasara*.

This is another inaccuracy, for Christians do not call themselves *Nasara*, and no one calls the Christians *Nasara* except Mohammed in his book, the Qur'an. Ibn Kathir quoted the rest of the verse in Qur'an 61:14: *...So a group from the children of Israel believed and another group became infidels....* Ibn Kathir interpreted this that when 'Isā called the Children of Israel and others to Allah, sometimes part of them believed and part became infidels, and other times the entire population believed, like the entire people of Antioch.

This statement is very surprising, for Jesus never went to Antioch. Instead, it was Paul who preached the Gospel to the people of Antioch. Ibn Kathir stated that Jesus sent three messengers to the people of Antioch, so they believed.[109] Obviously, Jesus did not send any of His disciples to Antioch. Instead, He sent His twelve disciples first to the house of Israel, and He clearly instructed them *not* to go to the Gentiles or the Samaritans (Matthew 10:5-6).

Another time Jesus did send seventy-two disciples, by twos, only in the land of Israel, for they went ahead of Him to prepare the Jewish people for the coming of Jesus (Luke 10:1-20). Then just before He ascended into heaven, Jesus gave the command to His disciples to go to Jerusalem, Judea, and Samaria. After the day of Pentecost,

---

[108]Ibid.
[109]Ibid.

Christianity spread to the ends of the world as instructed in the Great Commission by Jesus in Matthew 28:19-20.

Ibn Kathir skipped the rest of the verse when Allah said in Qur'an 61:14: ...*So we supported those who believed against their enemy, so they became triumphant.* There are a couple of questions we must ask here. *Who are those who believed in Jesus? Where are they today?* After all, the Qur'an clearly teaches that they triumphed over the infidels, for all the Christians we see today in the world believe in the word of God (the Bible) and in the Christian doctrine, which Mohammed in his Qur'an considered infidelity.

Ibn Kathir concluded this section by stating that other people of the Children of Israel became infidels, and they are the Jews.[110] Therefore, Allah supported whoever believed in him above whoever disbelieved in him as he said in Qur'an 3:55: *[55]When Allah said, "O 'Isā (Jesus), surely I am causing you to die, and I am raising you up to me and purifying you from those who became infidels and make those who follow you above those who became infidels, until the resurrection day. Then to me is your return, so I will judge between you about what you were differing.*

Ibn Kathir stated that this meant everyone who was near 'Isā was victorious. Because Muslims believe that the truth was in 'Isā, there is no doubt in him, since he was the slave of Allah and his messenger. That is why Muslims were victorious over the Nasara (Christians) who exaggerated about him. Because the Christians made Jesus the Son of God, or God, and the Jews did not believe in him, the Jews and the Christians are alike, the curse of Allah be upon them. Because the Christians believed in Jesus and the Jews did not, the Christians were victorious over the Jews until the time when Islam came to the world.

Once again, Ibn Kathir dodged the interpretation of the last verse in Qur'an 3:55. This verse clearly teaches that those who believe in Jesus (Christians) will be above those who became infidels (anyone who did not believe in Jesus) until the day of resurrection; notice he did not say until Mohammed comes. Once again, I ask two questions. *First, has the day of resurrection come yet? Second, where are those Christians today?* All the Christians who exist today, according to the teaching of Mohammed and the Qur'an, are nothing but infidels.

---

[110]Ibid., 103.

<u>The Bread of the Table</u>

Ibn Kathir began this section by quoting Qur'an 5:112-115:
[112]When the Hawārīyūn said, "O 'Isā, son of Mary, can your lord send down on us a mā'ida[111] from the heaven?" He said, "Fear Allah, if you were believers." [113]They said, "We desire to eat from it and to have our hearts assured and know that you indeed have told us the truth, and we will be witnesses of it." [114]'Isā, son of Mary, said, "O Allah our lord, send down a table on us from the heaven, that it becomes an 'id[112] for us, to the first of us and to the last of us, and a sign from you. And provide for us, and you are the best of the providers." [115]Allah said, "Surely I will send it down on you, so whoever among you becomes an infidel after that, so surely I will torment him a torment I will not torment any one of the worlds."[113]

Ibn Kathir interpreted these verses by stating that scholars said 'Isā commanded his disciples to fast thirty days.[114] When they completed it, they asked 'Isā to send upon them a table from heaven so they might eat from it and their hearts might be assured that Allah accepted their fasting and answered their request. Then it "may become a festival to break their fast with, and it would be enough for the first and the last of them, their rich and their poor."

'Isā preached to them and was afraid for them that they would not give thanks for it and also that maybe they would not do what was right toward it, so they just asked him to ask for them this request from his lord. Because they did not cease from this request, 'Isā stood up with a sackcloth over his hair, hung his head down, and his eyes filled with tears. 'Isā cried out to Allah in his prayer and requested they might receive what they were asking. Allah then sent down the table from heaven. The people were looking at it floating between two clouds and slowly, slowly it got nearer. Every time it got nearer, 'Isā asked his lord to make it a mercy, not a revenge, and to make it a blessing and peace. The table continued to come nearer until it sat still between the hands of 'Isā and was covered with a blanket.

Ibn Kathir then stated that 'Isā stood up to "remove the cover from it while he was saying, '…in the name of Allah the best of the providers.' So it was seven whales and seven pieces of bread. And it was said *vinegar* and it was said *pomegranate and fruit* and it had a

---

[111]table, non-Arabic word of Ethiopian origin
[112]festival, non-Arabic word of Syriac origin
[113]Ibn Kathir, 103.
[114]Ibid.

great smell. Allah said to it, 'Be,' so it was. Then he commanded them to eat from it. They said, 'We will not eat from it until you eat.' 'Isā said, 'You are the ones that started asking the question about it.' They refused to eat from it, so he ordered the poor, the needy, and the sick to eat; and there were almost thirteen hundred people who ate from it. Everyone who ate from it who had any handicap or prolonged illness was healed.

The people were sorry for not eating from it after seeing the good results that came to those who ate from it. Then it was said that the table used to come down once every day so people ate from it, and the last one of them used to eat as much as the first. It was said that seven thousand people used to eat from it. It used to come down day after day; it was the same as in the case of the story of the camel of Saleh whose milk the people drank day after day."[115]

Ibn Kathir stated that Allah commanded 'Isā to "only allow the poor and the needy to eat from it, not the rich, so this caused sadness among many of the people.[116] The hypocrites among them spoke against that, so the table was lifted completely, and all those who spoke against that were cursed into pigs." This was also supported with the hadith which was told by Ibn Abu Hatem who said that Amar Ibn Yasr said Mohammed said that "the table came from heaven, meat and bread, and they were commanded to not cheat on it and not save any of it and not to take any for the next day; so they cheated and they saved and they kept some for the next day. Therefore, they were cursed into monkeys and pigs."

To contradict all that was written concerning the table, with all the detailed information which is written above, Ibn Kathir stated in the conclusion that Ibn Jarir said Mujahid and others said that "the table never descended down, and they refused its descending to them when he said, 'so whoever among you becomes an infidel after that, so surely I will torment him a torment. I will not torment any one of the worlds.'"[117] That is why it was said that the Christians do not know the bread of the table, and it was not written in their book, even though its news was known. That's why we wrote about it, and Ibn Kathir ended his story by saying, *and Allah knows best*.

I will not blame Muslims who believe in these fabrications, if they do not have access to the true account of the Bible. The four

---

[115]Ibid.
[116]Ibid., 104.
[117]Ibid.

simple verses of Qur'an 5:112-115 do not give any details. However, as usual, Muslim scholars with the help of Mohammed in the hadith fabricated a long story with amazing details. Three stories from the Bible are mixed together.

Now let us look at the true account about Jesus and the Lord's Supper. As for the table, this is known to Christians as the Lord's Supper. It was the last Passover meal Jesus had with His disciples (Matthew 26:17-25, Mark 14:12-21, and Luke 22:7-13). Muslim scholars mixed it with the feeding of the five thousand men (Matthew 14:13-21, Mark 6:30-44, Luke 9:10-17, and John 6:1-15). Muslim scholars also mixed this story with a third story where Jesus fed the four thousand (Matthew 15:29-39 and Mark 8:1-10). In the feeding of the five thousand, the meal began with five loaves of bread and two fish, the leftovers were twelve baskets full, and the number of people fed did not include in the count the women and the children. As for the feeding of the four thousand, they began the meal with seven loaves of bread and a few small fish, the leftovers were seven baskets full, and the count of the number fed did not include the number of women and children.

As for the Lord's Supper, Jesus sent His disciples, Peter and John, to the city to meet with a specific person to ask this gentleman for the use of his place for the Passover meal. As we covered this before, when we talked about the ten plagues on the Egyptians which were performed by Moses, the last plague was to kill the firstborn of every family and of every animal of all the Egyptians' homes. As for the Hebrews' homes, they would be saved only if they sacrificed a lamb and added the blood of the lamb to the two posts and above the door so that when the Lord passed by their house, He would see the blood and pass over their homes. That is why it is called the Passover meal. As the Jews were inside their homes enjoying the meat cooked on the fire with the unleavened bread, the Egyptians inside their homes were wailing because of the loss of their loved ones.

What does that mean? It means that without the shedding of blood there is no forgiveness of sin. Without applying the blood to their doorframes (which means believing in God) there must be death as a consequence for their sin. Jews understand this. So do Christians, but Christians understand it fully, for Jesus is the True Lamb of God. He is the fulfillment of the prophecies and all that took place in the Old Testament concerning the shedding of blood.

Notice that the disciples were the ones who prepared the meal. After they met with Jesus and had their last Passover meal, Jesus established the Last Supper meal wherein Jesus once again showed His disciples what He was about to do for the sin of the world. The bread was broken, and He said that this was His body which was given for them. He prayed over it and then said to His disciples to take it and eat it. After the bread, Jesus took a cup of wine and blessed it. Then He gave it to His disciples and said that this was His blood which would be shed for the forgiveness of sin for many. He told His disciples to drink it from the cup and to do this in remembrance of Him.

It has been two thousand years, and the church still remembers the body of Jesus which was given for our sin and His blood which was shed for the forgiveness of sin. Sadly, Muslims for the last fourteen hundred years have no idea of what the Passover meal meant or what the Lord's Supper meant. All that the Muslim knows concerning the Lord's Supper is a fabricated interpretation, made up by Mohammed, Ibn Kathir, and other Muslim scholars as written above. There was no table that came from heaven; this is just another fairy tale, or shall we say an error in the Qur'an.

Jesus Going toward the Sea

Another funny fable written by Ibn Kathir was about 'Isā walking on the water.[118] He stated that Muslim scholars said that the disciples of 'Isā lost their Prophet 'Isā, so it was said to them that he went toward the sea. They went seeking him, and when they saw him at the sea, they saw him walking on the water. They saw the waves lift him up one time and go down with him another time. He had clothes on him; he was wearing half of his clothes and had the other half tied around his waist until he came to them. One of them said, "Will I come to you, O prophet of Allah?" 'Isā said, "Yes." So he (a disciple) put one of his feet on the water. As he put the other foot in the water, he said, "Oh, I am drowning, O prophet of Allah." 'Isā said, "Show me your hand, O you of little faith. If the son of Adam had a faith as big as a seed of the barley, he will walk on the water."

It was also said that 'Isā was asked how he walked on the water. He said it was by faith and assurance. They said, "We believe as you believe, and we are as sure as you are sure." 'Isā said, "Then walk." He said, "They walk in the waves so they drown." So 'Isā asked them, "What is the matter with you?" They said, "We feared the waves." He said, "Have you feared the lord of the waves?" So he got

---

[118]Ibn Kathir, 104.

them out. Then 'Isā struck the earth by his hand (meaning he took some of the earth in his hand). Then he stretched his hand before them. In one hand there was gold, and in the other was gravel. 'Isā said, "Which one is better in your hearts?" They said, "This gold." He said, "So surely they are the same to me."

What about the true account of Jesus walking on the water? We find the true story written in Matthew 14:22-36, Mark 6:45-56, and John 6:16-24. This miracle took place after the feeding of the five thousand when Jesus asked His disciples to take the ship and go across the Sea of Galilee (not like Ibn Kathir's statement that Jesus was lost). Then Jesus sent the crowd away and went up the mountain alone to pray. In the meantime, the disciples were tormented in the middle of the sea because the wind and the waves were rough, but later in the fourth quarter of the night (3:00 a.m.), Jesus, walking on the sea, went to His disciples.

First, they were afraid and shouted because they thought He was a ghost. Immediately, Jesus told them to not be afraid "that He is I Am." Then Peter (we know the name of this disciple, unlike Muslim scholars who, as usual, did not know the names of characters they wrote about) said that if He was Jesus, to command him to come to Jesus on the water. Then Jesus commanded him to come, so Peter left the ship and walked on the water to Jesus; but when he saw the strong waves, he feared and began to drown. He cried out for the Lord to save him.

Immediately, Jesus reached out His hand, held Peter, told Peter that he had very little faith, and then asked Peter why he doubted. After Jesus entered the ship, the waves calmed, and those who were in the ship worshiped Him saying that He truly is the Son of God.

Notice, although Muslim scholars rewrite the story with changes here and there, not one of them finished the story correctly. It is amazing how many times Muslims ask the question of where in the Bible Jesus said that He is the Son of God and to worship Him. If they would just read the Bible, they would discover that the disciples here in this passage above knew who Jesus was. That is why they confessed with their lips that Jesus is the Son of God. Jesus did not correct them by saying that He is just a prophet, a man, or a good teacher. Also, notice that they worshiped Him, and Jesus did not reject their worship.

Ibn Kathir continued by saying that 'Isā used to wear hair (clothes made out of hair) and eat from tree leaves.[119] He did not stay in homes or with families, he did not have money, and he did not store anything. He used to eat from his mother's food.

Ibn Asakir said that whenever 'Isā was reminded of the hour (the Day of Judgment), he used to shout and said that no one should even mention the hour in front of the son of Mary. Obviously, this was taken out of the Bible in Mark 13:32 as Jesus described in the entire chapter the signs of the end of time. (See also Matthew 24:1-35 and Luke 21:5-33.) In Mark 13:32, Jesus said that no one knows the day or the hour, not the angels who are in heaven or the Son; only the Father knows. That is one of the verses which Muslims use to say that Jesus is not God, for if Jesus is God, He would surely know everything. Notice that Jesus did not shout or say that no one should mention the hour in front of the son of Mary.

Most likely those who use this verse will use all the verses in the Bible which point to Jesus as a man. The fact is that most Muslims do not know that Christians believe that Jesus was fully man. He ate after being hungry, He drank because He was thirsty, and He went to relieve Himself after eating and drinking. When He got tired, He rested and slept. He cried when He was upset, and sometimes He wept when He lost a dear friend. He laughed when He was happy, and when He was upset, He got angry without sinning.

He lived as a man. He knows all things about men except one thing, which separates Him from all men. Jesus never sinned for He was a perfect man. Muslims need to know that Jesus is also fully God, for He fed the hunger of thousands from five pieces of bread and two fish, and He can feed the spiritual hunger of man as well as the spiritual thirst for Jesus is the Living Water and the Bread of Life. He wept when He lost His friend Lazarus. Four days after Lazarus's death, Jesus shouted, "Lazarus, come forth!" Lazarus came back to life. Since Jesus is the Creator of man, it is not hard for Him to fix the eye which cannot see or the ear which cannot hear, sometimes by spoken words and sometimes by simply putting mud on it.

Just imagine with me, if you were born blind and you went to the eye doctor's office and, instead of the doctor examining your eyes to see what was wrong with them, he spit in the flower bed of his office window and took the mud which he made and spread it over your eyes and then asked you to go wash in some lake. If you believed it,

---

[119]Ibid., 105.

you would have your sight back again. That is what my Jesus did. Sometimes He just said a word and healed whatever the sickness or disease was. He also accepted worship from people and forgave their sins.

If Muslims would say that Jesus was a bad teacher, a bad man, or a false prophet, that would match their beliefs about Christianity. What is amazing is that they believe that Jesus was a good teacher and profess to believe in His teaching. When I ask *what teaching*, they say that they do not know, or they do not agree that all His teaching was good. I quote what Jesus taught in John 14:6-8: *⁶Jesus said, "I am the way, the truth, and the life. No one comes to the Father except through Me. ⁷If you had known Me, you would have known My Father also; and from now on you know Him and have seen Him." ⁸Philip said to Him, "Lord, show us the Father, and it is sufficient for us."*

I will paraphrase John 14:9-11. Jesus asked Philip why he did not know who Jesus was even though He had been with him all this time. Jesus told Philip that whoever had seen Him had seen the Father, so how could Philip ask Him to show them the Father. Jesus also asked him if he believed that Jesus is in the Father and the Father in Jesus. He also told Philip that he did not speak on His own authority but by the Father who dwells in Him and does the work. Jesus told Philip to believe that He is in the Father and the Father in Him or else believe Jesus for the works themselves.

Do Muslims believe in this teaching? Absolutely not. They consider this teaching blasphemy. They say, *"How can Jesus be a good teacher if He is a blasphemer?"* Jesus taught that He is God.

When Jesus taught the Jews, in John 8:56-59, that Abraham rejoiced for seeing his days, the Jews guessed Jesus' age correctly. They asked Him how He could have seen Abraham since He was not even fifty years old. Jesus answered them by saying that before Abraham was that He was the I Am. Then the Jews picked up stones to kill Him. Maybe my Muslim friends do not understand the words "I Am," but the Jews understood it very well. That is the greatest blasphemy for a man to claim to be God.

Do Muslims believe that Jesus is God? Absolutely not. Therefore, Jesus cannot be a good man if He claims to be God. Last, Muslims believe that Jesus was a prophet. As a matter of fact, they believe in many people to be prophets. However, a prophet cannot be a prophet unless he prophesies, his prophecy must be fulfilled, and he must lead people to worship the true God. As we learn from Deuteronomy 13:1-

5, the true prophet must give a prophecy or a sign, this prophecy or sign must be fulfilled, and he must lead the people to worship the true God. God said that He will test His people to see if they will worship Him and love Him with all their heart and soul; however, the false prophet who leads them to worship false gods must be put to death.

Here are some places in the Bible where Jesus prophesied that He would die and rise again: Matthew 16:21-23; 17:22-23; 20:17-19; Mark 8:31-33; 9:30-32; 10:32-34; Luke 9:22; 9:43-45; 18:31-34; and John 12:20-36. *Do Muslims believe that Jesus died and rose again? Absolutely not.* Notice that Jesus' teachings, Jesus' identity, and Jesus' prophecy concerning His death and resurrection did not begin in the New Testament teachings. There are 330 prophecies written in the pages of the Old Testament hundreds of years before Jesus came in the flesh which prophesied this.

What about the statement that Jesus did not know the hour of His second coming? The simple answer is in Philippians 2:6-11. It is unacceptable to believe that a man can be God, but the opposite is true, meaning it is quite acceptable for God to be a man. I could not personally go and live or even spend a week in the White House, but the President of the United States of America can go and stay in anyone's home where they would be honored to host him.

The Bible says that, although Jesus is God, He did not claim His rights to be God. He emptied Himself by taking the form of a servant, and He lived among us. He humbled Himself and was obedient to the Father even to death on the cross. So you see, Jesus emptied Himself when He became a man; and, as the Son of Man, He did not know the hour of His return. Because of His obedience and because He humbled Himself, God raised Him up and gave Him the name that is above all names. For at the name of Jesus, every knee in heaven and on earth will bow down, and every tongue will confess that Jesus Christ is Lord for the glory of God the Father. Whenever you see a passage in the Bible that describes Jesus as a man, just remember that He is God who became a man, not a man whom some people made a god.

As I read many of the Muslim scholars' teachings concerning Jesus, I discovered that they claim in many of Jesus' sayings that some say one thing and some say another. I choose not to respond to all of this nonsense for I believe it is a waste of our time. One can find some of these teachings in Ibn Kathir's book which presents Jesus as a man who was sick, hungry, poor, and sometimes presented as a worshiper.[120] The entire purpose of Ibn Kathir's writing was to try to convince people that Jesus was just a man and not God.

One of the sayings of Mohammed revealed to 'Isā was this:

> O 'Isā, move from this place to that place, that you may not be known, so you will not be harmed by my glories and my honor; I will marry you to a thousand ever virgins, and I will *olamn* (a word written in Arabic letters with no meaning) four hundred years for you.

I believe the purpose of this hadith was to present Jesus as a mere human who would be exalted by marrying a thousand virgins in heaven.

Another hadith says that Jesus gave advice about what to eat and what to drink.[121] Some are close to what the Bible says as when Ibn Saeed said that he said, "Go through this world and do not fix it." Also, he used to say, "The love of this world is the head of every sin, and the look will plant the lust in the hearts." I believe, as the Scriptures teach, when Jesus said that anyone who looks at a woman with lust commits adultery in his heart with her (Matthew 5:27-28), and Paul stated that *the love of money is the root of all kinds of evil* (1Timothy 6:10b). This is similar to what Saeed said.

Some of the sayings are true, but Jesus never said what Abd Allah said that Jesus said: "Whoever desired this world will be like the one who drinks the water of the sea, the more he drinks from it the more he becomes thirsty, until it kills him."[122] Some of the blessings, which were written by Ibn Kathir, also are inconsistent with what Jesus said, as in the following sentences: "Blessed are those who cry for the remembering of his sin and who kept his tongue and enlarge his house" and "Blessed are the eyes who slept and did not speak to itself with iniquity and it gives attention to other than sin."[123] Many other sayings are similar to the ones I gave above.

The Ascending of 'Isā to the Heaven and the Lies of the Crucifixion

Ibn Kathir inserted a couple of passages from the Qur'an which clearly teach us about the nature of his god Allah.[124] I cannot see how Muslims can follow such teachings and such a god. First, Ibn Kathir quoted Qur'an 3:54-55: *[54]And they deceived, and Allah deceived.*

---

[120]Ibn Kathir, 105.
[121]Ibid., 106.
[122]Ibid.
[123]Ibid., 107-109.
[124]Ibid., 110.

And Allah is the best deceiver. ⁵⁵When Allah said, "O 'Isā (Jesus), surely I am causing you to die, and I am raising you up to me and purifying you from those who became infidels and make those who follow you above those who became infidels, until the resurrection day. Then to me is your return, so I will judge between you about what you were differing."

Then Ibn Kathir added the following passages from Qur'an 4:155-159: *¹⁵⁵So because of their breaking their covenant and being infidels in the verses of Allah and their killing of the prophets unjustly and their saying, "Our hearts are uncircumcised." Yet Allah has taba'a¹²⁵ on it for their infidelity so that they will not believe except for a few. ¹⁵⁶And because of their infidelity and their saying against Mary, a great slander.*

¹⁵⁷And their saying, "Surely we killed the Christ 'Isā, son of Mary, the messenger of Allah." And they did not kill him, and they did not salaba¹²⁶ him; but it was made to appear to them, and surely those who disagree about him are in doubt of him. They do not have any knowledge of him except following the conjecture, and they did not kill him for certain. ¹⁵⁸Yet Allah raised him up to himself. And Allah was dear, wise. ¹⁵⁹And none of the People of the Book¹²⁷ will believe in him before his death. And on the resurrection day, he will be a witness against them.

Ibn Kathir interpreted these passages by fabricating the following statement that Allah told us that he raised 'Isā up to the heavens after he caused him to die through sleeping, and he saved him from the harm of the Jews who desired to harm him through some infidel kings of that time.¹²⁸ Ibn Kathir said that Mohammed Ibn Isaac said this king's name was David Ibn Nora (King Ibn Nora). No king existed by this name, not in Jesus' time and not any time among the Jewish people. As a matter of fact, there was no king of the Jews at the time of the crucifixion of Jesus; that is why they put a sign on the cross: *Jesus, King of the Jews* (John 19:19).

The only king that existed in Israel during the time of Jesus had died more than twenty-five years prior to Jesus' death. He was Herod I or Herod the Great who was an Edomite Jewish Roman client king of the Roman provinces of Judea, Galilee, and Samaria (present-day

---

¹²⁵sealed, non-Arabic word of Syriac origin
¹²⁶crucify, non-Arabic word of Persian/Syriac origin
¹²⁷Bible
¹²⁸Ibn Kathir, 110.

Israel).[129] He was known for building the temple known as Herod's Temple and as being the king that ordered the murder of all male children under the age of two after Jesus' birth. After his death in AD 4, his kingdom was split up by the Roman ruler Augustus between Herod's sons, Herod Antipas, who was called a tetrarch (not king), and Herod Archelaus, who was called an ethnarch (not king). Antipas continued to rule Galilee and Perea as tetrarch until AD 39. However, in AD 6, Archelaus, who ruled Judea, Idumea, and Samaria, was judged incompetent by Augustus; and Judea province was formed under the direct Roman rule, governed by a prefect (not a king). Pontius Pilate was the prefect of Judea from AD 26-36, which covered the time of Jesus' crucifixion. There was, in fact, no king at the time of Jesus' crucifixion.

Ibn Kathir stated that Mohammed Ibn Isaac said King David Ibn Nora gave the order for Jesus' death by crucifixion. So they surrounded him in a house, in the holy house, and this was Friday night. When the time came for them to enter the house where Jesus was, the likeness of Jesus fell onto another of his companions who was with him, and Jesus was raised from a window of this house to heaven. The people of the house were watching, and when the soldiers entered, they found this young man who had received the likeness of Jesus and arrested him. They conjectured that he was Jesus, so they crucified him and put a thorn on his head to disgrace him. Then he was given to the Jews. Most of the Christians who did not see what happened went astray, for they thought that Jesus was crucified.

As for the saying in Qur'an 4:159: *[159]And none of the People of the Book[130] will believe in him before his death. And on the resurrection day, he will be a witness against them.* Ibn Kathir interpreted it to mean that they will believe in Jesus after he comes down to earth at the end of time before the hour of judgment. Surely he will come down, kill the pig, break the cross, establish a tribute tax, and believe in Islam. He will also kill the antichrist.

Ibn Kathir stated that Ibn Abbas said when Allah desired to lift up 'Isā to heaven, 'Isā, his head dripping with water, went to his twelve companions in the house.[131] He said to them, "One of you will become infidel in me twelve times after believing in me." Then he

---

[129]"Herod the Great," *Wikipedia*, last updated March 25, 2012, accessed March 28, 2012, http://en.wikipedia.org/wiki/Herod_the_Great.
[130]Bible
[131]Ibn Kathir, 110.

said, "Who among you will receive my appearance? Who will be killed in my place, so he will be with me in my reward?" One of the young men among them stood up, and he told him to sit down (meaning Jesus refused his offer as a substitution). When Jesus repeated the question again to them, the same young man stood up and said, "I." This happened three times, and Jesus refused him each time. Then Jesus said to him, "You are the one," so the likeness of Jesus fell onto this young man, and Jesus was lifted up to heaven from the window of this house.

Ibn Kathir continued, "The Jews came and asked for him, so they took the one that looked like Jesus. Then they killed him and crucified him. Some of them became infidels twelve times after they believed, and they broke into three groups (denominations): the Jacobites who believed that Allah was among them (they believed that Jesus is God) descended from heaven; the Nestorians, the second group, believed the Son of God was among them (meaning that they believed that Jesus is the Son of God) ascended to heaven; and the third group, the Muslims, who said the slave of Allah and his messenger was among us (which means they believed Jesus is just a man) and Allah raised him up."

The two infidel groups united and fought and killed the third group. The Muslims and Islam were hidden all these years until Mohammed, the apostle of Allah, came. Ibn Kathir proved his point by quoting Qur'an 61:14: *[14]So we supported those who believed against their enemy, so they became triumphant.* This verse does not support the teaching of Ibn Kathir above. *Therefore, how can he say that the true believers of Christianity, those who believe that 'Isā (Jesus) was a servant, just a man, were killed by the other two infidel groups and disappeared until Allah sent Mohammed?* This verse clearly teaches that Allah supported the believers. *Did the believers lose the war even though Allah supported them?*

Ibn Kathir stated that Ibn Jarir said 'Isā was praying to Allah that Allah might delay his time (death) because he wanted to continue sharing the message and invite more people to enter the religion of Allah.[132] Then he named the disciples with many errors in the listing. He named the last Yudas Karya Yota, and he said this was the one who led the Jews to 'Isā. Obviously, he meant Judas Iscariot (Matthew 26:47-56, Mark 14:43-52, Luke 22:47-53, and John 18:1-

---

[132]Ibid., 111.

11.) The actual names of Jesus' disciples can be found in Matthew 4:18-22, Mark 1:16-20, Luke 5:1-11, John 1:38-51, and Acts 1:13.

Ibn Kathir said that Ibn Isaac said there was a man among them (meaning among the disciples of Jesus) and his name was Sarjas, and the Christians hid him.[133] He was the one who took the likeness of Christ and was crucified instead of 'Isā. Some Christians claim that the one who was crucified instead of 'Isā was Yudas Karya Yota.

Ibn Abbas said that 'Isā asked Simeon to take his place, and the Jews killed Yudas (he meant Judas).[134] Ibn Jarir said, "'Isā came with seventeen of his disciples (This is in error for Jesus only had twelve disciples. *Where did the other five disciples come from?*), and the Jews surrounded the house. When they entered the house, Allah changed all the seventeen disciples of 'Isā to look exactly like 'Isā."

Then the Jews said to them, "You have bewitched us, so may 'Isā come out of you, or we will kill all of you." Then 'Isā said to his companions, "Who will purchase the garden today with his soul?" (He meant, "Who will die in my place to earn a place in heaven?") One of the men said he would. 'Isā (the one who looked like him) went out to meet with them and said, "I am 'Isā." So they took him and killed him and crucified him. Therefore, it appeared to them that they had killed 'Isā, so Jews conjectured that 'Isā was crucified. However, the truth is that Allah had raised him up on that day.

Ibn Jarir gave us another story.[135] When Allah told 'Isā, son of Mary, he was going out of this world, he feared death; and since it was a very hard time for him, he called his disciples and cooked food for them. Then he said, "Come to me tonight so surely I am in need of you." So when they met with him that night, he fed them dinner and stood up to serve them. So when they finished from eating, he washed their hands by his hand, and he dried their hands with his clothes so they became proud and hated it. Then 'Isā said, "Whoever rejected what I am doing this night, he is not of me and I am not of him, so they let him finish what he was doing." After 'Isā finished that, he said, "Whatever I did to you tonight, serving you the food and washing your hands by my hand, so do the same. You see that I am better than you so do not be proud against one another, and may every one of you give himself to one another as I gave myself for you. As

---

[133]Ibid.
[134]Ibid.
[135]Ibid.

for my need, for which I called to you, I want you to call on Allah. Pray hard that Allah may delay my death."

When they stood up to pray, sleep overtook them, so they could not pray. 'Isā tried to wake them up, and he said, "How great Allah is. Could you not have patience with me one night that you may help me in it?" They said, "We swear by Allah we do not know what is wrong with us. We swear by Allah fellowship all night, but tonight we can't. We are trying to pray, but it is hard." Then he said, "The shepherd will go, and the sheep will be scattered." He used to say words like that concerning himself. Then he said, "One of you will become an infidel in me before a rooster crows three times and one of you will sell me with few dirham and he will eat my price."

Then they departed, and the Jews were seeking him.[136] They took Simeon, one of his disciples, and they said, "This is one of his friends." He (Simeon) denied him, and he said, "I am not his friend." So they left him. Then some others took him; then he denied him again. Then he heard the voice of the rooster, so he cried and was sad. When it was morning, one of the disciples came to the Jews, and he said, "What will you give me if I lead you to the Christ?" They paid him thirty dirham. He took it and led them to 'Isā. He took the likeness of 'Isā before that so they took him, tied him with ropes, pulled him, and said to him, "You used to give life to the dead and rebuke demons and heal the demon possessed. Can't you save yourself from this rope?"

They spat on him and threw the thorns on him until they brought the wood with which they desired to crucify him on it. Allah raised him up to himself, and they crucified the one that was made to look like 'Isā. So he ('Isā) stayed with them. Muslim scholars disagree on how long 'Isā stayed with his disciples. Some said seven days, some said seven hours, and some said seven months, *and Allah knows best.*

Then his mother and the woman whom 'Isā used to heal, so Allah purified her from the demons, came to him crying and asking, "Where is the crucified?" 'Isā came to them, and he said, "Over whom do you cry?" They said, "Over you." He said, "Surely Allah has raised me up to him and nothing has touched me except good, and this (the crucifixion of the one who looked like 'Isā) was made to look like me to them." So he commanded the disciples to come to him in some place, and that is exactly what happened. The eleven disciples came to him in that place, and the one who sold him and led the Jews to

---

[136]Ibid., 112.

him was lost. 'Isā asked his companions about him (the betrayer). They said, "He became sorry, and he hung and killed himself." 'Isā said, "If he had repented, Allah would relent on him."

Then he asked about a young lad who used to follow them. His name was called Yahyah. He said, "He is with you, so go, for he will become every one of you and will speak with the language of his people. He will warn them, and he will call them." Ibn Kathir ended this fairy tale by saying that this was strange and wonderful, and it was more truthful than what was mentioned by the Christians (he meant what was written in the Bible). He was referring to when Christ came to Mary sitting and crying near him, and he showed her the scars of the nails on his body. He told her that his spirit was ascended to heaven and that his flesh was crucified. This was an astounding lie, a fabrication, misrepresentation, and false transposition of facts; it flies in the face of the specific facts and accounts provided by the Bible.

Wow! After reading so many small stories similar to those mentioned above concerning the crucifixion of Jesus and the long fabricated story, I am overwhelmed by the sheer number of these stories written by Muslim scholars. *Should I cry, or should I laugh?* Emotionally, I feel so sorry for all Muslims who do not believe the true account of the great work of Jesus on the cross for their sins, but at the same time neither Allah nor Gabreel nor Mohammed told of what really took place. For example, after reading all of their stories, we still don't know who died instead of Jesus and what actually happened. There is no information in the Qur'an or Mohammed's hadith; and in all the scholars' stories, no two stories match. If I translated all of these stories, this would go on and on for many pages concerning all that Jesus did before and after the crucifixion.

It is amazing how some of these stories give more details than a person can handle. I would think that the more details they give, the more believable their story would be, but this is simply not the case. For example, Muslim scholars said that Mary died five years after Jesus died and that she was fifty-three years old.[137] Another said that Jesus was thirty-four years old, but Fatmah said that Mohammed, the messenger of Allah, said that 'Isā lived 120 years. Mohammed told Fatmah, "That every prophet lived half of the age of the previous prophet, and I do not see myself to live sixty." Al Hafaz said that Fatmah said Mohammed said that Jesus lived forty years. Ibn Jarir

---

[137]Ibid., 113.

said Jesus lived forty years. The Prince of the Believers, Ali, said that 'Isā was ascended in the 22nd day of the month of Ramadan, and on a night like this night Ali died five days after he was stabbed. The lies go on and on and on, so I will stop here.

The True Story of the Crucifixion

In responding to the crucifixion of our Lord and Savior Jesus Christ, I would like to emphasize one important thing. The science of interpretation has never been taught to Muslim scholars, which is why I believe all their interpretations are nothing but fabrications. Proper interpretation means to understand what the original writer meant by what he wrote in the setting in which it was written, including the historical setting, as well the original recipients. The goal of proper interpretation is ultimately to apply that teaching into today's setting accurately. Throughout my study of the Qur'an, I cannot find any scholars that agreed on any one interpretation of almost every verse in the Qur'an because they begin their interpretation by stating, *scholars disagree.* Then they write different interpretations of what the verse means, many times their interpretations contradict each other completely, and finally they end their interpretation with the statement, *and Allah knows best.*

What a wonderful interpretation! When I said *fabrication,* it is simply because none of the words or information they share has any support in the verses of the Qur'an. As we saw in the previous case, the verses of the Qur'an which Ibn Kathir cited to prove that Jesus was not crucified were simply Qur'an 3:54-55 and Qur'an 4:155-159. However, Ibn Kathir's interpretation did not use any of these passages; he just made up stories without any historical, qur'anical, or archeological evidence. Crucifixion is the most important topic we can talk about, and there are many verses we will look at in the Qur'an. As we study all of these passages together, we will determine whether or not the crucifixion took place as the Qur'an states.

In Qur'an 3:185: *^{185}Every soul tastes the death…* means every person must die. I know we Christians believe that Enoch and Elijah did not die. However, the Qur'an teaches that they did, and that is what the Muslims believe. *Why not Jesus? Why did they not teach that the Jews killed Jesus?* The Muslim answer is that because he was a prophet and a messenger, and no one can kill the messengers of Allah. Therefore, I take my Muslim friends to Qur'an 5:70 where Allah said: *^{70}Indeed, we took the covenant of the children of Israel and sent messengers to them. Whenever a messenger* *came to them with what their soul did not desire, a group they denied and a group they are killing.* Also, in Qur'an 4:155: *[155]So because of their breaking their covenant and being infidels in the verses of Allah and their killing of the prophets unjustly and their saying, "Our hearts are uncircumcised." Yet Allah has taba'a[138] on it for their infidelity so that they will not believe except for a few.*

Notice the last two verses clearly teach that the Jews killed the messengers and the prophets of Allah. *Can any Muslim name any messenger or prophet the Jews killed?* Not even one, but as we will show you in the following paragraphs, Jesus Christ was killed, as even the Qur'an declared.

First, let us hear Jesus' own words as an infant, according to Qur'an 19:33-34: *[33]"And the peace be on me the day I was born and the day I die and the day I am raised alive." [34]This is 'Isā, son of Mary, the saying of truth about which they doubt.* A simple reading of the order of the words that baby Jesus spoke were the following: he was born, he would die, he would ascend alive into heaven, and these are exactly the words of truth. Some Muslims claim, as we have written above, that Jesus will come back, kill the pig, and break the cross.

Where do they come up with this fairy tale? If this were real, why didn't Allah or Gabreel insert these teachings into the Qur'an? Notice the same words here had been said earlier in the same book of the Qur'an by another prophet, as Muslims claim were in verse 15 concerning Yahyah (John the Baptist). *Does any Muslim believe that John the Baptist did not die; or that he will come back, kill the pig or some other animal, and break the cross or something else?* The answer is **absolutely not**, for all Muslims believe he did die. *Then why not Jesus?*

Second, we read in Qur'an 3:55: *[55]When Allah said, "O 'Isā (Jesus), surely I am causing you to die, and I am raising you up to me and purifying you from those who became infidels and make those who follow you above those who became infidels, until the resurrection day. Then to me is your return, so I will judge between you about what you were differing." What do we learn from this verse?* Here the word *motawafek* is in the present tense in the Arabic language meaning *I am causing you to die*, which

---

[138]sealed, non-Arabic word of Syriac origin

means the death of Jesus will take place at any time. Notice the order of the verse: death, rising, and purification.

Third, in Qur'an 5:117, 'Isā (Jesus) said: *¹¹⁷I did not tell them except what you had commanded me, 'That serve Allah, my lord and your lord,' and I was a witness among them as long as I was with them. So when you caused me to die, you were the watcher over them, and you are the witness of all things.*

This was the answer of Jesus to the question Allah asked in verse 116 which was whether or not Jesus had ever asked his people to worship him and his mother as gods. Here he denies this claim, which is an amazing question of Allah because no Christian ever believed in this lie. The important part here is the word of Jesus when he said to Allah, *falama tawafytany*, which when translated into English is *when you caused me to die*. This verb is written in the past tense which means the action of the verb had already been completed, which teaches that Jesus did die. Some Muslims lie in their modern translations (actually interpretations) and put the entire statement in the future tense meaning that Allah will ask Jesus in the future, as if this conversation between Jesus and Allah had not happened yet. I cannot imagine why people are so deceptive. They are purposely lying, even twisting the words of the Qur'an, in order to deny Jesus' death.

As for the verse which Ibn Kathir used above in Qur'an 3:54: *⁵⁴And they deceived, and Allah deceived. And Allah is the best deceiver. Is this how Muslims really view their god, that he is the best deceiver? Does he deceive all Christians when he performed some drama played out with his 'Isā (Jesus) and some of his followers?* If this were ever true, as I said earlier, this god must burn in hell. I believe 100 percent that the Allah of Mohammed is Satan who has deceived over a billion people and continues to deceive many millions more, by doing everything he can to tell the world that Jesus did not die for their sins, but he causes people to believe in Mohammed who is the so-called *Last Prophet.*

Now for the one single passage of the Qur'an which Ibn Kathir used to prove that Jesus did not die. We read in Qur'an 4:157-159: *¹⁵⁷And their saying, "Surely we killed the Christ 'Isā, son of Mary, the messenger of Allah." And they did not kill him, and they did not salaba[139] him; but it was made to appear to them, and surely those who disagree about him are in doubt of him.*

---

[139]crucify, non-Arabic word of Persian/Syriac origin

[203]

They do not have any knowledge of him except following the conjecture, and they did not kill him for certain. [158]Yet Allah raised him up to himself. And Allah was dear, wise. [159]And none of the People of the Book[140] will believe in him before his death. And on the resurrection day, he will be a witness against them.

We have already read how Ibn Kathir interpreted this verse above. I would like to ask a question. *Which came first, the killing or the crucifixion of Jesus?* It is amazing how the Qur'an puts these in the wrong order, and Muslim scholars do not admit the error of Mohammed's writings by his listing the killing before the crucifixion. This is obviously an error, for a person must be crucified first before death takes place. Even though I am not a Muslim scholar, I can easily interpret this verse in light of all the previous verses which I mentioned above as a true interpretation.

In the statement, *their saying*, who are *they*? They are the Jews. *Did the Jews say they killed the Christ? Or did they actually kill the Christ?* Both of these questions are answered by *no*. In simple words, it has been over two thousand years since Christ came, but Jews do not believe He came. As a matter of fact, they are still waiting for the coming of The Christ. *Who really killed Jesus?* Many people think that the Jews are the ones who killed Jesus, but that is not true. There were two persons involved in killing Jesus.

First, we must know that the Jews did not have any power to kill Jesus. We read this in John 18:31 where Pilate (the Roman prefect at the time) said to them to take Him and judge Him according to their law. The Jews answered him and said that they were not permitted to put anyone to death. However, it was necessary to fulfill the prophecy that He must be crucified. For example, we read in Psalm 22:16-18 that His hands and His feet must be pierced. If the Jews killed Jesus according to their law, they would have to have stoned him. If this would have happened, the Scripture would not have been fulfilled.

Pilate himself could not have killed Jesus. We see this in John 19:10-11 where Pilate asked Jesus if He didn't know that Pilate had the authority to free or crucify Him. Jesus answered him by telling Pilate that he had no authority over Him unless Pilate was given that authority from above. Notice Jesus' words clearly indicate that the authority of His crucifixion was given from above.

---

[140]Jews and Christians

So who took the life of Jesus? Clearly it was not the Jews or the Romans but God the Father Himself. Jesus (Yeshua) the Savior came to this world to do one thing and one thing only. He came to save His people from their sins, and He was crucified because God the Father sent Him to the cross. That was the first person who crucified Jesus. The second person who crucified Jesus was you and me. As it is written in John 3:16: *¹⁶For God so loved the world that He gave His only begotten Son, that whoever believes in Him should not perish but have everlasting life.* It was God and me. These are the two persons who crucified Jesus.

Now the questions I would like to ask are these. *Who does not want Jesus to be crucified? Who does not want anybody to be saved?* There's only one person, and his name is Satan. Since the only way we can be saved is through Jesus' death and resurrection, Satan will do everything he can to prevent people from believing in this truth. That's why I believe Mohammed has been led by Satan to deceive millions of Muslims.

It is amazing that we see 'Isā, the Jesus of Mohammed, not as a savior who came to save us from our sins, but a saved man who Allah saved from the cross when Allah caused someone else to die in his place. More than this, Allah did not save him openly, but he saved 'Isā in secret, which brought only deception for billions of Christians. After all, according to Qur'an 3:54, Allah is the best deceiver.

Therefore, I can interpret the rest of Qur'an 4:157-158 by saying that the Jews did not crucify 'Isā (Jesus) nor did they kill him. It was made to appear to them as if they had. They thought they killed Jesus with the help of Prefect Pilate. However, all their hope was gone as it is written in Qur'an 4:158: *¹⁵⁸Allah raised him up* with the true biblical language as we read in John 20, Matthew 28, Mark 16, and Luke 24, for Jesus had risen from the dead early Sunday morning. Although the Bible states that the Jews tried to do everything to spread the rumor that His body had been stolen, the Qur'an never made such a claim nor did any Muslim scholar's interpretation mention such a thing. Hundreds of eye witnesses saw Jesus alive with His resurrected and wounded body, with the nail marks in His hands and feet.

We can see this described in John 20:26-29, where Jesus asked Thomas, the disciple who doubted His resurrection, to put his finger in the wound scar on Jesus' hand and put his hand in the wound scar on Jesus' side. Then Thomas said, "My Lord and my God." At the time of the writing of the Gospel, which was more than twenty years later, there were at least five hundred eye witnesses still alive who saw Jesus, ate with Jesus, and touched Jesus (1 Corinthians 15:6).

Now, I would like to share with you a quick study of the crucifixion and resurrection of our Lord and Savior, Jesus Christ. All Muslims erroneously look at Judaism and the Old Testament as a religion. They claim that they themselves believe in the Torah of Moses and the Psalms of David. However, if you ask any of them if they have read these books, most likely they will answer that they have not because they believe these books are corrupted. They do not even know how many books are in the Old Testament. Muslims believe that Christianity is another separate religion which came to replace the Jewish religion. My prayer is that the following writings will help our Muslim friends to understand that neither Judaism nor Christianity is a religion but a faith.

Judaism is the foundation. In it we see the story of Creation, the fall of man to sin, and the Old Testament (the old covenant). It is a covenant between God and man. It is the sacrifice of pure animals, and through the shedding of their blood, men can receive covering for their sin and restoration. This can be seen throughout the Old Testament, as we have observed throughout this book. There are two common things about Adam, Abel, Noah, Abraham, Moses, Elijah, David, and others. First, they all sinned. Second, they all offered sacrifices for their sins. However, all of these sacrifices did not resolve the basic problem of the *sin nature* of men. The sacrifices offered by men were temporary and never sufficient in the eyes of God to the point that God hated these sacrifices of men.

God desired obedience rather than sacrifice (1 Samuel 15:22). Yet man never stopped sinning. Throughout the history of mankind, God spoke to men through other men called prophets. Promises were given from God to send a Savior, the Christ.

There are over three hundred prophecies written throughout the Old Testament concerning this Messiah, and I passionately believe that if Muslims were aware of theses prophecies and their fulfillment, their lives would be changed and many would accept Christ. The Christian faith is not a made-up religion by some early Christian apostles, but rather it is the fulfillment of all these prophecies. As I mentioned earlier, Christianity spread throughout the world in its first twenty years without one single line written in a New Testament section of the Bible, the Gospel. For that time, Christianity was simply the teaching of the prophecies of the Old Testament.

The spread of Christianity began after Jesus met with his disciples after the resurrection when He said to them (Luke 24:44-47) that this (all about the life of Jesus) is the word of which He spoke when He was with them and that all must be fulfilled which was written about Him in the law of Moses, the prophets, and the Psalms. Then Jesus opened their minds so that they could understand the books. He said that, as it was written, it must be fulfilled that Christ would suffer and rise from the dead on the third day and that repentance and forgiveness of sin must be preached in His name.

Therefore, I would like to point to some of the prophecies of the Old Testament, and I encourage you to read the entire Old Testament so you may see for yourself the truth of the only faith which can lead you to receive forgiveness for your sin and enable you to have eternal life.

We read what Mohammed wrote about the crucifixion of Christ in this one verse in Qur'an 4:157: *[157]And their saying, "Surely we killed the Christ 'Isā, son of Mary, the messenger of Allah." And they did not kill him, and they did not salaba[141] him; but it was made to appear to them, and surely those who disagree about him are in doubt of him. They do not have any knowledge of him except following the conjecture, and they did not kill him for certain.* We cannot find any information in this verse about how Allah saved Jesus or who the person was who allegedly died instead of him. This one lonely verse causes Muslim scholars to go in circles as they try to fabricate a story to fill the huge empty spaces of the Qur'an.

As we read above, all that the Muslims tried to do was unsuccessful just as it was when the Jews tried unsuccessfully to search for a false witness against Jesus. *Ask yourself the following question: Why does Islam reject the belief that Jesus would die on the cross on the behalf of someone else's sins, but at the same time, Allah teaches in the Qur'an that someone else died on the behalf of Jesus?*

A person might believe such lies if there was not a record of the true account in the Scriptures. As I mentioned earlier, the disciples of Jesus spread Christianity among the Jews with the written Scripture, meaning the Old Testament prophecies. What Muslims do not know about the Christian faith is that the crucifixion and resurrection of our Lord was not the invention of the disciples nor was it a surprise to Jesus or God the Father.

---

[141]crucify, non-Arabic word of Persian/Syriac origin

Jesus came to this world with the purpose stated in His name, Yeshua (Savior), to save His people from their sin. His purpose in coming was simply given in His name. We can easily read the prophecies of the Old Testament, even if we have no access to the New Testament. In the Old Testament alone, we see all the evidence needed to validate the deity, the crucifixion, the death, and the resurrection of our Lord and Savior Jesus Christ.

We will give a chart below showing some of the prophecies and the fulfillment of them. As for the record of what took place on that night before Jesus went to the cross, His burial, and His resurrection, it is recorded for us, not by one eye witness, but by many throughout the Bible. You can read the entire account in the Gospels, Matthew 26-28, Mark 14-16, Luke 22-24, and John 18-21. When you read this account in the Gospels, you will discover that there was no room for suggestion or fabrication because the record is clearly written. A simple reading will answer all questions.

Judas Iscariot betrayed Jesus for thirty pieces of silver. He died and the money was used to buy a cemetery (Matthew 27:6-8). This was simply to fulfill the following prophecies of the Old Testament: He was denied by Peter, judged before Caiaphas, Pilate found no sin in Him, but the Jews insisted that He must die. After scourging Jesus, Pilate gave the order to put Him to death.

He was crucified between two men. They took His garment and made four parts from it and cast lots for his coat without seams to fulfill the prophecy which was written a thousand years earlier. His mother and some other women were there near the cross. It was Jesus on the cross, not someone else, and He told the disciple whom He loved to take care of His mother. On the cross, Jesus asked God the Father to forgive those who crucified Him for they did not know what they were doing. Then He told one of the thieves who was crucified with Him that he would be with Jesus in paradise that day. He then said that He was thirsty, and they gave Him vinegar on a sponge. Then He said that He committed His spirit into the Father's hands. With these last words, Jesus gave up His spirit when He said, "It is finished."

Because it was the Sabbath, the soldiers decided to take the thieves off of the cross. They broke the legs of the thieves which caused them to die quickly due to suffocation since they could no longer lift themselves up to take a breath. As a soldier drew near to break Jesus' legs, he discovered that Jesus was already dead, so he pierced Jesus' side with a spear. Water and blood came out. This was to fulfill prophecies in the Old Testament in that no bones would be broken and that He must be pierced in His side. Joseph of Arimathea, after receiving permission from Pilate, took His body and buried Him. Nicodemus was there as well. Jesus was buried in Joseph's tomb which fulfilled another prophecy in the Old Testament. A huge rock was rolled over the door of the tomb.

On the first day of the week, after a great earthquake, an angel removed the rock from the door to the tomb. First, the women saw the empty tomb. The appearance of Jesus to the women is further evidence that this was not a fabrication. Then Peter and John saw the empty tomb. Even though they had access to the Scriptures, the disciples did not have the full understanding of the Scriptures. So they did not understand His death and resurrection.

Then Jesus appeared to Mary, and she told all of the disciples that she had seen the Lord. Jesus appeared to the disciples in a room even though the doors were closed because of their fear. He stood in the midst of them and said, "Peace be unto you." Jesus showed His disciples His side and His hands. It was not someone that looked like Jesus who went to the cross, but Jesus Himself, for He showed His hands and His side to the disciples, and they rejoiced. Thomas was not there, and he did not believe the other disciples. He said that he needed to see by his own eyes and touch by his own hands the print of the nails and pierced side of Jesus. Eight days later Jesus appeared to His disciples again, and He told Thomas to take his finger and touch the holes in His hands and His side. Thomas replied that Jesus was His Lord and God. Jesus appeared to His disciples many times.

There were over five hundred eyewitnesses who saw our resurrected Lord. Jesus opened their hearts to understand the Scripture, the Old Testament prophecies that He must suffer, be crucified, die, be buried, and on the third day He would rise from the dead. Then the disciples understood the Scriptures. Jesus met with His disciples and commanded them to meet Him at the mountain at Galilee. They worshiped Him. Jesus spoke to them and gave them the Great Commission.

Then He was taken up to heaven, and the clouds took Him from their sight. That was the beginning of the church. Please read the following prophecies of the Old Testament and their fulfillment in the New Testament, for the understanding of this information was what had been missing in the disciples. They did not have the full understanding of the Scripture and the prophecies in it, and it was only when Jesus opened these prophecies and explained them that they came to the full understanding of who Jesus is and all He had done. This could also be your situation.

As you read the Old Testament prophecy and its fulfillment in the New Testament, you will understand the true account of Jesus' birth, life, ministry, suffering, crucifixion, death, and resurrection.

Bible Prophecies and Fulfillments

	Prophecy	Description	Fulfillment
1	Genesis 3:15	The virgin birth ("seed of the woman") and He will bruise Satan's head	Luke 1:35 Hebrews 2:14
2	Genesis 12:3	As Abraham's descendant, He will bless all nations	Acts 3:25-26 Galatians 3:16
3	Genesis 22:8	The Lamb of God promised	John 1:29
4	Exodus 12:5	A Lamb without blemish	1 Pet. 1:19-20 Romans 5:8
5	Exodus 12:21-27	Christ is our Passover Lamb	1 Corinthians 5:7
6	Exodus 12:46	Not a bone of the Lamb to be broken	John 19:31-36
7	Numbers 21:9	The serpent on a pole pictured Christ lifted up on the cross	John 3:14-18
8	1 Chronicles 17:12-14	To reign on David's throne forever "I will be His Father, He will be my Son."	Luke 1:32, 33 Hebrews 1:5
9	Psalm 2:1-3	The trial and rage of kings and leaders against Christ	Acts 4:25-28
10	Psalm 2:7-8	Declared God's Son	Matthew 3:17
11	Psalm 16:9-11	Dead body was not to decay, the resurrection	Acts 2:31 John 20:9
12	Psalm 22:1	Forsaken because of the sins of others - Words spoken from the cross by Jesus, "My God..."	2 Corinthians 5:21 Mark 15:34
13	Psalm 22:7-8	They shoot out the lip and shake their heads - He trusted in God, let Him deliver Him	Matthew 27:39, 43

14	Psalm 22:14-15	Died of a ruptured heart Suffered agony on the cross - He thirsted	John 19:34 John 19:28
15	Psalm 22:16	His hands and feet to be pierced (an exact prediction of crucifixion hundreds of years before it was even invented)	John 19:16-18; 20:27
16	Psalm 22:17-18	They parted His garments They gamble for His clothing, "cast lots"	Luke 23:34-35 John 19:23-24
17	Psalm 27:12	Accused by false witnesses	Matthew 26:60-61
18	Psalm 31:5	"Into thy hands I commit my spirit"	Luke 23:46
19	Psalm 31:11	His own friends to flee	Mark 14:50
20	Psalm 35:19	He is to be hated without a cause	John 15:25
21	Psalm 55:12-14	Betrayed by a friend, not an enemy	John 13:18
22	Psalm 69:21	Given vinegar to drink for His thirst	Matthew 27:34
23	Psalm 72:10-11	Will be worshiped by foreign kings	Matthew 2:1-11
24	Psalm 72:17	In His name all nations shall be blessed	John 1:12-13 Acts 2:5-12, 41
25	Psalm 89:27	Emmanuel ("God with us") to be higher than earthly kings	Luke 1:32-33
26	Psalm 102:25-27	Messiah is the Preexistent Son, the Creator	Hebrews 1:10-12
27	Psalm 110:1	Ascends to the right-hand of God, the Father	Mark16:19 Acts 7:55
28	Psalm 110:4	A priest after Melchizedek's order	Hebrews 6:20-7:3
29	Psalm 118:22-23	The rejected stone becomes the head of the corner (foundational stone)	Matthew 21:42-43
30	Psalm 132:11	The Seed of David (fruit of His Body)	Luke 1:32
31	Proverb 30:4	Declared to be Son of God	John 3:13

32	Isaiah 7:14	He will be born of a virgin To be Emmanuel – "God with us"	Luke 1:35 Matthew 1:18-23
33	Isaiah 8:14	A stone of stumbling, a Rock of offense	1 Peter 2:8
34	Isaiah 9:1-2	His ministry to begin in Galilee	Matthew 4:12-17
35	Isaiah 9:6	A child born (His humanity) A Son given (His Deity)	Luke 1:31 Luke 1:32 John 1:14 1 Timothy 3:16
		Declared the Son of God with power The Wonderful One The Counselor The Mighty God The Everlasting Father The Prince of Peace	Romans 1:3-4 Luke 4:16-22 Matthew 13:54 Matthew 11:20 John 8:58 John 16:33
36	Isaiah 11:1	The Branch, A rod out of Jesse - (David's father)	Luke 3:23, 32
37	Isaiah 12:2	Called Yeshua (salvation)	Matthew 1:21
38	Isaiah 25:8	The Resurrection predicted	I Corinthians 15:53-54
39	Isaiah 40:3-4	To be preceded by a forerunner (John the Baptist)	John 1:23
40	Isaiah 42:1-4	The chosen one in whom God is pleased	Matthew 12:18-21
41	Isaiah 42:6	The Light (salvation) of the Gentiles	Luke 2:32
42	Isaiah 42:7	He will heal the blind	John 9:25-38
43	Isaiah 43:11	He is the only Savior	Acts 4:12
44	Isaiah 49:7	He is despised of the Nation	John 8:48-49
45	Isaiah 50:6	"I gave my back to the smiters." Jesus was flogged before His crucifixion He was beaten on the face He was spit upon	Matthew 27:26 Matthew 26:67 Matthew 27:30

46	Isaiah 52:13	The Servant exalted Behold, My Servant	Ephesians 1:19-22 Philippians 2:5-8
47	Isaiah 52:14	The Servant, Messiah, to be shockingly abused	Luke 18:31-34 Matthew 26:67-68
48	Isaiah 53:1	His own people would not believe Him	John 12:37-38
49	Isaiah 53:3	Despised Rejected Great sorrow and grief Men hide from being associated with Him	Luke 4:28-29 Matthew 27:21-23 Luke 19:41-42 Mark 14:50-52
50	Isaiah 53:4-5	He would bear the sins of the world Thought to be cursed by God His sacrifice would provide peace between man and God His back would be whipped	1 Peter 2:24 Matthew 27:41-43 Colossians 1:20 Matthew 27:26
51	Isaiah 53:6	He would be the sin-bearer for all mankind It is God's will that Jesus will bear the sin for all mankind	Galatians 1:4 1 John 4:10
52	Isaiah 53:7	Oppressed and afflicted Silent before accusers Sacrifice of the Lamb	Matthew 27:27-31 Matthew 27:12-14 John 1:29
53	Isaiah 53:8	Confined and persecuted He would be judged Killed Dies for the sins of the world	Matthew 26:47-27:31 John 18:13-22 Matthew 27:35 1 John 2:2

54	Isaiah 53:9	Buried in a rich man's grave	Matthew 27:57-60 Mark15:14 John 18:38
		Innocent & had done no sin No deceit in His mouth	
55	Isaiah 53:10	God's will that He die for mankind	John 18:11
		An offering for sin Resurrected & live forever He would prosper	Matthew 20:28 Mark 16:6 John 17:1-5
56	Isaiah 53:11	God fully satisfied with His suffering God's servant He would justify man before God The sin-bearer for all mankind	John 12:27 Romans. 5:18-19 Romans 5:8-9 Hebrews 9:28
57	Isaiah 53:12	Exalted by God because of His sacrifice He would give up His life to save mankind Grouped with criminals Sin-bearer for all mankind Intercede to God on behalf of mankind	Matthew 28:18 Luke 23:46 Luke 23:32 2 Corinthians 5:21 Luke 23:34
58	Isaiah 55:3	Resurrected by God	Acts 13:34
59	Isaiah 61:1-2	The Spirit of God upon him The Messiah would preach the good news Provide freedom from the bondage of sin and death Proclaim a period of grace	Matthew 3:16-17 Luke 4:17-21 John 8:27-33 John 5:24
60	Jeremiah 23:5-6	Descendant of David The Messiah would be God The Messiah would be both God and Man	Luke 3:23-31 John 13:13 1 Timothy 3:16
61	Daniel 2:34-35	Stone cut without hands	Acts 4:10-12

62	Daniel 2:44-45	His Kingdom Triumphant	Luke 1:33 1 Corinthians 15:24 Revelation 11:15
63	Hosea 11:1	His short stay in Egypt	Matthew 2:14
64	Micah 5:2	Born in Bethlehem From everlasting	Matthew 2:1-2 John 8:58
65	Zechariah 9:9	Greeted with rejoicing in Jerusalem Presented to Jerusalem riding on a donkey	Matthew 21:2-10
66	Zechariah 10:4	The cornerstone	Ephesians 2:20
67	Zechariah 11:12-13	Betrayed for thirty pieces of silver Thirty pieces of silver thrown into house of the Lord	Matthew 26:14-15 Matthew 27:3-5
68	Zechariah 12:10	The Messiah's body would be pierced The Messiah would be both God and Man The Messiah would be rejected	John 19:34-37 John 10:30 John 1:11

The Description of 'Isā

Ibn Kathir began this section by quoting three verses of the Qur'an.[142] First, he quoted Qur'an 5:75: *[75]The Christ, son of Mary, is nothing except a messenger; indeed, other messengers have gone before him, and his mother is a siddīqah.[143] They were eating the food. Look at how we show the verses to them, then look at how they turn away!* He interpreted this portion of the verse by saying that 'Isā was called the Christ, for He traveled throughout the land as a tourist. (The original Arabic verse is a play on words that the English reader cannot comprehend because of the language barrier.) Ibn Kathir claimed that 'Isā was escaping with his religion from the sedition of his time, for the Jews considered him a great liar

---

[142]Ibn Kathir, *Stories of the Prophets,*116.
[143]person of integrity, non-Arabic word of Aramaic origin

and treated him and his mother unjustly. It was said also that he was called the Christ because his feet were washed. Similar to the word *traveled*, the word *maseeh* is *Christ* in Arabic and is very similar to the word *mamsooh* which means *washed*.

Obviously, Ibn Kathir had no idea what *The Christ* meant, in the biblical languages, Hebrew and Greek. The word *Christ* means *the anointed one,* for kings in the Old Testament were anointed for a specific task, which was to lead God's people, the Jews. As we see Samuel anointed Saul as the first king in 1 Samuel 10 and when Samuel anointed David in 1 Samuel 16, these men and others were set apart as kings to lead the Jewish people for that specific time in history. Throughout the history of the Jewish nation, prophets came and prophesied of the coming of not *a* Christ but *the* Christ, which means that Jesus Christ was not just *a king* but, as the Scripture says, *the King of Kings, the Lord of Lords*.

His description was not given as a king to live in a castle or just to lead the people in wars to bring them victory over their enemies. Because the Jews misunderstood the prophecies, they did not believe in Him. They waited for the Christ who would deliver them from the Roman occupation, not the Christ who would deliver them from their own sin, the greatest enemy of all.

The reason the Jews were occupied and the reason war and chaos exists today is due to our one enemy, sin. The Scripture describes the Christ to be a suffering One, as it is written throughout the Old Testament prophecies. For example, the Prophet Isaiah wrote seven hundred years prior to the coming of Christ that He would suffer for the sin of the people. Through His suffering all would be healed, for all are as lost sheep, and the Lord put on Him the sin of the people (Isaiah 53).

One thousand years before Christ, King David also described Christ. As prophesied in Psalm 22, He would suffer exactly as it took place on the cross. This Christ was the answer for the cries of Job even hundreds of years before David when Job asked, ***Who can have his hand on both of us?***—meaning God and Job. In Job 9:33, Job was seeking an intercessor to reconcile himself with God, and this Intercessor is the man Jesus Christ. For there is one God, and there is one Mediator between God and man. His name is Jesus.

We can learn about this Intercessor in 1 John 2:1-2. He is the propitiation for the sin of the whole world. This is the Christ whom Muslim scholar Ibn Kathir did not know about. Christ is not the One who travels, but He came to fulfill the prophecies of the Old Testament. He is the One to reconcile man with God.

The second verse Ibn Kathir used to describe Jesus comes from Qur'an 5:46, but he mistakenly referenced it to Qur'an 57:47.[144] The correct verse is Qur'an 5:46: *[46]And in their footsteps we sent 'Isā, son of Mary, confirming what is between his hands of the Torah, and we gave him the Gospel, in it is guidance and light, and confirming what was between his hands from the Torah, and a guidance and a sermon to the fearer.* Amazingly, Ibn Kathir used this verse under the heading of the description of 'Isā, but he did not explain or interpret what is in it. Therefore, I would like to share some thoughts about it myself. Here the verse teaches that 'Isā, son of Mary, came to confirm the Torah which means that the Torah that existed in 'Isā's (Jesus') day was correct without any corruption. Therefore, Mohammed would not have said that 'Isā (Jesus) came to confirm a corrupt Torah. I personally believe that Jesus came not only to confirm the Torah, but as He said in His word, *to fulfill* the Torah. We read this in Matthew 5:17 when Jesus said, ***Do not think I came to destroy the law or the prophets but I came to fulfill.***

That is why I believe it is very important for Christians and Muslims to know what is written in the Old Testament concerning all the prophecies Jesus fulfilled. As for the words of the verse above saying that Jesus was given the gospel as guidance and light, once again Mohammed did not know the meaning of the word *Gospel.* Mohammed was thinking it was a book; in fact, it is the *Good News.* Jesus never received a book, for He is Himself the Word of God, and the Good News is that He came to fulfill the prophecies to die and to rise again, to be a substitute sacrifice for mankind, and through his resurrection we can be set free from the penalty of our own sin. This is the new covenant between God and man through the sacrifice of His own Son, Jesus Christ.

As for the last verse to describe 'Isā, Ibn Kathir used Qur'an 2:87: *...and we gave 'Isā,[145] son of Mary, the proofs and supported him by the qudus[146] spirit...[147]* This was another verse that Ibn Kathir listed but did not interpret. All he said after this verse was that "there are many verses that talk about the description of 'Isā, but from

---

[144]Ibn Kathir, 116.
[145]false name for Jesus, it would be Yasua in Arabic, non-Arabic word of Hebrew/Aramaic origin
[146]holy, non-Arabic word of Aramaic origin
[147]Ibn Kathir, 116.

[217]

this verse one can see that the proof has been given concerning who 'Isā is."

I would like to quote what Peter said in his first message when he stood to teach the truth about Jesus Christ's identity. I believe Qur'an 2:87 was an echoing of the words of Peter. Do not forget that as Peter finished his message, three thousand believed on Jesus' name and were baptized and added to the church. You can read his sermon in Acts 2:14-41. Here is a small portion of the message of Peter from verses 22-24: *²²Men of Israel, hear these words: Jesus of Nazareth, a Man attested by God to you by miracles, wonders, and signs which God did through Him in your midst, as you yourselves also know— ²³Him, being delivered by the determined purpose and foreknowledge of God, you have taken by lawless hands, have crucified, and put to death; ²⁴whom God raised up, having loosed the pains of death, because it was not possible that He should be held by it.*

We encourage the reader to read the entire message, but the important thing we must notice is who Peter was talking to and when. He was talking to the Jews, who were the ones who told Pilate the Prefect to crucify Jesus and the ones who said His blood would be on them and their children. That took place when Pilate said that Jesus was innocent. Also, this happened just a few days after the crucifixion took place.

These Jews knew exactly what Peter was talking about, and that's why the Bible said in verse 37 that when they heard this teaching, they were pierced to the heart and asked what they should do. Therefore, Peter said to them to believe in the name of the Lord Jesus Christ and be baptized. Not thirty or three hundred, but three thousand were saved and became Christians on that one day. Those people spoke at least thirteen different languages. Then they took the Gospel to their home countries, and that was the beginning of the church on earth.

Compared to Islam, this was not the same, for from the beginning of their religion until this day, almost 90 percent of Muslims have not heard the true message of Islam. Nor have they heard the truth about the Qur'an in their own language, and yet they are all Muslims without really understanding Islam.

Ibn Kathir listed many hadith stated by Mohammed that he saw Jesus, Moses, and Abraham. I do not believe Mohammed saw anyone, but he described seeing Jesus as being red, as if he came out of a hot shower, and having a large chest.[148] However, one hadith caught my attention where Mohammed said that Allah is not blind in one eye, but the antichrist is blind in his right eye. Mohammed claimed that he saw a man by the Kaaba. This man was a beautiful-looking man. His head was sweating, he was putting his hands on his shoulders, and he was circling the Kaaba; so Mohammed said, "Who is this?" They said, "The Christ, son of Mary." Then Mohammed saw another man, his right eye was blind, his hands were on his shoulders, and he was circling the house; so Mohammed asked, "Who is this?" They said, "This is the antichrist." In this hadith, Mohammed was saying that Allah does not have a blind eye. *Does this mean that Mohammed believed that the true Christ is God?* Jesus Christ did not have a blind eye, but the antichrist will.

Ibn Kathir included another hadith by Bukhari where he said that Abu Horyrah said, "Mohammed said 'Isā, son of Mary, saw a man stealing so he said to him, 'Did you steal?' He said, 'No. I swear by Allah there is no god but he.' So 'Isā said, 'I believe in Allah, and I call my eyes liars.'"[149] Ibn Kathir said that this is proof that Jesus was naïve with a good heart, for he believed that no one who would swear by the great Allah would lie. I would respond to this by saying that this is one of Mohammed's lies, for Jesus never saw such a person stealing and this conversation never took place. If it had happened, Jesus would not have had to see the man stealing or even to see that a theft had taken place because He knows such things without seeing them. If He had seen it, He would not change His mind just because the thief swore that he did not do it. Jesus was not just a simple naïve man. He is God in the flesh of man. He knows the mind of a man, even before a man speaks.

A good example of that can be found in Luke 7:36-50 when Jesus was invited for a meal at the Pharisee's house. While Jesus was eating the meal, a sinful woman from the city came to the house of the Pharisee and stood behind Jesus. She cried and began to wet Jesus' feet by her tears, she dried His feet by her hair, she kissed His feet, and she anointed His feet with perfume. The Pharisee who saw this happening thought to himself, speaking to himself in his mind, "If this was a prophet, he should know what kind of woman she is. She is a sinful woman."

---

[148]Ibid.
[149]Ibid., 116-117.

Surprise, surprise. Jesus knew what this Pharisee, Simon, was thinking. Then He taught Simon a good lesson about forgiveness. He also taught Simon that He knew what Simon was thinking. At the end of the story, Jesus told the woman that her sins were forgiven and to go and sin no more. We encourage the reader to read the entire story in the Scripture, for this story alone is another great proof that Jesus is God who forgives sin and that God knows what man is thinking; for the Scripture states that no one can read the mind of man, for only the Lord knows the thoughts of men (Psalm 94:11).

Another hadith given by Abu Horyrah that Mohammed said that all prophets are paternal brothers and their religion is one and they have different mothers and he was preferred over 'Isā, son of Mary, because there was no prophet between him and 'Isā.[150] And he ('Isā) will descend from heaven, so if you see him, then know him. He is red and white. Water dropped off his head even if he did not get wet. He would break the cross, he will kill the pig, and he will establish the tribute tax. He will end the religion in his time except for Islam. In his time, Allah will destroy the antichrist. Peace and security will take place on earth. The camels will lay down with the lions, tigers with the cow, and wolves with the sheep. Young boys will play with snakes, and they will not harm them. He will dwell wherever Allah will allow him to dwell, and then Allah will cause him to die. So all the Muslims pray over him, and they will bury him.

Some other scholar stated that 'Isā (Jesus) will live on earth forty years. Then Ibn Kathir closed with this portion of his interpretation of Qur'an 4:159: *[159]And none of the People of the Book will believe in him before his death. And on the resurrection day, he will be a witness against them.*

When we read this verse, we see that if Christ did not die, no one should believe in Jesus today, for the verse teaches that no one will believe in Jesus until He dies. When we read Qur'an 3:55 where Allah said: *...and make those who follow you above those who became infidels, until the resurrection day...*, we discover that Allah promised 'Isā that his followers will be above the infidels until the day of resurrection. *I ask, once again, where are these believers in Jesus? Did He die, or did He not? If He didn't die, how can He have followers who believed in Him? He had followers; therefore, He must have died.*

---

[150]Ibid., 118.

Ibn Kathir stated that Ibn Haban said Mohammed said Allah took the life of David while he was among his companions.[151] So they did not commit any sedition or change, and the companions of Christ (Christians) stayed on his religion (Christianity) and on his guidance for two hundred years. According to Ibn Haban and Ibn Kathir, this hadith alone proves that Christianity was true without any corruption for at least two hundred years. As we know historically, during this time, Christianity spread abroad in many languages. This proves that Christians in the world, who were in accord with the Christianity of the Bible, could not be infidels.

It is impossible for anyone to collect all the manuscripts, change them, and then bury them again. The manuscripts which have been discovered recently, date back before the end of the first two hundred years after Christ. They are an amazing match to the Bible we have in our hands today.

Ibn Kathir said that Ibn Jarir said before 'Isā ascended "he encouraged his disciples to call the people to worship Allah alone without any partner.[152] He appointed to everyone a country between Sham (Lebanon, Syria, Jordan, and Israel) and the countries of the West. They mentioned that each one of them speaks the language of those whom the Christ sent them to." Perhaps Ibn Jarir here was talking about the Great Commission which is recorded in Matthew 28:19 where Jesus said to his disciples to: ***Go therefore and make disciples of all the nations, baptizing them in the name of the Father and of the Son and of the Holy Spirit.***

This was what happened when Jesus sent his disciples to all the nations. As for the language that they spoke, perhaps Ibn Jarir is hinting at Acts 2 which tells of what took place on the day of Pentecost. The problem here was that the disciples did not go to different countries to speak the different languages, but people from different countries with different languages went to Jerusalem. Even though the disciples were all Galileans, they were able to speak the language of all those visitors in Jerusalem because the Holy Spirit filled the disciples and caused them to speak different languages and different dialects. That was how three thousand people were saved on the first day after hearing the first message of Apostle Peter, as we mentioned previously.

---

[151]Ibid., 120.
[152]Ibid.

Ibn Kathir stated that Ibn Jarir continued by saying, "And someone said that the Gospel was written by four: Luke, Matthew, Mark, and John. These four Gospels vary. Some of them are big, and some of them are small. Two of these four men knew the Christ and saw Him, and they were Matthew and John. And two were companions of his companions, and they were Mark and Luke."[153]

What a great way to find the truth and evidence of Muslims writing of the existence of the four Gospels. They even named them correctly and gave us more details correctly and truthfully that Matthew and John were disciples of Jesus. As for Mark, he was a disciple of Peter who wrote the Gospel of Mark. As for Luke, he was a disciple of Paul who wrote the Gospel of Luke and the book of Acts. Many times I have heard Muslims make fun of the four Gospels, for they believe that these four Gospels are a fraud because they simply believe that there is only one gospel, the gospel of Jesus. I wish such people would read what Ibn Kathir and Ibn Jarir wrote.

Let us see what else Ibn Jarir said. He wrote that there was one of the men (Daynan) who believed in Christ from the people of Damascus, and he was hiding inside a cave near the Church of the Crucifix. He was afraid of Paul the Jew, who was unjust and hated Christ, so when Paul came to him, Paul stoned him until he died, may the mercy of Allah be on him. When Paul heard that Christ went to Damascus, he prepared his mule and went to fight Christ. So he met him at a star (the author has no idea the meaning of the previous statement), so when Paul met the companion of Christ, an angel came to him and struck his face with the tip of his wings.

The angel blinded Paul so when he became blind, he believed in Christ. So Paul came to 'Isā (Jesus) and apologized for what he had done and believed in 'Isā, and so 'Isā accepted his apology and Paul asked 'Isā if he will wipe out his eyes that Allah may return his sight. He said to him to go to Damascus at the edge of the market from the east, and he would pray for him. He came to him and prayed for him so he gained his sight back, and the belief of Paul in Christ was good. He was the servant of Allah and his messenger, and a church was built by his name, the Church of Paul, the famous one in Damascus. From the time it was invaded by the companions, may Allah be pleased by him until it was destroyed. *I wonder if you can guess who destroyed this church?* Oh, it was the Muslims!

---

[153]Ibid.

When I read such a long story, it reminds me of the Qur'an itself, for Mohammed, in the writing of the Qur'an and the stories of the prophets, did exactly what Ibn Jarir did here. He picked names and stories and mixed them together. Since most Muslims do not really know what is written in the Bible, they do not realize that Mohammed just made up stories in his Qur'an.

First, I am assuming Ibn Jarir is talking about the stoning of Stephen. Paul, who was known as Saul at that time, was involved in the stoning of Stephen, for he stood by the clothes of the men who stoned Stephen. Stephen did not hide in some cave near the church as Ibn Jarir claimed, for there was no church building built at this time, and he was not afraid of Paul or anyone. We encourage the reader to read the entire account in Acts 6:9-7:60. It is a great testimony of the wonderful first Christian martyr for Jesus.

Second, Ibn Jarir moved to Saul's story when he went to Damascus to seek and to persecute all the Christians there. Saul did not go to Damascus to find Jesus for Jesus had already ascended to heaven after the resurrection. We also encourage the reader to read the testimony of how Paul met Jesus on his way to Damascus, found in Acts 9.

I believe the confusion of Ibn Jarir concerning the meeting of Jesus and Paul is the misunderstanding of the conversation which took place after Saul (Paul) became blinded from the bright light. When we Christians say that Paul met Jesus on his way to Damascus, it is the same when people come to know Jesus (get saved). We say that they *met* Jesus. It is a figure of speech to mean "know/believe" in Jesus. However, in Paul's testimony, he met Jesus and actually talked with Jesus, even though he could not see Jesus. Paul said to the voice he was hearing, "Who are you, Lord?" And the answer was, "I am Jesus whom you persecute."

As for how Paul received his sight, it was not Jesus who healed him, as Ibn Jarir erroneously stated, but he was healed by a Christian man in Damascus by the name of Ananias. As for the life of Paul and his ministries, read the rest of Acts and the wonderful letters he wrote throughout the New Testament. One third of the New Testament was written by Paul.

It is amazing how many books have been written lately to belittle Apostle Paul. These Muslim authors attack Christianity by claiming that the Christianity of Paul is not the Christianity of Jesus. Sadly, all of these Muslims have not read Paul's writings or the writings of any of the apostles of Jesus. The Christianity of Paul is the same

Christianity of Peter, John, James, Jude, Matthew, Mark, and Luke; they all teach the same message, the Christian faith message – God loves you. He sent His son, Jesus Christ, to die for you. He rose from the dead on the third day. All of this was the fulfillment of all that had been written through the Torah, the prophets, and the Psalms.

The Disagreement Among the Companions of Christ

Ibn Kathir stated that Ibn Abbas and others said some of the Christians believed that 'Isā was the servant of Allah and his messenger and that he was ascended to heaven.[154] The second group said that he was god, and the third group said that he was the son of god. The first group was the true believers; as for the other groups, they were infidels. Ibn Kathir continued by stating that they were in disagreement in passing down the gospel with four sayings, one they added, another they took away, the third way they changed, and the fourth one they exchanged. Then he stated that three hundred years later, the great disaster took place when the leaders of the church, elders, pastors, deacons, and monks, disagreed about Christ on numerous disagreements and could not be fixed. They assembled before King Constantine, and this was the first council.

The king agreed with the saying of the large group, and they destroyed those who were against them from the group who followed the servant of Allah, Ibn Adyos. This proved that 'Isā was a slave among the servants of Allah and a messenger of the messengers of Allah. They lived in the desert and valleys. They built places to live and places to worship, and they had a simple way of life. They did not mingle with the other groups who built the big churches, they matched what it was from the buildings of the Greeks, and they took their places of worship to the east and the west.

Since the beginning of the church, just as Paul wrote, there have been many heresies from within the church. I believe that our greatest enemy is not those who are outside of the faith like Muslims, but rather those from within the church who claim to be Christians. Our Lord Jesus and Apostle Paul both described such false believers as wolves in sheep's clothing. The church has done a great job of disputing such heresies in the past, but even today heresy exists.

One of the new heresies that exists in the West which has flourished in the past ten years is called the interfaith denomination or the coexist cult. This is when Christians, Muslims, Jews, Buddhists,

---

[154]Ibid., 121.

and other religions get together and hold hands and sing "Kumbaya" or the purple dinosaur Barney's famous hymn: "I love you, you love me, we're a happy family!"

Another group flourishing for the last few years is Chrislam. That is where liberal Christians and Muslims join together and worship together.

During the month of January 2012, I attended an interfaith meeting which took place at the University of Orlando, Florida. There were roughly thirty-five people at the meeting. This was a group which had been meeting for around ten years. That night, they had their largest group because at least half of those attending were my friends. We had two cameras in the room, which was a public place. The leader of the meeting that night was a minister, a wolf in sheep's skin, from a large church in the Orlando area. He was the same gentleman who kicked me out of his church a year earlier.

He prolonged the meeting by having each person introduce themselves and tell some information about themselves. When the meeting started, he said, "I noticed that there are two cameras here today. In our previous meetings, we have not had cameras." He continued by asking the question, "Does anyone here object to having these cameras?" The Muslim imam, who used to be a Christian minister, and the lady in hajab (Muslim dress) said that they objected to having cameras in the room; therefore, he gave the order that the cameras must be shut down. However, the people that were with me said to leave the cameras on. He said, "We will turn off the cameras."

I stood up and spoke very loudly and clearly. "These two cameras will not be turned off until the end of the meeting. Anyone who is uncomfortable to be on camera, he or she is welcome to leave the meeting." Another gentleman in the room stood up and said to me, "Who do you think you are to make this decision?" With a firm voice, I said to him, "I am a citizen of the United States of America, a resident of the state of Florida, and I know what the law says concerning the use of a public place." He thought that the cameras were mine, but I assured him that they were not my cameras. I also stated that as a taxpayer that even the electricity being used in that room was costing me money. I told him that the best thing that he could do was to dial 9-1-1, and I assured him that when the police would come that they would explain to him that this is a public place, a public meeting, and the owners of these cameras have all the rights to record the meeting.

Two of their men came to speak with me privately and tried to persuade me to change my mind. I asked them, "Are you speaking against the Constitution of the United States of America? Are you saying anything illegal in the meeting?" They had no answer. The wolf in sheep's skin said that the meeting was adjourned, and then he, along with the leaders of these cults, left the room. One man asked what I was going to do with the videos. I said, "In a few moments they will be on YouTube," and they are. You can go online and watch at here: http://www.youtube.com/watch?v=PAAPYkNdPvQ.

Dear readers, how can you stop such wicked cults in the West? It is very simple. You need to attend these meetings, take your cameras with you, and expose their lies on the internet and in your churches. I promise you, every time a camera shows up in any of these meetings, the leaders of the meeting will cancel it. If not, please send me a copy of the video.

The gathering of different cults is, first, the direct result of not knowing the Christian doctrine. Second, they are ignorant of other cults and religious beliefs. For example, Christians who worship with Muslims, believing that we worship the same God, are not aware that Jesus Christ is God Almighty, come in the flesh, the second Person of the Trinity. Third, they do not know that the Qur'an does not teach that Jesus is God or the Son of God. As a matter of fact, those who believe that Jesus is God or the Son of God are called infidels and must be put to death.

How can they, from opposite beliefs, get together and worship? Some of the early heretics, as mentioned by Ibn Kathir above, were those who claimed that Jesus was just a man, simply because they looked at all the verses in the Scripture that clearly teach the humanity of Jesus. Other heretics, such as those who look at Christ as being only divine and without flesh, support their heresy by using only the verses that attest to His power, authority, and sinlessness. The church addressed these heresies by balancing the written Word because Christianity is not what someone claims or does but what is expressed in the Scripture.

The saying of Ibn Kathir that the leaders of the church in the fourth century were in chaos, not knowing Christian doctrine, cannot be any further away from the truth. The claim that Christianity was changed to what it is today as a result of King Constantine's authority also is a twisted view of what happened at the Council of Nicaea.[155]

---

[155]Ibid., 121-122.

The truth is that Constantine became a Christian, and the persecution of Christians ended as he declared Christianity to be the accepted faith. All he did at this council included inviting all Christian bishops (not pastors, deacons, elders, or priests as Ibn Kathir claims) to meet at the council. There were around 318 bishops out of 1,800 who were invited that attended the council. Many Muslims claim that there was a large division; but the truth is that the vote, after the reading of the Scripture concerning the nature of Christ, was only two in favor of the heresy (both from Libya) and the other 316 in favor of the Christian truth.

Arianism developed around AD 320, in Alexandria, Egypt, concerning the person of Christ and was named after Arius of Alexandria.[156] For his doctrinal teaching, he was exiled to Illyria in 325 after the first ecumenical council at Nicaea condemned his teaching as heresy. It was the greatest of heresies within the early church that developed a significant following. Some say it almost took over the church. Arius taught that only God the Father was eternal and too pure and infinite to appear on the earth. Therefore, God produced Christ the Son out of nothing as the first and greatest creation. The Son is then the one who created the universe. Because the Son's relationship to the Father is not one of nature, it is, therefore, adoptive. God adopted Christ as the Son.

Though Christ was a creation, because of his great position and authority, he was to be worshiped and even looked upon as God. Some Arians even held that the Holy Spirit was the first and greatest creation of the Son. At Jesus' incarnation, the Arians asserted that the divine quality of the Son, the Logos, took the place of the human and spiritual aspect of Jesus, thereby denying the full and complete incarnation of God the Son, second Person of the Trinity. In asserting that Christ the Son, as a created thing, was to be worshiped, the Arians were advocating idolatry.

Docetism was an error with several variations concerning the nature of Christ.[157] Generally, it taught that Jesus only appeared to have a body, that he was not really incarnate (Greek, "dokeo" = to seem). This error developed out of the dualistic philosophy which viewed matter as inherently evil, that God could not be associated with matter, and that God, being perfect and infinite, could not suffer.

---

[156]Matt Slick, "Arianism," *Christian Apologetics and Research Ministry*, accessed January 29, 2011, http://carm.org/arianism.
[157]Matt Slick, "Docetism," *Christian Apologetics and Research Ministry*, accessed January 29, 2011, http://carm.org/docetism.

Therefore, God as the Word, could not have become flesh. In John 1:1, 14: *¹In the beginning was the Word, and the Word was with God, and the Word was God. ¹⁴And the Word became flesh and dwelt among us, and we beheld His glory, the glory as of the only begotten of the Father, full of grace and truth.* This denial of a true incarnation meant that Jesus did not truly suffer on the cross and that He did not rise from the dead.

The basic principle of Docetism was refuted by the Apostle John in 1 John 4:2-3. *²By this you know the Spirit of God: Every spirit that confesses that Jesus Christ has come in the flesh is of God, ³and every spirit that does not confess that Jesus Christ has come in the flesh is not of God. And this is the spirit of the Antichrist, which you have heard was coming, and is now already in the world.* Also, in 2 John 7: *For many deceivers have gone out into the world who do not confess Jesus Christ as coming in the flesh. This is a deceiver and an antichrist.*

This erroneous belief was refuted and defeated by early fathers of the church like Ignatius of Antioch (died around 110) and Irenaeus (AD 115-190) and Hippolatus (AD 170-235) who wrote against the error in the early part of the second century. Docetism was also condemned at the Council of Chalcedon in 451.

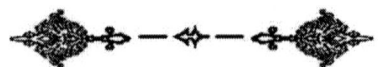

33 *The Story of*
The Building of Bethlehem and
the Church of the Crucifixion

When Ibn Kathir wrote that the king of Constantinople built Bethlehem, he obviously meant the Church of the Nativity, the same place where Christ was born, and that his mother Helana built Al Kmamah, a word in Arabic which means *trash*.[1] I researched this word in Ibn Kathir's online book and in his printed book, and in both places it is written the same way. I assume that this was either an error in writing the word or, quite possibly, a play on words as an intentional insult to Christians because the word in Arabic is not Al Kmamah (The Trash), but **Al Kyamah** which means *The Resurrection*. Ibn Kathir said these people became infidels, they made new laws and the judgments, and some of them disagreed with what was written in the Torah.

Ibn Kathir continued by saying that the Christians made many things lawful which were forbidden, such as eating pigs, praying towards the east, and having pictures in the church. They set their doctrines; and their children, their women, and their men had to memorize it. They called it faithfulness, but it is in fact the biggest infidelity and betrayal of all. Many different denominations believe in it, but they disagree in its interpretation.

Ibn Kathir continued by saying that he "[is] here to recite the recitation of the infidelity, but this will not be a sin" for him because it is just full of words without value and words of infidelity, which causes the one who believes it to go to hell.[2] They (Christians) say the following creed:

> We believe in one God, the Father, the Almighty maker of heaven and earth, of all that is seen and unseen. We believe in one Lord, Jesus Christ, the only Son of God, eternally begotten of the Father, God from God, Light from Light, true God from true God, begotten, not made, one in being with the Father. Through Him all things were made. For mankind and for our salvation He came down from heaven by the power of the Holy Spirit, He was born of the Virgin Mary, and became man. For our sake, He was crucified under Pontius Pilate; He

---

[1] Ibn Kathir, *Stories of the Prophets*, vol. 2, Abo Al Fida Ishamail Ibn Kathir Al Kurashi Al Damashce (Beirut: Dar Al-Arab Heritage, 1408 AH, 1988), 121.
[2] Ibid., 122.

suffered, died, and was buried. On the third day He rose again in fulfillment of the Scriptures; He ascended into heaven and is seated at the right hand of the Father. He will come again in glory to judge the living and the dead, and his kingdom will have no end. We believe in the Holy Spirit, the Lord, the giver of Life, who proceeds from the Father and the Son. With the Father and the Son, He is worshiped and glorified. He has spoken through the prophets. We believe in one holy catholic and apostolic Church. We acknowledge one baptism for the forgiveness of sins. We look for the resurrection of the dead, and the life of the world to come. Amen.

Here we see Ibn Kathir calling our Christian faith, our doctrines, our beliefs *infidelity and sin*. Muslims do not see any wrongdoing for repeating what their Muslim scholars claim. I do not believe any Christians have asked for or demanded an apology. I do not believe that the church has commanded the Muslims to remove such a great insult to all Christians out of their books. Therefore, with the freedom of speech and freedom of religion, I believe Christians have the right to express their feelings freely, concerning the wicked cult of Islam and the falsehood of Mohammed's prophecy and the error of his Qur'an, and I will not give an apology for what is written in this book or what is yet to come in the following pages.

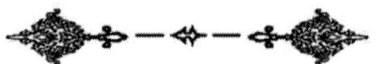

The Story of Alexander the Great

Ibn Kathir stated that Allah mentioned Za Al Qarnain[1] (Alexander the Great), who was a just man as he traveled to the east and the west as an invader, and that he ruled over the world.[2] Ibn Kathir bragged about him. He stated that Zu Al Qarnain was a prophet, and others stated that he was a messenger. What is even stranger is that Ibn Kathir stated that others believed that he was one of the angels. It was stated by the Prince of the Believers, Omar, that he heard a man calling another, "'O Zu Al Qarnain,' so he said, 'Isn't it enough that you name your sons after the prophets that you now name yourself after the angels?'" It was said by Abu Horyrah that Mohammed said that he did not know whether Zu Al Qarnain was a prophet or not.

Isaac Ibn Bashier stated that Ibn Abbas said that Zu Al Qarnain was a righteous king and The Green (Al Kadar, the prophet in chapter 18) was like a prince in his army and took advice from him.[3] Al Azroqee mentioned that Zu Al Qarnain became a Muslim by the hand of Abraham and circled the Kaaba with Ishmael and Abraham. Odeida said that Zu Al Qarnain performed the pilgrimage walking on foot.[4] When Abraham heard of his coming, he met with him and called on Allah for him. Allah subjugated the clouds for him so they carried him wherever he wished to go. This baloney reminds me of Aladdin and the flying carpet. He ended this lie by saying, *and Allah knows best.*

Scholars disagree why he was named Zu Al Qarnain. Some say he used to have on his head what looked like two horns which is the meaning of the name Zu Al Qarnain. Wahab Ibn Monabah said he used to have two horns of brass. Some Muslim scholars claim that the People of the Book said that it was because he was king over Rome and Persia; it was also said it was because he was in control of the sun and the west and the east and that he was a king over all the land in

---

[1]Notice the name of this character has different spellings as written in Arabic in the Qur'an.

[2]Ibn Kathir, *Stories of the Prophets*, vol. 2, Abo Al Fida Ishamail Ibn Kathir Al Kurashi Al Damashce (Beirut: Dar Al-Arab Heritage, 1408 AH, 1988), 123.

[3]Ibid., 123.

[4]Ibid., 124.

between the east and the west. Of course, this is a surprising claim, since the People of the Book (Christians and Jews) do not consider Alexander the Great a prophet. Al Hasan said that because he had two braids, he was called Zu Al Qarnain. Many other fabrications have been given for why he was named Zu Al Qarnain. Some Arabs have written poetry for Zu Al Qarnain. Many Muslims have given him many names, which is another proof that they do not truly know the identity of this man.[5]

Some say his name was Marzipan Ibn Marzbah, Afriedon Ibn Assfayan, Hermes, or Horwes. Ibn Kathir ended these fabrications by stating, *and Allah knows best*. Isaac Ibn Bashier said that Qatadah said that he was Alexander, that his father was the first czar, and that he was a descendant of Shem Ibn Noah. He apparently suggested that there were two Zu Al Qarnains (Alexanders the Great) when he said that as for the second Zu Al Qarnain, he was Alexander Ibn Philips, Ibn Masreem, Ibn Hermes, and the names go on and on. He was the Greek, Macedonian, and Mizrain who built Alexandria of Egypt, and he came later after the first Alexander. This was around three hundred years before the days of Christ. He was the one who had victories over many kings. Mohammed, the self-proclaimed prophet of Islam, said that he was the one who built the city of Alexandria in Egypt and that this was great evidence that he was Alexander the Great.[6]

Another proof that Muslims believed that there were two Zu Al Qarnains comes from Ibn Kathir, who said that the first Zu Al Qarnain was a servant, righteous believer, and just king; this is the one that Allah mentions in the Qur'an.[7] As for the second Zu Al Qarnain, Ibn Kathir continued by saying that he was a polytheist, a philosopher, and a minister; and the distance between these two Zu Al Qarnains was two thousand years.

Obviously, there is much confusion about who Alexander the Great, Zu Al Qarnain, was. Historically, there was only one Alexander the Great, who is well known. A simple online search will bring solid facts and plenty of information which is readily known to any historian. As for the fabrication of the existence of two Alexanders, it is a cover-up by Muslim scholars to tie such a character to Abraham, who obviously lived fifteen hundred years or so earlier than Alexander the Great. Alexander the Great was not a prophet, a

---

[5] Ibid., 125.
[6] http://quran.al-islam.com/Page.aspx?pageid=221&BookID=13&Page=302, accessed February 4, 2011.
[7] Ibid., 126.

messenger, or an angel; nor did he or anyone else claim that he was. He was not a just leader; he claimed to be a god. Instead, he was an ungodly invader. All of the historical pictures or statues do not show any horns. He died at age thirty-two. He never met with Abraham, and he was not a Muslim. As for the claim of Ibn Kathir that there were two Alexanders the Great, the first being a righteous believer and just king while the second was alleged to be an ungodly polytheist philosopher, the timeline between them was two thousand years.[8]

What is so amazing is that Ibn Kathir stated that they were not equal, they were not alike, and anyone who confuses themselves between the two does not know the facts of the matter and is foolish! The fact is that the foolish ones are Ibn Kathir and those who follow these lies. There was only one Alexander the Great historically, and it cannot be proven otherwise. As we study the story of the Qur'an, this evidence will become even stronger.

Qur'an 18:83 states: *[83]They ask you about Ze Al Qarnain.[9] Say, "I will recite to you an account of him."* The reason this verse was given was because the Jews of Quraish asked to examine the knowledge of Mohammed. That is why Allah sent down the story of Zu Al Qarnain. Allah stated that he made his kingdom the width of the countries. Ibn Kathir stated that Qatadah said that a man asked Ali Ibn Abu Talb about Zu Al Qarnain as to how he reached the easts and the wests.[10] He answered the man by saying that Allah subjugated the clouds to him. Allah made the light to cover the night so that it became like day to him. Allah also stretched the roads for him (which is allegedly another proof that it was Alexander the Great because, in his time, Rome made roads all over the known world). *Doesn't this sound like a fairy tale, my dear readers?*

Ibn Kathir went on and on to tell the story about four kings who ruled the world.[11] Two were believers, and two were infidels. He counted King Solomon and Alexander the Great to be the believers. Nimrod and Nebuchadnezzar were the infidel kings. Ibn Kathir said that Abi Isaac al Subaie said that he used to invade the cities and

---

[8]Ibid.

[9]the one with two horns and according to Muslim scholars this is Alexander the Great. See http://quran.al-islam.com/Page.aspx?pageid=221&BookID=13&Page=302, accessed October 2, 2011.

[10]Ibn Kathir, 126.

[11]Ibid., 127.

collect the treasures, so if anybody followed him and converted to his religion, that person would live; otherwise, he would kill him.

Here we find the real reason Mohammed picked up the story of Alexander the Great in order to make him a great prophet. It was used as leverage to justify Mohammed's actions of invading countries and people around him because if it was good for Alexander the Great, it was good for Mohammed. Perhaps Mohammed idolized Alexander the Great because he dreamed of being a great military leader, conqueror, and plunderer like Alexander who could force others to accept his religion.

Continue reading in Qur'an 18:84: *[84]Surely we established him on the earth, and we gave him from everything a way.* Scholars gave different interpretations of this verse. Ibn Abbas stated that Alexander the Great was given knowledge. Abd Al Rhoman said Allah gave Alexander the knowledge of the languages; therefore, he spoke to the people he invaded in their own languages. Qatadah stated that he knew the landmarks of the earth and where it (the earth) was located. The truth is that Alexander took what he needed for his kingdom from every place he went. He used to take supplies, food, and goods, which enabled him to take over other regions. Ibn Kathir said that the People of the Book (Christians and Jews) mentioned that he lived sixteen hundred years traveling all over the earth calling the people to worship Allah alone without any partner. He concluded that he was not sure of the length of this time, *and Allah knows best.*

What about the People of the Book? What Christian or Jew made such a claim? With all types of fabrication and nonsense, Ibn Kathir doubted a lie concerning the time period of the life of Alexander the Great, which he himself made up! I wonder if Muslims really believe that Christians or Jews made up such a lie. Once again, I assure readers that not one Christian or Jew believes that Alexander the Great, or anyone, lived sixteen hundred years!

Qur'an 18:85-86a continues by stating: *[85]So he followed a way, [86]until when he reached the setting of the sun, he found it set in a muddy spring....* Ibn Kathir did his best to interpret these words so as to remove a great error of Allah in the Qur'an, the error of the setting of the sun in a muddy spring.[12] He interpreted it by stating that Alexander the Great traveled on the earth until he reached the far west of the earth where the earth begins and the west ocean is and that he saw the setting of the sun through his eyes. The meaning of the

---

[12]Ibid., 127-128.

setting of the sun in the muddy spring is that it looked like it was setting in the mud. Ibn Kathir said that Allah did not say that the sun was setting in the muddy spring, but that it *looked like it was setting in the muddy spring.*

Obviously, Ibn Kathir's attempt was not very successful, for Allah's words are in the Qur'an, and it is very clear, for it is written that "he found it set in a muddy spring." Allah did not say that it was in the west ocean as Ibn Kathir claimed, but he found it had set in a muddy spring. When Mohammed saw the sun set, he said, "In the raging fire of Allah, the hot. If Allah did not move it with his command, it will burn all that is on the earth." Also, in the interpretation by Al Bydawy, he stated that the word *hamayah* (muddy) means water and mud.

In Al Tabari's interpretation of this verse, he mentioned that Ibn Abbas said that the sun set in black mud.[13] Ibn Kathir said that some claim that Zu Al Qarnain traveled beyond the setting of the sun with his army in the darkness for many years.[14] He said that whoever believed in such a lie has been misled, for this teaching stands against reality and understanding. Ibn Kathir said that another fairy tale concerning Zu Al Qarnain was that he used to have one of the angels as a friend. He asked this angel about this place of the spring of life. The angel told him about this place, and he went to search for it with The Green. The Green arrived there before him, and it was in the valley of darkness. He drank from it, but Zu Al Qarnain was not able to find the place.

Then in Qur'an 18:86-87, Allah said: *[86]... and he found a people by it. We said, "O Za Al Qarnain, either that you torment them or that you do good to them." [87]He said, "As for those who are unjust so we will torment. Then he will be returned to his lord, so he will torment him with a horrible torment.* Ibn Kathir interpreted this by stating that the torment of the world's life and of the hereafter will be joined against the infidel. Then Allah began by the torment of this world.

As for verse 88: *[88]And as to him who believed and did good deed, so he will have the reward of the good, and we will say to him from our easy command."* Ibn Kathir interpreted this by stating that Allah began by saying that what is important is the reward

---

[13]"Hadith 17561," accessed October 29, 2011, http://quran.al-islam.com/Page.aspx?pageid=221 &Book ID=13& Page=303.
[14]Ibn Kathir, 128.

of the hereafter, and he added to it his goodness. That is the proof of the justice and the knowledge and the faith.

Continuing with verses 89-90: *[89]Then he followed a way, [90]until when he reached the rising of the sun, he found that it rose on a people to whom we had given no shelter from it.* Ibn Kathir interpreted that Zu Al Qarnain traveled from the west to the east.[15] It took twelve years, and those people who lived at the east section did not have any homes or covering to shelter them from the heat of the sun. The sun became so hot that they used to seek refuge in a mirage in the earth that looked like graves.

Verse 91 states: *[91]Likewise, and indeed, we were aware of what he had of news.* Ibn Kathir said that Allah meant that he knew what circumstances he went through and that Allah was keeping and watching over him in all this traveling from the west of the land to the east of the land.

Verses 92-93 continues: *[92]Then he followed a way, [93]until he came between the two mountains under which he found a people who could not understand a saying.* Ibn Kathir interpreted this by stating that these people were dumb. It was said that they were Turkish and the cousins of Gog and Magog. So they mentioned to him that Gog and Magog had encroached upon them and vandalized their land. Then they offered Alexander the Great tribute that he might help them build a barrier between them and Gog and Magog. However, he refused to take their tribute for he was satisfied with the money which Allah had given to him.

This is what is written in verses 94-97: *[94]They said, "O Za Al Qarnain, surely Ya'juj[16] and Ma'juj[17] are vandalizing in the land. Shall we make to you a tribute that you make between us and them a barrier?" [95]He said, "That in which my lord has established me is better, so assist me with strength. I will make a barrier between you and them. [96]Bring me blocks of iron," until it equalizes between the two sides. He said, "Blow," until when he made it a fire. He said, "Bring me brass that I may pour over it." [97]And they were not able to scale it, neither were they able to dig through it.*

Ibn Kathir interpreted these verses by stating that they asked them to gather the men and equipment to build the barrier between the two

---

[15]Ibid., 129.
[16]Gog
[17]Magog

mountains. Ibn Kathir also stated that instead of brick, he used iron; and instead of mud, he used brass, which was smooth outside, so that they were not able to go above it with ladders nor were they able to dig through it with shovels, for it was built very strong.

Also, in verse 98: *[98]He said, "This is a mercy from my lord. So when the promise of my lord comes to pass, he will make it dust. And the promise of my lord was true."* Ibn Kathir interpreted this verse by stating that the mercy of Allah to his servants was to forbid the aggression of Gog and Magog against these people.[18] He stated also that this barrier which Alexander the Great built would become dust in the day of resurrection; this must be done, for the promise of his lord is true.

I would like to ask the reader some questions. *First, how can Allah in the Qur'an, in verse 93, say that the people could not speak, but in the following verses they were able to talk in full sentences to Alexander the Great? Second, who are these people? Third, what happened to this great barrier which was made out of iron and brass?* Today we can travel the whole world, and no such barrier can be found. *Notice that the day of resurrection has not come yet, so how can the promise of Allah be true?*

Ibn Kathir wrote some strange statements concerning what took place at the time of the death of Alexander the Great.[19] One was that he advised his mother to prepare a feast that she might gather the women of the city. She put the food between their hands (in front of them) and gave permission for them to eat of the meal unless they were widows. When Alexander the Great's mother did that, none of the women put their hands in the food because all of them were widows, and this served as a comfort for his mother.

Ibn Kathir stated that Ibn Bashier said the People of the Book (Christians and Jews) said that Alexander the Great died when he was 3,000 years old. Ibn Kathir said that was strange, and he also said that Ibn Asakir said Alexander the Great lived thirty-six years, while others said thirty-two years, and that he lived 740 years after David. He lived 5,181 years after Adam, and his kingdom was sixteen years, *and Allah knows best.*

Obviously, there are many errors in these stories. First, no Christian or Jewish scholar believes that Alexander the Great lived 3,000 years. Methuselah, who was the oldest living person, lived 969

---

[18]Ibn Kathir, 129-130.
[19]Ibid., 130.

years according to Genesis 5:27. Second, no Christian or Jewish historian believes in the existence of two Alexanders the Great. The time distance between Alexander the Great and David was around 770 years. The time distance between him and Adam was roughly 3,700 years. Such numbers cannot be proven by the Qur'an or the hadith, but it can be easily be proven by the biblical account when it is tied to the historical account. Since Alexander the Great was not a prophet, I could not find a specific rebuttal from the biblical account. The errors in the qur'anical account, however, are obvious when we compare them with the historical account.

Alexander the Great was born on July 20, 356 BC and died in the year 323 BC in Babylonia.[20] He died at the age of thirty-two, as stated above, from a poison or some disease resulting from a wound he received in India. He was not a prophet; he was an invader. There is no such thing as two Alexanders the Great as some Muslims claim with the distance of two thousand years between them. Even if this were true, there would be no chance for either one of them to have met with Abraham since Abraham was born roughly nineteen hundred years before Christ. Abraham lived 175 years. If there were two Alexanders the Great with the distance of two thousand years between them, that would make the birth of the first Alexander the Great in 2,356 BC. This would be around 450 years before the birth of Abraham, which means that there was no chance for them to meet and for Abraham to become a Muslim. Therefore, Abraham never met with Alexander the Great, either the first or the second.

Gog and Magog Nations and the Description of the Barrier

Although the Qur'an does not mention any details concerning Gog and Magog, Ibn Kathir stated that the inhabitants of Gog and Magog were the descendants of Adam without any disagreement.[21] Ibn Kathir proved this point from the following hadith:

> [when] Mohammed said, "On the day of resurrection Allah will say, 'O Adam.'" So Adam will say, "Here I am to please you, and the news is in your hand." Allah will respond, "Arise and send to the fire those who come from your descendants." Then Adam will ask, "Who are the ones to be sent to the fire?" Allah will say, "For every one thousand,

---

[20] "Alexander the Great," *About.com,* accessed November 5, 2011, http://ancienthistory. about.com/od/alexander/a/Alexander.htm.
[21] Ibn Kathir, 130.

nine hundred and ninety-nine people will go to hell and one will make it to heaven." Then the young will turn gray from the fear and every pregnant woman will give birth. The people will appear to be drunk even though they are not drunk, but the torment of Allah will be severe. So he said that this was so hard for them. They said, "O apostle of Allah, is there any among us that will go to heaven?" Mohammed said, "Good news. For from among you is the one (that will go to heaven), and from Gog and Magog one thousand people will go to hell."

What a strange hadith. The error here is in the calculation of the numbers. *If for every one thousand of the descendants of Adam, only one will make it to heaven and nine hundred and ninety-nine will go to hell, how can Mohammed state that one thousand of the Gog and Magog will make it to hell for every one Muslim?* The total is one thousand and one. This makes no sense when we know, as it is written in the following hadith, that Gog and Magog are one group of many of the descendants of Adam. The questions we must ask here are as follows: *What about the rest of the descendants of Adam? Will they be counted as a portion of the one thousand?*

Let us take a quick look at this hadith which states that Noah had three sons, Shem, the father of the Arabs; Ham, the father of the Sudanese; and Japheth, the father of the Turks. Gog and Magog are a Turkish sect, and they are the harshest people and the most corrupt.[22] It was said that the Turkish people were named Turks because when Zu Al Qarnain (Alexander the Great) built the barrier and forced Gog and Magog from behind the barrier, there was a sect from among them which was not as corrupt. They were left, and that is why they were called *Turks*, a word in Arabic that literally means *left*. However, that is a lie, because the name *Turks* is an Arabic word given to the people. Their original name is *Al Tatar* (plural), and the singular is Turkish, which has nothing to do with either *left* or *left behind*. Moreover, neither the Turks nor Zu Al Qarnain spoke Arabic, so the meaning giving in Arabic is irrelevant.

A second opinion as to who Gog and Magog are is offered by Ibn Kathir, who said that Abu Zakariyya and others said that some of the sperm of Adam fell on the dirt, so they were created from that and not from Eve.[23] My response to this is that I believe that Ibn Kathir had

---

[22]Ibid., 131.
[23]Ibid.

no common sense. Even if man's sperm is mixed with dirt to produce a baby, this fetus would still need a womb in which to grow and to develop for nine months. What nonsense this is from those who are called Muslim scholars.

Ibn Kathir also claimed there is no proof of this. This is also in disagreement with what the Qur'an said, for all people are the descendants of Noah. Some people claim that the Turkish were in different shapes and different heights; some of them were very long like a very long palm tree, while others were very short. Some of them would spread one of their ears as a blanket and cover themselves with the other ear. (This reminds me of Dumbo the Elephant. Had Ibn Kathir written a resume, Disney would have hired him on the spot.)

Ibn Kathir said all of these are words without proof. The truth is, they were the descendants of Adam, they looked like him, and they were in the same shape. The so-called prophet of Islam, Mohammed, said that when Adam was created, he was ninety feet tall, and from his days until today, people are getting shorter. It was said that none of them die until they see a thousand of their descendants. Ibn Kathir did not agree with that because he did not know what was true and what was not. He ended by stating, *and Allah knows best.*

Ibn Kathir repeated a similar hadith to the one above, wherein Mohammed said that Gog and Magog were the descendants of Adam; and if they were sent to the people, they would corrupt their lifestyle and that no one would die from Gog and Magog until they left a thousand of their descendants.[24] There were three nations that came after them. They were Taweel, Tarrisse, and Minsk. Ibn Kathir stated that this hadith was very strange and very weak and very questionable.

If it was a weak, strange, and questionable hadith, why did Ibn Kathir bother to put it in his book? So far, everything he put in his book is nothing but strange, weak, and questionable. It is amazing when he talks about the length of Adam being ninety feet tall, Ibn Kathir did not see anything strange or questionable about these statements. As we have seen before, all numbers in the hadith and in the interpretations of the Muslim scholars are no different at all from the previous numbers. I could easily believe that a man could have a thousand descendants, especially if he lived as long as Adam or Methuselah and had multiple wives. However, describing Adam as

---

[24]Ibid., 132.

being ninety feet tall is nonsense; this could only be seen in fiction movies or in cartoons.

Another example of nonsense, that Ibn Kathir did not see any weakness in, involved a long fairy tale of Mohammed ascending to the seventh heaven, as the Qur'an and hadith stated. Ibn Kathir said that when Mohammed was ascending to heaven, he went and met with the people of Gog and Magog and invited them to Allah.[25] They refused to answer his call or to follow him. Mohammed then called to the three nations of Taweel, Tarrisse, and Minsk, and they believed in him. Ibn Kathir said that this hadith was fabricated by Abu Naaeem, one of the big liars. One must ask a question here. *If Abu Naaeem is such a big liar, why did Ibn Kathir use him many times throughout his book?* Ibn Kathir concluded with *and Allah knows best.*

Ibn Kathir quoted a big liar, and he knew he was a big liar. Maybe this hadith of the big liar is not a big lie, *only Allah knows best. Why did he not quote someone who had the truth?* The answer is very simple, as we will see in the conclusion. There is no truth, except in the Bible, because Ibn Kathir, all Muslim scholars, Mohammed, his Angel Gabreel, and Allah do not know any truth about Gog and Magog.

The contradictions continue as Ibn Kathir stated in the hadith which all agree that Gog and Magog will be the substitutions for the believers on the day of resurrection. They will be in the fire of hell instead of the Muslims. Allah did not send to them any messengers as it is written in Qur'an 17:15: ... *And we were not tormenting until we sent a messenger.* The answer will be that there will not be torment until Allah shows the proof against them and their excuses. So if they were before the days of Mohammed, indeed, the messenger came to them from among them. The proof against them is given, but if Allah did not send to them any messenger, he will judge them according to their instincts as well as those who did not receive invitations. Other hadith assured that on the day of resurrection, Allah will examine the people. Those who answer the caller will enter the garden (paradise), and those who refuse and do not answer the caller will go to the fire (hell).

Ibn Kathir continued by stating that this exam will not require their salvation nor go against the telling that they were the people of the fire because Allah will inform his messenger, Mohammed, of what he will, concerning the matter of the unseen. In more detail, Ibn

---

[25]Ibid.

Kathir said that Allah has informed his messenger that those are the people of misery, and they will not accept the truth or be led to it. They will not answer the caller on the day of resurrection. Some people when they see the fire in hell will fall into belief, but because they did not accept it in their worldly life, their repentance will not be accepted on the Day of Judgment.

The Barrier

As for the barrier, Ibn Kathir stated that Zu Al Qarnain (Alexander the Great) built it from iron and brass.[26] He made it the same height of the tallest mountain, to the point that there was not one building on the earth that was stronger or more useful to the people than it. Ibn Kathir's interpretation stated that the people of this land did not have any trees or houses that could deliver them from the heat of the sun.[27] Therefore, whenever the sun rose, they would go in the water until the sun set, and then they could come out of the water. They were red from the sun, and they were a short people. No plants grew in the land. Al Bukhari said a man told Mohammed, "I have seen the barrier." Mohammed said, "What did it look like?" The man replied, "It is like striped hail." So Mohammed said, "I saw it like that." *Really?* What a wonderful "proof" that this barrier did exist in Mohammed's day*!*

Al Bukhari said a man came to Mohammed and said, "O messenger of Allah, indeed I saw the barrier of Gog and Magog." Mohammed said, "Describe it to me." The man said, "It was like striped hail with black and red stripes." Mohammed said, "Indeed, you have seen it."

That means Mohammed agreed with this man because Mohammed had seen this barrier. It is amazing, as we have stated before, that there is no evidence of the existence of such a barrier. Alexander the Great did not build any barrier; and if there was such a barrier with this description, it should still exist, especially when we read that the Qur'an said that it will be there until the day of resurrection (Qur'an 18:95-101) which has not taken place yet. Such a mountain does not exist, nor is there any archaeological evidence to prove its existence. Moreover, there is not any biblical reference to such a barrier. The only barrier or wall that is known to the world is

---

[26]Ibid., 133.

[27]http://quran.al-islam.cor/pae.aspx?pageid+221&bookID+11&Page+303, accessed November 3, 2011.

the Great Wall of China, which still exists today and is very well documented in history. This proves that these men in this hadith and Mohammed are liars.

Caliph Al Wask sent messengers from his place and wrote letters to the kings for permission to travel to the countries they visited until they arrived at the barrier. They investigated the news about this barrier, how Zu Al Quarian built it, and a description of it. When they returned, they told the caliph about this information, described the barrier, and said that it had a great door with many locks. The building was very high and strong. The remainder of the iron bricks and the equipment of the tower were there. The story goes on and on to describe the nature of the people and the kingdoms which existed there. Their different way of life included farming and fishing from the wilderness and from the seas. The people were huge in number, but no one knows the number except for Allah.

Many hadith have been written concerning Gog and Magog. These are nothing but myths. Ibn Kathir continued on with more fairy tales.[28] I see nothing but a waste of time and space to translate such lies and made-up stories, which end with Ibn Kathir's infamous statement, *and Allah knows best.* No, my dear readers and Muslim friends, Allah does not know anything; but you and I can know all the truths, not only about Gog and Magog but all that we need, by simply reading the Bible.

In Genesis 10:1, we learn that Japheth was a son of Noah. Genesis 10:2 states: *[2]The sons of Japheth were Gomer, Magog, Madai, Javan, Tubal, Meshech, and Tiras.* In this verse we learn that Magog was an individual descended from Noah. At a much later time, we learn in Ezekiel 38:1-9 that Magog was designated as a people (it was typical for a people to be named after a founding father, such as the Magog of Genesis 10:2), and Gog was defined explicitly as the office of prince of Meshech and Tubal. Both Meshech and Tubal were sons of Japheth (Genesis 10:2; 1 Chronicles 1:5) and were closely associated in the mind of Ezekiel (Ezekiel 27:13; 32:26; 39:1).

Therefore, when Gog and Magog appear together, they are an individual and a nation, not two nations as Mohammed in the Qur'an and hadith describe them. In the biblical reference Ezekiel 38:2, Gog was the name for a leader, Magog was the land of Rosh Meshech, and Tubal was the name of his kingdom. As for what is written in Ezekiel 39:1-2, the Bible gives a prophecy concerning Prince Gog and his

---

[28]Ibn Kathir, 133-134.

countries that will come from the far north to the mountains of Israel. From this verse we can know for sure that these countries are located further north than Israel. There are different opinions of what locations they are in the present world; some say Turkey, and others say Northern Russia. I personally believe they could both be the descendants of Japheth (Magog), as described in Genesis 10:2. There is so much that has been written concerning the end time prophecy or the interpretation of Ezekiel 38 and 39. We encourage the reader to search it online and study Jewish and Christian interpretations.

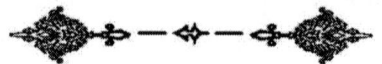

The Story of the Companions of the Cave

The story of the companions of the cave is written in Qur'an 18:9-26. Ibn Kathir stated that the reason these verses were descended on Mohammed was because the Jews used to test Mohammed, and that is why Allah gave this story to the people.[1] Shoaib Al Jubba'i stated that the name of the young men's cave was *Hayzm*, and Ibn Abbas stated that he did not know what Allah meant by the word *rakim* as it is written in Qur'an 18:9: *⁹Or did you think that the companions of the cave and al rakim[2] were of the wonders of our signs?* Ibn Abbas said different names have been given for the cave by different Muslim scholars, and as usual, Ibn Kathir ended this information by stating, *and Allah knows best.*

In his book, *Stories of the Prophets*, Ibn Kathir did not mention verses 10-12, but on an internet site Muslims posted his interpretation of these verses.[3] These young men escaped with their religion from the people and sought refuge, and that was why they said: *¹⁰When the young men took refuge in the cave, so they said, "Our lord, grant us mercy from you and prepare a right course for us in our affair." ¹¹So we struck on their ears in the cave for many years. ¹²Then we raised them up so that we might know which of the two parties could best discern the time they stayed.* Ibn Kathir interpreted this by stating that Allah raised them from their sleep, and one of them left the cave with dirhams (money) to buy food and also to know which one of them was right concerning the time they stayed sleeping in the cave.

Shoaib Al Jubba'i said that their dog's name was Hamran and that these young men lived after Christ and were Christians. Their people were idolaters. The young men refused to worship the idols of their people, and they worshiped Allah alone. They met together in one place. That is why Allah said: *¹³We will relate to you their*

---

[1] Ibn Kathir, *Stories of the Prophets*, vol. 2, Abo Al Fida Ishamail Ibn Kathir Al Kurashi Al Damashce (Beirut: Dar Al-Arab Heritage, 1408 AH, 1988), 135.

[2] a word without meaning

[3] http://quran.al-islam.com/Page.aspx?pageid=221&BookID=11&Page=294, accessed November 3, 2011.

news with the truth. Surely they were young men who believed in their lord, and we increased them guidance. *14And we tied on their hearts when they stood up, so they said, "Our lord is the lord of the heavens and the earth. We will not call any god other than him; indeed, if we did, then we said a transgression." 15Those our people have taken other gods than him. Were it not that they had brought to them a clear authority. So who is more unjust than one who forged a lie against Allah?*

They decided to leave their people's religion, and they became innocent of what their people served other than Allah. That is why they escaped to the cave. These young men escaped because they desired to save their flesh, but Allah will protect them and will reward them. This was Ibn Kathir's interpretation of verse 16: *16And if you separate from them and what they serve except Allah, so take refuge in the cave. Your lord will unfold his mercy to you and will prepare a way for your affair.*

Ibn Kathir interpreted 18:17: *17aAnd you see the sun when it rose bending to the right of their cave, and when it set going from them on the left side….* He stated that the cave in which they were hiding had a gate which was facing the east.[4] So the sun in the summertime and other similar times used to rise in the cave from the west side of the cave, and it came out of the cave slowly towards the right side.

Then when the sun was about to set, it shone towards the cave from the east side slowly, slowly until it set. That is how a person inside the cave can see it, and the wisdom of entry of the sunshine coming into the cave was to keep the air from going bad, to keep fresh air inside the cave. As for the rest of verse 17: *… and they are in a wide space in it. This is from the signs of Allah. Whomever Allah guided, so he is the guided. And whomever he leads astray, so you will not find for him a guided friend.* Ibn Kathir interpreted this by stating that they stayed all these years inside of the cave in this condition even though they had not eaten or drunk, and that "is a great proof that Allah has power and great might." Some said that their eyes were open so their eyes would not go bad.

Let us continue with Qur'an 18:18: *18And you think that they were awake, but they were sleeping. And we turned them to the right and to the left. And in the entry lay their dog with paws outstretched. Had you looked at them, you would surely have*

---

[4]Ibn Kathir, 136-137.

turned away from them in flight, and you would have been filled with fear of them. Ibn Kathir interpreted this by stating that they used to be turned to the right and to the left once a year or maybe more than that, *and Allah knows best.* It was also said that their dog did not go with them inside the cave for angels do not enter a house when there is a dog in it. Muslim scholars disagree about the location of the cave. Some said that it was in Nineveh; some said it was in Byzantine land, *and Allah knows best.* Ibn Kathir stated that if you had seen these young men in the cave, you would have run away from them because of the awe and glory in their situation.[5]

Continuing with the story, Allah said in Qur'an 18:19-20: *[19]And likewise, we raised them up that they might ask one another. One of them said, "How long have you stayed here?" They said, "We have stayed a day or part of a day." They said, "Your lord knows best how long you have stayed. So send now one of you with this your paper[6] into the city. So let him see who in it has the purest food, so he will bring to you a provision from it. And let him be courteous, and let not anyone feel you. [20]Surely if they prevail against you, they will stone you or turn you back into their religion, and then you will never prosper."*

Ibn Kathir interpreted this verse by stating that Allah praised these men back to life after they had been asleep for 309 years, as written in 18:25-26: *[25]And they abided in their cave three hundred years and add nine. [26]Say, "Allah knows how long they abided." To him are the unseen things of the heavens and the earth. See by him and hear. They do not have any friend other than him, and no one partners in his judgment.*

When they woke up, they questioned one another about the length of time they had slept. Later, they sent one of them with money, which Ibn Kathir called *dirhams*, to a city by the name of Dafassos that he might buy food. That is obviously because they thought they had only been asleep for a day or just a part of a day, but the country had changed over the years. It was said that one of them by the name of Tezoses disguised himself so that he would not be known. Some said that the people of the city carried him to their leaders because they were afraid that he might be a spy.

It was said that he escaped from them, and it was said that he told them about his story and those who were with him. They went with

---

[5]Ibid., 138.
[6]money

him to the cave to see his brethren. They knew the length of time they had been sleeping inside the cave. This was Allah's command. It was said that they continued to be asleep, and it was said that they died after that. As for the people of the city, it was said that they were not guided to this place where the cave was located because Allah had hidden their situation from them.

As for verse 21: *²¹And likewise, we made their adventure known⁷ so that they might know that the promise of Allah is true and that the hour, there is no doubt in it. When they disputed among themselves concerning their affair, so they said, "Build a building over them, their lord knows best about them." Those who prevailed in the affair said, "We will surely raise over them a place of worship."* Ibn Kathir stated that the people of the city disagreed among themselves.⁸ Some said to build a building above them, meaning to close the gate of the cave so that they would not be harmed. Others said to put a place of worship above them, meaning to have a place of worship near these righteous people.

Ibn Kathir inserted that Mohammed said Allah cursed the Jews and the Christians for they took the tombs of their prophets as a place of worship. This statement is not true, but to the contrary, it is commonly known among Muslims to have mosques where Muslims visit the burial places of their dead religious leaders, beginning with Mohammed's tomb. True Christians and Jews do not worship the relics of their dead.

Let us ask a question. *How many men were sleeping inside the cave for these 309 years?* The answer can be found in Qur'an 18:22: *²²They will say, "Three, their dog is their fourth." And they say, "Five, their dog is their sixth," guessing of the unseen, and they say, "Seven, and their dog is their eighth." Say, "My lord knows best their number; no one knows them except a few." So do not dispute in them except with reference to that which appeared, and do not consult anyone about them.* So obviously, from the words of Allah, no one knows how many there were.

Perhaps there were three, five, or even seven? Most importantly, there was only one dog, even though Mohammed clearly taught that angels would not enter a house that has a dog in it. That is why Mohammed and his followers killed the last dog in Mecca. Saudi Arabia is the only country on the planet earth to have a widespread

---

⁷to their fellow citizens
⁸Ibn Kathir, 139.

ban on dogs. However, here we see in the Qur'an the contradiction to Mohammed's claim that the angel of Allah used to go inside the cave to turn these men to the right and the left while they were asleep 309 years. Even though Muslim scholars tried to fabricate an interpretation that the dog was outside the cave, which is a lie, we see that the dog was their fourth or sixth or their eighth. *Why did Allah count the dog with them if he was not with them?*

From the information of the Qur'an, we do not know where this story took place, when the story took place, who these men were, or how many people were in the cave. What a wonderful fairy tale. The fact is that this story is not true. It never took place. This story was written years before Mohammed was born. Mohammed thought when he heard the story that it was a true story, and that is why he added it to the body of the Qur'an just like the stories of Adam, Noah, and Moses. *So what did we really learn from this story?* The answer is *absolutely nothing*, but this story is great evidence that Mohammed's Qur'an is not a revelation from heaven but only a miscopying of the stories of the Bible with many fairy tales added. The true source of this story of *the several sleepers* is a fifth century myth which was taken from a Greek book by Gregory of Tours, *The Glory of the Martyrs.*[9]

Someone may say there is a good lesson to learn from Qur'an 18:23-24: *[23]And do not say about anything, "I will surely do it tomorrow." [24]Only if Allah wills. And remember your lord when you forget and say, "Perhaps my lord will guide me so that I may come near the right answer of this."* I will respond to this by saying that there is nothing that we can learn from the Qur'an, if we know the original source of comments in the Qur'an. For even the advice Mohammed gave in this verse is copied from the Bible. We, as Christians, should never say that we will do anything in the future unless we add to it "if God wills." These are not my words, but words from the Bible, which Mohammed copied when he recited verses 23-24. These words are written in the book of James 4:13-15: *[13]Come now, you who say, "Today or tomorrow we will go to such and such a city, spend a year there, buy and sell, and make a profit"; [14]whereas you do not know what will happen tomorrow. For what is your life? It is even a vapor that appears for a little time and then*

---

[9]Gregory of Tours, *The Glory of the Martyrs*, Translated Texts for Historians, vol. 4, trans. Raymond Van Dam (Liverpool: University of Liverpool Press, 1988).

vanishes away. [15]Instead you ought to say, "If the Lord wills, we shall live and do this or that."

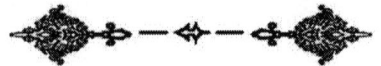

36 The Story of the Believer and the Infidel

In Qur'an 18:32-44, Mohammed mentioned the parable of two men. No names were given, and the parable was written without any purpose. Mohammed was obviously trying to copy the method which Jesus used to teach. Just as Jesus taught with parables, Mohammed included parables, or what he thought were parables, in his Qur'an.

Ibn Kathir stated that these two men were friends; one of them was a believer, and the other was an infidel. It was said that each of them had money.[1] The believer spent his money with obedience to Allah and to please him seeking his face. (However, we could not find this in any verse in the Qur'an.) The infidel spent his money buying two gardens which are mentioned in a story of the Qur'an. There were grapevines and palm trees in the gardens. They were near rivers which he used for irrigation. The owner of the garden, the infidel, was bragging to the poor believers. He bragged, "I have more money than you and mightier followers." Ibn Kathir stated the purpose of this comment was that the infidel was making fun of the believers and how they wasted their money by giving it to the poor and not investing it as the infidel had done.

The infidel man walked in his garden according to verse 18:35: *[35]And he entered his garden, and he was unjust to himself. …* Ibn Kathir stated that when the infidel man entered the garden, he saw the width of the garden, the large amount of water in it, and the beauty of its trees. Then he thought in his mind that if one of these trees died, he could replace it with a better tree. Then he said *[35b] …"I do not think that this will ever perish…."* Ibn Kathir interpreted that the infidel man was assured with the life of this world and denied the existence of the life of the hereafter.

The infidel man said, "I do not think that the hour is coming, and even if I be taken back to my Lord, I will surely find a better place than that." Ibn Kathir interpreted this verse by stating that the infidel

---

[1]Ibn Kathir, *Stories of the Prophets*, vol. 2, Abo Al Fida Ishamail Ibn Kathir Al Kurashi Al Damashce (Beirut: Dar Al-Arab Heritage, 1408 AH, 1988), 140.

was proud in thinking that Allah had not given him his riches except for Allah's love for him and because the infidel thought he deserved it.

Ibn Kathir stated that this foolish man became proud with what he had in this world, so he denied the hereafter by stating, "If the hereafter exists, he will find with his Lord better of what he got."[2] His companion, the believer, argued with him when he said to him in verse 37- 38: ..."*Did you become an infidel by him who created you from dust, then from nutfah, then fashioned you as a man?* [38]*But as for me, he is Allah my lord....* Ibn Kathir stated that the believer meant, "I say the opposite of what you say, and I believe the opposite of what you believe." Verse 38 continues with: ... *I will not partner anyone with my Lord.* Ibn Kathir interpreted this:

> I will serve Him alone, and I believe He will raise the dead body after it is decomposed, so he will bring back the dead and cause the bones to be gathered. I know that Allah has no partner in his creation or his kingdom. There is no god but him.

Then Ibn Kathir continued and advised the infidel by stating that, as stated in verse 39: [39]*And were it not that if you entered your garden said, 'What Allah wills. There is no might except by Allah.'* Notice here there is an error in the Qur'an, for in the beginning of the story, the Qur'an states that the infidel man had two gardens, but here the believer stated that he entered a single garden. It would be correct as *gardens*. Ibn Kathir said that is what anyone should say when he sees anything he likes of his wealth or his family. Then Ibn Kathir mentioned a hadith by Mohammed as follows: Anas said that Mohammed said, "Whatever Allah graced on a servant of family, money or son, so he must say, 'What Allah wills. There is no might except by Allah.'"[3]

Then the believer said to the infidel in verse 40: [40]*so perhaps my lord may give to me better than your garden and will send on it his counting (judgment) from the heaven so that it will become a barren wasteland.* Ibn Kathir stated that he meant in the hereafter. *How did Ibn Kathir know that this is what he meant?* Ibn Abbas and others stated that the meaning is a torment from heaven as a destructive strong rain which will pull up the trees and plants from the ground so that the garden will become a barren wasteland. Verse

---

[2]Ibid., 141.
[3]Ibid., 142.

41 states: *⁴¹or its water will become sinking so that you are unable to seek it."* Ibn Kathir stated he will not be able to get the water out of the ground. Ibn Kathir also stated that Allah said that the infidel man was surrounded with his fruit, so when he remained alternating his hands (clapping hand action by Middle Eastern people to show sorrow) over what he had spent on it, it was empty on its trellises. In the last part of verse 42: *⁴²...And he said, "Oh, I wish I had not partnered anyone with my lord."* Ibn Kathir interpreted that all the land was ruined and that the man was sorrowful of all that he said before because he was an infidel of Allah the great. Allah said in verses 43-44: *⁴³And there was not a group to help him other than Allah, and he was not helped. ⁴⁴Thereupon is protection from the true god, and he is best for reward and best for the final end.*

Ibn Kathir concluded the story by stating that we learn lessons from this story in that no one should depend on the life of this world, be proud of it, or trust in it; but one should be obedient to Allah and depend on him in every circumstance and that man should have the belief of whatever is in the hand of Allah is more assured than what is in our hands.[4] In the story, whatever we do not offer or give in obedience to Allah, we will be punished by it, or perhaps it will be taken from us.

Another lesson that we learn from the story is that Ibn Kathir stated we should take the advice from the brothers in not accepting the advice that will bring destruction and regret, which does not work when the opportunity is passed. We depend on Allah, for the judgment belongs to him.

It is amazing that the story in the Qur'an is similar to a parable in the Bible because I believe that Mohammed heard the biblical story and was influenced by it as usual when he copied and changed the stories of the Bible to be put in poetry form as newly revealed Qur'an verses. This parable is named by Christian scholars as "The Parable of the Foolish Rich Man" which can be found in the book of Luke 12:15-21. We encourage the reader to read the entire parable as it is written in the Scripture.

Let us look at what Jesus teaches in this parable. Jesus has taught his followers to take heed and beware of covetousness, for no one's possessions are considered as valuable as his life. This is the purpose of this parable about the rich man. The ground of this rich man

---

[4]Ibid., 143.

brought forth plenty. He thought to himself, because he ran out of space to store all of his bounty, that he would tear down his barns and build a greater storehouse. He said to himself, "O my soul, you have plenty for many years. Relax and eat and drink and be merry." Then God said to him, "O you foolish man, today your soul will be taken so all that you have prepared, to whom will it go?" Jesus ended the parable by stating that the one who lays up earthly treasures for himself is not rich in the eyes of God; he will be in the same situation as this foolish rich man. Obviously, here we see the similarities between Jesus' parable and Mohammed's verses in the Qur'an. However, Mohammed garbled the message somewhat!

What is amazing to me, although the Qur'an says it is a parable, Muslim interpreters like Ibn Kathir and others do not understand what a parable is. They interpret this parable as if it were a true story. One can see this clearly when we read the statement of *who* this man was and *what* he was not. As Muslim interpreters usually do, they add to the verses of the Qur'an. If Ibn Kathir and other Muslim scholars had understood that this was only a parable, they would not have added all the details and information to the parable as if it were a real story about real people.

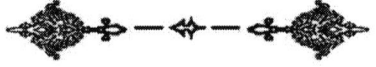

The Story of the Companions of the Garden

Once again, Mohammed made up this story; yet, "The Story of the Companions of the Garden" is written in the Qur'an as if it were a true story. There was no mention here of who these people were, where they lived, or when this took place. According to Muslim scholars, they were a true people. Ibn Kathir stated that they were from the people of Yemen. Saeed Ibn Jaber said that they were from a village named Darwan, which is located six miles away from Sana'a, the capital of Yemen. Ibn Kathir also said that they were Ethiopians. They were among the People of the Book (Jews or Christians).

Their father was a good man. He used to give to many charities. When he died, his children inherited his garden. They said that their father was a fool because he used to give to the poor from his garden. "If we forbid them from having any fruit of the garden, we will have more for us. This is what took place in the story; this is the basis for our story." On the other hand, Ibn Abbas contradicted the previous interpretation by stating that Allah gave this parable to the people of Quraish for he clearly teaches that this is a parable, not a true story.[1,2] And I will add, *and Allah knows best.*

This story can be found in Qur'an 68, beginning in verse 17 and continuing through verse 33. Here is the story as it is written.
[17]*Surely we have tested them as we tested the companions of the garden when they swore that they would cut its fruit in the morning.* [18]*And they did not set aside a portion.* [19]*Then a visitation from your lord encircled them while they were asleep.* [20]*So it[3] became like a harvested field.* [21]*So they called each other in the morning:* [22]*"Go early to your harvest, if you were binding."* [23]*So they went, and they were whispering:* [24]*"That surely no poor will enter it to you today."*

[25]*And they went out at daybreak with this settled purpose.* [26]*So when they saw it, they said, "Surely we have gone astray.*

[1]Ibn Kathir, *Stories of the Prophets*, vol. 2, Abo Al Fida Ishamail Ibn Kathir Al Kurashi Al Damashce (Beirut: Dar Al-Arab Heritage, 1408 AH, 1988), 143.
[2]http://quran.al-islam.com/Page.aspx?pageid=221&BookID=11&Page=565, accessed November 7, 2011.
[3]the garden

²⁷Yet, we are destitute." ²⁸The one in the middle of them said, "Have I not said to you, 'Were it not that you had praised.'" ²⁹They said, "Praise be to our lord. Surely we were unjust." ³⁰So they came to one another, blaming. ³¹They said, "O woe to us, surely we were rebellious. ³²Perhaps our lord will exchange a better one than it for us. Surely we desire our lord." ³³Likewise is the torment, and the torment of the hereafter is bigger, if they were knowing.

Muslim scholars do not know the difference between a true story and a parable as we saw previously in "The Story of the Believer and the Infidel," which was written as a parable in the Qur'an. However, Ibn Kathir and other scholars interpreted it as if it were a true story. Here in the Qur'an, "The Story of the Companions of the Garden" is given as a true story, but Ibn Kathir interpreted it as a parable. Ibn Kathir continued by stating that Allah had sent the generous great messenger (Mohammed) to them, the people of Quraish, but they called him a liar and disagreed with him. Ibn Abbas explained that it was a garden with all kinds of plants and fruits ready to be harvested. They swore to harvest it in early morning when no poor could see them, for they chose not to give any of the fruit to the poor. So Allah prohibited them by singeing the garden, leaving nothing.

Ibn Kathir stated, "When they woke from their sleep, early in the morning, they were whispering to one another. They agreed, with one another with evil intent, not to give any of the harvest to the poor."[4]

Akramah said that they were angry against the poor people; and when they got to the farm and saw what had happened to it, they said, *"Surely we were unjust,"* meaning that they were punished because of their evil intentions and were forbidden the blessing of their harvest.

Ibn Abbas and Mujahid and others said that *"the one in the middle"* meant the most just and good one among them who said, *"Were it not that you had praised."* So they regretted, and their regret did not help them. It was said these men were brothers and had inherited this garden from their father, who used to give plenty of charity to the poor. However, when they took this land, they disregarded the command of their father and did not give to the poor. That is why Allah punished them with a strong punishment on the day of the harvest.

---

[4]Ibn Kathir, 144.

I personally believe this story is just a made-up story, without any details, and those scholars tried hard to make it a true story by adding extra details. Ibn Kathir ended the story by quoting, "Likewise the great torment, for Allah will torment whoever disobeys his commands and does not show compassion to the needy of whom he created, and the punishment of the hereafter is greater."

Obviously, this is not true, for there are thousands, and we can even say millions, of ungodly people throughout the history of mankind who are richly blessed materially but who did not give to the needy ones; and Allah, the god of Mohammed, did not punish them for many generations. On the other hand, the God of the Bible tells us that God brings the sunshine on the evil and the good, and He brings His rain on the just and the unjust. That is why the true God of the Bible commands His believers to love their enemies, bless those who curse the believers, and pray for those who persecute them so that the believers may be like their Father, who is God in Heaven. Moreover, the unbelievers may become the children of their Father. Please read Matthew 5:44-48.

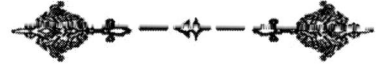

38 — The Story of Those Who Transgressed on the Sabbath

This story, "The Story of Those Who Trangressed on the Sabbath," is mentioned in three different locations in the Qur'an. Two of these locations contain no specific details. The first is in Qur'an 2:65-66 where Allah said: *[65]And indeed, you know those of you who transgressed in the Sabt[1]; so we said to them, "Become despised monkeys." [66]So we made that[2] an example to what is between her hands[3] and what is behind her[4] and a sermon to the fearers.* The second is in Qur'an 4:47: *[47]O you who have been given the book, believe in what we have sent down[5] confirming what is with you[6] before we hide faces and turn them on their backs or curse them as we cursed the companions of the Sabbath.[7] And the command of Allah was accomplished.*

The long story, with a little bit more information, can be found in Qur'an 7:163-166: *[163]And ask them about the village which was present by the sea, when they transgressed on the Sabbath (Saturday), when their whales came to them appearing openly on their Sabbath day; and the day they did not have Sabbath, they (their whales) did not come to them. Likewise, we tempted them because they were transgressors. [164]And when one nation of them said, "Why preach to people whom Allah will destroy or torment them with severe torment?" They said, "[As] an excuse for your lord, and perhaps they may fear." [165]So when they forgot what they had been reminded of, we delivered those who had been forbidden from the evil, and we seized those who did injustice with an evil torment because they were transgressors. [166]So when they revolted against what they were forbidden to do, we said to them, "Become despised monkeys."*

Ibn Kathir quoted Ibn Abbas and other scholars by telling the readers that those people were the people of Aylah who lived between

---

[1]Saturday, non-Arabic word of Aramaic/Hebrew origin
[2]that, i.e. Allah's punishment
[3]now—the present
[4]the following generations
[5]the Qur'an
[6]the Bible
[7]i.e. the Jews who have been changed to monkeys

Midian and the mountain.[8] They were following the teachings of the Torah by keeping the Sabbath. Therefore, the whales became familiar with them, so that they were able on the Sabbath to move freely in the water, knowing that they would not be caught, for the whales knew that it was forbidden for people to catch them on that day. During the rest of the week, the whales disappeared because they could only be caught on the other days, not on the Sabbath.

Ibn Kathir continued by stating what Allah said in the Qur'an: *Likewise, we tempted them because they were transgressors.*[9] He interpreted these words by saying that Allah caused plenty of the whales to come out on the Sabbath because of the people's transgressions. The people began to let down their ropes and nets and dig out trenches and lakes where they prepared factories. Now when the fish swam into the lakes, they could not come out of them. Notice that Ibn Kathir used the word *fish* in the last sentence and not the word *whales* as in the Qur'an. Ibn Kathir continued by stating that they did that on Fridays so when the whales came out on Saturdays, they would get caught in the trap. So when the people came out on Saturdays, they took their catch. Allah became angry with them and cursed them because they disobeyed his command.

When the people broke the Sabbath by working, those who did not break the Sabbath split into two groups. One group denied what the sinful ones did. The other group did not deny it, and they did not forbid what was done. They said, "Why preach to people whom Allah will destroy them or torment them with severe torment?" Ibn Kathir interpreted this by stating that they asked, "What is the profit you will gain by rebuking those who broke the Sabbath?" Indeed, they deserve the punishment; so the other group responded by saying, "As an excuse for your lord, and perhaps they may fear." This meant perhaps the sinful may repent and stop working on the Sabbath.

Ibn Kathir stated that Allah said in Qur'an 7:165: *[165]So when they forgot what they had been reminded of....*[10] He stated that this meant that when they gave any attention to those who forbade them from the evil act which they had done, *...we delivered those who had been forbidden from the evil, and we seized those who did injustice with an evil torment because they were transgressors.* Ibn Kathir interpreted this verse by stating that those

---

[8]Ibn Kathir, *Stories of the Prophets*, vol. 2, Abo Al Fida Ishamail Ibn Kathir Al Kurashi Al Damashce (Beirut: Dar Al-Arab Heritage, 1408 AH, 1988), 145.

[9]Ibid.

[10]Ibid., 146.

who sin against Allah would be punished with a severe, painful punishment. Then Allah explained the torment which he caused them by saying, *[166]So when they revolted against what they were forbidden to do, we said to them, "Become despised monkeys."*

Ibn Kathir explains here that Allah told us that he destroyed the unjust and delivered the believers who spoke against the sinners, and he did not talk about those who were quiet. Scholars disagreed among themselves concerning what took place with the third group. Some scholars said they were among the delivered ones, but others said they were among the destroyed ones. The reason that some scholars said the third group was not delivered was because even though they denied in their hearts what the wicked did, they did not show it in action, for the denying of evil must be by action, the tongue, and the heart.

Ibn Kathir stated that Ibn Abbas and other scholars said the people of the city separated themselves from those who did not keep the Sabbath. They spent the night by themselves, locked their own doors, and then sat and waited to see the destruction which would come upon them. One morning, they opened their doors, and in the middle of the day the people of the city commanded a man to go up a ladder and look upon the evil ones to see what happened to them; and behold, they became monkeys with tails. The people opened the doors for the monkeys, and they began to meet the other relatives of other monkeys.

The people said to the monkeys, "Did we not forbid you from doing what you were doing?" The monkeys nodded their heads, meaning *yes*. Then Abd Allah Ibn Abbas said, "Surely we see many evils, and we do not deny them or speak against them." Al Ofey stated that Ibn Abbas said the youth of this village became monkeys and the elders became pigs. Ibn Abbas also said they did not live long, and they did not have descendants, for they did not live more than three days. Mojahid, on the other hand, said that these people were changed in their hearts and were not changed into real monkeys and pigs, for this was only a parable given by Allah and not a true story. Ibn Kathir said this was a very strange interpretation because it disagreed with the word of Allah in the Qur'an, *and Allah knows best.*

Obviously, this is a made-up story by Mohammed in the Qur'an, and Muslim scholars, as usual, disagree on its interpretation. Not only does this story not exist in the Bible, but it disagrees with the nature of the God of the Bible, for here in the Qur'an, Allah tempted the Jewish people and caused them to break the Sabbath. He controlled the whales to show up on the Sabbath days and not on the weekdays which resulted in the Jews sinning. Then he punished them by turning them into monkeys and pigs. In this case, Allah tempted with evil, and this is a clear contradiction to the Bible which teaches that God does not tempt anyone with evil. See James 1:13-14.

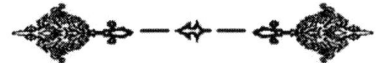

39 The Story of Lokman

Although the story of Lokman is not mentioned in the Bible, Mohammed mentioned it in one location in the Qur'an, in 31:12-19, a portion of revelation which, amazingly, is named after him. The name Lokman is used in verse 12 and only one time: *[12]And indeed, we gave Lokman the wisdom: "That give thanks to Allah." And whoever gives thanks, so surely he only gives thanks to himself, and whoever becomes an infidel, so surely Allah is rich, praised.*

When we ask who Lokman was, sadly Muslim scholars do not know. For example, Ibn Kathir stated that Lokman was Ibn Ankaa Ibn Sadoon.[1] Ibn Kathir also said that Ibn Jarir stated that he was called Lokman Ibn Tharan. On the other hand, Ibn Kathir said that Al Sohale said that he was from Nubia from the household of Elah, that he was a righteous man who had worshiped Allah, and that he had great wisdom. Ibn Kathir also stated that he was a judge in the days of King David, *and Allah knows best.*

On still another hand, Ibn Kathir stated that Ibn Abbas said that he was a slave from Ethiopia and a carpenter.[2] Qatadah stated that Lokman was a short man with a snub nose from Nubia. Ibn Kathir stated that Yahya said Saeed Ibn Almoseeb said that Lokman was from Sudan, and Allah gave him the wisdom and forbade him the prophethood.[3] A man came to Saeed, and he was sad because he was black. Saeed told him, "Do not be sad, for some of the best people from the land of Sudan were black." He named them, Belal and Mohjaa and Lokman, the wise man. Mohjaa said that Lokman was a black slave with big lips and cracked feet.

I am amazed at how Muslim scholars offered many different descriptions of Lokeman with inherent contradictions among them. *Was Lokman a judge in David's time, or was he a slave carpenter? Was he from Ethiopia or from Nubia? How did these Muslim scholars know that he was short or had big lips?* The verses of the Qur'an do

[1]Ibn Kathir, *Stories of the Prophets*, vol. 2, Abo Al Fida Ishamail Ibn Kathir Al Kurashi Al Damashce (Beirut: Dar Al-Arab Heritage, 1408 AH, 1988), 147.

[2]Ibid., 152.

[3]Ibid., 148.

not give any of these descriptions. All that we know from verse 12 is that Lokman was given wisdom. Much other information had been given about him in a series of contradictions to the previous information, but here he was a shepherd.

Ibn Kathir stated that Ibn Abu Hatem said Lokman did not have family, money, or position; he was a quiet man, a deep thinker, and a deep meditator.[4] He never slept during the day. No one ever saw him spit, "harrumph," urinate, excrete, wash, laugh, or have a temper; and he always spoke with wise sayings. He continued by stating that Lokman did marry and have sons. However, they all died, and he did not cry over them. It was also said that the prophethood was offered to him, but he was afraid that he could not fulfill its duties. Therefore, he chose wisdom because it was easier for him, *and Allah knows best.*

Then Ibn Kathir contradicted himself by stating that Ibn Jarir said that Akramah said Lokman was a prophet.[5] We must ask a question here. *Was he a prophet or not?* Ibn Kathir thought he was a wise man and *not* a prophet. Ibn Kathir stated that Allah mentioned him in the Qur'an with some of his words from what he had preached to his son, whom he loved more than any other creature and to whom he was more compassionate than to anybody else.

The first thing that he preached to his son is in Qur'an 31:13: *[13]And when Lokman said to his son while preaching to him, "O my son, do not partner with Allah, surely the partnering is a great injustice."* Then Allah commanded the son to honor the parents, and he proved their rights over the son and commanded the son to do good to his parents, even if the parents were polytheists. However, they must be disobeyed if they ask the son to follow their religion, as Allah told about Lokman when he was preaching to his son. Qur'an 31:14-15 states: *[14]We have commanded the human concerning his parents. His mother carried him with weakness on weakness and his weaning in two years: "That be thankful to me and to your parents. To me is the final return. [15]And if they perform jihad against you to get you to partner with me of which you have no knowledge, so do not obey them and be in companionship with them in this world with kindness. And follow a way of him who turns to me. Then your return is to me, so I will inform you of what you were doing.*

---

[4]Ibid.
[5]Ibid., 149.

As for the statement in verse 16: *¹⁶O my son, surely if it is the weight of the grain of the mustard seed, so it will be in a rock or in the heavens or on the earth, Allah will bring it. Surely Allah is kind, aware.* Ibn Kathir interpreted this verse by stating that Lokman forbade his son from doing injustice to the people, even if it was a little bit of injustice the size of a mustard seed, for Allah would require an answer concerning any injustice; and on the Day of Judgment, he would put it on the scale.

Al Saddi claimed that what Allah meant by the rock, mentioned in the above verse, was the rock below the seven earths.[6] Here we see Al Saddi's inconsistency with the Qur'an, which teaches that there are seven earths and seven heavens. In the following verses of 17-19, Lokman gave his son advice: *¹⁷O my son, perform the prayer and command with the right and forbid from the evil and be patient under whatever will befall you. Surely this is from the determination of the affairs.* Ibn Kathir interpreted this verse by stating that Lokman advised his son to perform the prayer with all its requirements, with its exact time, with kneeling, with respect, and to stay away from what is forbidden from it. When he commanded the right and forbade the disgrace, then he must do all that he could by his hand if he could; and if not, by his tongue; and if not, by his heart. Lokman commanded him to be patient, for things would happen, and there was no way to change them.

As for verse 18: *¹⁸And do not turn your cheek to the people,[7] and do not walk in the land arrogantly. Surely Allah does not love every arrogant, proud.* Ibn Abbas and others said that this means that the son of Lokman was advised not to be proud and not to walk boastfully.[8]

Now, the final verse of the story, verse 19: *¹⁹And let your pace be moderate and lower your voice, surely the most hideous voice is the voice of the donkeys."* Ibn Kathir said that Lokman advised his son to be humble, for he assured him that Allah does not love the people who are arrogant and proud; therefore, he advised him to not walk hurriedly and also asked him to speak with a soft voice.[9] Then, amazingly, Mohammed said that Lokman said to his son that the most hideous voice was the donkey's. What a great "proof" that

[6] Ibid.
[7] with pride
[8] Ibn Kathir, 150.
[9] Ibid., 150-151.

Lokman was a wise man, for I personally like the voice of the donkey and believe the donkey is very wise.

So many people think donkeys are stupid. That is why, in the Middle East, when people try to insult someone, they call that person a donkey as a way to describe that person as being not very smart. However, that is not true, for I remember one time, when I was a child, that there was a line of donkey carts on the side of the road. I had gone to the market to buy some flour. The owner of the donkey cart left the cart and the donkey in the middle of the street. There was a big trailer coming in the middle of the street. The driver stopped in front of the donkey, angrily blowing his horn, for there was no one to remove the donkey and the cart. From a distance, I saw what happened, and I moved toward the cart so that I could remove it from the street. Before I could reach the donkey, however, I was shocked to see the donkey himself back the cart into the right lane to fit just right between two other donkeys and their carts. It surprised both the driver and me. Three or four people laughed, for sometimes some people cannot park a car in one attempt, but the donkey parked it correctly the first time.

Another time, I was visiting my cousin in Upper Egypt, and I went with him to the farm, which is roughly 4-5 kilometers from home, with him riding his donkey. At the farm my cousin put enough grass (hay) on the back of the donkey, hit the donkey on the back with his hand, and spoke to the donkey saying, "Go home." An hour later when we arrived home, I was shocked to see that the donkey was already home. He had traveled all the way from the farm to the home by himself because donkeys are really smart.

They are not stupid as people may think. However, Ibn Kathir stated in the hadith that Mohammed said when people hear the donkey bray, they must seek refuge from Allah, especially if this happened at night, for Mohammed claimed that donkeys bray when they see Satan at night.[10]

Many things have been written about Lokman. For the sake of time and space, I choose to leave this part of the section of Ibn Kathir's book behind, but I want to share the following information contained elsewhere in the section on Lokman.

In one of the stories, Lokman was a slave in Ethiopia, and his master asked him to kill a sheep and to bring from this sheep the best

---

[10]Ibid., 151.

two pieces of meat so that he may eat.[11] Lokman brought him the tongue and the heart, so his master asked him, "Was there any better meat than these two things?" Lokman said, "No." Then his master asked him to kill another sheep. He said to him, "Bring to me the worst two pieces of meat." So Lokman brought him the tongue and the heart. The master was surprised and asked him, "When I asked you to bring me the two best pieces of meat, you brought me the tongue and the heart. Then when I asked you to bring me the worst two pieces of meat, you still brought me the tongue and the heart." Lokman answered him, "Yes, because if the heart and the tongue are good, they would be the best; and if they were bad, they would be the worst." According to the claims of Muslim scholars, a great amount of advice was given by Lokman to his son; however, there is no mention of such advice anywhere in the Qur'an or the hadith.

Ibn Kathir stated that Qatadah said Allah gave Lokman the choice between wisdom and the prophethood, and Lokman chose wisdom over the prophethood.[12] It was also said that Angel Gabreel came to him while he slept and increased his wisdom so that when he woke up in the morning, he started speaking with wisdom. Lokman said, "Allah has sent on me the prophethood. I would have taken it, and I would have done the best; but since he gave me the choice, I took wisdom. I was afraid that I would be too weak to be a prophet, so I loved wisdom more than the prophethood." Qatadah also stated that when Allah said, "And indeed, we gave Lokman the wisdom," he meant jurisprudence and Islam, but he was not a prophet and did not receive revelation.

How did Muslim scholars come up with these various descriptions of Lokman? As usual, Ibn Kathir ended his story by the famous words, *and Allah knows best.*

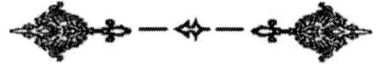

---

[11]Ibid., 152.
[12]Ibid., 154.

40 The Story of the Companions of the Moat

Muslim scholars give many stories as interpretations for the following verses in Qur'an 85:1-10: *[I swear] by the heaven with the constellations ²and by the promised day ³and by the witness and the witnessed. ⁴Killed are the companions of the moat, ⁵the fire with the fuel. ⁶When they sat in it, ⁷and they were witnesses of what they did to the believers. ⁸And they did not take vengeance on them, except that they may believe in Allah, the dear, the praised. ⁹To whom the kingdom of the heavens and the earth, and Allah is witness over all things. ¹⁰Surely those who seduced the believing men and believing women, then they did not repent. So for them is the torment of hell and for them is the torment of the fire.*

Ibn Kathir told two different stories concerning the people of the moat (fiery pit).[1] He began by stating that Muslim scholars disagree about when these people (companions) existed. Some said that they existed before the time of Christ, while others said it was after the time of Christ.

The first of the two stories was about a young man who had been taught to be a sorcerer. This young man was beaten by his family. When he went to the man who had taught him sorcery, he would beat the young man, too. The young man was able to take the advice of a monk. The young man decided to test Allah to see who was right, the monk or the sorcerer. One day he saw a huge beast which prevented people from traveling the road in safety, for this beast had brought fear to the people. The young man held a rock in his hand and said that if he threw it at the beast and the rock killed the beast, then the monk was more loved by Allah than the sorcerer. He killed the huge beast. He was also able to perform miracles. He was able to heal many sicknesses of the people.

The king asked a blind man who had received his sight back, who it was that opened his eyes. The blind man said that it was his lord. The king was upset that the man believed in another god and not the

---

[1] Ibn Kathir, *Stories of the Prophets*, vol. 2, Abo Al Fida Ishamail Ibn Kathir Al Kurashi Al Damashce (Beirut: Dar Al-Arab Heritage, 1408 AH, 1988), 154-157.

king himself, so he beat the man until he confessed that the young man had healed him by the power of Allah. He brought the young man and beat him until he told the king about the monk. Then the king found the monk who refused to leave his religion, and the king killed him by cutting him with a saw. The king asked the healed blind man to recant his religion, but he refused, so the king killed him with the saw. The king asked the young man to leave this religion, but he refused, so the king tried to kill him by throwing his body from the top of the mountain.

They took him to the mountain, but the mountain shook with them.The young man came back to the king, and he told the king that Allah had saved them. Then the king sent him with other people to the sea so that if he did not leave his religion, they would drown him; however, Allah saved him, and the others all drowned. Then the young man came back to the king, and he told the king that the only way that he could kill him was to do what he told him to do:

> You need to gather all the people in one place, and then you crucify me on the trunk of a tree. Next you take an arrow from my quiver, and you kill me by it as you say, 'In the name of Allah, the lord of the young boy.' If you do that, you will kill me.

The king did as instructed, and he hit the young man in his temple. Thus the young man died. Then all the people said, "We believe in the lord of this young man. We all believe in the lord of this young man." It was said to the king, "See you have done what you have been afraid of. Indeed, Allah has brought down on you what you feared." Then all the people believed in Allah. Afterward, the king ordered the people to dig a moat, and they put a fire in it. He gave the order that the people would pass through the fire if they did not renounce their religion, but people were racing into the fire. There was a woman with a son whom she was breastfeeding. When she was about to fall into the fire, the little boy said, "O be patient, my mother; surely you are on the right path."

The same story was repeated by Ibn Kathir but with different details. In this second version, some of the people of Nagran were worshiping idols. A sorcerer came from the next village to teach sorcery to a young man. A man came and built a tent between his village and the people of Nagran. Al Tamer sent his son, Abd Allah Ibn Al Tamer, with all the other young men, to learn sorcery from the sorcerer. His son stopped by the tent to see what was in it. He saw a man who worshiped Allah, the holy god, and he asked this man about

Islam. Abd Allah Ibn Al Tamer believed in Islam. He asked the man who owned the tent about the great name, but he kept the name a secret. Abd Allah Ibn Al Tamer began to learn the names of god, and he wrote the names on some cups. Then he gathered all the cups, started a fire, and began to throw the cups into the fire until he came to the cup with the greatest name. He took the cup and told his friend about the great name. His companion asked him how he knew the great name. He told the friend what he had done in the burning of the cups, and the only one that had leaped out of the fire was not harmed by the fire at all.

Then he began to tell all the people of the village about his god, Allah. The king sent Abd Allah Ibn Al Tamer to be thrown from the top of the high mountain. He fell on his head, but there was no harm done to him. Then he was sent to be thrown into water, where if anyone would be thrown into this water, he would die.

However, he came out of the water with no harm at all. Then he told the king, "You will not be able to kill me unless you believe in my god, Allah." So the king said the *shahadah* (the statement that he testified in one Allah, the god of Abd Allah Ibn Al Tamer). Then the king struck Abd Allah Ibn Al Tamer with a rod which was in his hand and scratched Abd Allah Ibn Al Tamer with a small scratch. He was killed, and also the king died where he stood. As a result, the people of the city believed in the god of Abd Allah Ibn Al Tamer, and they believed in the religion of Abd Allah Ibn Al Tamer. Then a man named Zo Noas came with his army and gave the people of the city a choice between converting to Judaism or being killed. So they chose to die. They dug the moat and burned the fire. So he killed them by the sword, and he burned around twenty thousand people. That is why Allah gave the story in the Qur'an where he said, *[4]Killed are the companions of the moat, [5]the fire with the fuel.*

Ibn Kathir said that some said this story happened in many places in the world. Some said it happened in Yemen, and then they burned the Christians in the moat. However, others said that it happened in Iraq, in the land of Babylon, when King Nebuchadnezzar made a huge statue and commanded the people to worship it. Daniel and his friends, Azrya and Mshayl, built a furnace. They put the wood and the fire in it. Then the king threw Daniel and his friends into the fire. Then "Allah made the fire cold and in peace," and Allah saved them from it. However, those nine who were against them were thrown into the fire, and the fire consumed them. Ibn Kathir stated that Al Saddi said that the companions of the moat were the three in Shem, Iraq, and Yemen.

Obviously, these stories are nonsense. As usual, the verses of the Qur'an do not have enough details, and Muslim scholars interpreted these verses by fabricating many stories. If you read the verses above, simply as written, you would not understand what Mohammed was talking about. However, if this were a true story about some people who had been thrown into the fire, no one would believe such a fairy tale. Maybe Mohammed was alluding in these verses to the story of Daniel and his friends, as written in the Bible in Daniel 3. I will paraphrase it below, but we encourage the reader to read the entire story in the Bible.

King Nebuchadnezzar made a statue of gold, sixty cubits high and six cubits wide, and then commanded the people of his kingdom to bow down and worship the statue when they heard the sound of the music. Anyone who did not worship the statue would be thrown into the burning, fiery furnace. Some of the Chaldeans went and complained that the Jews were not worshiping the statue. They said to the king that Shadrach, Meshach, and Abed-Nego had not shown any respect to the king and his god.

The king was very angry with them and threatened them with being thrown into the fire if they did not worship him the next time. He boldly said, "There is no god to deliver you from my hand." However, they told the king, "Our God is able to deliver us from your fire, and He is able to deliver us from your hand, O King." Then they told the king, "We will not serve your gods, and we will not worship your statue." Then the king was very angry and commanded that the furnace be made seven times hotter. Then he commanded his most mighty men to tie Shadrach, Meshach, and Abed-Nego and throw them into the fire.

They were thrown into the fire, and the flames of the fire burned these mighty men who threw Shadrach, Meshach, and Abed-Nego into the fire. Then the king saw in the fire four men, and the fourth looked like the Son of God. The king called Shadrach, Meshach, and Abed-Nego to come out of the fire. Then the king and the people saw these men, and the fire had not harmed them. The fire did not even harm their clothes or their hair, and they did not smell like smoke.

So the king blessed the God of Shadrach, Meshach, and Abed-Nego, and he gave the command that anyone who would speak evil of the God of these men would be cut into pieces. Then the king promoted these three men in his kingdom.

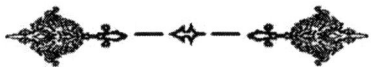

On September 11, 2012, Muslim believers attacked the American consulate in Benghazi in Libya, killing four Americans, including Ambassador J. Christopher Stevens. The illegal Muslim President of the United States, Barack Hussein Obama, and his administration were quick to blame this attack and many other riots by angry mobs of Muslims all over the world on a fourteen minute video cobbled together from trailers of a movie by the name of *Innocence of Muslims* which had been posted on YouTube. Liberals continue to defend Islam, as Republicans did under President George W. Bush eleven years earlier when he invented the title of *radical Islam*, claiming that the September 11, 2001, crime had nothing to do with Islam, but rather it was the action of a few extremists. Now, Obama and his administration are echoing the lies of Bush by stating that almost every Muslim terrorist act has nothing to do with Islam or the teaching of Mohammed, the prophet of Islam, but is simply a result of a movie which insulted the prophet of Islam.[1]

I believe we are living in the last days, for the Scripture has told us that *evil* (Islam) will be called **good** and *good* (Christianity) will be called **evil**. The truth will be called an insult, and the insult will be called the norm. I sat and watched the fourteen minute trailer, and I found that there is only one reason for which those who were involved in this movie should be arrested, and that is for the very poor quality of this film production. On the other hand, I found the message of this movie to be 100 percent truthful.

Now, because of the ignorance of the American people about Islam, Muslims in America are in a better place than they were before September 11 came and went because the truth was never told. Today there are more Muslims in the important offices of the United States of America. That is why we have Muslims in the White House, Pentagon, FBI, CIA, Senate, Congress, as mayors, and all over our military branches. Just name it, and they are there. My prediction is that because we as American people do not know Mohammed, the so-

---

[1]Nakoula Basseley Nakoula, *Innocence of Muslims* (movie trailer), accessed November 16, 2012, https://www. youtube.com/watch?v=wuPRB XnXn2M, (may no longer be accessed in US, but available in other countries).

called prophet of Islam, most likely Muslims here in America will use this movie about Mohammed to literally demolish our freedom of speech.

This can be stopped if the American people learn the truth about Mohammed. That is why I recorded a documentary, *Revealing the Truth behind the Mohammed Movie,* which is available on our website at http://thestraightway.org, as well as on YouTube. That is also why this chapter on Mohammed is so important to show why Muslims do what they do. It is foolish to believe that there will ever be peace in the Middle East or for democracy to ever have a place in the Muslim world. As Turkish Prime Minister and Muslim Brotherhood front man Erdogan once said, "Democracy is like a streetcar that you take to your destination; then you get off."[2] Or more accurately put, it is like a streetcar that you take only as long as you believe it will get you to your destination; otherwise, you hop off.

I believe that Muslim riots and anger all over the world about the Mohammed movie were a result of one or both of the following two reasons. First, they are ignorant about their prophet. Second, they will just use any reason to do what they have been told to do by the word of Allah in the Qur'an and the command of Mohammed in the hadith. So let us begin to learn the truth about Mohammed, the prophet of Islam.

Muslims believe Mohammed was the most perfect man who ever lived, as well as the greatest of the prophets, and he is to be emulated in every way. Muslims also believe that prophets do not sin. However, as we have discovered in *Exposing the Truth about the Qur'an: The Revelation of Error* that all men, prophet or not, have sinned; the only one who has not sinned is our Lord and Savior, Jesus Christ. Throughout the Qur'an, Mohammed was a sinful man. For example, we read in Qur'an 47:19: *...and ask forgiveness for your sins, and for the believing men and believing women....* Also in Qur'an 48:2: *[2]that Allah may forgive you for your past sins and your future sins and to fulfill his grace on you....* Mohammed committed murder, adultery, theft, blasphemy, and other sins. I refer you to the Qur'an and the hadith (Mohammed's own sayings) to see the many sins of Mohammed.

---

[2]quoted in H. D. Munn (blog), "Democracy," September 20, 2012, accessed December 14, 2012, http://hdmunn.net/2012/09/20/democracy.

The story of Mohammed is extensive and could be a book of its own. For our purposes, we will only provide a summary sufficient to introduce the reader to the story of his life.

Who was Mohammed? To begin, we must recognize that Mohammed is the reason why we have *Exposing the Truth about the Qur'an: The Revelation of Error* because of his concocted religion of Islam and his recitation of the Qur'an.

Some Muslims may say, "We believe in all of the prophets, Abraham, Moses, Jesus, and Mohammed. They are all equal in the sight of Allah, and we worship one god." *Is that true?* When reading Qur'an 2:253, Allah said: *[253]These are the messengers; we favored some of them above the others....* Obviously, to Muslims the prophets are not equal. Muslims believe Mohammed to be the final prophet, as it is written in Qur'an 33:40: *[40]Mohammed was not the father of any man among you, but is the messenger of Allah and the khātam[3] of the prophets. And Allah was the knower of all things.* Moreover, Mohammed said, "...I am the last of the Prophets."[4] Mohammed is the greatest prophet because he came with the final religion of Allah, the religion of Islam, the only religion accepted by Allah. We can see this clearly in Qur'an 3:85: *[85]And whoever desires any other religion except Islam, so it[5] will not be accepted from him, and in the hereafter he will be of the losers.*

Notice that Muslims believe that the Bible has been corrupted but that the Qur'an is the perfect word of Allah. All this leads to this final thought which is that Islam is the only accepted religion and Mohammed is the final prophet; therefore, he must be the greatest prophet of all. I would like to pose a question. *According to the Qur'an, can Mohammed even be a prophet?* In the Qur'an we read that the prophethood was given to the Children of Israel, the descendants of Jacob. In Qur'an 45:16: *[16]And indeed, we gave the book and the wisdom and the prophethood to the children of Israel, and we provided them with the good things. And we favored them above the worlds.* In Qur'an 29:27: *[27]And we granted him Isaac and Jacob, and we assigned the prophethood and the book to his descendants. And we gave him his wage in this world, and surely in the hereafter he is*

---

[3]seal, non-Arabic word of probable Aramaic origin
[4]Sahih Bukhari, Hadith 735.
[5]any other religion

among the good. Was Mohammed a descendant of Israel?
Obviously, he was not. Therefore, according to the Qur'an, he cannot
be a prophet.

Introduction to Sheik Mohammed Ibn Abd Al Wahab

Unlike Ibn Kathir, Sheik Mohammed Ibn Abd Al Wahab, in his
book, *A Summary of the Life of the Messenger,* gave a quick summary
of the stories of the prophets.[6] He began with the story of Adam, how
Allah created him in heaven, and then how Allah sent him to earth.
Then he mentioned that after him, Allah sent many messengers, some
givers of good news and some warners. This author stated that the
first messenger was Noah and the last messenger was Mohammed.
The writer advised Muslims to know the line of prophets, and he
stated that if people could identify Mohammed's heritage with this
line of prophets, they would be safe. Otherwise, they would be lost.

He also advised Muslims to know what happened to their father
Adam and to their enemy Satan and what happened to Noah, Houd,
Saleh, Abraham, Lot, Moses, 'Isā, and Mohammed along with their
people.[7] Notice, he wrote about Noah through 'Isā, and he only
mentioned seven names before Mohammed. Perhaps he forgot there
were more prophets than these.

Sheik Mohammed stated that Adam and his descendants, for ten
generations, were all Muslims.[8] Then they became infidels because
they elevated some of the good people to the point of worshiping
them as gods.

In Qur'an 71:23: *[23]And they said, 'Do not forsake your gods
and do not forsake Wadd nor Sowah nor Yaghuth and Yahuk
and Nasr.'* (Some scholars state that these were pagan Arab gods).
As we mentioned before, these were the five righteous men who died,
and people worshiped them. That is why Allah sent his Prophet Noah
to them. Allah saved Noah and his people on the ship, and they spread
all over the earth.

The people became polytheists again. Allah sent many
messengers to them. Qur'an 16:36: *[36]And indeed, we have sent to
every nation a messenger that: "Serve Allah, and turn away
from the idolatry." So some of them Allah guided, and some of*

---

[6]Mohammed Ibn Abd Al Wahab, *A Summary of the Life of the Messenger, Sirat Rasul Allah,* 2nd printing, recorded by Solomon Ibn Sahman, 1309 After Mohammed's Immigration (Damascus: Dar Al Salam), 7.
[7]Ibid., 8.
[8]Ibid., 9.

them, the error established over them. "So walk on the earth, so see how was the end of the deniers."

Is this true? Did God send a messenger to every nation? The statement that Allah sent a messenger to every nation is not true. We can write a list of all of the nations who never received a messenger. As a matter of fact, the only nation to which God used to send messengers is the nation of Israel. Sometimes God sent a messenger from Israel to a Gentile nation, as in the case of the people of Nineveh. Jesus, on the other hand, sent his disciples and Christian believers to the ends of the world.

From reading the Bible, we know that people believed their prophets. Either Mohammed did not know that or he did not read the Bible. The Bible states that people believed Moses and respected him. They respected Jesus and still worship Him.

Then Sheik Mohammed said that the messenger of Allah, Mohammed, used to narrate the stories of these early messengers to his companions so that they might learn from his stories in order that we may know the good and the evil.[9] The author confessed that there were many messengers and their people about whom nothing is known, for "Allah did not tell us anything about them. Allah did tell us about Ad and their Prophet Houd and how the companions of Houd believed in one god. We do not know how long their belief lasted." Then he mentioned Prophet Saleh and his companions, stating he did not know how long they were believers.

Sheik Mohammed mentioned the story of Abraham, which we covered in detail in chapter 7.[10] He then addressed Qur'an 29:27: *[27]And we granted him Isaac and Jacob, and we assigned the prophethood and the book to his descendants. And we gave him his wage in this world, and surely in the hereafter he is among the good.* Based on this verse, Sheik Mohammed asserted that all the prophets and the messengers, except Mohammed, came from the descendants of Isaac. As for Ishmael, he stated that Allah did not send from his descendants anyone except his prophet of Islam, Mohammed, whom Allah sent to all the worlds (remember they claimed there were seven earths). The prophets who came before him went only to their own people. Allah's favorite prophet, Mohammed, was sent to all the people, and Allah favored him over all other prophets with many other things which he did not mention.

---

[9]Ibid., 10.
[10]Ibid., 16-20.

We covered these statements previously, but I will summarize. All the other prophets were Jews, but Mohammed was not a descendant of Ishmael but of Keturah. We know though, that Jesus was not sent only to the Jews but to the whole world. *For God so loved the world that He gave His only begotten Son, that whoever believes in Him should not perish but have everlasting life* (John 3:16).

The Qualifications that Make a Person a Prophet

What is a prophet? It is a person who receives prophecies (of future events) from God, shares them with his people, and then these prophecies come to pass. Additionally, he will lead the people to worship the true God of the Bible. These are the three major markers of a true prophet. *Did Mohammed meet such standards?* Obviously, he did not!

From the Qur'an we can clearly see that he was not a prophet. Qur'an 3:179 reads: *[179]It was not in Allah to leave the believers in the condition in which you are in, until he distinguishes the bad from the good. And it was not of Allah to show you the unseen, but Allah chooses of his messengers whom he wills. So believe in Allah and his messengers, and if you believe and fear, so you will have a great wage.*

What does the Bible teach concerning the proof of prophethood? How can we know if a prophet is a true prophet? Moses gave us an answer. He said the person who claims to be a prophet must prophesy, which is to predict what will happen in the future, or he is no prophet. We will cover Mohammed's so-called prophecies in more detail later, but the bottom line is that Mohammed did not give any prophecies, so he failed the first test.

Deuteronomy 13:1-5: *[1]If there arises among you a prophet or a dreamer of dreams, and he gives you a sign or a wonder, [2]and the sign or the wonder comes to pass, of which he spoke to you, saying, "Let us go after other gods"—which you have not known—"and let us serve them," [3]you shall not listen to the words of that prophet or that dreamer of dreams, for the Lord your God is testing you to know whether you love the Lord your God with all your heart and with all your soul. [4]You shall walk after the Lord your God and fear Him, and keep His commandments and obey His voice; you shall serve Him and hold fast to Him. [5]But that prophet or that dreamer of dreams shall be put to death, because he has spoken in order to turn you away from the Lord your God, who brought you out of the land of Egypt and redeemed you from the house of bondage, to entice you from the way in which the Lord your God commanded you to walk. So you shall put away the evil from your midst.*

The second important test concerning the proof that a man is a prophet is that some of his prophecies must be fulfilled during his lifetime. Other prophecies could be given for future fulfillment. Since Mohammed did not have any prophecies that were fulfilled, he failed the second test.

Not only does the Bible teach that the man who claims to be a prophet must prophesy and his prophecy must be fulfilled, he must lead the people to worship God, the true God of the Bible. Here someone may say, "Allah and God are the same." This is what many claim and many millions accept, especially those who have never read the Bible and the Qur'an. That is why I believe this book which you are reading has given you the answer. I pray that by now you will open your eyes and open your mind and will save your heart and the hearts of those you care about from falling for the teachings of Islam.

Although there are many false prophets who came after our Lord and Savior Jesus Christ, we decided to write only on the prophet of Islam (Mohammed) in this book, *Exposing the Truth about the Qur'an: The Revelation of Error,* because of the dire issues with which the world now struggles resulting from his role as the founder of the cult of Islam and the creator/fabricator of the stories about the prophets in the Qur'an. We chose to use Ibn Isaac's book, *The Life of Muhammad,* which is a large book with over eight hundred pages, to summarize the important portions and to shed enough light to know Mohammed as Muslims view him.[11] I will also add my views as we go through this summary, as written in the Qur'an and its interpretations by Muslim scholars and Mohammed's own words. Another source we will be using is Mohammed Ibn Abd Al Wahab's book, *A Summary of the Life of the Messenger, Sirat Rasul Allah.*

Genealogy of Mohammed, the Prophet of Islam

One of the more humorous writings found throughout the internet is the genealogy tree of Mohammed. Muslims created a lengthy genealogy of their prophet of Islam, Mohammed, which begins with Adam, as we discussed before in chapter 2 of *Exposing the Truth*

---

[11]Guillaume, Alfred, *The Life of Muhammad,* The Translation of Ibn Israq's *Sirat Rasul Allah* (Karachi: Oxford University Press, 1978).

about the Qur'an: The Revelation of Error. Every time we read any genealogy Ibn Kathir or some other Muslim scholar has given for any of the so-called prophets in the Qur'an, we must ask this question. *Where did they get this genealogy?* As in most of these occasions, the answer is the Bible. Here we must ask the question once again. *If Muslims cannot prove to us who Mohammed's father was, as we will explain shortly, then how can they tie Mohammed to this imaginary family tree?* The matter is laughable. Of course, these Muslim scholars had access to the Bible, and there in the pages of the Bible, they discovered that Christians can tie Jesus' genealogy to Adam. Therefore, Muslims fabricated a genealogy tree to bring greatness to their prophet of Islam, Mohammed; but, as we will see, their attempt was most unsuccessful.

Mohammed's Birth

Mohammed was born around AD 570 in Mecca, Saudi Arabia. His named father was Abd Allah which means the servant of Allah. His mother was Aminah Bint (daughter of) Wahb. Both parents were non-Christian, non-Jewish, and probably idol worshipers, as were most of the people around Mecca. Mohammed, in the hadith, wept before his mother's tomb, asking Allah to forgive his mother, but Allah refused to do so. We know from the hadith that Mohammed had siblings because Mohammed said that his mother said, "When I was pregnant with him (Mohammed), I had never had such a light pregnancy as in his case, and I saw in my sleep when I was pregnant with him that light came out of me...."[12] We have no knowledge of these siblings; however, Mohammed's birth in the year AD 570 was four years after his named father, Abd Allah, died!

Some might say, *"How can a child be born four years after his father's death?"* The answer is simple. Abd Allah was called his father, but he was not.[13] This is one of the pieces of information shared in the trailer of the Mohammed movie which will be discussed in more detail in the following pages.[14]

In an apparent effort to explain Mohammed's birth being so long after his father's death, Muslim scholars Ibn Kathir and Al Qurtobi both asserted that a pregnancy could be as short as six months and

---

[12]Imam Al Suoty, *The AL Kasa's AL-Kubra VI* (n.p., n.d.), 132-135.

[13]Christian Prince, *Deception of Allah* (Venice, FL: Usama K. Dakdok Publishing, 2011), 11.

[14]Nakoula, *Innocence of Muslims.*

dispute over the maximum length of between two or five years.[15,16] This is in their interpretations to Qur'an 13:8: *[8]Allah knows what every female bears, and how much their womb lessens and enlarges. And with him everything is by measure.* In a video shown on YouTube about the gestation time of pregnancy, a question was asked of the Mufti of Egypt.[17] The Mufti of Egypt stated that a woman can be pregnant for four years, and no one can accuse her of committing adultery because that is the teaching of Muslim scholars. Some may claim that this was the thinking only in the days of Mohammed, but that is not true for this belief continues today in the Muslim world.

Mohammed's real name was Qathem.[18] He later changed his name to Mohammed. The Qur'an also stated that his name was Ahmad in Qur'an 61:6: *[6]And when 'Isā, son of Mary, said, "O children of Israel, surely I am a messenger of Allah to you, confirming what is between my hands from the Torah and to give you the good news of a messenger to come after me. His name is Ahmad."[19] So when he came to them with the proofs, they said, "This is obvious sorcery."*

Mohammed claimed that 'Isā (wrong name, he meant Jesus) prophesied that there would be a messenger after him and his name would be Ahmad. Some Muslims cite the Gospel of Barnabas, a fifteenth century forgery by Muslims, which obviously shows that Muslims do not understand what *is* and *is not* canonical text, where it is written that Jesus answered that the name of the Messiah is admirable, for Allah himself gave him the name when he had created his soul and placed it in celestial splendor.

Then Allah said: "Wait, Mohammed; for thy sake I will create paradise, the world, and a great multitude of creatures, whereof I make thee a present insomuch that whoso blesses thee shall be

[15]"Interpretation of Qur'an 13:8," accessed February 19, 2012, www.Quran.al-islam.com/Page.aspx? pageid=221&BookID=13&Page=250.
[16]"Interpretation of Qur'an 13:8," accessed February 19, 2012, www.Quran.al-islam.com/Page.aspx? pageid=221&BookID=14&Page=250.
[17]http://www.youtube.com/watch?v=ttgl74W0vvY, accessed December 19, 2012.
[18]http://romanos.150m.com/nasab_mo7amad.htm, original Arabic sources are 1) Altbakat al-Kobrya to Ibn Sad *The Book of the Marriage* of Abdulah Ibn al-Motulab to Amnah bent Wahub; 2) al-Sayrah al-Halabiah, *The Book of the Marriage* of Abd Allah the father of Mohammed to Amnah and The Digging of the Zamzam Well; 3) *The Discrimination Between Friends* by Ibn Abd al-Bar, *The Book of Mohammed, The Messenger of Allah*; and 4) *The Lion of the Forest,* accessed March 14, 2012.
[19]Muslims claim that Ahmad is the same name as Mohammed, which is not true, and that 'Isā, whom they claim to be Jesus, prophesied his coming.

blessed and whoso shall curse thee shall be accursed. When I shall send thee into the world, I shall send thee as my messenger of salvation; and thy word shall be true, insomuch that heaven and earth shall fail, but thy faith shall never fail. Mohammed is his blessed name." Then the crowd lifted up their voices, saying: "O god, send us thy messenger: O admirable one, come quickly for the salvation of the world!" (Barnabas 97:9-10)

They claim that the Italian manuscript replaces *Admirable One* with **Mohammed**. They also claim Old Testament references to Mohammed: "I will raise a Prophet from amongst their brothers (the brothers of the Israelites). I will reveal My Speech upon him." These verses refer to Deuteronomy 18:15, 18-19. Also, in John 16:6-8, 12-13, Muslims misunderstand the *Counselor* (Paraclete) to be Mohammed which will be discussed in detail later. Neither the name Ahmad nor Mohammed should be given to men for such a name means *praised one*. This name should only be given to God alone.

Who then was Mohammed's father? Muslims claim that he was the son of Abd Allah. In the above sources we found that Abd Allah (Mohammed's father) married Amnah and Abd Al Motlab (Mohammed's grandfather) married Halah on the same day. Mohammed's mother, Amnah, became pregnant immediately after the marriage, and then Mohammed's father died while she was pregnant. Abd Al Motlab (Mohammed's grandfather) had a son from his wife, Halah, who was named Hamzah. Hamzah was four years older than Mohammed, even though Mohammed's father died after living only a few months with Mohammed's mother. Therefore, his son Mohammed could not actually be his son, unless he was inside his mother's womb for four years.

One might ask this question. *How did we know that Hamzah, Mohammed's uncle, was four years older than Mohammed?* The answer can be determined by knowing the age at death of both Mohammed and his uncle, Hamzah. Muslim scholars say that Mohammed died eight years after his uncle, Hamzah, died at the age of sixty-three. If they were born at the same time, Hamzah would have died at age fifty-five. However, scholars also record that Hamzah died in the third year of the emigration[20] at the age of fifty-nine (59+8=67-63 [Mohammed's age at death] = 4 years younger). This proves that Hamzah was born four years prior to the birth of Mohammed. *Who then was Mohammed's father?* Since it is

---

[20]Mohammed died eight years after Hamzah's death, at the 11th year of emigration.

impossible, except in Islamic science, for a woman to be pregnant for over four years, we must conclude that *only Allah knows best* for no one knows for sure who Mohammed's father was.

Mohammed's Childhood and Upbringing

Although we do not know much about his childhood or upbringing, Muslims stated that Mohammed suffered epileptic fits beginning at age five. Mohammed's mother, Aminah, died when he was six years old.[21] He then lived with his grandfather, Abd Al Motlab, until his grandfather died two years later when Mohammed was eight years of age. Mohammed then lived with his uncle, Abu Talib. He worked as a shepherd, as well as a merchant for his cousin, Khadijah, a wealthy business woman who had been married three times or so. He acted as a trading agent for her caravans. Notice that, before Islam, women used to own businesses, and Mohammed actually worked for his boss/wife for some twenty years before he claimed to be a prophet. Muslims in the West claim that Islam gives women more rights than they had before Islam, which obviously is a lie, for now, under Islamic law (Sharia), it is forbidden for women to work.

In Saudi Arabia, King Fahd Bin Abdul Aziz passed a law, #11651, dated 16-5-1403. (This date is according to the Muslim calendar which is dated starting in the year after Mohammed's emigration from Mecca to Medina; this corresponds to around 1980.) This law stated that women are not allowed to work in any institution, public or private, or any government offices, no working whatsoever. The reason given was because it is unlawful and stands against Islamic law and the tradition of the country.

Mohammed's Marriages

Khadijah, the owner of the caravans, liked Mohammed because he was a faithful worker. That is why she proposed marriage to him when he was twenty-five and she was in her forties. She is reported to have had six children, two sons who died in childhood and four daughters who lived to adulthood. They were reportedly Mohammed's children. However, it is noted that with the many subsequent wives and concubines, he was unable to produce any other children. Their marriage lasted for twenty-five years and was reported

---

[21]"Muhammad," *Wikipedia,* last updated February 9, 2013, accessed February 10, 2013, http://en.wikipedia.org/wiki/Muhammad.

to be a happy one. Mohammed and Khadijah adopted a son by the name of Zaid who married a woman by the name of Zanab Bint Jahash whom we will discuss later in this chapter.

Khadijah died when Mohammed was fifty years old. It was after her death that he began to take multiple wives. He had at least thirteen wives and numerous concubines.[22] After the death of Khadijah, Mohammed had a wife by the name of Soudah Bint Zamah who was not an attractive woman, but whose purpose was to raise Mohammed's third and favorite wife Aisha, whom he married at the age of fifty-one when she was only six years old. This was documented in the Mohammed movie and is another portion of the movie which causes Muslims to be angry, for there we see Mohammed as a pedophile.[23]

Mohammed went and asked for her hand from her father, Abu Bakr. Abu Bakr refused to give Mohammed his daughter, as he said, "You are my brother." Mohammed answered, "Yes, you are my brother in faith, but I want her as a wife." Mohammed claimed that Allah dropped Aisha to him on a blanket of silk from heaven and that Allah had given her to Mohammed as a wife.[24] *(Does this remind you of the vision in the Bible of Peter and the blanket?* You can read that story in Acts 10:10-17.) When Abu Bakr could not dispute with Mohammed any more, he gave his daughter to Mohammed as a wife. Aisha's mother went outside the house and brought her daughter, who was holding a doll, from the swing as she was swinging. She washed Aisha's face with water and then put her on Mohammed's lap.

What would we call a man who enters into such a marriage but a child molester and a sex offender? Muslims may protest and say that Mohammed did not actually penetrate her until she turned nine years of age and he was fifty-four. Mohammed is cited for being a man of exceptional self-control because he only touched her from outside without full intercourse for this period of three years. In other words, Mohammed used this little child-wife for sexual gratification in every way short of actual penetration until she was nine years old.

---

[22]From the following books 1. Vol. 2 from the book Ahya Alluom El dean, 2. The Women of the Prophet, 3. El Sumpt El Samean, 4. Sahih Bukhari, 5. The Wife of the Prophet).

[23]Nakoula, *Innocence of Muslims*.

[24]http://www.dorar.net/enc/hadith?skeys=%D8%A3%D8%B1%D9%8A%D8%AA%D9%83+%D9%81%D9%8A+%D8%A7%D9%84%D9%85%D9%86%D8%A7%D9%85+%D8%AB%D9%84%D8%A7%D8%AB+%D9%84%D9%8A%D8%A7%D9%84%D9%8A&xclude=&degree_cat0=1, accessed March 6, 2012.

If we say this was child molestation, Muslims say this is not true because she was his wife. Another good excuse Muslims give for such a marriage is that children in Saudi Arabia, with its high climatic temperature, mature at an early age, especially in Mohammed's days. Therefore, she was not really a child. However, note that the Qur'an teaches even today that Muslim men can not only marry children but even have sexual relations with them at such an age, as it is practiced in many Muslim countries around the world. The waiting period to determine if a divorced wife is pregnant is given in Qur'an 65:4 where Allah said: *⁴And for those of your women who despair of the menstruation,*[25] *if you doubt [that they may be pregnant], their prescribed waiting time is three months, as well as for those who have not yet begun menstruation.*[26] Al Qurtobi interpreted the phrase "not yet begun menstruation" to mean little children.[27] Therefore, when a man divorces a child-wife, the waiting period to determine if she is pregnant, is three months.

Another excuse Muslims give for Mohammed is that he had the right to such a young child because it was normal during his days, for many men married children. I would like to respond by stating that, in Lot's day, many men enjoyed other men sexually and that was the norm in that culture, but this did not give Lot the right to enjoy another male sexually. Sin is sin, and Mohammed, the great noble messenger or prophet, as stated in the Qur'an, should not indulge in such ungodly desires simply because it is the norm for his day.

When Mohammed later desired to divorce Soudah Bint Zamah, she begged him not to divorce her because she desired to be one of his wives on the Day of Judgment. She knew how much Mohammed loved his favorite child-wife Aisha, so she made him an offer which she was sure he could not refuse. She told him that she did not have the woman's desire of sexual needs and offered to give her night to Aisha. He accepted her offer, and she was kept as one of his wives.

A few of Mohammed's other wives are worth noting. One of these was Zanab Bint Jahash. We can read her story in Qur'an 33:37-38: *³⁷And when you said to whom*[28] *Allah had graced on and you graced on, "Keep your wife to yourself and fear Allah." And you hide in yourself[29] what Allah would reveal. And you feared the people,[30] and Allah is more worthy to be feared. So when Zaid had satisfied his desire from her,[31] we married her to you so that it would not be a shame on the believers to marry the wives of their sons[32] when they have settled the affair[33] concerning them. And the command of Allah was accomplished. [38]There was no shame on the prophet where Allah had ordained for him. The custom of Allah with those who have gone before and the command of Allah was a predetermined decree.*

When I read such words, my heart breaks for all Muslims who put their trust in such a man. What kind of father was this man to take the wife of his son because of his lust after her, which began when he went to visit them (Zanab and Zaid) and he caught a glimpse of her exposed flesh? Some Muslims would defend Mohammed's action here by saying that Zaid was not a real son, he was just an adopted son, and Allah (conveniently for Mohammed) canceled the practice of adoption in Islam after questioning Mohammed about his actions. This was also shown in the Mohammed movie.[34]

This convenient cancelation of adoption freeing Mohammed from criticism is written in Qur'an 33:4-5: *[4]Allah did not make to man two hearts inside his body, and he did not make your wives which you turn your back from them your mothers. And he did not make your adopted sons your sons. This is your saying with your mouth, and Allah says the truth. And he guides the way. [5]Call them[35] to their fathers, this will be more just with Allah. So if you do not know who their fathers are, so they are your brothers in the religion and your friends. And there is no fault against you in what you have sinned in, but what your heart purposely intends. And Allah was forgiving, merciful.*

I would say to them: shame on you. The Bible says that if a man looks at a woman with his eyes and lusts in his heart, he commits adultery with her. One of the noblest acts, which was practiced in the Arab world before Islam, was to adopt a child; however, because of

---

[29]his lust for Zanab
[30]what they would think of Mohammed marrying Zanab
[31]divorcing her
[32]in adoption
[33]divorce
[34]Nakoula, *Innocence of Muslims.*
[35]the adopted sons

his lust, Mohammed and his Allah canceled adoption. *How long will Muslims defend a man like this?*

Another portion of the movie which causes Muslims to be angry is Mohammed's treatment of another wife, Safiyya Bint Huyayy, was also very disturbing. Muslims often excuse Mohammed's many wives by saying there were so many widows of war that he married many out of compassion. Of course, they do not mention that he created many of those widows, as in the case of Safiyya Bint Huyayy. While she was still a new seventeen-year-old bride of a Jewish man, Mohammed killed her father, brother, and husband—in fact, her whole family.

Then Mohammed took her as his wife, after she had been taken captive and dragged through the carnage. He had a large wedding feast and had sex with her that same night.[36] During this night while Mohammed was having sex with Safiyya, a man by the name of Abu Ayyub protected the place where Mohammed was with his sword. Mohammed saw him in the morning and asked him what he had been doing. He responded that he was fearful for Mohammed's safety with this woman whose father, husband, and people Mohammed had killed.[37]

This was Mohammed as a father, a husband, and the prophet of Islam. We can go on and on with many more stories about Mohammed's other forced or sorrowful marriages. We will stop here, but the reader may investigate more on his own.

Mohammed's Sexual Lifestyle

If we open the Qur'an and discover that Mohammed, the greatest prophet that walked on earth as Muslims claim, had sinned in the form of killing and adultery, will this demolish and end the claim that the Qur'an is a holy book? Quickly, let us look at Qur'an 66:1: *[1]O you prophet, why do you forbid what Allah has made lawful to you, seeking to please your wives? And Allah is forgiving, merciful. What does Allah is forgiving mean?* The meaning of this verse is not immediately clear, but when we read the interpretation of Muslim scholars, we discover that Mohammed had repeatedly committed the sin of adultery with Mary the Coptic woman.[38]

---

[36]Sahih Bukhari, Hadith 6160.

[37]*Biography of Ibn Hisham*, http://sirah.al-islam.com/display.asp?f=hes2452.htm, accessed February 10, 2013.

[38]Nakoula, *Innocence of Muslims.*

Unlike King David who repented when he committed adultery with Bathsheba and covered his bed with tears, Mohammed did not do any repentance. Unlike God, Allah did not send any prophet or any friend to advise Mohammed to repent of his sin, but Allah himself told Mohammed NOT to stop his sexual sin. Allah instructed Mohammed by stating that it was not wrong, it was not sin, and it was lawful for Mohammed to do so.

Mohammed gave himself permission to be with an unlimited number of women sexually without marriage, as is written in Qur'an 33:50: *⁵⁰O you prophet, surely we have made it lawful for you, your wives whom you have given their wages and those that your right hand possesses which Allah has granted you and the daughters of your paternal uncle and the daughters of your paternal aunts and the daughters of your maternal uncle and the daughters of your maternal aunts, those who emigrate with you. And a believing woman if she gives herself to the prophet, if the prophet desires to have sex with her, this is a privilege for you but not for any other believers. Indeed, we know what we ordain for them in their wives and what their right hand possessed, that there may be no shame on your part. And Allah was forgiving, merciful.*

Some Muslim scholars changed the words *have sex with* to read ***to marry,*** but that is dishonesty in the translation. *Why?* First, in Islamic law if any believing woman offers herself to any man, he can marry her. *So where is the privilege for Mohammed here?* The verse said that it is a privilege for Mohammed alone. Second, the verse ended with *that there may be no shame on your part. Why would Mohammed be ashamed to have another wife?* He already had at least thirteen wives, which superseded the law of Allah in the Qur'an which clearly teaches that a man could only have four wives. Finally, Allah said in Qur'an 33:52: *⁵²It is not lawful for you the women[39] after that, nor to exchange your present wives for other women though their beauty charms you, except what your right hand possesses. And Allah was watcher over all things.*

How could the command of Allah in verse 50 concerning the statement, "have sex with" mean in a marriage relationship, if Allah did not allow Mohammed to marry any new women in verse 52? The obvious conclusion is that in verse 50, Allah is giving Mohammed permission to be involved sexually with any believing women who

---

[39]in marriage

offer themselves to him without marrying them. This was shown in the Mohammed movie to describe Mohammed as an adulterer and as a womanizer.[40]

The Qur'an lists a large number of female family members Mohammed could lie with, but then he said it would be additionally lawful in 33:50: ... *And a believing woman if she gives herself to the prophet, if the prophet desires to have sex with her....* Notice that Allah did not say "if a single believing woman," but "*a believing woman*" which means that Mohammed was given permission to have sex with any woman, single or not.

All of the Muslim scholars, in their sugar-coated English translations of the Qur'an, actually tried to cover up the command of Allah to Mohammed that gave him permission to be with all these women sexually (by claiming a marriage relationship). Here are some examples:

> Khan stated: "... and a believing woman if she offers herself to the Prophet, and the Prophet wishes to **marry** her..."
>
> Maulana said: "...and a believing woman, if she gives herself to the Prophet, if the Prophet desires to **marry** her."
>
> Pichthall translated this: "and a believing woman if she gives herself unto the Prophet and the Prophet desire to ask her in **marriage**."
>
> As for Rashad, he translated it to be: "Also, if a believing woman gave herself to the prophet - by forfeiting the dowry - the prophet may **marry** her without a dowry, if he so wishes."
>
> Sarwar translated it to be: "...The believing woman, who has offered herself to the Prophet and whom the Prophet may want to **marry**, will be specially for him, not for other believers."
>
> Shakir said it was: "...and a believing woman if she gave herself to the Prophet, if the Prophet desired to **marry** her-- specially for you, not for the (rest of) believers."
>
> Sherali stated: "...and any other believing woman if she offers herself for **marriage** to the Prophet provided the Prophet desires to **marry** her; this provision is only for thee."
>
> Then Yusufali translated the verse to be: "...and any believing woman who dedicates her soul to the Prophet if the

---

[40]Nakoula, *Innocence of Muslims.*

Prophet wishes to **wed** her; - this only for thee, and not for the Believers (at large)."

Notice all of the above translators added the word *marriage* or *marry* into it, which does not exist in the Arabic language. In the Qur'an it is literally stated by Allah *If the prophet desires to "f___ her,"* which, in order not to offend readers, we translated as "to have sex with her." There is no *marriage* mentioned in the verse. Even though all these Muslim scholars deceived the English reader by fixing the previous verse to replace the crude words for having sex with the word *marriage*, they all forgot to correct verse 52, as we read in their own following translations, which goes on to discuss limitations on actual marriage.

Khan translated it as: "It is not lawful for you **(to marry other) women** after this, nor to change them for other wives even though their beauty attracts you, except those (captives or slaves) whom your right hand possesses. And Allah is Ever a Watcher over all things."

Now Maulana translated it to be: "**It is not allowed to thee to take wives after this**, nor to change them for other wives, though their beauty be pleasing to thee, except those whom thy right hand possesses. And Allah is ever Watchful over all things."

Pichthall translated it to be: "**It is not allowed thee to take (other) women** henceforth, nor that thou shouldst change them for other wives even though their beauty pleased thee, save those whom thy right hand possesseth. And Allah is ever Watcher over all things."

Then Rashad wrote that it meant: "Beyond the categories described to you, you are **enjoined from marrying any other women**, nor can you substitute a new wife (from the prohibited categories), no matter how much you admire their beauty. You must be content with those already made lawful to you. GOD is watchful over all things."

Sarwar translated: "Besides these, **other women are not lawful for you to marry** nor is it lawful for you to exchange your wives for the wives of others (except for the slave girls), even though they may seem attractive to you. God is watchful over all things."

Shakir translated that: "**It is not allowed to you to take women afterwards**, nor that you should change them for other wives, though their beauty be pleasing to you, except what your right hand possesses and Allah is Watchful over all things."

Sherali translated: "**It is not allowed to thee to marry women after that,** nor to change them for other wives even, though their goodness please thee, except any that thy right hand possesses. And ALLAH is Watchful over all things."

Yusufali translated: "**It is not lawful for thee (to marry more) women after this,** nor to change them for (other) wives, even though their beauty attract thee, except any thy right hand should possess (as handmaidens): and Allah doth watch over all things."

As you have seen, these translators were able to change the wording in verse 50, but they all missed verse 52 and contradicted themselves. *How can Allah give permission to his great noble messenger and prophet to marry any believing woman in Qur'an 33:50 and, at the same time, not allow him to marry any other women than the wives which he already has?* Yes, indeed, liars are forgetful. They lie in their translations. The final conclusion is Mohammed was a womanizer, a man who likes to be with multiple women, and who also encouraged the believers to do so, even with married slaves and prostitution, as written in Qur'an 4:24 which we will be discussing later.

Mohammed's Call to Prophethood

On a cold winter night, Mohammed ran from the cave of Hara after he saw a spirit. He was sweating with fear, crying, "Zamalony, Zamalony," which means *cover me, cover me.* When he reached home, his wife Khadijah comforted him and told him that the next time the spirit appeared she would perform some tests, so they would know whether it was a godly or demonic spirit. Depiction of these ridiculous tests is another portion of the Mohammed movie which causes Muslims to be upset.

On another night the same spirit appeared to Mohammed, and he told his wife, so she performed her tests.[41] She told him to sit on her left thigh, and then she asked, "Do you see the spirit?" He replied, "Yes." Then she asked him to sit on her right thigh and repeated her

---

[41]Readers can go online and read about the tests of Khadijah and the proof of Mohammed's prophecy. See http://www.islamweb.net/newlibrary/display_book.php?bk_no= 58&ID =192&idfrom=261&idto=274&bookid=58&startno=7, accessed April 2, 2012.

question. He replied, "Yes, I see him." She held him on her lap and asked him a third time, "Do you still see him?" He answered, "Yes." At that point she sighed and uncovered herself. She asked Mohammed one last time, "Do you still see the spirit?" He said, "No."

Then she rejoiced and announced to him, "O Mohammed, good news. You are the apostle of Allah, and this spirit is nothing but an angel."[42] Later she took Mohammed to her cousin, Waraka Ibn Nawfal, who was a heretic monk who assured Mohammed that this was Angel Gabreel. That is how Mohammed proved his prophethood. Reference in the Mohammed movie to the assistance this individual gave Mohammed in creating the Qur'an further incited Muslims.

Let us examine this proof of prophethood. First, note in the following verse that the witness of a woman in Islam is only equal to half of men. In Qur'an 2:282, we read: *[282]... So if the debtor was mentally deficient or weak or cannot dictate, so let his friend dictate with fairness and call two witnesses from your men; so if there were not two men, so one man and two women of those among whom you are pleased for witnesses so that if one of them[43] should make an error, the other may cause her to remember....*

According to this verse, the requirement for a witness is two men or one man and two women.[44] We see, in resolving the proof of Mohammed's prophecy, half of a man, that is, his wife Khadijah, was enough. This is unacceptable, according to the teaching of the Qur'an. We must ask the following question. *How could she be a witness to something she herself had not seen?* This was a very basic and vital witness case, but this testimony would not stand in any court, especially a Muslim court.

We have to ask another question. *How did she know that this was an angel and not a demon?* Muslims claim that angels would not be in the presence of uncovered women, while demons would not mind. Since the spirit left the room when she uncovered herself, the implication was that this was a godly angel. *How can we know this*

---

[42]Notice this is Gabreel, as his name was originally spelled. This is not the angel Gabriel.
[43]the women
[44]In the case of adultery, the requirement for a witness is four. Qur'an 24:4: And those who accuse virtuous women, then they cannot bring four witnesses, then scourge them with eighty stripes, and do not receive their testimony forever, and those are the transgressors.

was not a demon who left the room on purpose to deceive Khadijah and Mohammed?

How then did she or her cousin know for sure that this was the Angel Gabreel and not Mika'il or any other angel? She just said these things, and that settled the case of Mohammed's prophethood for him, for all his followers, and for all the scholars forevermore. Another question is this. *Is this the way to prove someone is a prophet?*

There was no mention of the coming of Mohammed as a prophet in the Bible. However, Jesus clearly taught that there will be false prophets who will come after him; for example, in Matthew 24:11: *[11]Then many false prophets will rise up and deceive many.* Muslims still do anything they can to find some mention of Mohammed in the Bible to the point that some claim that Jesus' prophecy of the coming of the Holy Spirit in John 14:16-17 is a prophecy about Mohammed: *[16]And I will pray the Father, and He will give you another Helper, that He may abide with you forever— [17]the Spirit of truth, whom the world cannot receive, because it neither sees Him nor knows Him; but you know Him, for He dwells with you and will be in you.*

They interpreted these two verses to be a prophecy of their prophet of Islam, Mohammed, even though these two verses' words cannot fit to (describe) any human but only the Holy Spirit. Mohammed was never a comforter. Mohammed did not stay with the Muslims forever. Mohammed was never called the spirit of truth. Mohammed was received by the people of the world. People saw Mohammed and knew Mohammed. Mohammed did not dwell with the disciples. Mohammed was not ever with the disciples.

According to Jesus' words in John 14:26: *[26]But the Helper, the Holy Spirit, whom the Father will send in My name, He will teach you all things, and bring to your remembrance all things that I said to you.* Jesus clearly taught that the Holy Spirit would be sent from the Father in Jesus' name. Muslims do not believe in such a teaching, and Mohammed did not teach the disciples and did not remind them of what Jesus taught them, but the Holy Spirit did. Acts 1:4: *[4]And being assembled together with them, He commanded them not to depart from Jerusalem, but to wait for the Promise of the Father, "which," He said, "you have heard from Me."*

This is yet more evidence that the Comforter is the Holy Spirit, not Mohammed, for Jesus commanded his disciples to wait in Jerusalem until the Holy Spirit came to them. Jesus' disciples did not wait six hundred years in Jerusalem for Mohammed, but it was actually on the Day of Pentecost as we read in Acts 2:4: *[4]And they were all filled with the Holy Spirit and began to speak with other tongues, as the Spirit gave them utterance.*

Remember, Mohammed claimed to have a vision of a spirit when he was alone in a cave. He was confused, afraid, and ran to his wife Khadijah, who with the help of her cousin, Waraka Ibn Nawfal, convinced him that the spirit was the Angel Gabreel and that Mohammed was the prophet of Allah. Notice that for every great event in Mohammed's life, he did not have a second witness.

Mohammed did not have any great success in the first thirteen or so years of preaching, during which he used a peaceful method to reach out to the people of Mecca. Muslims claim that he had approximately seventy-two followers at the end of these thirteen years during which he lived and preached in Mecca.

The Beginning of the Revelation

Sheik Mohammed wrote that the first thing that was described as the beginning of the revelation descended on Mohammed.[45] This is written in Qur'an 96: *¹Read, in the name of your lord who created. ²He created the human from a clot. ³Read, and your lord is the generous ⁴who taught with the pen. ⁵He taught the human what he did not know. ⁶Certainly not, surely the human is rebellious; ⁷that he sees himself as self-sufficient. ⁸Surely the return is to your lord. ⁹Have you seen the one who forbids ¹⁰a servant when he prays? ¹¹Have you seen that he was upon the guidance? ¹²Or commands with piety? ¹³Have you seen if he denies and then turns away? ¹⁴Did he not know that Allah sees? ¹⁵Certainly not, if he does not stop, then we will take him by his forehead, ¹⁶a lying, sinful, forehead. ¹⁷So he will call on his company. ¹⁸We will call the zabānī.[46] ¹⁹Certainly not, do not obey him. And worship and draw near.*

As usual, Muslim scholars disagreed, for some claimed that Qur'an 74 was the first portion of revelation revealed to Mohammed. However, others said that Qur'an 6:151 was the first verse revealed. Others said that it was Qur'an 1. The amazing thing about how Mohammed received the revelation was that "the spirit used to squeeze Mohammed until he lost his strength, and then the spirit would release him. This was repeated many times. Every time the spirit asked Mohammed to read, Mohammed answered every time,

---

[45]Mohammed Ibn Abd Al Wahab, *A Summary of the Life of the Messenger*, 29.
[46]guardians, non-Arabic word of probable Syriac origin

'I am not reading.'" This shows the extent of the nonsense written in the interpretation of Qur'an 96.

Then Sheik Mohammed stated that the second revelation was Qur'an 74 when Mohammed warned the people; a few people answered him, but the majority did not follow him. At the same time, they did not deny him until he showed them the shortcomings of the religion and the falsehood of their gods.

Therefore, enmity began to take place between Mohammed and the Arabs of Mecca, and this became difficult for him and his early Muslim followers. The Arabs began to torment him severely, and they desired to take him away from his religion by offering him riches, but Mohammed insisted that he would fulfill his duty before Allah as a messenger.

Then the story of Mohammed's uncle, Abu Talib Ibn Abd Al Motlab, began.[47] He protected Mohammed with his life, money, children, and tribe. He suffered because of that, but he was patient. He loved those who loved him and showed enmity to those who hated Mohammed. He did not accept Mohammed's religion, holding to the religion of his fathers. Mohammed desired to ask forgiveness for him, but Allah said in Qur'an 9:113: *[113]It was not for the prophet or those who believed to ask forgiveness for the polytheists, even though they were closest relatives, after it has been made clear to them that they are the companions of hell.* I believe that this could be good evidence that Mohammed was not a prophet because his uncle, who suffered for him and raised him and protected him, never believed him to be a prophet.

The Early Believers of Mohammed

The first man who believed in Mohammed was Abu Bakr. His wife also believed in him, and many of his early believers were slaves, many of whom they owned. Then Ozmond believed, followed by Talhah and then Saad and Mohammed's first wife Khadijah and Ali Ibn Abu Talib, who was eight years old when he believed, according to some scholars.[48]

Sheik Mohammed told the story of Zaid Ibn Harisah, who was bought by Mohammed's first wife Khadijah and given to Mohammed when they married.[49] His uncle and his father came to take him away

---

[47]Mohammed Ibn Abd Al Wahab, *A Summary of the Life of the Messenger*, 30.
[48]Ibid., 80.
[49]Ibid., 81.

from Mohammed, so Mohammed gave him the freedom to choose between Mohammed and his own family. He chose to stay with Mohammed. Then Mohammed stood up and asked all the people to witness that Zaid was his son. He would inherit him, and he would be inherited by him. That is when Zaid's father and uncle left in peace. Zaid was called the son of Mohammed until Allah came with his new command, as written in Qur'an 33:5: *⁵Call them (the adopted sons) to their fathers, this will be more just with Allah....*

Then Waraka Ibn Nawfal became a Muslim. After that, people entered the religion of Islam one after another, until Mohammed began to insult their gods. Then they became enemies of his. They began to harm and torment him and those who believed him. Abu Bakr Al Sadeek used to buy slaves and set them free, and they became Muslims. Because of the persecution, Sheik Mohammed stated that Mohammed, the prophet of Islam, ordered some of the believers to immigrate to Ethiopia where their "men who do not do injustice to the people." Twelve men and four women emigrated there. Notice the Ethiopian people at that time were Christians.

Sheik Mohammed explained that the believers returned from Ethiopia when they heard that the people of Quraish, who were the dominant tribe of Mecca, had become friends with Mohammed after Mohammed had praised their gods.[50] Mohammed pleased them by writing what were later called the satanic verses of the Qur'an. Then they were persecuted again. That is when Mohammed gave the believers permission to again immigrate to Ethiopia. This time there were thirty-three men and nineteen women.

The Deaths of Khadijah and Abu Talib
Sheik Mohammed stated that Khadijah died a few days after Mohammed's uncle, who had been protecting him, so the hardship became severe on Mohammed and his people.[51] As the Arabs of Mecca met to plan to kill Mohammed, Abu Bakr stood up and cried, "Would you kill a man because he said, 'Allah is my Lord'?"

The Story of Mohammed and the People of Quraish
Sheik Mohammed[52] mentioned that Mohammed recited Qur'an 53:19-20: *¹⁹Have you seen Al Lat and Al Ozza? ²⁰And another,*

---

[50]Ibid., 89.
[51]Ibid., 103.
[52]Ibid., 31.

the third one, Manat? Then Satan cast in his recitation, *"These are the exalted cranes [intermediaries] whose intercession is to be hoped for."*

When the people of Quraish heard, they rejoiced greatly, saying, "That is what we believe, and that is what we desire. Allah is the creator, the provider, and we desire the intercession of our gods with Allah. If Mohammed agreed with that, there is no disagreement between us and him." Mohammed continued to recite these verses and worshiped with them (prayed with them). The people of Quraish worshiped with him, and the news spread that the people of Quraish united with Mohammed. The news spread all the way to Ethiopia. His companions came back to Mohammed to see about this news.

Mohammed became very afraid of Allah until Allah sent the following verse which is written in Qur'an 22:52: *[52]And we did not send before you any messenger nor prophet except that when he wishes, Satan casts in his wishes, so Allah abrogates what Satan casts. Then Allah fixed his verses. And Allah is knowing, wise.* This verse is not true, for Mohammed tried to save himself and those who believed in him from among the people of Quraish. He praised their gods intentionally until he became strong. Then he decided these verses were given to him by Satan, not Allah. He deceived the people of Quraish. There was not one prophet or messenger in the Bible who gave one word, let alone verses, by the power of Satan.

The fact is, what happened in Mohammed's days, with the people of Quraish, is what is repeated in the West by Mohammed's followers, the Muslims. When they are weak in a land, they lie and deceive the people of those countires by stating that they believe in Jesus, they believe in Moses, in Buddha, or whatever god your neighbor worships until they have the ***upper hand***. That is when they will practice the hate of the verses in the Qur'an of Islam as written in Qur'an 47:35: *[35]So do not be weak and do not call for peace when you have the upper hand. And Allah is with you, and he will not leave from[53] you [for] your works.*

The Emigration from Mecca to Medina

Sheik Mohammed asserted that Mohammed, the prophet of Islam, gave the Muslims permission to immigrate to Yathrib, later called Medina by Mohammed after he killed and conquered the Jewish

---

[53]phrase indicating *will reward*

inhabitants.[54] One by one they began to go, except Mohammed and his father-in-law. Mohammed and Abu Bakr were prepared to immigrate when the people of Quraish united to kill the messenger of Allah. When they saw that the believers had immigrated to Medina, they were afraid that Mohammed himself would leave and become strong against them. They gathered together in a meeting, and Satan joined them in the shape of an old man. The final decision was to pick a young man from every tribe. As they carried swords, they would strike Mohammed once each. In that case, the tribe of the children of Abd Monaf (Mohammed's people), could not fight the rest of the tribes. They decided to give Mohammed's blood money to his family.

Angel Gabreel told Mohammed what had been planned, and he commanded Mohammed not to sleep in his bed that night. In the middle of the day, Mohammed told Abu Bakr to leave because Allah had given him permission to emigrate from Mecca and go to Yathrib, a Jewish city Mohammed took over and then changed its name to Medina, which means *the city*. Mohammed ordered his cousin Ali, Abu Talib's son, to sleep in his bed. The people of Quraizah were waiting and watching from the door for Mohammed to sleep. Mohammed came out of the house, and he threw dust over them while he was quoting the two verses of Allah, 36:9: *⁹And we made between their hands a barrier and from behind them a barrier, so we cover them so they do not see,* and 8:30: *³⁰And when those who became infidels deceive you to detain you or to kill you or to expel you. And they deceive, and Allah deceives. And Allah is the best deceiver.*

Mohammed went to Abu Bakr by night, and they both traveled to Medina. A man came by the house of Mohammed and asked the young men with swords in their hands planning to kill Mohammed why they were waiting. They told him they were waiting for Mohammed. He said, "You have lost, for he has passed by you and spread the dust over your heads." They swore by Allah that they did not see him and began to remove the dust from over their heads. We must ask a question here. *How can they swear by Allah if they did not believe in him or in his prophet, Mohammed?* They came to Ali on Mohammed's bed and asked him, "Where is Mohammed?" He said, "I do not know."

---

[54]Mohammed Ibn Abd Al Wahab, *A Summary of the Life of the Messenger,* 129-131.

Mohammed and Abu Bakr stayed in the cave of Sor, and the spider built a house at the entry of the cave. (It was a miracle that the spider could build the house in such a short time.)

It is amazing how Muslim scholars fabricated miracles for their prophet, Mohammed, and here is a good example.[55] They claimed that Allah performed a miracle by causing the spider to build a web in a short time, not knowing that it takes about one hour for a spider to construct an elaborate web of silk thread, called an orb web. An orb web consists of a series of roughly circular, concentric outlines, with spokes extending from a hub. Orb webs, which are most noticeable in the morning dew, are constructed by many species of spiders. Notice that Mohammed and Allah also made another huge error concerning the strength of the web of the spider when Allah stated in Qur'an 29: 41: *[41]The parable of those who took friends without Allah is like the 'ankabūt[56] that took a house. And surely the frailest of all the houses is the house of the spider, if they were knowing.* The Qur'an here claims that the spider web is a frail house! This is in error. It is on record that a spider web is strong enough to capture hummingbirds and will hold them long enough for the spider to kill and eat them.[57]

Sheik Mohammed continued that because of this web, the people of Quraizah would not have thought the two men were inside the cave. The people of Quraizah searched for Mohammed and Abu Bakr. They stood at the entrance of the cave but did not see the men, even though the two men could hear them. Allah had blinded their eyes. Mohammed and Abu Bakr stayed in the cave three days. Then they continued their trip to Medina.

There were many more stories about the trip of the two men from Mecca to Medina, but I will discuss only one more. Sheik Mohammed said that, as Mohammed traveled to Medina, they stopped at the home of a woman named The Mother of Mabad. They asked if they could buy food from her, but she did not have any. Mohammed asked her about a sheep he saw, and he asked if he could get any milk out of it. She said, "The sheep does not have any milk," but Mohammed prayed to Allah and then began to milk the sheep. He

---

[55]"How Long Does it Take the Average Spider to Weave a Complete Web?" *enotes.com*, October 9, 2011, http://www.enotes.com/science/q-and-a/-long-does-take-average-spider-weave-complete-286282, accessed November 15, 2011.

[56]spider, non-Arabic word of Aramaic origin

[57]*Character Sketches: From the Pages of Scripture*, illustrated in the *World of Nature*, vol. 2, (Chicago: Rand McNally & Company, 1976), 48.

got a large amount of milk. The woman drank enough, and everyone had enough. Then he filled the pitcher again.

Her husband came in and asked where she had gotten the milk, and she told him all that had taken place. As she described Mohammed to him, her husband said, "I swear by Allah, this was the companion of Quraizah whom they are seeking, and I have decided to follow him (meaning, he believed Mohammed)." Mohammed arrived in Medina, and the people were happy to have him. Mohammed built a mosque where his camel rested. He bought the land for ten denarii after the people offered him the land for free.

Sheik Mohammed stated that a Jewish rabbi named Abdullah Ibn Salam became a Muslim, but most of the Jewish people chose infidelity over Islam.[58] There were three tribes, Kankaa and Nadyer and Quraizah. They broke the covenant with Mohammed. That is why he engaged in war with them. He showed mercy to Kankaa, he removed Nadyer, and he killed Quraizah. This is shown in another portion of the Mohammed movie. Qur'an 59 was descended (written) about Nadyer and Qur'an 33:26-27 was descended (written) about Quraizah. When Muslims claim that these tribes broke a covenant with Mohammed, this is not true. Like Muslims always do, they rewrote history to make Islam look good and to give excuses for what Mohammed did.

A good example is the story of the killing of the Benne Quraizah.[59] This happened in the first year after the emigration.

After Mohammed won the Battle of Handak, he was washing in his house when Angel Gabreel came to him and said that Allah commanded him to go and fight the Jewish tribe of Benne Quraizah, the descendants of Quraizah. So Mohammed sent a call to the Muslim men and said, "Whoever is obedient, the prayer of the afternoon will be in the land of Benne Quraizah." So Mohammed put on his clothes of war and rode on his horse to the land of Benne Quraizah. The Muslims and Mohammed surrounded the people of Quraizah and launched rocks by catapult. Mohammed's men shot their arrows, and the Jews also shot their arrows until nightfall.

A Jewish man by the name of Nabash Ibn Quis came to Mohammed and offered to give Mohammed their entire city and all their money if Mohammed would allow the men to walk out of the

---

[58]Mohammed Ibn Abd Al Wahab, *A Summary of the Life of the Messenger,* 141.
[59]http://bint-hawa.blogspot.com/2006/11/blog-post.html, accessed 11/10/2011.

city with their wives, children, and whatever they were able to carry; and they would leave their weapons behind. The loving, peaceful prophet refused the Jewish offer.

When the siege became too harsh, the Jews surrendered to Mohammed, who commanded the prisoners of war to be chained by their ankles. All the women and children were put to one side. Their goods, furniture, weapons, and clothes were also put aside. This included fifteen hundred swords, five hundred shields, one thousand spears, fifteen hundred of another type of shield, and lots of wine. The wine was poured out. There were also lots of camels and other livestock.

The tribe of Oas asked Mohammed if he would give them the descendants of Quraizah. Mohammed gave the judgment to a man from among them. This man had been wounded from the previous invasion; his name was Saad Ibn Maaz. He had been praying to Allah that he would live to judge the descendants of Quraizah. He judged that every man, including grown-up boys who had ever shaved to be killed, the women and children to be taken as concubines, and the money to be shared. Then the messenger of Allah, Mohammed, said, "You have judged with the judgment of Allah from the seven heavens." On the following day, Thursday, the seventh day of the month of Zo Al Hijjah, Mohammed commanded for trenches to be dug by the people of Quraizah. Then Mohammed struck the necks (decapitated) of the teenagers and men, everyone who grew hair, beards, or mustaches. They killed the men of Quraizah until evening. Between 600 and 750 men were killed, and their bodies were buried in the trenches.

According to other sources, the Muslims forced the women and children to walk through the corpses for the purpose of terrorizing them. Mohammed chose two of these women. One was Rihanna, daughter of Amro. She accepted Islam. The second woman was Safiyya Bint Huyayy, who had only been married a short time to her husband and was very beautiful. Mohammed killed her husband, father, and brother. He then took her and consummated his marriage to her that very same night, as we mentioned previously. *What a loving, considerate husband.*

Let me conclude this section by mentioning a few more actions that took place during the second year after emigration. Bilal began to call for prayer. The next thing was that they began the fast for

Ramadan and abrogated the fast of Aashoraa. Mohammed married Ali to his daughter Fatima.

The Messenger Settles in Medina

Sheik Mohammed stated that when Mohammed settled in Medina and Allah gave him and the believers a victory, he united their hearts with friendship after hate.[60] Their enemies from among the Arabs and the Jews wanted to go to war with them. Allah commanded Mohammed to forgive and to pardon until the thorn became strong. Then Allah gave him permission to engage in war, as written throughout the Qur'an. In Qur'an 22:39: *[39]Permission is given to those who engage in war because they were wronged, and surely Allah is capable of helping them.* In Qur'an 2:190: *[190]And engage in war for the sake of Allah against those who engage in war against you, and do not transgress. Surely Allah does not love the transgressors.* Also, in Qur'an 9:36: *[36]... and engage in war with all the polytheists as they engage in war with all of you....*

When the Supporters (The People of Medina) Became Muslim

Sheik Mohammed stated that the Jewish scholars who desired Mohammed's coming and who were waiting for him to believe in him, knew that the honor would be for those who would believe Mohammed and would follow him.[61] It is written in Qur'an 2:89: *[89]And when a book[62] came to them from Allah confirming what they have,[63] and they were previously praying for assistance against those who became infidels, so when what they knew came to them, they became infidels in it. So the curse of Allah is on the infidels.*

When the supporters accepted Islam, Mohammed ordered the believers to emigrate from Mecca and go to Medina. That is why Allah said in Qur'an 8:26: *[26]And remember when you were few and weakened on the earth, you feared that people might snatch you, so he sheltered you and supported you with his victory and provided you from the good things, perhaps you may give thanks.*

---

[60]Mohammed Ibn Abd Al Wahab, *A Summary of the Life of the Messenger*, 145.
[61]Ibid.
[62]Qur'an
[63]the Torah

There is not one true Jew who believed in Mohammed or Islam because they were waiting for him as a prophet. Jews were and are waiting for the Christ, not Mohammed; they were awaiting a Jewish prophet, not an Arab prophet. The fact is that some Jews believed him because he bribed them or they feared for their lives as written in Qur'an 9:60: *⁶⁰Surely alms are only to the poor and the needy and those who collect them and to those whose hearts are inclined⁶⁴ and for the necks [ransom for slaves] and for debtors and for the sake of Allah and the son of the way, an ordinance from Allah. And Allah is knowing, wise.*

The Marriage of Mohammed to The Mother of Habebah

The Mother of Habebah was a woman who emigrated with her husband, Abd Allah Ibn Jahsh.⁶⁵ Her husband became a Christian and died as a Christian. Mohammed wrote to Al Nageshe, the leader of Ethiopia, that he might give The Mother of Habebah to him and send to him the rest of the believers who immigrated to his country. This was during the seven years after Mohammed's emigration. Al Nageshe sent the woman and the companions in two ships, and they met with Mohammed in Khaybar which they invaded. When Al Nageshe died, Mohammed prayed over him.⁶⁶

The Legalization of Jihad in Medina

Sheik Mohammed stated that after Muslims emigrated from Mecca to Medina and gathered with those who emigrated earlier with the helpers of the people of Medina, Allah enacted the law for them to perform jihad.⁶⁷ Before that, Allah had forbidden them to perform jihad. In Qur'an 4:77: *⁷⁷Have you not seen those to whom it was said, "Withhold your hands⁶⁸ and perform the prayer and bring the legal alms." So when it was prescribed for them to engage in war, behold, a group of them feared the people like the fear of Allah or a greater fear. And they said, "Our lord, why did you prescribe for us the engagement of war? Were it not that you delay us to a near time." Say, "Little is the enjoyment of this world, but the hereafter is better for him who fears. And you will not be dealt unjustly a thread."*

⁶⁴the people whom Mohammed bribed to bring to Islam
⁶⁵Mohammed Ibn Abd Al Wahab, *A Summary of the Life of the Messenger*, 99.
⁶⁶Ibid., 94.
⁶⁷Ibid., 37.
⁶⁸from waging in war

The statement *"Withhold your hands"* meant to *not* perform jihad. Then Allah sent down on them the new verses of the Qur'an which teach to perform jihad, as in Qur'an 2:216: *[216]War is decreed to you, and it is hated by you. And perhaps you may hate something, and it is good for you; and perhaps you love something, and it is evil for you. And Allah knows, and you do not know.*

Sheik Mohammed continued to name some of the famous fights or invasions which Mohammed led, as they are written about throughout the Qur'an. See the table in the section titled "Mohammed's Battles." This is also seen in the Mohammed movie.[69] After the Arabs drew near to Mohammed and entered Islam by huge numbers, Mohammed and his followers began engaging in war against the foreigners or non-Muslims.

New Life in Medina and Mohammed's Militant Lifestyle

Mohammed began forming an army and raiding local villages and caravans, so he became rich and powerful in Medina. During this time he changed his message and teaching, for the language of the Qur'an became harsh, violent. That is when the doctrine of abrogation began to take great roots in the teaching of the Qur'an. He was bluntly commanding his followers to engage in war until there was no further rebellion and the religion of Islam was supreme over all for Allah; if they ceased fighting, there would be grave consequences from Allah. We see this in Qur'an 8:39: *[39]And engage in war with them until there will not be sedition and the religion[70] will be completely to Allah. So, if they cease, so surely Allah sees what they do.* His riches were also built on Qur'an teachings for he was able to gain 20 percent of the spoils as he claimed that Allah said in Qur'an 8:41: *[41]And know that whatever you take of spoil of anything, so a fifth part to Allah and to the messenger....* This is also shown in Mohammed's teachings in the hadith when he states, "I descended by Allah with the sword in my hand, and my wealth will come from the shadow of my sword. And the one who will disagree with me will be humiliated and persecuted...."[71]

Then Mohammed died at the age of sixty-three, after living in Medina for around ten years during which time he conquered Mecca

---

[69]Nakoula, *Innocence of Muslims*.

[70]Islam

[71]Ibn Hisham, *The Life of Muhammad*, author's translation, 3rd ed., pt. 6, vol. 3 (Beirut: Dar-al-Jil, 1998), 8.

and virtually all of Arabia. He had fulfilled his purpose of giving the message of Islam. Then the War of Apostasy began.

Sheik Mohammed stated that when Mohammed died, most of those who believed in Islam left the religion.[72] Great sedition took place. However, Allah strengthened those to whom he showed grace because Abu Bakr Al Sadeek (Mohammed's father-in-law) fought the seditionists. He also reminded the companions (the believers) what they forgot, and he taught them what they did not know. He encouraged them concerning the things they feared. So Allah strengthened the religion of Islam by Abu Bakr Al Sadeek.

The Doctrine of Abrogation

One of the amazing mysteries of the Qur'an is the doctrine of abrogation. Ironically, this doctrine actually stands against the teaching of the Qur'an itself, which clearly says in Qur'an 4:82: [82]*Do they not consider the Qur'an? If it was from other than Allah, they would have found in it many inconsistencies.* This verse clearly tells us that the Qur'an is free from any inconsistencies. Moreover, Qur'an 6:34 states: [34]*...no one can change the words of Allah....* Qur'an 85:21-22 reads: [21]*Yet, it is a glorious Qur'an* [22]*in a kept board.* (What is being stated here is that the Qur'an is written on a board in heaven and is being guarded from change.)

From such verses one might think that the words of the Qur'an are written consistently and without any contradiction or any change. *But how does one reconcile this concept with the numerous verses in the Qur'an which obviously teach about the doctrine of abrogation?* For example, in Qur'an 2:106: [106]*Whatever verse we abrogate, or cause it to be forgotten, we bring a better [verse] than it or like it. Do you not know that Allah has might over all things?* Also, Qur'an 16:101 states: [101]*And if we exchange one verse in a place of another verse, and Allah knows what he sent down....* Such verses teach that there is a change in qur'anic verses and abrogation truly exists. Abrogation in the Qur'an is actually the only way to explain the inconsistencies throughout the Qur'an.

*What do we mean by **abrogation**?* According to Ibn Kathir's interpretation, abrogation is defined as "the removal of a verse or the change of a verse with another (newer) verse or to make something

---

[72]Mohammed Ibn Abd Al Wahab, *A Summary of the Life of the Messenger*, 37-38.

lawful which was unlawful or vice versa."[73] *How many portions of revelation in the Qur'an contain abrogation?* Seventy-one portions of revelation contain abrogation, which is over 60 percent of the Qur'an. Sometimes it is just one verse. For example, Qur'an 9:5, which is called the Verse of the Sword by all Muslim scholars, abrogates 124 verses of the Qur'an that speak softly about other religions and other people such as the People of the Book (Christians and Jews). There are three different types of abrogation in the Qur'an.

The first type of abrogation is when the verse is removed from the Qur'an and Muslims are not required to practice its teaching. These are verses that Muslims and Mohammed could no longer remember because Allah caused them to be forgotten. It should be noted that there was no effort to compile Mohammed's recitations during his lifetime. Rather, they depended primarily on the memory of Mohammed and his followers, so it is not surprising that some of the verses were forgotten.

The second type of abrogation is when the verse exists but has been superseded by a newer verse and, therefore, is no longer practiced. This type of abrogated verse includes those verses that Muslims try hard to use in the West to prove that the Qur'an is not a hateful, barbaric book. These are typically the Meccan or early Medinan verses recited prior to Mohammed becoming a strong military leader. According to Muslim scholars, the verses which Mohammed received later supersede the earlier verses, in the event of a contradiction.

A sample of such superseded verses is Qur'an 2:62 which says: *[62]Surely those who believed[74] and those who are Jews and the Nasara[75] and the Sābeen,[76] whoever believed in Allah and the last day and did good deed, so they will have their ajoor[77] with their lord and no fear on them, and they will not grieve.* Such a verse teaches that Christians, Jews, and idol worshipers will have a place in heaven, but this verse was abrogated when Allah says in Qur'an 3:85: *[85]And whoever desires any other religion except*

---

[73]Ibn Kathir, *Stories of the Prophets*, vol.1, Abo Al Fida Ishamail Ibn Kathir Al Kurashi Al Damashce (Beirut: Dar Al-Arab Heritage, 1408 AH, 1988), 134.

[74]Muslims

[75]word made up to mean Christians

[76]Sabians—idol worshipers—uncertain what specific people this represents; may have been a word play on the name of the Sabaean Christians of S. Arabia, non-Arabic word of unknown origin

[77]wage, non-Arabic word of possible Syriac origin

Islam, so it[78] *will not be accepted from him, and in the hereafter he will be of the losers.*

Notice in Qur'an 2:62, Mohammed showed respect for Jews, Christians, and idol worshipers, but then he called Christians infidels, as it is written in Qur'an 5:72: [72]*Infidels, indeed, are those who said, "Surely Allah is the Christ, son of Mary."...* Also in Qur'an 5:73, when he stated: [73]*Infidels, indeed, are those who said, "Surely Allah is the third of three."...* And he commanded his Muslim followers to engage in war with the People of the Book.

Other examples are in Qur'an 8:61 which says: [61]*And if they lean toward peace (Islam), so lean toward it....* And in Qur'an 2:256 which states: [256]*No compulsion in religion....* These and many other such verses will give the unknowing reader the impression that the Qur'an is a kind book. But the fact is that all of these verses have been abrogated by Qur'an 9:5 which is known as the Verse of the Sword, one of the last portions revealed to Mohammed, when Allah said: [5]*So when the forbidden months are passed,*[79] *so kill the polytheists wherever you find them, and take them [as captives] and besiege them and lay wait for them with every kind of ambush; so if they repent*[80] *and perform the prayer and bring the legal alms, so leave their way free. Surely Allah is forgiving, merciful.*

Also, in Qur'an 9:29, Allah says: [29]*Engage in war with those who do not believe in Allah nor in the last day. Nor forbid what Allah and his messenger forbid, nor believe in the religion of the truth*[81] *among those who have been given the book until they pay the jizya*[82] *out of hand and they are subdued.*

Such newer verses abrogate the previous verses, and Muslims are commanded to live by the new verses, not the old verses. Therefore, we must conclude that there is no such thing as soft, kind verses in the Qur'an because Allah has changed his mind and abrogated such verses.

The third type of abrogation is when the written verse is gone but Muslims are still commanded to practice such verses, as we see in practicing the ordinance of stoning the adulterer. When women commit adultery in Islam, the Sharia (Islamic law) commands them to

---

[78]any other religion
[79]pre-Islamic tradition of not fighting during a four month period
[80]convert to Islam
[81]Islam
[82]tribute, non-Arabic word of Aramaic origin

be punished by stoning them to death even though the written verse of the Qur'an has been removed. What a strange god! What strange words of this god in *The Generous Qur'an.*

In Matthew 5:17-18, Jesus said: *¹⁷Do not think that I came to destroy the Law or the Prophets. I did not come to destroy but to fulfill. ¹⁸For assuredly, I say to you, till heaven and earth pass away, one jot or one tittle will by no means pass from the law till all is fulfilled.* What a difference the true Word of God makes!

Mohammed's Methods

Notice the great change in Mohammed's life before leaving Mecca and after arriving in Medina. He was quiet, peaceful, and without any army; but after he escaped to Medina, he began raiding caravans and later villages and killing innocent people in the name of Allah and Islam. He became rich and forced people to convert to Islam as he practiced such a barbaric way of life, stating that these were the words and the commands of Allah.

We can gain great insight into the character of a man or prophet by considering carefully what he believes, how he behaves, and especially what he teaches. As we have seen earlier in our book, the errors about the prophets' stories provide great evidence that Mohammed was not a true prophet. I would like to share a quick summary of Mohammed's teachings as written in the Qur'an and the hadith.

What Mohammed Taught about Allah

Mohammed taught that god (Allah) is unknowable and unapproachable. He is only to be feared. This type of fear is not the fear of reverence as the Bible commanded, but it is a trembling fear as stated at the end of Qur'an 2:196: *¹⁹⁶...And fear Allah, and know that Allah is severe the punishment.* Other evidence that Mohammed's god is not the God of the Bible can be found in Qur'an 3:54: *⁵⁴And they deceived, and Allah deceived, and Allah is the best deceiver.* This verse clearly teaches that Allah is nothing but Satan, the Great Deceiver. See also Qur'an 8:30: *³⁰And when those who became infidels deceive you to detain you or to kill you or to expel you. And they deceive, and Allah deceives. And Allah is the best deceiver.*

He also taught that Allah leads people astray, as we find in Qur'an 35:8: *⁸...So surely Allah leads astray whom he wills and guides whom he wills....* We also see that Mohammed taught that

Allah desires to fill hell with people, as it is written at the end of Qur'an 32:13, where Allah stated, *[13]..."I will surely fill hell with jinn and people together."*

What Mohammed Taught about Jesus

Mohammed taught that Allah has no son because, obviously, Allah did not have a girlfriend. We see written in Qur'an 6:101: *[101]The inventor of the heavens and the earth, how can he have a son when he has no female companion?* Mohammed taught that Jesus was a good man, good teacher, and good prophet. Muslims in the West speak highly of Jesus, of His virgin birth, and of His many miracles. As we have described earlier in the section on Jesus, what Westerners do not know, is that when Muslims say that they believe in Jesus, they mean Prophet 'Isā. We must acknowledge the fact that as simply as Mohammed changing Jesus' name from the Hebrew name Yeshua (Savior) to the non-Arabic name 'Isā (name which means nothing), this simple change by Mohammed can be defined by a complete denial of who Jesus is and why He came to our world.

Jesus cannot be a good man when He claimed to be God; for if he is not God, then that means that He is a blasphemer. Jesus cannot be a good teacher if all that He taught were false teachings, especially if we know what He taught about Himself throughout the Gospels. Finally, Jesus cannot be a good prophet if His prophecy of dying and rising again was never fulfilled. It is very easy for Mohammed or Muslims to say that they believe in Jesus, but if we think deeply of the Muslims' true understanding and beliefs about Jesus, we will come to the conclusion that the Jesus of Mohammed and Muslims has nothing to do with the Jesus of the Bible. As a matter of fact, all that is written by Mohammed in the Qur'an and the hadith is nothing but the greatest insult to Christ, Christianity, and the God of the Bible.

According to Mohammed, Jesus will burn in hell forever and so will all the Christians who worship Him. As mentioned in chapter 32, we can see this clearly in Qur'an 21:98-99: *[98]Surely you and whatever you serve, without Allah, will be the fuel of the fire for hell, and into it you will arrive. [99]If those were gods, they would not enter it, and everyone in it will abide there forever.*

What Mohammed Taught about Himself

From reading the Qur'an (Allah's words) and the hadith (Mohammed's words), we can conclude that Mohammed was favored by Allah over all other prophets and all humans. As written in Qur'an 2:253: *253These are the messengers; we favored some of them above the others. Some of them spoke to Allah, and he exalted some of them by degrees....* Mohammed claimed that he was the seal of the prophets as in Qur'an 33:40: *40Mohammed was not the father of any man among you, but is the messenger of Allah and the khātam*[83] *of the prophets. And Allah was the knower of all things.*

He also claimed to be the last prophet and that no other prophets would come after him. "...I am the last of the Prophets."[84]

Mohammed claimed that he is the cornerstone when he said, "My similarity in comparison with the other prophets is that of a man who has built a house nicely and beautifully, except for a place of one brick in a corner... I am that brick..."[85]

There are two simple facts about Mohammed that I would like to share with you. If Muslims were to realize the message in these sayings of Mohammed, they would know exactly who he was. Mohammed said, "I have been commanded to fight against people till they testify to the fact that there is no god but Allah, and believe in me [that] I am the Messenger and in all that I have brought."[86] From statements such as this, we can summarize the ministry of Islam as a cult that is spread by the sword.

What Mohammed Taught about Mankind

Mohammed taught that Allah controls the fate of all men. Eternal destiny is up to the fickle whim of Allah, not up to men. This is shown clearly in Qur'an 14:4: *4...So Allah leads astray whom he wills and guides whom he wills, and he is the dear, the wise.*

He also taught that every man is surrounded by two angels. The angel of the right side writes in his book all the good deeds a man can perform. The angel on the left side keeps records of all of the sins that a man commits. Even though Allah controls the destiny of men, Mohammed stated that the more good deeds that a man has, the better his chance is to make it to the garden.

Men are favored above women. Men are in charge of women. Men can even beat their women as written in Qur'an 4:34: *34... And of whom you fear rebellion, so preach to them and separate*

---

[83]seal, non-Arabic word of probable Aramaic origin
[84]Sahih Bukhari, Hadith 735.
[85]Ibid.
[86]Muslim: C9B1N31.

from them in the beds and scourge them. So if they obey you,
so do not seek a way against them. Surely Allah was higher,
big.

What Mohammed Taught about the Bible

Muslims throughout the world believe that the Bible has been
corrupted and has been changed, but I could not find anywhere in the
Qur'an or in Mohammed's teachings to support their claim that the
Bible has been corrupted. According to the Qur'an, the Bible is the
inspired word of Allah as in Qur'an 16:43: *[43]And we did not send*
before you any except men that we inspired, so ask the people
of the reminder,[87] if you were not knowing. Here we discover that
the entire Bible was written by inspired men. Of course, someone
may say that the Bible *used to be* the Word of God but is not any
longer. There are then questions that must be asked. *Who destroyed*
it? When, where, why, and how was it destroyed? Muslims have been
asked these questions ever since the beginning of Islam. Today we are
still waiting for their answers.

Mohammed said that the Bible cannot be changed. According to
Qur'an 15:9: *[9]Surely we have sent down the reminder,[88] and*
surely we will be its keeper. Allah is the one who sent the reminder
(Bible/Qur'an), and he is the one who is responsible to guard and
protect it. Someone may claim that the word *reminder* here is the
Qur'an, not the Bible. I will say this, read Qur'an 21:48: *[48]And*
indeed, we gave Moses and Aaron the discriminator and a light
and a reminder for the fearer, and read also Qur'an 16:44: *[44]With*
proofs and the scriptures, and we sent down to you the
reminder,[89] that you may reveal to the people what has been
sent down to them, and perhaps they may reflect.

Also, Allah in the Qur'an stated that no one can change his words
as written in Qur'an 6:34: *[34]And indeed, the messengers before*
you were denied, so they were patient on being denied, and
they were harmed until our victory came to them. And no one
can change the words of Allah. And indeed, some of the news
of the messengers came to you.

Much more can be said about this topic, but I would like to state,
if Muslims claim that the Bible has been corrupted, then they must

---

[87]Jews and Christians
[88]the Bible
[89]Qur'an

realize that their Qur'an confirmed a corrupted Bible and failed to guard it as we read in Qur'an 5:48: *⁴⁸And to you⁹⁰ we have sent down the book⁹¹ with the truth, confirming what is between his hands of the book⁹² and as guardian over it....*

I would like to conclude with this point, that their prophet, Mohammed, knew for sure that the Bible was excellent, without any corruption, when Allah said to Mohammed in Qur'an 10:94: *⁹⁴So, if you were in doubt concerning what we have sent down to you, so ask those who are reading the book before you; indeed, the truth came to you from your lord, so do not be of the doubters.*

Mohammed consistently affirmed the validity of the Bible because he was pretending to be a prophet and did not have to worry about his followers having access to anything like a complete Bible in their language. Now that Muslims are confronted with the Scriptures, they are frantically scrambling to explain away the falsehood of the Qur'an.

What Mohammed Taught about Prayer

After traveling between the fourth and seventh heavens, Mohammed negotiated the amount of prayers per day from fifty down to five times per day. He was given a very specific pattern of five public prayers each day. Prayers are to be repetitive and formal. Qur'an 4:103 states: *¹⁰³So when you will have completed the prayer, so remember Allah, standing and sitting and reclining; so when you are secure, so perform the prayer. Surely the prayer is prescribed at fixed times for the believers.*

Concerning the change of the direction of prayer, Sheik Mohammed stated that in Medina, Mohammed worshiped toward Jerusalem sixteen months.⁹³ He prayed that Allah would let him pray toward the Kaaba (Mecca). He asked Gabreel if he would ask Allah to do so, but Gabreel told him to ask for himself. That is why in Qur'an 2:144, Allah gave them the right to pray toward Mecca: *¹⁴⁴Indeed, we have seen you turning your face toward the heaven. So we will have you turn to a direction which will please you. So turn your face toward the forbidden mosque.⁹⁴ And wherever you are, so turn your faces toward that place. And surely those who*

---

⁹⁰Mohammed
⁹¹the Qur'an
⁹²Bible
⁹³Mohammed Ibn Abd Al Wahab, *A Summary of the Life of the Messenger,* 143.
⁹⁴Masjid ul Haraam at Mecca

have been given the book know for sure that this is the truth from their lord. And Allah is not unaware of what they were doing. Sheik Mohammed continued, "There was great wisdom and hardship for people." As for the Muslims, they said, "We believed in him."

As for the polytheists, they said, "He is coming back to our direction of prayer. Soon he will return to our religion."[95] As for the Jews, according to Qur'an 2:142: [142]*The fools among the people will say, "What has turned them from the direction*[96] *which they were?" Say, "The east and the west to Allah. He guides whom he wills into a straight way."* As for the hypocrite, they said, "If the first direction of prayer was true, that means Mohammed is praying in the right direction. If the new direction is true, that means Mohammed was in error."

A majority of Muslims memorize their prayers and repeat them in the Arabic language because Arabic is the only language that Muslims can use in their prayers. What is astonishing is that most Muslims repeat the words of their prayers without having a clue as to what they are saying because about 87 percent of Muslims do not speak the Arabic language. Before I came to America, I thought that it was the norm for Third World country people to pray in Arabic without knowing what they were saying because so many are uneducated. They just obey the commands of the leaders of the mosques and the leaders of their tribes. However, after traveling to the West, I was shocked to see the new converts of Islam, those in Europe and in the United States, are no different than the Third World Muslims. I think by now you may realize that Muslims do not use their logic or common sense within the Islamic religion, even as they perform the prayers.

What Mohammed Taught about Good Works

Mohammed taught in some of his words that good works will erase sin. We can find this in Qur'an 11:114: [114]*...Surely good deeds drive away the evil deeds....* When Muslims perform their ritualistic prayer, give zakāt (legally required alms), fast, or perform the pilgrimage of hajj, they believe this will counteract their evil. deeds and provide forgiveness of their sins. Mohammed taught that,

---

[95]http://quran.al-islam.com/Page.aspx?pageid=221&BookID=11&Page=22, accessed October, 27, 2011.
[96]of prayer

although a Muslim may do all of the above, there is no guarantee of paradise.

Even Mohammed himself did not know if he would make it to the garden (paradise) or not. But there is one way of assurance we can find throughout the Qur'an which encourages Muslims to commit suicide for Allah through jihad, and then only if the Muslim dies while performing jihad. Consider Qur'an 3:169: *¹⁶⁹And do not think that those who were killed for the sake of Allah⁹⁷ dead. Yet they are alive with their lord, receiving their provision.*

Mohammed either forgot or never understood that the Scripture, the Holy Bible, the true Word of God, clearly teaches in Hebrews 9:22 and Isaiah 64:6 that without the shedding of blood, there is no forgiveness of sin and all our good deeds are like filthy rags in the eyes of God. A good passage I would like to share with you is Ephesians 2:8-9: *⁸For by grace you have been saved through faith...it is the gift of God, ⁹not of works...*

What Mohammed Taught about Forgiveness

Mohammed's teachings regarding forgiveness include that Mohammed could not forgive sin nor could he ask Allah to forgive the sins of others. We see this recorded in Qur'an 9:80: *⁸⁰Ask forgiveness for them, or do not ask forgiveness for them; if you ask forgiveness for them seventy times, so Allah will not forgive them.* Mohammed taught that only Allah determined who to forgive and who not to forgive. This is found in Qur'an 3:129: *¹²⁹...He forgives to whom he wills, and he torments whom he wills. And Allah is forgiving, merciful.* Notice throughout the Qur'an contradictory statements can fall in the same verse. We must ask a question. *How can Allah be forgiving, merciful, when he torments whom he wills?* Men have no choice in this action.

What Mohammed Taught about Rejection

Mohammed ordered Muslims to attack and kill anyone who rejects Islam. Mohammed claimed that he was only a messenger and only did what Allah commanded him to do. In a simple reading of the final verses of Allah in the Qur'an (the late Medina verses), we will see that there are over 300 verses in which Allah commands Mohammed and Muslims to spread Islam with the sword. For example, in Qur'an 9:5: *⁵... so kill the polytheists wherever you*

---

⁹⁷in jihad

find them, and take them [as captives] and besiege them and lay wait for them with every kind of ambush; so if they repent[98] and perform the prayer and bring the legal alms, so leave their way free. Surely Allah is forgiving, merciful.

<u>What Mohammed Taught about Women</u>

Mohammed taught that women are inferior to men and that men are in charge of women as it is written in Qur'an 4:34: *[34]Men are in charge of women by what Allah preferred some of them above the others....* He also taught that women are unclean as written in Qur'an 4:43: *[43]O you who have believed, do not come near the prayer while you are drunk until you know what you are saying, nor after sexual orgasm except that you are merely passing by, until you wash. And if you were sick or traveling or one of you has relieved himself <u>or you have touched the women</u>, so you did not find water, so rub your faces and your hands with good dirt. Surely Allah was pardoning, forgiving.* He is saying that women are not only unclean, but they are dirtier than dirt. After a man touches a woman, if he cannot find water with which to wash, he can become clean by rubbing his hands and face with clean dirt. This makes dirt like soap. One may ask the following question. *What is clean dirt?* I do not know exactly what Mohammed meant by clean dirt, but I guess it is loose dirt without camel urine or feces.

Another teaching in the hadith states that Mohammed clearly taught that 99 percent of women are in hell, according to the hadith which reads, "One woman, of 100 women, is in heaven, and the rest of them are in Fire."[99] Also, Mohammed said, "As I stood by the gate of Hell, I saw that most of those who enter the gate are women."[100]

<u>What Mohammed Taught about Marriage</u>

Mohammed's teaching concerning marriage allows Muslim men to have four wives at a time and an unlimited number of concubines and slaves. In Qur'an 4:3: *[3]And if you fear that you cannot deal fairly among the orphans, so have sex (marry) what appeals to you from the women, two and three and four. So if you fear that you will not treat them equally, so one [wife]; or [have sex with]*

---

[98]convert to Islam
[99]*Kanzu al-'ummal*, 22:10.
[100]Sahih Bukhari, Hadith 5251.

what your right hand possesses,[101] *this is near that you may not have hardship.*

Mohammed even allowed his male followers to have another sort of marriage: temporary sexual liaisons as short as a few minutes to a few days, known as *marriage for fun*, a formalized type of prostitution. He also allowed his followers to have sexual relations with married slaves. Qur'an 4:24 is the verse which clearly teaches marriage for fun: [24]*And married women [are also forbidden], except all that your right hand possesses. This is the decree of Allah for you. And it is lawful to you, besides this, to seek out women with your money, chaste without fornication. So, whatever you enjoy by it (their sexual parts) from them, so give them their wages; it is an ordinance. And there will be no sin on you about what you have mutually agreed on after the ordinance. Surely Allah was knowing, wise.* This is also supported by the hadith.[102]

This type of marriage can be ended by agreement, and it can be purchased for a limited time. This is still practiced today by Shi'a Muslims, although Sunni Muslims argue by claiming that this type of marriage is abrogated. However, Shi'a Muslims insist that it was never abrogated, and there is no verse in the Qur'an to support the Sunni claim.

What Mohammed Taught about Divorce

Mohammed taught that only men can divorce their wives, and it is an instant divorce because when a man looks at his wife and says this statement, "You are divorced," that will end the marriage on the spot. The ex-husband can return to his ex-wife if he chooses, within three months after saying the above statement. This can be clearly seen in Qur'an 2:229: [229]*The divorce is twice. So keep them in fairness, or put them away in fairness. And it is not lawful for you to take what you have given to them of anything unless they fear that they cannot keep the limits of Allah....*

If a husband divorces his wife a third time, he cannot return to her again until she marries another man and that husband has sex with her. If the new husband divorces her, then it is lawful for the first husband to marry her again. This can be clearly seen in Qur'an 2:230:

---

[101]concubines and slaves
[102]Musnad Abd Allah, Hadith 4195, Sahih Muslim, Hadith 3479, and Sahih Bukhari, Hadith 5173, 4559.

[230]So if he divorces her [a third time], so it is not lawful for him to take her again until she has sex with another husband. So if he divorces her, then there will be no sin on them if they return to each other if they think that they can keep the limits of Allah. And these are the limits of Allah; he shows them to people who know.

I wonder how many Muslim women in the last fourteen hundred years got pregnant from the middle husband (the second husband). I also wonder how many Muslims who claim to believe Moses and the book of Moses have read this next passage in Deuteronomy 24:1-4:

[1]When a man takes a wife and marries her, and it happens that she finds no favor in his eyes because he has found some uncleanness in her, and he writes her a certificate of divorce, puts it in her hand, and sends her out of his house, [2]when she has departed from his house, and goes and becomes another man's wife, [3]if the latter husband detests her and writes her a certificate of divorce, puts it in her hand, and sends her out of his house, or if the latter husband dies who took her as his wife, [4]then her former husband who divorced her must not take her back to be his wife after she has been defiled; for that is an abomination before the Lord, and you shall not bring sin on the land which the Lord your God is giving you as an inheritance. For what the Bible calls in Moses' writing an abomination, Mohammed taught in the Qur'an to be lawful.

What Mohammed Taught about Heaven

Mohammed taught that heaven is a physical garden such as the garden of Adam and Eve, except that his garden is full of sensual pleasures that are denied on earth. Men will enjoy an eternal paradise filled with renewable virgins, both females and young males. The description of the female virgins is unimaginable in the hadith. In Qur'an 55:70, 72, and 74, Mohammed claimed that Allah said: *[70]In them, good and beautiful maidens. [72]Hūr[103] confined in the khaima.[104] [74]No human nor jinn has ever had sex with.* As for the boys, the Qur'an says in 56:17: *[17]Going around them immortal young boys....* In this garden, Muslims will be able to experience fleshly pleasures which are forbidden on earth such as being able to drink wine. As written in Qur'an 47:15: *[15]The description of the garden which Allah has promised the fearer: in it rivers of water*

---

[103]the ever-virgins of the gardens with white skin, large dark eyes and large breasts
[104]tents, non-Arabic word of Abyssinian origin

which are not corrupted and rivers of milk which taste does not change and rivers of wine delicious to those who drink it and rivers of clarified honey....

What Mohammed Taught about Hell

Mohammed taught that all Muslims will go to hell temporarily, and then Allah will remove from hell those whom he chooses to go to his garden as we see in Qur'an 3:185: *[185]Every soul tastes the death, and surely you will only receive your wages on the resurrection day. So whoever is removed from the fire and enters the garden, so indeed, he becomes triumphant. And what is the world's life except the enjoyment of the proud.* Therefore, there is an eternal, fiery punishment of all those who are cursed by Allah, and even Muslims will be there for some period of time.

Mohammed taught that Allah ultimately decides whom he will forgive. A person can do nothing to affect this final decision as it is written in Qur'an 3:129: *[129]... He forgives to whom he wills, and he torments whom he wills....* In the hadith, Mohammed, responding to a question, indicated that even he would go to hell unless Allah covered him with his mercy.[105]

As we read previously in the hadith, Mohammed clearly taught that 99 percent of the women are in hell. "One woman out of 100 women is in the garden, and the rest of them are in Fire."[106] Again, in the hadith, "As I stood by the gate of Hell, I saw that most of those who entered the gate are women."[107] Also, "I also saw the Hell-fire and I had never seen such a horrible sight. I saw that most of the inhabitants were women."[108] Mohammed's description of the character of Allah leads us to the conclusion that the Allah of Mohammed is the Satan of the Bible.

Mohammed and Miracles

Muslims claim today that Mohammed performed many miracles, even though the Qur'an clearly taught that Mohammed did not perform any miracles. The only miracle of Mohammed we know of is the Qur'an itself, but as we have seen in *Exposing the Truth about the Qur'an: The Revelation of Error,* this miracle, the Qur'an, is nothing

---

[105]Sahih Bukhari, Hadith 6463, 5673.
[106]*Kanzu al-'ummal*, 22:10.
[107]Sahih Bukhari, Hadith 5251.
[108]Sahih Bukhari, Hadith 161.

but a chain of errors, one after another. Muslims say that the miracle of every prophet was given by Allah to match what was going on at the time when the prophet of Allah was sent. In Moses' day, there were the sorcerers. Therefore, Moses performed his magic to compete with the sorcerers. The case with Jesus is the same.

There were doctors and medicine, and so that is why Jesus was performing healing and raising the dead. In Mohammed's day, people were reciting poetry. Therefore, Mohammed came with his Qur'an to compete with their poetry. This claim could be true if Mohammed's Qur'an was correct, but as we have seen so far, the Qur'an is a book full of errors and fabrication. The last opinion by Muslims is that Mohammed truly did perform miracles, for they claim that he split the moon and ascended to the seven heavens, as we read below.

The Split of the Moon

Some Muslims claim that Mohammed performed miracles, like cutting the moon in half. When you ask for evidence, they will cite Qur'an 54:1: *[1]The hour has approached, and the moon has been split.* Muslims claim that Mohammed divided the moon, but the infidels still would not believe. However, the verse did not say that Mohammed divided the moon, but the verse simply says that "the moon has been split." This verse is actually a plagiarized portion of a poem written by the poet Emra Al Kaise who died in AD 540. Note that Mohammed was born in AD 570.

Mohammed's Ascension to the Seven Heavens

Another claim that Mohammed performed miracles was his ascension to the seven heavens while riding on his mule. According to Qur'an 17:1: *[1]Praise be to him who took his servant by night from the forbidden mosque[109] to the farthest mosque,[110] whom we have blessed that which surrounds him, that we might show him some of our signs. Surely he is the hearing, the seeing.* This passage describes Mohammed's trip to Jerusalem and to the seven heavens.

Mohammed claimed that he was miraculously taken from his house in Mecca to Jerusalem to the Temple of Solomon. There he prayed with all the prophets. However, that temple was actually demolished 550 years earlier. It is amazing that Mohammed, in the

---

[109]of Mecca
[110]Solomon's Temple in Jerusalem

hadith, described the temple with its details as if the temple still existed.

According to the hadith, Mohammed ascended to the seven heavens riding a mule after his miraculous visit to the temple. Notice in Qur'an 17:93 when the people requested that Mohammed ascend to heaven as a proof for them to believe in him, his response was not, "I have already been to heaven," but rather, "I am just a human."

A lengthy but very important hadith concerning the Angel Gabreel and Mohammed's trip to the seven heavens must be shared here. It is written that Mohammed claimed that he was cleansed with water and filled with wisdom then transported from Mecca to Jerusalem, then to the first heaven, then to the second heaven, and then to the third heaven until he arrived at the seventh heaven.[111] All this took place while he was riding his mule. In the first heaven, he met with Adam. He moved from heaven to heaven, meeting with different prophets (Joseph, Moses, and others) along the way. When Mohammed met with Adam, he described him as a ninety-foot tall man. *Does this make sense to you?* Every time this man looked to the right side, he laughed. Every time he looked to the left side, he cried. When Mohammed asked Angel Gabreel who the tall man was, he told Mohammed that this was Father Adam. Then Mohammed asked why Adam was laughing and crying. Gabreel told Mohammed that every time Adam looked on his right side, he saw those who believed Mohammed, and they are rejoicing in paradise. Every time Adam looked on his left side, he saw all those who did not believe in Mohammed, and they were burning in hell. That's why he was crying. Notice that Adam was crying in heaven which proves that the story is a fairy tale because the Bible clearly states that there are no tears in heaven.

As mentioned earlier, when Mohammed arrived at the seventh heaven, he was commanded to pray fifty times per day. He accepted this command and later met with Moses. Moses suggested that fifty prayers per day were too many. As Mohammed continued traveling between the fourth and seventh heavens, he negotiated with Allah after each time he returned to Moses, who said that the number of prayer was too high. After making ten trips, the number was reduced, eventually reaching five times per day. Mohammed claimed he made

---

[111]Sahih Bukhari, Hadith 3207, repeated in 3430 and 3878.

ten trips between these heavens. Then Mohammed returned to his house, and amazingly, his bed was still warm!

This miracle contradicts other teachings of the Qur'an. Qur'an 70:4 states that *⁴The angels and the spirit ascend to him in a day; its duration was fifty thousand years.* Also in Qur'an 32:5: *⁵He arranges the affair from the heaven to the earth. Then it ascends to him in a day, its duration was one thousand years from what you count.*

From the previous two verses, we discover that Mohammed believed the distance between heaven and earth is 1,000 or 50,000 years of traveling, as we count here on earth. According to him, these are the times that angels take to travel from heaven to earth. This by itself is a great contradiction. Here one must ask a question. *How could Mohammed have left his house, go all the way to Jerusalem, go all the way to the first heaven, go to the fourth heaven, then go back and forth between the fourth and seventh heavens ten times, come back to his own bed, and find that the bed was still warm?* Some may say that it was just a miracle. My response is that if Mohammed was alone without Angel Gabreel, this could perhaps be what happened. Since Angel Gabreel was with Mohammed, and according to the previous two verses of the Qur'an, Gabreel could not make it any faster than the speeds to which Allah had limited the angels in regards to their traveling from heaven to heaven. The conclusion must be that this is a fairy tale.

This story is repeated by many Muslim scholars with a few changes here and there. For example, according to Sheik Mohammed, Mohammed was taken to the holy site from Mecca riding on his mule. He traveled with Angel Gabreel.[112] There Mohammed prayed with all the prophets and led them in the prayer as the imam. He tied the donkey at the gate of the temple. Then he ascended on his mule to the heaven of the world. There he met with Adam. In the second heaven, he met with 'Isā and Yahyah. In the third heaven, he met with Joseph. In the fourth heaven, he met with Idris; in the fifth heaven, he met with Aaron. In the sixth heaven, he met with Moses.

Notice here that Mohammed met with Moses in the sixth heaven, not in the fourth heaven as stated previously, and do not forget that the Bible clearly declares that there are only three heavens. When he met with Moses, Moses was crying. Mohammed asked him why he was crying. He said, "I cry because a young man comes after me.

---

[112]Mohammed Ibn Abd Al Wahab, *A Summary of the Life of the Messenger*, 120.

More of his people (meaning more Muslims who believe in Mohammed) will enter the garden than the Jews who believe in me." Notice that Moses was crying in heaven which proves that the story is a fairy tale because the Bible clearly states that there are no tears in heaven, as we already mentioned.

Then Mohammed went to the seventh heaven and saw Abraham. That is when he saw Angel Gabreel with his 600 wings. *How can he meet Angel Gabreel when he was traveling with him the entire time?* Then he talked with his lord, and he gave him whatever he gave him. (This is a strict translation of these pronouns.) When it was morning, Mohammed told his people about his trip to the holy city and the heavens, but people called him a liar. They asked him to describe the holy house, and he did. They had no response to that. My response is, what Sheik Mohammed and those ignorant people who argued with Mohammed did not know, is that Mohammed could not possibly have described this holy house for the simple reason that it was completely demolished in the year AD 71. That was more than five hundred years before Mohammed claimed to visit or to tie his donkey at its door.

What is amazing about these miracles is that there is no second witness. It is only Mohammed's own words. *What is the purpose of a miracle if no one has seen it?* As we have seen throughout Scripture, miracles were performed before people so people would see them and believe.

Mohammed performed no miracles. The only miracle that Muslims can claim that Mohammed provided to the world is the Qur'an. We have already discussed why that was not a miracle. The reason why Mohammed did not perform miracles is given in Qur'an 17:59: *[59]And nothing prevented us from sending the signs except that the ancients denied them....* Mohammed claimed that when Allah sent miracles with the early prophets, people did not believe in the miracles. Common sense then would tell us that there was no reason for Allah to perform any type of miracle with his final messenger/prophet. This interpretation is not credible because when we read the Qur'an and the Bible, we discover that people believed in the prophets after the prophets performed miracles. Miracles are the evidence that the prophet is a true prophet, for the miracles supported the message of the prophets as we have seen in the cases of Moses, Joshua, Elisha, Elijah, and Jesus, as well as His disciples.

Most noteworthy are the striking contrasts between Mohammed and Jesus Christ. Mohammed made seeing eyes blind (as in the interpretation of Qur'an 5:33 and Bukhari vol. 8, p. 520); Jesus made the blinded eyes to see (Luke 18:35-43). Mohammed made the walking lame (Qur'an 5:33); Jesus made the lame to walk (Matthew 9:6). Mohammed cut off the hands of others (Bukhari vol. 8, p. 520 and Qur'an 5:33); Jesus healed the withered hand (Matthew 12:10-13). Mohammed had the living killed (Ibn Hisham p. 308 and Qur'an 5:33); Jesus raised the dead (John 11:1-45). Moreover, Mohammed's reaction to a blind man was exactly the opposite of Jesus' reaction. In the Qur'an, it is recorded that when a blind man called on Mohammed, instead of Mohammed seeking to help or heal him, he ran away from him. Qur'an 80:1-2 records: [1]*He (Mohammed) frowned and turned away* [2]*when the blind man came to him.*

<u>Mohammed and Demons</u>

Mohammed was demon-possessed as can be seen in the description of the condition of Mohammed each time he received a revelation. Muslims described him as fainting, foaming at the mouth, sweating heavily, seizing (having seizures), and shaking. He reported hearing loud ringing bells, and people reported hearing the sound of bees coming from his face. They would wrap him in blankets before he received revelations and unwrap him after his receiving such revelations. Thus we have the Arabic names of two Qur'an portions of revelation, portion (chapter) 73 named "The Wrapped" and portion (chapter) 74 named "The Cloaked." Aisha stated that Mohammed was bewitched by a Jewish woman.[113] He also had suicidal moments when Waraka Ibn Nawfal, a heretical Christian monk, whom I believe was helping Mohammed to construct the stories of the Bible in qur'anic poetry form, died. When Waraka Ibn Nawfal died, the revelations stopped. During this time, Mohammed went to the top of the mountain three or four times to commit suicide, as seen in the Mohammed movie, but it is said that Angel Gabreel called on him, "Do not kill yourself, you are truly the prophet of Allah."[114]

Mohammed invented characters in his Qur'an called *jinn*. Muslim scholars like Ibn Kathir, as mentioned previously in "The Creation of Jinn" in the section on Creation, stated that the jinn were created by Allah two thousand years before the creation of Adam. The singular form of the word is *jinni* (jínnee); I am assuming that is where the *genie* came from in the stories of Aladdin. I personally believe that jinn are nothing but demons, ungodly spirits (Satan's angels). We

---

[113]Sahih Muslim, Hadith 5832.
[114]Nakoula, *Innocence of Muslims.*

know from the Qur'an that they were Muslim believers. Qur'an 72:1-3 states: *¹Say, "It was revealed to me that a company of the jinn listened, so they said, 'Surely we have heard a wonderful Qur'an. ²It guides to the right way, so we believed in it, and we will not partner anyone with our lord. ³And that he is exalted much, our lord did not take a female companion nor a son.'"* Wow! The jinn are good Muslims and do not believe that Jesus is the Son of God. This is great evidence that jinn are demons. This is a quick and simple study. An in-depth study would be another book. When we connect all this together, we conclude that Mohammed was demon-possessed. The demons believed in the god of Mohammed, Allah. He is their god, and demons rejected the Sonship of Christ. Mohammed is the prophet of Allah, who, like Satan, is the best deceiver; and the Qur'an is the work of the devil.

Mohammed's Prophecies

To provide evidence of Mohammed having been given successful prophecies, Muslims most often allude to various verses in which Mohammed promised victory to his army. The passage from the Qur'an most often cited as proof of Mohammed's prophecy is Qur'an 30:2-4: *²The Rūm[115] are defeated. ³In a near part of the land and after having been defeated, they will be victorious. ⁴Within a few years, to Allah is the affair, before and after and on that day, the believers will rejoice.* This is said to predict that after an initial victory by the Persians, the Romans would be victorious over the Persians after a few years. However, there were no details for this prophecy. *When, where, who*, and *how* are missing from this claim of prophecy. Imagine if I tell you that in the next nine years the rain will fall near your house. *Would you consider my statement to be a prophecy?* That is what Mohammed did.

Moreover, the words which are written in the verse above, the Rūm *are defeated...after having been defeated*, can be read in the Arabic language as *jholbat* (lost) or *jhalbat* (won), depending on how the word is pronounced. Both are in the past tense, but obviously give differing meanings to the verse.

Since the Qur'an was originally written without *tashkeel* (Arabic diacritical marks), a person can pronounce the word either way, as *lost* or as *won*. In verse 3, the same word can be read the following ways: *sayaghlibuna* (they shall defeat) or *sayughlabuna* (they shall be

---

[115]Byzantines, a non-Arabic word of Greek origin

defeated), both in the future tense. This in itself can end the claim that
Mohammed gave a prophecy. No matter what took place in the
battlefield, Mohammed's prophecy was fulfilled.

Look at this one prediction or prophecy made in Qur'an 30:2-4
regarding the Roman Empire having been defeated in a land close by;
but they, even after this defeat of theirs, would soon be victorious
within a few years. The Persians defeated the Romans at the capture
of Jerusalem about AD 614. The counter-offensive began about 622
and resulted in victory in 625, which was at least ten or eleven years
after the prediction and possibly closer to thirteen or fourteen.

Uthman's edition of the Qur'an (after he burned the original
copies of the Qur'an) was written after this battle was won, after the
claim of the prophecy was fulfilled. His interpretation has no vowel
points, and these were added much later. Therefore, the word
sayaghlibuna (they shall defeat) could have been rendered
sayughlabuna (they shall **be** defeated) which makes this prediction
suspect. Moreover, a perceptive reading of the trends of the time
could very well have led to the conclusion that the Romans would
bounce back. Compare this with certain biblical prophecies, which are
amazing in their details of time, place, and people, to the extent that
individuals have been called by name before they were born.

Some totally failed prophecies which the Muslims try to ignore
are written in Qur'an 59:14 *[14]They will not engage in war together
against you except in fortress villages or from behind walls....*
The nation of Israel certainly proved that wrong in the twentieth
century when the Muslim nations attempted to wipe them out. They
certainly "engaged in war against" them, and very successfully!

I would like to share such an obviously false prophecy that is
written in the Qur'an. In Qur'an 109, Allah said: *[1]Say, "O you, the
infidels, [2]I do not serve what you serve, [3]and you do not serve
what I serve. [4]And I will not serve what you have served, [5]and
you will not serve what I serve. [6]To you your religion, and to me
is my religion."*

Notice in verse 5, Allah said that the people of Quraish will not
serve Allah. What is amazing is that soon after Mohammed wrote
theses verses, almost all the people of Quraish believed in
Mohammed and served Allah.

Mohammed's Education

Some Muslims claim that Mohammed was a great prophet and his
prophecy is proven by the beautiful poetry of the Qur'an or by the

accuracy of his Qur'an, especially when they declare that Mohammed was illiterate and did not have access to the Bible. However, they claim that he was still able to tell many of the stories of the Bible. I would like to respond to the claim that Mohammed wrote beautiful stories of the Bible without access to the Bible.

First, the stories of Mohammed, as you have already read, were corrupted with many errors and confusion because very important information was missing as stories were mixed together from different times and places. This in itself is proof that Mohammed was not a true prophet but rather a plagiarist.

Second, the claim that Mohammed did not have access to the Bible is not true, for when we read in Qur'an 10:94: *[94]So, if you were in doubt concerning what we have sent down to you, so ask those who are reading the book before you....* According to the reading of this verse, one must come to the following two conclusions. The first conclusion is that the Bible was available in Mohammed's day because Christians and Jews could not read a book that did not exist. The second conclusion is that the Bible was not corrupted but was in excellent condition because Allah, the knower of all things, would not have asked Mohammed to check the validity of his Qur'an with a corrupt book.

Third, in the hadith, when the Jews asked Mohammed concerning the judgment on older men and women who commit adultery, Mohammed asked them to bring the Torah. To show his respect for the Torah, Mohammed put his pillow in front of him, placed the Torah on it, and was able to read from it that they should be stoned.[116]

The claim that Mohammed could not read and write is invalid for the following reasons. First, he was a merchant for the wealthiest woman in Mecca, and an important part of performing this job was keeping records and accounting for goods. This job could not have been performed by an illiterate person.

Additionally, I believe that the original problem is in the wording of the Qur'an. In Qur'an 7:157: *[157]Those who follow the messenger, the Gentile prophet whom they will find described for them in the Torah and the Gospel....* The word *omey* in the Arabic language has two meanings. It could mean Gentile, for all of the non-Jews are Gentiles as we see in the Bible. For example, Paul was the apostle to the Gentiles, and we can say in Arabic that the Apostle Paul was an *omey* apostle. No one can claim that Paul was

---

[116]Sahih Bukhari, Hadith 3635.

illiterate; he was a highly educated man. The second meaning of the word *omey* is illiterate. Therefore, we can conclude that Mohammed was a Gentile prophet. He was **not** illiterate. That is why I chose to use the word *Gentile* in my translation of the Qur'an, as seen in the above verse, as the accurate translation for the word *omey*.

If we say that Mohammed was illiterate, then we must ask this question. *If so, then were all the Arabs who believed him also illiterate?* In Qur'an 62:2: *²He is who raised a messenger in the Gentiles from among them, who recites his verses on them and purifies them and teaches them the book and the wisdom, and though they were in obvious error before….* Here are the people to whom Mohammed was sent, and they became Muslims. Here the word is Gentiles, not *illiterates*, unless Muslims believe that all Muslims who believed were illiterate, which does not make sense. See also Qur'an 3:75: *⁷⁵And some of the People of the Book who, if you trust him with a qintār,[117] he will pay it back to you. And some of them, if you trust him with a dīnār,[118] he will not pay it back to you unless you keep demanding it. This is because they said, "There is no way upon us in the Gentiles." And they say the lies against Allah, and they know.* Another point I would like to share is that writing poetry does not require an education. Even today many people can write poetry without a formal education.

There have been many great poets throughout the history of man. Although their large body of works is excellent and millions have studied their work and given applause to their excellent work, neither these poets nor the people who love their poetry can claim that these poets are prophets. As mentioned before, good examples of these poets are Shakespeare, whose work is some of the best poetry in the English language, and Voltaire, who wrote many beautiful pieces of French poetry.

Poetry is not evidence of the prophethood; rather, the message in the poetry is the evidence of the prophecy. If the message has the truth in it, this means that it will be a true prophecy, the prophecy will be fulfilled, and the man who gives the prophecy will lead the people to worship the true God of the Bible. As for the case of Mohammed, when we look at his message in the Qur'an, as we have seen in *Exposing the Truth about the Qur'an: The Revelation of Error*, the writing of the Qur'an does not show any truth concerning the stories

---

[117]a measure, non-Arabic word of Greek origin
[118]dinar, a coin, non-Arabic word of Greek origin

of the prophets. It is actually a ridiculous counterfeit and plagiarism of the writing of the Bible and many other books. It does not contain any prophecy, and it does not lead the Muslims to worship the true God of the Bible, but rather Allah (Satan), the god of Mohammed.

Mohammed's Battles

Muslim sources vary widely on the number of battles and raids in which Mohammed was personally involved until he was wounded. Subsequently, he appointed a prince to lead more battles and raids on his behalf. To this day, Muslim powers all over the world carry on the message of Mohammed to terrorize the world and kill infidels wherever they are able to do so. Mohammed was involved in twenty-eight battles in which he led the army in the battle during an eight year period beginning from the second year after emigration to the ninth year.[119] He directed an additional thirty-eight campaigns in which he did not directly participate.[120] A basic outline of some of these battles follows:

Year (AD)	Place or person(s) attacked	Leader	Purpose
623	Waddan	Mohammed	Robbery
623	Lower Thaniyatu'l-Mara	Ubaida b.al-Harith	Robbery
623	Al-'Is on coast	Hamza b Abdul-Muttalib	Robbery
623	Buwat	Mohammed	Robbery
623	Dul-'Ashir	Mohammed	Attempted Robbery
623	Ushayra	Mohammed	Robbery
623	Al-Kharrar	Sa'd b. Abu Waqqas	Robbery

---

[119]Arabic Wikipedia
(http://ar.wikipedia.org/wiki/%D8%BA%D8%B2%D9%88%D8%A7%D8%AA_%D8%A7%D9%84%D8%B1%D8%B3%D9%88%D9%84_%D9%85%D8%AD%D9%85%D8%AF#.D8.BA .D8.B2.D9%88.D8.A7.D8%AA_.D8.A7.D9.84.D8.B1.D8.B3.D9%88.D9%84_.D8.B5.D9.84.D9.89_. D8.A7.D9.84.D9.87_.D8.B9.D9.84.D9.8A.D .87_.D9%88.D8.B3.D9.84.D9%85), accessed October 23, 2012.

[120]http://www.1000mistakes.com/1000mistakes /index. php? Page=011_012_001_001, accessed September 17, 2011.

623	Safwan (1. raid on Badr)	Mohammed	Revenge, recapture goods. Pursuit Kurz b. Jabir
623?	Nakhla (Bahran)	Abdullah b. Jahsh b.Riab al-Asadi	Spy, robbery
624, Jan.	Battle of Badr	Mohammed	Intended to rob, met army
624	Ka'b b. al-Ashraf	Mohammed b. Malama	Murder
624?	Al-Qarada	Zayd b. Haritha	Rob
624	Bani Salim	Mohammed	Rob
624	"Eid/Zakat-ul-Fitr"		
624, Feb.	Bani Quainuga	Mohammed	Kill or expel Jews and rob them
624	Sawiq	Abu Safyan b.Harb	Rob
624	Gahtafan (Dhu Amarr)	Mohammed	Rob
624	Bahran	Mohammed	Rob
625	Uhud	Mohammed	Battle of defense in a war of aggression
625	Humra-ul-Asad		
625, June	Banu Nadir	Mohammed	Kill, expel, rob Jews
625	Dhatul–Riqa of Nakhl	Mohammed	Rob
626	Badr – 3. Raid	Mohammed	Meet Abu Sufyan
626	Badru-Ukhra		
626	Dumatul-Jandal	Mohammed	Rob
627, Feb.	The Trench (Medina)	Mohammed	Defense in war of aggression
627	Ahzab		
627, March	Bani Quraiza	Mohammed	Rob Jews
627	Bani Layhan	Mohammed	Avenge and rob
627	Ghaiba		

627? (628?)	Banu Mustalaq Nikah	Mohammed	Kill, expel, rob Jews
627, Aug.	Khaybar	Mohammed	Kill, enslave, rob Jews
628	Al-Hudaibiya	Mohammed	War not intended but perhaps provocation.
629	Khaybar	Mohammed	Kill, rob, enslave Jews
630, Jan.	Mecca	Mohammed	Conquest
630, Feb.	Hunain (Hunsin?)	Mohammed	
630	Auras		
630	Taif	Mohammed	Conquest
630, Sept.	Tabouk	Mohammed	Pre-emptive attack

This list demonstrates that Mohammed was not a prophet of peace and love. If he was a prophet of peace and love as Muslims claim, he would not been involved in all of these battles, even if other people desired to engage in war with him. Mohammed did not seek reconciliation; instead, he called all those who lived around him his enemies, and he started the fights. He lived, pretending to be a loving and peaceful prophet, when he was weak militarily, in his early years in Mecca after claiming to be a prophet; however, when he became strong, he performed all these battles. Let us not forget that Mohammed was a noble example for Muslim believers to follow as Allah stated in Qur'an 33:21: [21]*Indeed, there was in the messenger of Allah a noble example for you, for him who was hoping in Allah and in the last day and remembers Allah much.* That is why we see Muslim imams and believers in the West, when they do not have the upper hand, imitate Mohammed's early years while he was in Mecca. I hope and pray that the people of the West will wake up before the true color of Islam appears because then it will be too late.

Sheik Mohammed stated that Mohammed, the apostle of Islam, used to speak with his people to get their opinion about the jihad, he used to invade people, he used to prepare his army to go and fight from every side of war, he used to do swordfights, and he wore the clothes of war.[121] When he called out, "Allah Akbar," (which means *Allah (Satan) is bigger*, not as Muslims claim it means *god is great*) and if the people responded by saying, "Allah Akbar," that meant they accepted Islam. However, if they did not respond, then Mohammed would fight them. Sheik Mohammed named many of the invasions or wars which Mohammed led. These were previously listed.[122]

Dividing the Spoils of Badr

Mohammed ordered the believers to gather the spoils of war. The people who gathered it said, "It is ours." But the people who fought the war said, "No, it is ours. If it had not been for our fighting, you would have no spoils." It was given to Mohammed, and he divided the spoils among the Muslims. That is why Allah said, in Qur'an 8:1: *[1]They ask you about the spoils, say, "The spoils to Allah and the messenger." So fear Allah and do good among yourselves and obey Allah and his messenger, if you were believers.*

The Prisoners of the War of Badr

Mohammed asked the opinion of his companions concerning the seventy prisoners of the war of Badr.[123] Abu Bakr said, "We will take a ransom from them and let them go. Perhaps Allah will lead them to Islam." Another believer named Omar said, "No, by Allah, I do not see that. We will strike their necks. They are the leaders of the infidels."

The following morning, Omar met with Abu Bakr and Mohammed, and he saw them both crying. He asked them why they were crying. Mohammed said, "Because of what your companion's opinion was, to take ransom from the prisoners of war. It was revealed to me by Allah that I must torment them. If the torment is sent, no one will be saved from it." (Omar was the one to come up with the right answer.)

Sheik Mohammed mentioned many of Mohammed's battles and invasions, which he supported with plenty of verses from the Qur'an and in which Allah commanded Mohammed to go out and kill.[124] All

---

[121]Mohammed Ibn Abd Al Wahab, *A Summary of the Life of the Messenger*, 146.
[122]Ibid., 147-157.
[123]Ibid., 158.
[124]Ibid., 159-221.

these pages describe the nature of Mohammed and how Islam was founded on so much shedding of blood.

Sheik Mohammed stated that after Mohammed finished the invasion of the war of Tabuk and after the Sakeef tribe accepted Islam, the camels were coming to Mohammed from every direction in the ninth year of emigration.[125] The Arabs knew then that they would not be able to deny Mohammed, and they could not be his enemy; therefore, people began to accept Islam in throngs, as Allah said in Qur'an 110:1-3: *¹When the triumph of Allah and the conquest comes ²and you see the people entering the religion of Allah by throngs, ³so praise with your lord's praise and seek his forgiveness, surely he was ever-relenting.*

Many more tribes and people came to Mohammed and Islam. When I say to the Muslims in the West or the Westerners in general that Islam is spread by the sword, they cannot comprehend this fact. Yet, we read the words of Muslim scholars in their own books. I wonder if people can see this fact, as it is written in the history of Islam and in the life of Mohammed, the prophet of Islam.

Additional Errors

Many errors have already been addressed throughout *Exposing the Truth about the Qur'an: The Revelation of Error*; however, I would like to mention a few additional errors here, which will bring us to the logical conclusion that Mohammed could not be a true prophet when such errors exist in the Qur'an or the hadith. Consider the olive tree on Mount Sinai mentioned in Qur'an 23:19-20: *¹⁹So we produce to you by it gardens of palm trees and grapes. You have in it much fruit, and from it you eat. ²⁰And the tree that grows up on Mount Sainā,[126] which yields oil and a juice for eaters.* Have you ever been on Mount Sinai? Have you ever seen pictures of Mount Sinai? It is a granite mountain where no olive tree can grow. This is a botanical error because Mohammed had never been there and did not know what it was like.

In Qur'an 16:106, Allah gives permission for Muslims to deny their faith if they are compelled: *¹⁰⁶Whoever becomes an infidel in Allah after he believed, except one who was compelled and his heart is secure in faith; but whoever opens his chest to the infidelity, so on them wrath from Allah, and they will have great*

[125]Ibid., 222.
[126]Sinai, non-Arabic word of Syriac origin

torment. This is what most Muslims do when they travel in the West, especially when they attempt to infiltrate an important office as in the case of Barack Hussein Obama who has denied many times that he is a Muslim, even though, according to the Qur'an and the hadith, he is without doubt a Muslim man. Note that the Bible, in Luke 12:9, clearly teaches that whoever denies Christ before men will be denied before the angels of God. Millions of Christians were slaughtered by Muslims in the last fourteen hundred years simply because they refused to deny Jesus.

What about the verse in the Qur'an which teaches Muslims that it is lawful to lie in their swearing? In Qur'an 2:225 we read, *[225]Allah will not hold you responsible for your mere utterance in an oath, but he will hold you responsible for that which your hearts gained.[127] And Allah is forgiving, forbearing.* I remember when I stood before the judge in Tampa, Florida, and raised my right hand, giving allegiance to the United States of America. There were goose bumps all over me, as the hair stood up on the back of my neck, while I had one eye on the judge and the other on the flag of the United States of America. I was honored to do so. (Do not forget, however, I am even more honored to be a Christian than to be an American.)

There were around three hundred people there on that day to give allegiance to America. Of those, around fifty were Muslim men and women who also raised their right hands and repeated the words of the judge. The women were covered in hijab; that is how I knew they were Muslim. Their husbands were growing their beards. In Islam this is a sign of being a true believer. In my home country and around the world, Muslims, when they become jihadists, grow beards. Muslim men do not grow facial hair for their looks or for fashion as Westerners do; they grow it because of the *sunnah,* in obedience to Mohammed and to imitate him and the Muslim way of life.

I asked myself then, and I ask you now: *Do you believe these Muslims meant what they swore to?* My answer is *absolutely not*, for the Muslim's allegiance must first be to Allah, second to Mohammed, third to the Muslim Ummah (supra-national Muslim community), fourth to their native Muslim country, fifth to the neighboring Muslim countries with which they are friendly, and sixth to the Muslim countries with which they are enemies. By this point, you can kiss allegiance to the United States of America *good-bye.* To illustrate this fact, when the judge in a New York court asked Faisal Shahzad, the

[127]what your heart meant

Times Square bomber, "Didn't you swear allegiance to this country when you became an America citizen?" He answered, "I did swear, but I did not mean it." The judge then asked, "You took a false oath?" Shahzad replied, "Yes."[128]

This leads us to the third point which Mohammed taught in the Qur'an concerning lying. In a hadith, Mohammed said, "It is lawful to lie in three cases: A man to his wife that she will be pleased with him or at a time of war because war is deception or to make peace between people."[129] What a wonderful relationship between a Muslim man and his wives when he is encouraged to lie to them, and the encourager was Mohammed himself. Note that the Bible clearly teaches *"Thou shall not lie."*

Throughout the Qur'an, Mohammed stated that Allah swears. It is amazing the things by which Allah swears; sometimes he swears by trees or some mountain or the dawn or other things. For example, in Qur'an 89:1-5: *[I swear] by the dawn ²and by the ten nights ³and by the even and the odd ⁴and by night when it departs. ⁵Is there an oath in this to one who possesses a stone?*[130] What a great internal proof that this god of Mohammed is not the true God of the Bible.

As Jesus taught us in Matthew 5:34-37: *³⁴But I say to you, do not swear at all: neither by heaven, for it is God's throne; ³⁵nor by the earth, for it is His footstool; nor by Jerusalem, for it is the city of the great King. ³⁶Nor shall you swear by your head, because you cannot make one hair white or black. ³⁷ But let your "Yes" be "Yes," and your "No," "No." For whatever is more than these is from the evil one.* When God in the Bible swears, He swears by nothing but Himself, for one must swear by the greatest thing, not a perishable thing.

Another immoral teaching in Islam can be found in Qur'an 8:41: *⁴¹And know that whatever you take of spoil of anything, so a fifth part to Allah and to the messenger....* Again in Qur'an 8:69: *⁶⁹So eat of the spoils you have taken lawfully and good, and fear Allah. Surely Allah is forgiving, merciful.* To *fear Allah* is to make sure that Allah, and especially Mohammed, get the fifth part of the spoils.

---

[128]Michael Wilson, "Shahzad Gets Life Term for Times Square Bombing Attempt," *New York Times,* October 5, 2010, accessed February 21, 2013, http://www.nytimes.com/2010/10/06/nyregion/06shahzad.html?_r=0.

[129] Musnad Ahmed, Hadith 26315.

[130]Muslim scholars interpret this as *understanding*, equating it to hardheadedness.

I grew up in Upper Egypt which is the southern part, and I was always astonished by the culture in which I grew up, which is the culture of revenge or retaliation. That is seen when somebody is killed in a family, and instead of the family seeking judgment by the court of law, they take the matter into their own hands by killing a person from the guilty family who is equal to the person whom they have lost. For example, if a twenty-year-old man was killed by an older man or a woman from another family, the deceased family will not kill the older man or woman who killed the young man but rather kill another innocent member of the family of close age to the person that was killed. What a terrible culture.

Later in my life when I started to study the Qur'an, I was shocked to my bones of what took place in Upper Egypt. This culture of retaliation was not a culture at all but the religion of Islam, the teaching of Allah in the Qur'an. This can be found in Qur'an 2:194: *[194]The forbidden month for the forbidden month[131] and all the forbidden things are retaliation, so whoever commits transgression against you, so transgress against him similar to how he transgressed against you....* Also, note Qur'an 2:178: *[178]O you who have believed, retaliation is decreed on you for the murdered, the free man for the free, and the slave for the slave, and the female for the female....*

Mohammed regularly urged his followers to use the sword. In Qur'an 47:4: *[4]So when you meet those who became infidels, so strike the necks (decapitating) until you have made a great slaughter among them....*

Much more could be told about the life of Mohammed, but as mentioned previously, it would require a large book to cover everything about him. My prayer is for you to investigate my writings in this book. Then, after knowing for sure that it is true, that you will share it with as many people as you can, Americans and foreigners alike, Christians or non-Christians alike, for we are in a war, and it is spiritual warfare. It is a war of truth against lies. If we allow the lies to spread because of political correctness or ignorancy, we will be destroyed, and this spiritual warfare will turn into a physical war led by Muslim believers, the terrorists. Americans will lose their freedoms, and many who will not know the truth will lose eternity.

---

[131]Mohammed probably meant *months* since there are four months during which engaging in war is suspended

However, if we hold on to the truth, we will be set free and democracy will flourish, not only here in America but around the world. For now we know for sure that Mohammed was a terrorist and Islam is the religion of tyranny as stated in Qur'an 33:26-27: *26And he brought down the People of the Book who backed them from their strong places and cast the terror into their hearts. A group of them you are killing, and a group of them you are taking captive. 27And he made you to inherit their land and their homes and their money and a land which you had never set foot on. And Allah was mighty over all things.* See also Qur'an 3:151; 8:12; and 59:2.

The Pilgrimage of Abu Bakr with the People

The reason Mohammed sent Abu Bakr to perform the first hajj in the ninth year after the hijrah (when Muslims fled from Mecca to Medina), while he himself did not go to lead the Muslims, was because there were infidels and polytheists who performed the hajj with their females, and they were all naked. There was a cease-fire between Mohammed and the people of Quraish, the polytheists, until the eighth year of emigration; then Mohammed claimed to receive the final revelation, Qur'an portion (chapter) 9 in the ninth year of emigration. That's when Allah and Mohammed cancelled his covenant with the people of Quraish, and after that the house belonged to the state of Islam and the one god, Allah. No longer could polytheists or infidels or naked persons perform the hajj. That is why Mohammed sent someone else in his place. When Qur'an portion 9 *conveniently* descended, Mohammed sent this portion of revelation with Ali Ibn Abu Talib, and he read it to all the people. That is when Mohammed took over the house (Kaaba).

The Farewell

Sheik Mohammed wrote that Mohammed was prepared to perform the hajj, and he ordered the people to prepare for him.[132] He commanded them to meet with him at Medina, and all the people, near and far, met with him on the way to Mecca. He led the people in this final hajj or pilgrimage as he taught them the performance of the hajj. He repeated to them his statement, "O people, learn from me the tradition of the hajj. Perhaps you will not see me after this year." He

---

[132]Mohammed Ibn Abd Al Wahab, *A Summary of the Life of the Messenger,* 228.

preached to the people again, "O people, hear my speech. For surely, I do not know if I will meet you after this year. O people, your blood and your money and your possessions…I left among you what, if you hold to it, you will never go astray: the book of Allah and my sunnah (way of life)." He pointed with his finger to the heaven and to the people three times as he said, "O Allah, bear witness."

Another important fact we must mention here is that Mohammed was dying from poison which had been mixed with some mutton meat and served to Mohammed and another man by a Jewish woman. The other man died immediately after swallowing the meat, but Mohammed was able to spit the meat out of his mouth. However, the poison caused Mohammed to become feverish and later caused his death.

The Deployment of Osama Bin Zaid to Al Baka

It was Monday, four days before the end of the month Safar of year eleven of the emigration, when Mohammed ordered the people to prepare to invade the Byzantine Empire. On the following day, Mohammed called Osama Bin Zaid to go to the place where his father Zaid Bin Harsah was killed to prepare the people there to be able to begin his invasion. The "hypocrites" rejected the leadership of Osama Ibn Zaid, so the apostle of Allah got very angry even though he was very sick. He stood up on the pulpit as stated by Sheik Mohammed and preached to the people, stating, "If you reject Osama's leadership, then you reject his father's leadership." Mohammed assured them that he loved Osama's father more than any other human. Then Mohammed left the pulpit, and his pain became very strong. Osama went out with his armies, and he camped at Jarf.

The Sickness of the Apostle of Allah

Sheik Mohammed said that Ibn Isaac said Osama said that when Mohammed became sick, the people went with Osama to the city.[133] Osama entered into the presence of Mohammed, and Mohammed became quiet. He did not speak. He raised his hand to the heaven. Then he put it on Osama, as Osama said, "I know he was praying for me." When the pain came hard on Mohammed, he called his wives and asked their permission to continue his sickness in the house of Aisha, his favorite wife. They gave him permission.

---

[133]Ibid., 229-231.

Aby Saeed Al Khadry said that Mohammed gave a speech in which he said, "Allah gave a servant the choice between this world's life and what is with Allah, so this servant chose what is with Allah. Then Abu Bakr cried, so we wondered why he cried. So he said, 'The servant is Mohammed, and he was going to the garden.' Mohammed then spoke highly of Abu Bakr, and he said, 'If I would choose a friend, rather than my lord, I would take Abu Bakr as a friend.'"

In the Sahih hadith of Abu Moses Al Ashare, he said, "When the sickness of Mohammed was very strong, Mohammed asked Abu Bakr to lead the people in prayer; so Aisha said, 'O apostle of Allah, he is a very tender man. If he stood in your place to lead the people in the prayer, people could not hear him. Ask Omar to lead the people in prayer.' Mohammed said, 'Ask Abu Bakr to lead the people in prayer.' Then Aisha returned, and she said, 'Ask Abu Bakr to lead the people in the prayer.'" So Mohammed came to him, and Abu Bakr led the people in prayer during the life of Mohammed.

The Death of Mohammed

Let us now turn our attention to his death. He contracted a fever which required Muslims to shower him with cool water to lower his temperature to enable him to lead them in their prayers. Some claim that this sickness was the result of eating poison meat which had been given to him and a companion by a Jewish lady. His companion died immediately after swallowing the meat, but Mohammed spit out the meat and did not eat it. The conclusion is that Mohammed died from poisoning. His body was placed in a tomb and is still there. Muslims traditionally visit his tomb when performing the pilgrimage of hajj. In conclusion, I would like to quote a verse written concerning Mohammed when Allah said in Qur'an 39:30: *[30]Surely you (Mohammed) are dead, and surely they (the Muslims) are dead.* We compare this to Jesus Christ who said in John 11: 25: ***Jesus said to her, "I am the resurrection and the life. He who believes in Me, though he may die, he shall live."***

According to Sheik Mohammed, Al Zohare stated that Anis said it was Monday when the spirit of the messenger of Allah was taken.[134] Mohammed came after the people as they were praying the morning prayers. When Muslims met with him, they rejoiced, and they were coming to be with him. However, Mohammed pointed to them to continue in their prayer. Anis continued that the apostle of Allah

[134]Ibid., 231.

smiled when he saw their position in the prayer. He saw the best of everything in that hour. Then he returned, and the people left. Abu Bakr left his people, and Mohammed died in the afternoon that day.

Sheik Mohammed stated that Ibn Isaac said Abu Horyrah said when the messenger of Allah died, Omar rose up and said that some hypocritical men claimed that the messenger of Allah died.[135] "I swear by Allah, he did not die; but he returned to his lord, as Moses Ibn Amran was absent from his people forty nights. Then he returned to them, and it was said that he died. I swear by Allah, surely the messenger of Allah will return after a while, as Moses returned. Surely he will cut the hands and the feet of the men who claim that he died."

Abu Bakr came by the mosque when he heard the news (while Omar was still speaking to the people). He did not look at anything, but he entered the house of Aisha. He uncovered the face of Mohammed, and he kissed him. Abu Bakr came out, and Omar still spoke to the people. He said, "Listen, O Omar," but he refused to listen. Because Abu Bakr saw that Omar refused to listen, he spoke to the people. The people listened to Abu Bakr, and they did not listen to Omar. That is when Abu Bakr said, "Whoever served Mohammed, so surely Mohammed is dead; and whoever served Allah, so Allah is surely alive. He will never die." Then Abu Bakr quoted Qur'an 3:144: *[144]And Mohammed is not but a messenger; indeed, the messengers passed before him. If he dies or is killed, will you turn on your heels? And who turns on his heels will not harm Allah anything. And Allah will reward the thankful.* After Mohammed died, the people went in different directions.

The Killing of the Apostate

Muslims who left Islam moved to different sects. Some left and returned to the worship of idols.[136] Others said, "We believe in Allah, but we will not pray." Others believed and prayed, but they would not pay the *zakāt* (legally required alms). Others believed in Allah and Mohammed, but they also believed in Mosylamh, meaning that he and Mohammed were partners in the prophethood. Some of the people of Yemen believed in the Black Al Ansee, who claimed to be a prophet. Others believed in Calyha Al Asdee, but the companions of Abu Bakr decided to wage a campaign against all of them. They

[135]Ibid., 231-232.
[136]Ibid., 239.

disagreed about killing those who were Muslim but refused to pay the zakāt (giving alms). The ones who refused to go and fight quoted what Allah said in the hadith and other places.[137] Mohammed said, "I have been commanded to wage a war on people until they say, 'There is no god but Allah.' If they say it, their blood and their money will be safe from me," except for *just cause,* that is, if they do not obey Allah.

That is why Abu Bakr said that the zakāt is a portion of their belief. He swore by Allah, if they stopped giving anything which they used to give to the apostle, he would engage in war against them. That is why they fought the apostates, and Allah gave them victory. They killed "whom they killed from them," and they took the spoils of their women and their children. This war did not end there, but it continued throughout the history of Islam. Sheik Mohammed continued in his book that Muslims continued to kill each other.[138] Different people at different times and different places came with different cults, but the true Muslim believer caught them and killed them.

Conclusion

As I continued to read Sheik Mohammed's book, I saw that many of the Muslim tribes were forced into Islam, which fits perfectly with the words of Mohammed in Qur'an 49:14: *[14]The Bedouins said, "We believed." Say, "You did not believe. But say, 'We surrender (became Muslim as a result of fear).' And the faith has not entered your hearts. And if you obey Allah and his messenger, he will not decrease anything from your works. Surely Allah is forgiving, merciful."* This is the fact about Islam and the Muslim. There is nothing for people to believe in. As we have seen in this book, the only miracle Mohammed could use to prove his prophethood is the Qur'an. The book is full of errors, a ridiculous counterfeit of the stories of the Bible and other stories as well, such as the stories of the made-up prophets and the story of the cave which we covered previously.

Why do people believe in Islam? They were forced to become Muslims or be killed by the sword. If Mohammed was a true prophet, he would easily have had thousands of followers to believe in him in the first ten years of claiming to be a prophet. Surely his message was

---

[137]Sahih Bukhari, Hadith 1335; Sahih Muslim, Hadith 20.
[138]Mohammed Ibn Abd Al Wahab, *A Summary of the Life of the Messenger,* 241.

powerful; his lifestyle would be the greatest. Remember that Muslims say that Mohammed was the greatest prophet who ever walked on planet Earth; therefore, they claim that Mohammed must be greater than Jesus.

Jesus ministered for three short years, and thousands followed Him. After His resurrection, on one occasion, when one of His disciples by the name of Peter preached, three thousand people were saved and became Christians in one day. Then the following day, two thousand more believed in Jesus. It seems that surely Mohammed should have had hundreds of thousands of followers in his thirteen years of preaching. That is not the case. He only had a few followers.

Muslims claim, in the writing of their history, that Mohammed and his followers were persecuted. I cannot see this anywhere, for if the people of Quraish were really persecuting Mohammed and his follows, they could have easily killed them all in one day since they were clearly the dominant tribe in Mecca. That is not what took place. When the early church was persecuted, all of Jesus' disciples were killed except John, who was not a free man for he was imprisoned on an island. Today, two thousand years later, the church is still alive. Whenever or wherever persecution exists, there is always revival in the church, for I believe persecution is the fuel which causes the church to be strong and keep going.

When did Mohammed's believers grow in number? That is when Mohammed began to use his sword and when he began to kill Jews, Christians, and Arabs. That is the opposite of how the church grew. The church flourished during persecution. *What happened when Mohammed died?* Almost all the Arabs who believed in Mohammed left Islam. They apostatized. *How did the people of Islam get united and become strong again?* It was when Abu Bakr began the War of Apostasy.

How did Islam spread from the Saudi Arabian Peninsula to the rest of the Arab world? This was through the wars that started from Saudi Arabia with Osama Bin Zayd and the twelve armies of men who traveled throughout the land to Jordan, Syria, Iran, Iraq, Afghanistan, Pakistan, Turkey, Egypt, Libya, Tunisia, Algeria, from Morocco to Spain, and from Turkey to France. That is how Islam was about to take over Europe thirteen hundred years ago. It was the armies who practiced the teaching of Allah in the Qur'an until people believed, as stated in Qur'an 9:5: [5]*So when the forbidden months are passed,*[139] *so kill the polytheists wherever you find them, and take them [as captives] and besiege them and lay wait for them with every kind of ambush; so if they repent*[140] *and perform the prayer and bring the legal alms, so leave their way free. Surely Allah is forgiving, merciful.* That is compulsion in religion.

Compare this to Christianity in which no army, no sword, and no blood were used. All these countries which Muslims invaded were Christian lands before they fell by the sword of Islam to the cult of Islam.

How about the way Muslims are spreading Islam in the West? It is in no other way but invasion and deception. First, let us look at how invasion is taking place in the West. I see Muslims coming from the Middle East every day, romancing infidel females of the West (whom Muslims view as trash) and marrying them, not because they love them, but simply because they can serve as the mothers of their Muslim children. They are the ticket to the green card and to citizenship.

The second way is deception as they teach that Islam is a loving, peaceful religion in which they worship the same god of the Bible and that women are very much respected in Islam and equal to men. These are all lies.

Thousands of Westerners are coming to believe in Islam. If we had the freedom today in the world to teach openly and Muslims had the opportunity to learn the truth about Islam, that is, to teach Muslims the Qur'an in their own language and all the facts which we have put in this book, *Exposing the Truth about the Qur'an: The Revelation of Error,* Muslims could be saved, that is, to leave the cult of Islam and believe in the Christian faith. Obviously, if Muslims had the freedom to leave Islam without being killed by their family members or by the good believer in the mosque, as Abu Bakr did after Mohammed's death when almost all the Muslims left Islam, there would not be any Muslims on the earth today.

The killing of Muslims who are apostate to Islam is known in the Qur'an as honor killing, which there are thousands of cases all over the world each year according to the United Nations.[141] You can

---

[139]pre-Islamic tradition of not fighting during a four month period

[140]convert to Islam

[141]Phyllis Chesley, "Worldwide Trends in Honor Killings," *Middle East Quarterly* (Spring 2010): 3-11, accessed October 21, 2013, http://www.meforum.org/2646/worldwide-trends-in-honor-killings.

search the words *honor killing* to see pictures and stories about this. Honor killing is stated in Qur'an 6:151: [151] *...And do not kill the soul which Allah forbids except with a just cause....* This same teaching is also repeated in Qur'an 17:33 and 25:68. *The question we must ask here is who are the people whom Allah forbade to be killed?* The answer is found clearly in Mohammed's own words in the hadith by Bukhari, volume 9, #17 where Mohammed said, "The blood of a Muslim cannot be shed except in three cases; for murder, adultery, and the one who becomes an Apostate (leaves) from Islam."

Muslims who claim to be insulted by the truth we are exposing need to know that Mohammed himself is insulting to the Muslims, especially as we have seen that all that has been said by Mohammed and Allah and Muslim scholars are shameful and disgraceful writings. As for those who claim that burning the Qur'an is very insulting, my response is that reading the Qur'an is the most insulting thing a man or a woman does to Islam. As a matter of fact, burning the Qur'an is an honorable thing to do to Islam. It is actually like hiding the evidence of a crime which any criminal wishes to do. I always ask myself this question. *Why do Muslims get upset when someone burns a copy of the Qur'an, but not one Muslim ever got upset when the second Caliph Othman Ibn Affan burned the first seven original manuscripts of the Qur'an?* Perhaps this is a great proof of what I have shared earlier in that Muslims will use any excuse to practice the violence of Allah's word in the Qur'an towards infidels.

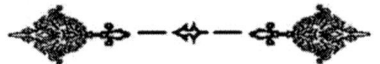

What will you do with Jesus?

It is no accident that you are reading this particular page at this particular moment in time. The Library of Congress contains nearly 30 million books on over 500 miles of shelves, receiving nearly 20,000 new items per day. Adding all other printed materials, the number would surely climb into the hundreds of millions. Yet, today, at this moment, you are reading this. Is it an accident? I say *NO*.

When it comes to ultimate questions, there are three basic issues that we all need to answer. First, "Who am I?" Second, "Is there a purpose in life?" And finally, "Where am I going when I die?" These are the real questions that we hear deep down inside, during quiet moments, moments when we stop the background noise of the distractions of the day. Many people run from these questions, but *don't*. Let's take a few minutes and *think*.

RANDOM CHANCE OR INTELLIGENT DESIGNER?

Atheism, a belief system that denies that there is a God, tries to dismiss these deep questions by speculating about a universe with no cause, no purpose, and no Creator. Atheism defines our existence as an incredibly improbable cosmic accident: a galactic fluke, a nearly limitless chain of biological mutation miracles, called evolution, to arrive at the beauty and complexity of life that we see all around us. However, recent research into DNA, the building code of life, shows that evolution is not only *mathematically* impossible in terms of time, number of mutations, and specified complexity, it is *genetically* impossible due to built-in error correction in our DNA.

Some skeptics will say, "Well, the universe could be billions of years old, so surely it could have happened!" Considering the possible age of our universe and the age of our planet, doesn't it sound reasonable to think there might be enough time for almost anything to occur by chance? Using statistics, the mathematical science of probability and chance, is this within the realm of possibility? The answer is an overwhelming *NO*! It is not even *close*.

Mathematicians who study probability say that any event with a chance less than 1 in 10^{50} is effectively *ZERO*. Life by chance is not 1 in 10^{50} but *quadrillions* of times far less likely than that. In other words, ZERO chance. In 1991, John Horgan, an atheist and senior staff writer for *Scientific American*, after reviewing the status of *all* existing scientific theories for the origin of life, said that there is *still no plausible way life could have begun by chance*.

The only logical conclusion is that an intelligence far beyond our own has *designed life*.

Eminent scientist and British mathematician Sir Fred Hoyle had this to say about the evidence: "A common sense interpretation of the facts suggests that a *super intellect* has monkeyed with physics, as well as chemistry and *biology*, and that there are no blind forces worth speaking about in nature" [emphasis mine] ("The Universe: Past and Present Reflections," *Annual Reviews of Astronomy and Astrophysics* 20, 1982, 16). He also says: "The notion that not only the biopolymer but the operating program of a living cell could be arrived at by chance in a primordial organic soup here on the Earth is evidently *nonsense* of a high order" [emphases mine] ("The Big Bang in Astronomy," *New Scientist*, 19 November 1981, 527).

IN THE BEGINNING...NOTHING?

But atheism's problems go much farther than just concerning the nearly unimaginable intricacies of life. In defiance of logic and science, atheism imagines that the entire universe either exploded out of nothing for no reason or that it has always existed (eternal). Both of these scenarios are now being rejected due to recent discoveries. Robert Jastrow (Ph.D. in physics), former head of NASA's Goddard Institute for Space Studies, proclaimed: "Astronomers now find they have painted themselves into a corner because they have proven, by their own methods, that the world began abruptly in an act of creation... That there are what I or anyone would call supernatural forces at work is now, I think, a scientifically proven fact" ("A Scientist Caught Between Two Faiths," Interview with Robert Jastrow, *Christianity Today*, August 6, 1982).

Dr. Arthur Compton who was awarded the Nobel Prize for Physics offered this conclusion: "For myself, faith begins with the realization that a supreme intelligence brought the universe into being and created man...for it is incontrovertible that where there is a plan there is intelligence" (Arthur Compton, *Chicago Daily News*, 12 April 1936).

NOT THE *HOW*, BUT THE *WHO*

As we have seen, scientific evidence points to an intelligence, or as one scientist said a *super intellect* and another defined as a *supreme intelligence* which led to the formation of the universe, and ultimately to life itself. But just *WHO* is this intelligence, and what is *he/she/it* like? Does this Creator care about the universe, about life, or even about *me*? There are a variety of religions, namely Islam, Hinduism, Taoism, Mormonism, as well as others, with various views of what God is or is not like and who or what that God is. The facts of the universe prove that there is a God, but to identify that God among the many worshiped requires further investigation.

There are several things, though, that we can know about God, using logic and inference. Does it make sense to believe that a God *without intelligence* could create people *with intelligence*? *NO*. Therefore, God must be intelligent, even incredibly so, to create the universe around us. By sheer observation, we can also surmise that God must be powerful beyond anything we have ever seen. Could a God *without personality* create people *with personality*? The answer again: *NO*. In like manner, could a God who cannot or *will not* communicate create a race of people who can and do communicate? *NO*.

WHAT ABOUT EVIL?

Let me interject one caution at this point. Using this line of reasoning, some wrongly conclude that if there is evil in the world, then God must also be partially evil, which is the Hindu view of God. This is illogical for two reasons. First, if God is all wise and all good, God would know all things, including how things would be if they weren't good. For example, I have never murdered anyone, but that doesn't mean I don't know what murder is. The fact that God should allow evil, as He obviously does, does not mean that He is evil. His allowing the possibility of evil is actually evidence of the highest good. Let me explain.

God created us as choice-makers, with free wills, so that we would not be robots. At stake was whether we would be able to freely love versus whether we would be robotic androids, *machines that look like people yet which do not have free choices*. To illustrate this, what if I told you, "I'll take you out for lunch, and you can have whatever you want. You can have pizza, pizza, or pizza. What do you want?" That's no choice. For real love and goodness to exist, without us merely being robots, there had to be an alternative, a real choice besides love and goodness: evil, or rebellion against the Creator, also known as sin.

The second reason God could not be evil is because He wrote the rule book. By definition, God is the only one who can truly label good *good* and evil *evil*. Whatever He says goes. Our judgments of God matter little. If He created us, who are we to sit in judgment of Him? We would be using brains He created to criticize the One who made us. Nonsense.

A PERSONAL GOD

Therefore, as we return to the original point about what God is like, as popular as is the notion that God is some sort of impersonal *FORCE* who merely set things in motion and then stepped out of the picture, as in deism, fate, or Taoism, such a view does not hold up to reason. God is much more that a FORCE.

Since God is most likely personal (He has created personal beings) and has the ability to communicate (He has created beings who use communication constantly), the next question is whether God has ever communicated with mankind. This would truly be the only way to know what God is like in His character, apart from logically deduced attributes. There are many different religions which claim that God has spoken to them, usually through one of their prophets or founders. One of the first logical steps would be discovering which of the world religions might possibly be true. One simple test would be to determine which of the world religions believe in an all-powerful, personal, moral God who has communicated with mankind.

Only three of the major world religions believe in such a God: Judaism, Islam, and Christianity. The infinitely personal God does not fit the description of the impersonal Brahma who is the World Soul of Hinduism and is both good and evil. Nor does it fit the *Buddha Consciousness* in which Buddhism seeks to suppress human desires as harmful.

COULD ISLAM BE TRUE?

Could Islam be the true religion, just because many of its views of their god Allah seem right and that many of its adherents are very sincere? Logically, Islam cannot be the one true religion as it professes. **WHY?** Because Islam's founder Mohammed said that the Bible is to be *believed*, including the teachings of Jesus. In the Qur'an, Mohammed said, "Say, 'We believed in Allah and in what has been sent down on us and what has been sent down on Abraham and Ishmael and Isaac and Jacob and the tribes and in what was given to Moses and 'Isā and the prophets from their lord. We do not differentiate between any one of them. And to him we are Muslims.'" (Qur'an 3:84. See also Qur'an 4:136; 5:50, 68). Mohammed said that we should *believe* the writings of the Bible, which contain the Law, the Prophets, and the New Testament; yet in reality, Mohammed denied many of the major teachings of the Bible, both Old Testament and New Testament, and doctrines which Jews and Christians have always held to be true. For example, if you read the New Testament, you will discover that the historical crucifixion of Jesus as payment for the sins of the world is the central theme of the entire New Testament (Matthew 27:35, Mark 15:32, Luke 24:20, Acts 2:36, Philippians 2:8, 1 Corinthians 1:23). However, Mohammed denied that Jesus was crucified (Qur'an 4:167).

Another contradiction between the Qur'an and the Bible is that in the New Testament and the Old Testament, Jesus is called the *Son of God* (e.g., John 3:16; Matthew 14:33; John 1:34; and Acts 9:20). Mohammed emphatically taught that Jesus was *not* the Son of God and that anyone who believes that Jesus *is* the Son of God is cursed (Qur'an 9:30); the list of contradictions goes on and on. In the New Testament, Jesus is worshiped as God Who has come in the flesh (John 1:1-14), yet this is condemned and forbidden in the strongest language in the Qur'an.

How could Mohammed say that the teachings of Jesus are to be *believed* and then deny most of the major doctrines of the New Testament? Such irreconcilable contradictions make Islam untrue, definitely not a perfect revelation from a perfect God.

CHRISTIANS OR CHRIST?

Don't judge the Christian faith by hearsay or negative encounters you might have had with Christians. This would be like saying that *all* food is bad because you have experienced bad or rotten food.

Christianity stands or falls based upon *CHRIST*, not *Christians*. God does not ask you to have faith in *Christians*; He asks that you have faith in *CHRIST*. You can read the truth about Jesus Christ in the New Testament of the Bible.

CAN CHRISTIANITY BE PROVEN?

Also, some think of Christianity as *escapism* or as *wishful thinking for those who have a need to imagine a god*. The real issue, of course, is whether or not it is *true*. To say, "There is a tunnel under this prison" may be an escapist idea, but it may also be true. So how can you determine whether Christianity is true? Actually, it is not as hard as you may think. Unlike most other religions which are based upon philosophies and dogmas in which nothing can be proven or disproved, Christianity is a *historical* faith based upon historical facts which can be investigated.

In a spirit of open-mindedness, I urge you to take a fresh look at the history-changing individual known as Jesus. I will show you evidence which proves that Jesus is who He claims to be.

Suppose one day a Man walked this earth claiming to be God, saying, "I am the way, the truth, and the life. No one comes to the Father but by me" (John 14:6). Any person claiming to be the only way to get to God would have to be one of three things: psychotic with delusions of grandeur, a deceiver out to pull off one of the greatest scams of all time, or He might be *GOD.*

C. S. Lewis, once an atheist who studied evidence that eventually led him to become a Christian, wrote, "A man who was merely a man and said the sort of things Jesus said would not be a great moral teacher. He would either be a lunatic on a level with the man who says he is a poached egg or else he would be the Devil of Hell. You must make your choice. Either this man was, and is, the Son of God or else a madman or something worse..." (C.S. Lewis, *Mere Christianity,* New York: Macmillan Publishing, 1978, 56).

Most people do not realize that in the New Testament Jesus is called almost every major name and attribute used to describe God in the Old Testament. For example: Jesus is called *God* (Romans 9:5; John 1:1, 14), *Jehovah* (John 8:58), *Lord* (Acts 10:38) *Creator* (Colossians 1:15-18; Hebrews 1:1), *Savior* (Titus 2:13), *King of kings*

(Revelation 19:16), *the Alpha and the Omega* (Revelation 1:17-18; 22:13), *Holy One* (Acts 3:14), and many more.

You could take Buddha out of Buddhism, and it would remain basically unchanged. You could take Mohammed out of Islam, and it would continue to exist. But, if you took Jesus Christ out of Christianity, it would collapse because Christianity is not merely a *religion* or *philosophy* of life but an encounter with a Person who claimed to be God and who said that He was going to die for us and then rise from the dead to prove His claims: Jesus Christ. Christianity is not an *it* but a *WHO*. Christianity is not a set of rules; it is not a religion of "do this" and "don't do that." It is essentially coming to grips with the claims of Christ and how those relate to you personally.

EVIDENCE FOR JESUS' CLAIMS

Before I go on, some of you are no doubt asking about the evidence for Jesus. Some say: "If you want me to trust Christ, I need to know if there are solid reasons to do so." Absolutely. Let me summarize some of the major reasons that Jesus was telling the truth.

The first is the historical evidence for the resurrection of Jesus. If anyone could disprove the resurrection, they could disprove Christianity. However, to do so, they would have to explain what happened to His mutilated body; how the tomb, which was guarded by Roman soldiers, got empty; how over 500 people saw Him physically alive; and several other equally difficult questions. For further reading, I highly recommend Josh McDowell's book *The Resurrection Factor.*

Another line of evidence involves the trustworthiness of the eyewitnesses themselves. Of the original twelve disciples, excluding Judas the betrayer, history tells us that all but John were *killed* for their belief and bold profession that Jesus had conquered death, that they had seen Him alive after the crucifixion, and that He was the one hope for mankind. Some people such as suicide bombers will die for what they *think* is true, but the apostles would have died for something they *knew* that they made up. In other words, the apostles would have had to die for a lie that *they invented.*

A third piece of evidence is the reliability of the Bible as a historical document. Did you know that there are over 24,600 partial or complete manuscripts of the New Testament? The second-best documented manuscript of antiquity is *The Iliad and The Odyssey* by Homer. It has around 600 manuscripts. Most ancient documents have fewer than ten original copies still in existence. Using standard literary tests, the New Testament we have today is over 99.9 percent reliable. Not one word in a thousand is in question, and no major doctrine is in doubt.

The last and perhaps most conclusive piece of evidence is *fulfilled prophecy*. There were many prophecies in the Bible foretelling Christ's coming, including where He was to be born (Micah 5:2), and that He would die having His hands and feet pierced (Psalm 22:16; cf., Isaiah 53; Zechariah 12:10); it also pinpointed the exact week and year He would die (Daniel 9:25, 26). Read *Daniel's Prophecy of the 70 Weeks* by Alva J. McClain (Winona Lake, IN: BMH Books, 2007) to better understand this prophecy. The Bible also predicted that Jesus would conquer death by being resurrected (Psalm 16:10; cf., Acts 2:22-27). There are, in fact, over 300 prophecies about the coming Messiah in the Old Testament.

How could the Bible predict such astounding things hundreds of years in advance if the Bible wasn't true and Christ wasn't who He claimed to be? It was God's way to be sure we wouldn't mistake His coming. Please refer to our special section about the prophecies of Jesus to read about more of this evidence.

THE REAL PROBLEM

Like a perfect physician, Jesus was very clear when diagnosing our deepest problem; in fact, He said that He was going to die to heal our *disease*. That destructive condition is known as *SIN*. The Bible is clear that, although God created mankind to live in perfect fellowship with Himself, humanity has rebelled against our Creator; this is called sin. God reveals, "For ALL have sinned and have fallen short of the glory of God" (Romans 3:23). In other words, no one is able to reach *His perfect standard.*

Of all the truths of Christianity, the universal sinfulness of mankind is rarely questioned. Why? One word: HISTORY. One does not have to look very far into the annals of human history to witness extreme decadence, hatred, greed, and abuse multiplied millions of times over. But actually, we do not even have to look that far; each one of us is reminded of our own sinfulness every time we honestly look into the mirror.

Take heart. A necessary fact of His justness and goodness is that God hates sin; however, He still loves the *sinner*. That is why God Himself has provided the way for us to be forgiven from our sins. He wants to restore you to a right relationship with Him. But He has left the choice up to you. He has given you a free will to choose or reject His offer of love and salvation.

STEPS TO KNOWING GOD

Principle #1: God is a God of love (I John 4:16). He loves you (John 3:16). What God wants for you is awesome beyond belief (Ephesians 3:14-21). What could be more incredible than a relationship with the Creator of the Universe, knowing that He loves you deeply?

Principle #2: So, what went wrong? Why aren't more people experiencing what God intended? It is because our sin separates us from a holy God (Isaiah 59:2; Romans 6:23). Sin is active or passive rebellion against God. It is missing God's mark of perfection. Because God is *holy*, meaning He's pure and blameless, and totally without sin (Isaiah 6:1-5; I John 1:5), we cannot just come into His presence. We all fall short of God's standard of perfection.

According to the Bible, we all stand guilty before God, no matter whether we have sinned a little or a lot (James 2:10). It is like the man who was caught stealing a car who said to the judge, "But look at all the *other cars* that I didn't steal!" The point? None of us deserves to go to Heaven. Scripture teaches that we have all sinned against an eternal God and committed eternal crimes.

Principle #3: Jesus died to pay the penalty for our sin; therefore, Christ is the only way to a right relationship with God (II Thessalonians 1:8-9; John 3:16; Romans 5:8; Acts 20:28). Jesus is the bridge that connects a holy God with sinful man (I Timothy 2:5).

The Bible says that the penalty for sin is death (Romans 6:23). When we stood condemned before God as the Judge, without hope, deserving death and hell, God, in a very real sense, took off His *judicial robe* of glory, He put on a *humble robe* of humanity, became a man in the person of Jesus Christ, and died for us. The scripture says that God took on human flesh (John 1:1, 14). He lived the perfect life that we could never live, and then He died for us accomplishing what we could never do for ourselves (Romans 5:6).

Principle #4: Just *knowing* the first three principles is not enough. It takes a response on our part. Salvation is something we must *RECEIVE* (John 1:12). The Bible makes it very clear that salvation is a *FREE GIFT*; there is nothing we can do to earn it or deserve it (Ephesians 2:8-9). "For the wages of sin is death, but the *GIFT OF GOD* is eternal life through Jesus Christ our Lord" (Romans 6:23).

How much do you have to pay to get a *FREE* gift? Well, *NOTHING*. A gift is to be received, not earned, not bought, nor bargained for. It is to be received, accepted. But God will not force you to accept His offer of salvation. Many people look at their sinful lives and think that God wants them to first *clean up their act* or to *become worthy* of salvation. NO. He wants you to admit that you *can't* fix your sin problem and then to receive His divine forgiveness in faith, turning away from your sinful rebellion against Him.

Someone once said that we are born with our backs to God; in other words, we are naturally sinful, always turning away and running from God, even if we appear to be outwardly *religious*. We might even be in a church or synagogue nearly every Saturday or Sunday. Maybe we feel like we are living better lives than many other people, but this is missing the entire point. Regularly sitting in a church can't make you a Christian any more than sitting in a garage will make you into a car. Let's face it; we have already blown it. If we are to be saved, then only God can save us.

WHAT MUST I DO TO BE SAVED?

So, now the real question comes: *How* do you receive the gift of salvation? First, you must believe that Jesus really did die for your sins and that He arose from the dead (I Corinthians 15:3-5; Romans 10:9). Some have asked: "*Why* does God require *belief*?" It is because He is asking us to *trust* Him, for that is the essence of faith. He wants us to trust Him.

Since it is your sin which has been keeping you from God, you must acknowledge your sin and be willing to turn away from it as well (Mark 1:14, 15). The Bible calls this *repentance*, which simply means to turn around. If you are headed down a one-way street in the wrong direction, away from God, then turn around. As you turn back to God, ask God to forgive you and receive you back. The Bible says that if you will confess or *admit* your sins, no matter how great or small they are,

God will forgive you (Isaiah 1:18; I John 1:9) based upon what He has done for you on the cross.

The story is told of a man who skillfully walked a tightrope over and back across Niagara Falls with a heavy sack of sand on his shoulders. Upon successfully completing a two-way trip across the falls without even the slightest problem, he turned to a spectator and asked, "Do you believe that I could do that with a person on my back instead of a sack of sand?" The person said, "Of course!" The tightrope walker tossed down the bag of sand and said, "Then climb on my back." *Wow.* Real believing is more than giving mental assent to the claims of Christ. God asks you to *climb on board* and commit yourself to Him. It is more than merely believing something to be true in your head. It is a commitment of the heart.

A TIME OF DECISION

If you feel God speaking to you, deep down, and you have become convinced in your heart and in your mind that what I have shared is true, then you face a decision.

Think about it. some day you will stand before God, either forgiven or unforgiven. Hell is one of those horrible realities we don't like to discuss. However, Jesus talked about it more than all the other Bible writers put together. Not to choose God, and accept His offer of forgiveness, is to choose a life of eternal separation from Him (Revelation 20:11-15; II Thessalonians 1:8-9; Matthew 13:40-43). God is serious when it comes to sin. God is holy, and He judges sin.

But remember: there is no sin too great for God to forgive. He loves you. He died for you. Whatever you have done, whatever guilt you are carrying, God is willing to forgive. God does not lie. He promises to forgive you if you will receive Christ as Savior (Isaiah 1:18; I John 1:9).

This may be a hard decision for you. Much is at stake. If you receive Jesus as Lord, it will cost you. You may be misunderstood. Friends and family members may reject you. *Welcome to the club. Jesus was also misunderstood and rejected. But He was willing to die for you. Are you willing to live for him?*

When you are ready to make your peace with God, perhaps you could pray something like this: "Dear Jesus, I thank you for loving me. I am sorry for the ways that I have sinned against you. I believe that you died on the cross for my sin. As best as I know how, right now, I invite you to come into my life. Please forgive me, and cleanse me from all my sin. Make me the person you want me to be. I need you. Thank you for hearing my prayer. Amen."

May the Lord encourage your heart with His truth and His love.

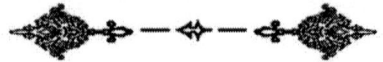

[355]

The Generous Qur'an

An Accurate, Modern English Translation of the Qur'an, Islam's Holiest Book

Get your copy today!

The need for a clear understanding of what this ideology/religion of Islam actually teaches is more important at this time than ever before, now that Islam is controlling an increasing portion of the world and dramatically gaining influence in Europe and the United States. Islam is being welcomed with open arms and in general ignorance by the West.

To further assist the reader in understanding Islam, Usama Dakdok, working with a team of scholars around the world, has created an accurate, modern English translation of the Qur'an, Islam's holiest book. This valuable resource combines an accurate verse by verse translation with annotations throughout the text to help the reader better understand what the content actually means and how it relates to relevant biblical verses. Additional exposition and tables further aid the reader in understanding Islam.

Features:
1. Accurate English Translation
2. Study Notes for the Reader
3. Errors and Contradictions
4. Comparison with Biblical Accounts
5. Points to Original Sources
6. Highlights Non-Arabic Words & Idioms in the Qur'an
7. Table of Bible Prophecies about Jesus
8. Gospel Invitation
9. Index

ORDER TODAY!

Print Version: http://www.thestraightway.org/booksdvds/
E-Book Version: https://www.smashwords.com/books/view/491841